THE CAMBRIDGE COMPANION TO THE AMERICAN SHORT STORY

This *Companion* offers students and scholars a comprehensive introduction to the development and the diversity of the American short story as a literary form from its origins in the eighteenth century to the present day. Rather than define what the short story is as a genre, or defend its importance in comparison with the novel, this *Companion* seeks to understand what the short story does – how it moves through national space, how it is always related to other genres and media, and how its inherent mobility responds to the literary marketplace and resonates with key critical themes in contemporary literary studies. The chapters offer authoritative introductions and reinterpretations of a literary form that has re-emerged as a major force in the twenty-first-century public sphere dominated by the Internet.

MICHAEL J. COLLINS is Reader in American Studies at King's College London, where he teaches nineteenth- and twentieth-century fiction, life writing, and music. He is the author of *The Drama of the American Short Story, 1800–1865* (Michigan, 2016) and *Exoteric Modernisms: Progressive Era Literature and the Aesthetics of Everyday Life* (Edinburgh, forthcoming).

GAVIN JONES is the Frederick P. Rehmus Family Professor of the Humanities at Stanford University, where he has taught American literature since 1999. He is the author of four monographs, most recently *Failure and the American Writer: A Literary History* (Cambridge, 2014) and *Reclaiming John Steinbeck: Writing for the Future of Humanity* (Cambridge, 2021).

D1554325

THE CAMBRIDGE
COMPANION TO THE
AMERICAN SHORT STORY

EDITED BY

MICHAEL J. COLLINS

King's College London

GAVIN JONES

Stanford University

CAMBRIDGE
UNIVERSITY PRESS

CAMBRIDGE
UNIVERSITY PRESS

Shaftesbury Road, Cambridge CB2 8EA, United Kingdom

One Liberty Plaza, 20th Floor, New York, NY 10006, USA

477 Williamstown Road, Port Melbourne, VIC 3207, Australia

314–321, 3rd Floor, Plot 3, Splendor Forum, Jasola District Centre, New Delhi – 110025, India

103 Penang Road, #05-06/07, Visioncrest Commercial, Singapore 238467

Cambridge University Press is part of Cambridge University Press & Assessment, a department of the University of Cambridge.

We share the University's mission to contribute to society through the pursuit of education, learning and research at the highest international levels of excellence.

www.cambridge.org
Information on this title: www.cambridge.org/9781009292818

DOI: 10.1017/9781009292863

© Cambridge University Press & Assessment 2023

This publication is in copyright. Subject to statutory exception and to the provisions of relevant collective licensing agreements, no reproduction of any part may take place without the written permission of Cambridge University Press & Assessment.

First published 2023

A catalogue record for this publication is available from the British Library.

Library of Congress Cataloging-in-Publication Data
NAMES: Collins, Michael J. (Michael James), 1984- editor. | Jones, Gavin Roger, 1968- editor.
TITLE: The Cambridge companion to the American short story / edited by Michael J. Collins, King's College London ; Gavin Jones, Stanford University.
DESCRIPTION: New York, NY : Cambridge University Press, 2023. | Series: Cambridge companions to literature | Includes bibliographical references and index.
IDENTIFIERS: LCCN 2022040183 (print) | LCCN 2022040184 (ebook) | ISBN 9781009292818 (hardback) | ISBN 9781009292849 (paperback) | ISBN 9781009292863 (epub)
SUBJECTS: LCSH: Short stories, American–History and criticism. | LCGFT: Literary criticism.
CLASSIFICATION: LCC PS374.S5 C36 2023 (print) | LCC PS374.S5 (ebook) | DDC 813/.0109–dc23/eng/20221020
LC record available at https://lccn.loc.gov/2022040183
LC ebook record available at https://lccn.loc.gov/2022040184

ISBN 978-1-009-29281-8 Hardback
ISBN 978-1-009-29284-9 Paperback

Cambridge University Press & Assessment has no responsibility for the persistence or accuracy of URLs for external or third-party internet websites referred to in this publication and does not guarantee that any content on such websites is, or will remain, accurate or appropriate.

Contents

Figures

Tables

Contributors

MARK ALGEE-HEWITT is Associate Professor of Digital Humanities and English at Stanford University, where he directs the Stanford Literary Lab. His work combines digital and critical methods to explore aesthetic phenomena in literature from the eighteenth century to the present. His work has applied network theory to dramatic plotting, used neural networks to explore the phenomena of suspense, and traced the history of the sublime through large-scale embedding models of eighteenth- and nineteenth-century literature.

LOLA BOORMAN is Lecturer in American Literature and Culture at the University of York. Her research interests include twentieth- and twenty-first-century American writing, literary institutions, the intersections between literature and linguistics, the short story form, the essay, and African American film and literature. She is currently completing her first monograph, *Make Grammar Do: Grammar and Twentieth-Century American Fiction*.

OWEN CLAYTON is Senior Lecturer in English Literature at the University of Lincoln. His specialism is late-nineteenth- and early-twentieth-century US and British literature, and his current research interests are the representation of vagrancy and homelessness. He is the author of *Literature and Photography in Transition, 1850–1915* (Palgrave Macmillan, 2015) and *Vagabonds, Tramps, and Hobos: The Literature and Culture of US Transiency 1890–1940* (Cambridge, forthcoming). He is also the editor of *Representing Homelessness*, a multidisciplinary volume that was published as part of the *Proceedings of the British Academy* series (Oxford, 2021), and of a book of primary-source letters titled *Roving Bill Aspinwall: Dispatches from a Hobo in Post-Civil War America* (Feral House, 2022).

MICHAEL J. COLLINS is Reader in American Studies at King's College, London where he teaches nineteenth-, twentieth, and twenty-first-century fiction and life writing. He is the author of two monographs: *The Drama of the American Short Story, 1800–1865* (Michigan, 2016) and *Exoteric Modernisms: Progressive Era Literature and the Aesthetics of Everyday Life* (Edinburgh, forthcoming). His essays have been published in *Textual Practice*, the *Journal of American Studies*, *Amerikastudien*, *English Language Notes*, and elsewhere.

BRAD EVANS is Professor of English at Rutgers University. A specialist in nineteenth- and twentieth-century American literature, he is the author of two books, *Before Cultures: The Ethnographic Imagination in American Literature* (Chicago, 2005) and *Ephemeral Bibelots: How an International Fad Buried American Modernism* (Johns Hopkins, 2019). He co-produced the restoration of *In the Land of the Head Hunters*, a 1914 silent feature film directed by the photographer Edward Curtis and starring an all-indigenous cast from the Kwakwaka'wakw community of British Columbia, Canada. He leads the Pragmatism Working Group at the Rutgers Centre for Cultural Analysis, and his new project is tentatively titled *Missed Connections: "Relational Aesthetics" from Henry James to Felix Gonzales Torres*.

JARED GARDNER is Professor of English at the Ohio State University. He has authored or edited several books, including *The Rise and Fall of Early American Magazine Culture* (Illinois, 2012) and, forthcoming, a Norton Critical Edition of Will Eisner's graphic short fiction and, with Elizabeth Hewitt, an MLA-CSE textual edition of the final writings of Charles Brockden Brown.

AMINA GAUTIER is Associate Professor of English at the University of Miami. She is the author of the short story collections *At-Risk* (Georgia, 2011), *Now We Will Be Happy* (Nebraska, 2014), and *The Loss of All Lost Things* (Elixir, 2016), and is a recipient of the Pen/Malamud Award for Excellence in the Short Story. Her critical essays and reviews have appeared in *African American Review*, *Critical Insights: Frederick Douglass*, *Daedalus*, the *Journal of American History*, *Libraries and Culture*, *Nineteenth Century Contexts*, and *Whitman Noir: Essays on Black America and the Good Grey Poet*.

LOREN GLASS is Professor and Chair of English at the University of Iowa, specializing in the twentieth- and twenty-first century literatures and cultures of the United States, with an emphasis on book history and literary institutions. He is the author of *Counterculture Colophon: Grove Press, the Evergreen Review, and the Incorporation of the Avant-Garde* (Stanford, 2013), republished in paperback by Seven Stories Press under the title *Rebel Publisher: Grove Press and the Revolution of the Word*, and the editor of *After the Program Era: The Past, Present, and Future of Creative Writing in the University* (Iowa, 2016). He is currently working on a literary history of Iowa City. He is a member of the Post45 collective and co-edits their book series.

SYLVAN GOLDBERG is Assistant Professor of English at Colorado College, where he teaches and writes on US literature of the long nineteenth century and the environmental humanities. He has published essays on environmental affect, the interrelation of literary and geologic form, and the roles that climate and environment have played in western American literature.

COLEMAN HUTCHISON is Associate Professor of English at the University of Texas at Austin, where he teaches courses in nineteenth- and twentieth-century US literature and culture, bibliography and textual studies, and poetry and poetics. A past president of the Society for the Study of Southern Literature, he is the author of *Apples and Ashes: Literature, Nationalism, and the Confederate States of America* (Georgia, 2012); co-author of *Writing About American Literature: A Guide for Students* (Norton, 2014); editor of *A History of American Civil War Literature* (Cambridge, 2015); and co-editor of *The Cambridge Companion to the Literature of the American Civil War and Reconstruction* (Cambridge, 2022).

GAVIN JONES is the Frederick P. Rehmus Family Professor of the Humanities at Stanford University, where he teaches courses on nineteenth- and twentieth-century American literature. He is the author of *Strange Talk: The Politics of Dialect Literature in Gilded Age America* (California, 1999), *American Hungers: The Problem of Poverty in U.S. Literature, 1840–1945* (Princeton, 2007), *Failure and the American Writer: A Literary History* (Cambridge, 2014), and *Reclaiming John Steinbeck: Writing for the Future of Humanity* (Cambridge, 2021).

LEE KONSTANTINOU is Associate Professor of English at the University of Maryland. He is the author of *Pop Apocalypse* (Ecco/HarperCollins, 2009), *Cool Characters: Irony and American Fiction* (Harvard, 2016), and *The Last Samurai Reread* (Columbia, 2022). He co-edited the collections *The Legacy of David Foster Wallace* (Iowa, 2012) and *Artful*

Breakdowns: The Comics of Art Spiegelman (Mississippi Press, forthcoming). He is currently working on a new project called *Platform-Art: Graphic Storytelling in the Age of Social Media.*

LONG LE-KHAC is Assistant Professor of English at Loyola University, Chicago. His research and teaching focus on American literature, relational race studies, Asian American studies, Latinx studies, migration studies, narrative theory, social movements, and digital humanities. He is the author of *Giving Form to an Asian and Latinx America* (Stanford, 2020). His other published work appears in *Post45*, the *Journal of Cultural Analytics, American Literature, MELUS, Victorian Studies,* and the pamphlets of the Stanford Literary Lab.

MICHAEL LUNDBLAD is Professor of English-Language Literature at the University of Oslo, Norway. He is the author of *The Birth of a Jungle: Animality in Progressive-Era U.S. Literature and Culture* (Oxford, 2013); co-editor, with Marianne DeKoven, of *Species Matters: Humane Advocacy and Cultural Theory* (Columbia, 2012); and editor of *Animalities: Literary and Cultural Studies Beyond the Human* (Edinburgh, 2017) and of a special issue of *New Literary History* on "Animality/Posthumanism/Disability" (2020).

ALEXANDER MANSHEL is Assistant Professor of Twentieth Century and Contemporary American Literature at McGill University. His writing on contemporary fiction and literary institutions has appeared in *PMLA, MELUS, Post45, Public Books,* and *The Atlantic.*

CODY MARRS is Professor of English at the University of Georgia. He is the author of *Melville, Beauty, and American Literary Studies* (Oxford, 2022), *Not Even Past: The Stories We Keep Telling About the Civil War* (Johns Hopkins, 2020), and *Nineteenth-Century American Literature and the Long Civil War* (Cambridge, 2015), as well as numerous articles that have appeared in journals such as *American Literature, American Literary History,* and *J19.* He is also the editor of *The New Melville Studies* (Cambridge, 2019), a co-editor of *Timelines of American Literature* (Johns Hopkins, 2019), and the General Editor of the four-volume series *Nineteenth-Century American Literature in Transition* (Cambridge, 2022).

ANNA MUKAMAL is Assistant Professor of Digital Culture and Design in the Department of English at Coastal Carolina University. Her work synthesizes new formalism and narrative medicine to show how writing and reading have served as a form of psychotherapy from modernism to the contemporary. She has used computational methods to analyze discussions of feminist novels across online interpretive communities; applied linear discriminant analysis to contemporary therapy sessions and literature; and asserted the value of intergenerational feminist collaboration in Digital Humanities project management. Her current work examines mental health and social justice in the generational cohort Gen Z.

SIMONE MURRAY is Associate Professor in Literary Studies at Monash University, Melbourne, Australia. She is author of four monographs: *Mixed Media: Feminist Presses and Publishing Politics* (Pluto Press, 2004); *The Adaptation Industry: The Cultural Economy of Contemporary Literary Adaptation* (Routledge, 2012); *The Digital Literary Sphere: Reading, Writing, and Selling Books in the Internet Era* (Johns Hopkins, 2018); and *Introduction to Contemporary Print Culture: Books as Media* (Routledge, 2021).

WILL NORMAN is Reader in American Literature and Culture at the University of Kent, where he specializes in twentieth-century American literature and culture, and has held Fulbright and Leverhulme fellowships. He is the author of *Nabokov, History and the Texture of Time* (Routledge, 2012) and *Transatlantic Aliens: Modernism, Exile and Culture in Midcentury America* (Johns Hopkins, 2016). His articles on crime fiction have appeared in *American Literature*, *Modernism/modernity*, *Post45*, and the *Journal of Modern Literature*.

J. D. PORTER is Digital Humanities Project Specialist in the Price Lab for Digital Humanities at the University of Pennsylvania. He combines text mining and other digital approaches with specialties in modernism, race and ethnicity theory, jazz studies, and contemporary literary reception. His recent work investigates historic changes in the contents of literary anthologies; applies network theory to genre detection in music reviews; and examines the uses of distributional semantics for addressing problems in ordinary language philosophy.

GABRIELLA SAFRAN is Eva Chernov Lokey Professor in Jewish Studies in the Department of Slavic Languages and Literatures at Stanford University. Her most recent monographs are *Wandering Soul: The Dybbuk's Creator, S. An-sky* (Harvard, 2010) and *Recording Russia: Trying to Listen in the Nineteenth Century* is forthcoming (Cornell, 2022). She is beginning a book about the rise of the notion of Jewish speech style, in multiple languages, as comical.

OLIVER SCHEIDING is Professor of North American Literature and Culture in the Obama Institute for Transnational American Studies at the University of Mainz, Germany. His research focuses on magazine studies, print culture, and material culture studies. He is currently working on a monograph titled *Print Technologies and the Emergence of American Literature* (Wiley-Blackwell, forthcoming). His periodical research projects are funded by the German Research Foundation.

SHELLEY STREEBY is Professor of Literature and Ethnic Studies at the University of California, San Diego. She is the author of *American Sensations: Class, Empire, and the Production of Popular Culture* (California, 2002), which received the American Studies Association's Lora Romero First Book Prize; *Radical Sensations: World Movements, Violence, and Visual Culture* (Duke, 2013); and *Imagining the Future of Climate Change: World-Making through Science Fiction and Activism* (California, 2018). She received a 2021 American Council of Learned Societies Faculty Fellowship to support her current project on the memory-work and world-making of Judith Merril, Ursula K. Le Guin, and Octavia E. Butler.

MYKA TUCKER-ABRAMSON is Associate Professor of English and Comparative Literary Studies at the University of Warwick. Her first book, *Novel Shocks: Urban Renewal and the Cultural Origins of Neoliberalism* (Fordham, 2018), argued for the centrality of post-World War II American urbanization projects in the transformation of both the modernist novel and the emergence of neoliberalism. She is currently working on a book on the road novel and the uneven geographies of American empire.

HERTHA D. SWEET WONG is Professor of English and Associate Dean of Arts and Humanities at the University of California, Berkeley, where she teaches and writes about autobiography, visual culture, and American literature, particularly Indigenous literatures. She is the author of *Picturing Identity: Contemporary American Autobiography in Image and Text* (North Carolina, 2018) and *Sending My Heart Back Across the Years: Tradition and Innovation in Native American Autobiography* (Oxford, 1992), as well as the editor or co-editor of three anthologies of essays on Native American literatures and the author of numerous essays in this field.

Chronology

1644 Puritan governor John Winthrop publishes *A Short Story of the Rise, Reign, and Ruine of the Antinomians, Familists and Libertines, that Infected the Churches of New England*; this tract against heresy is one of the earliest recorded uses of the term "short story" in an American context.

1692 Clergyman Cotton Mather includes the supernatural tale "A Narrative of an APPARITION which a Gentleman in Boston, had of his Brother, just then Murdered in London" in *The Wonders of the Invisible World*.

1722 Ben Franklin adopts the pseudonym Silence Dogood, under which he publishes an essay series in the *New-England Courant*. Franklin's contributions are emblematic of how short fiction was integrated into early American periodical culture, laying the groundwork for the form's nineteenth-century explosion in popularity.

1787 Ben Franklin's tale "Origin of Tobacco," a satirical appropriation of a Susquehannock myth, runs in several North American newspapers and magazines.

1787 "Sir Bertrand: A Fragment," a short gothic narrative by English writer Anna Lætitia Barbauld, appears in *The Columbian Magazine*. It was common for narratives like Barbauld's to be reprinted in North American newspapers, helping to establish the short story tradition in the United States.

1819 Washington Irving publishes "Rip Van Winkle" and "The Legend of Sleepy Hollow" in *The Sketch Book*.

1821 The first issue of the *Saturday Evening Post* is printed in Philadelphia.

1826 The first American literary annual, the *Atlantic Souvenir*, begins publication in Philadelphia. The elaborately illustrated and decorated volumes, intended to be given as gifts or tokens of friendship, featured short stories, poetry, and essays.

1830 Catherine Sedgwick publishes "Cacoethes Scribindi" in the *Atlantic Souvenir*.

1832 Nathaniel Hawthorne anonymously publishes "My Kinsman, Major Molineux" in the *Atlantic Souvenir*. His authorship of the story was not made public until 1837.

1837 Sarah Josepha Hale becomes the editor of *Godey's Lady's Book* and advocates for printing contributions only from American authors. Hale publishes Lydia Sigourney, Nathaniel Hawthorne, Edgar Allan Poe, and several other prominent writers during her forty-year tenure as editor.

1841 Edgar Allan Poe publishes "The Murders in the Rue Morgue," the first of his detective stories to feature Auguste Dupin.

1842 Lydia Maria Child contributes the short story "The Quadroons" to *The Liberty Bell*, an abolitionist gift book published annually from 1839 to 1858.

1842 Edgar Allan Poe reviews the second volume of Nathaniel Hawthorne's *Twice-Told Tales* in *Graham's Magazine*.

1845 Edgar Allan Poe publishes "The Facts in the Case of M. Valdemar" simultaneously in both the *Broadway Journal* and the *American Review*; it is later reprinted by Hugo Gernsback, who views it as an early example of "scientifiction" – a forerunner of today's science fiction.

1853 Frederick Douglass publishes his long short story "The Heroic Slave," which appears first as a serial in *Frederick Douglass' Paper* and later as part of *Autographs for Freedom*, edited by Julia Griffiths.

1856 Herman Melville publishes his collection *The Piazza Tales*, featuring "Bartleby, the Scrivener," "Benito Cereno," and four other stories previously published in *Putnam's Magazine*.

1857 The *Atlantic Monthly* is founded in Boston.

1859 Frances Ellen Watkins Harper publishes "The Two Offers" in the *Anglo-African Magazine*. The tale is often considered to be the first published short story by an African American woman in the United States, though this claim is disputed.

1864 Henry James anonymously publishes his first known short story, "A Tragedy of Error," in *Continental Monthly*.

1868 *Overland Monthly* is founded in California. The publication was an early incubator for regionalist short stories, including several by its first editor, Bret Harte.

1882 Frank A. Munsey founds *Argosy*, the first American pulp magazine.
        Seven years later, in 1889, he starts *Munsey's*, an illustrated
        magazine which also prominently featured short fiction.

1884 Brander Matthews publishes "The Philosophy of the Short-Story"
        in *Lippincott's Magazine*. Matthews will later revise and expand this
        important contribution to early short story criticism.

1884 Mary Murfree publishes her first story collection, *In the Tennessee
        Mountains*.

1884 Mary Wilkins Freeman publishes "On the Walpole Road" in
        Harper's Bazar.

1886 *Cosmopolitan* is founded in New York City.

1892 Charlotte Perkins Gilman publishes "The Yellow Wall-Paper" in
        the *New England Magazine*.

1893 Grace King publishes *Balcony Stories*, a collection of tales about
        Louisiana women who lost family, money, and status in the
        Civil War.

1894 Kate Chopin publishes her first collection of short stories, *Bayou
        Folk*.

1895 Sherwin Cody publishes one of the earliest guides to writing short
        stories, *How to Write Fiction, Especially the Art of Short Story
        Writing*. By the early decades of the twentieth century, several
        guides to writing and selling short fiction will be available on the
        American market.

1896 Sarah Orne Jewett publishes *The Country of the Pointed Firs*.

1896 *Argosy* begins to exclusively publish fiction.

1896 *Munsey's* begins their "storiettes" monthly feature – a collection of
        short stories each around a column in length.

1896 The University of Chicago offers the first course in story writing,
        "The Art of the Short Story," taught by E. H. Lewis.

1898 Paul Laurence Dunbar publishes *Folks from Dixie*, his first
        collection of short stories.

1899 Charles Chesnutt publishes *The Conjure Woman*, a collection of
        trickster stories featuring Julius McAdoo, a formerly
        enslaved character.

1899 While imprisoned for embezzlement, William Sydney Porter
        publishes "Whistling Dick's Christmas Stocking" in *McClure's
        Magazine* – his first short story under the pen name O. Henry.

1899 George Horace Lorimer becomes editor of the *Saturday Evening
        Post*, a position he will retain until 1936. During his tenure, the

Post's circulation skyrockets; by the 1920s, it is one of the highest-paying markets for short fiction in the United States.

1900 Pauline Hopkins publishes "Tamla Gordon," the first mystery story by an African American author, in *The Colored American Magazine*.

1900 Literary magazine *The Smart Set* is founded.

1901 Zitkála-Šá publishes *Old Indian Legends*, a collection of traditional Sioux stories.

1909 Though still producing short fiction, Henry James chafes against the 5,000-word limit – "detestable number!" – which is standard for most periodicals of the time.

1910 German writer Paul Heyse, "writer of world-renowned short stories," is awarded the Nobel Prize in Literature.

1911 E. Pauline Johnson publishes *Legends of Vancouver*, a collection of Native oral stories.

1914 H. L. Mencken and George Nathan become co-editors of *The Smart Set*. Under their editorship, Mencken and Nathan will publish several important authors, including James Joyce, whose fiction makes its first US appearance in the magazine ("A Little Cloud" and "The Boarding House" from *Dubliners*).

1915 American editor Edward J. O'Brien publishes the first-ever installment of *The Best American Short Stories* (as *The Best Short Stories of 1915 and the Yearbook of the American Short Story*). He will continue to edit the series until his death in 1941, helping to establish the careers of Sherwood Anderson, Ernest Hemingway, William Faulkner, Thomas Wolfe, and Dorothy Parker, among others.

1919 The O. Henry Award, given annually to a short story of exceptional merit, is established. The first winner is Margaret Prescott Montague for her "England to America."

1919 F. Scott Fitzgerald sells his first short story, "Babes in the Woods," to *The Smart Set* for $30. Fitzgerald's relationship with the magazine will become instrumental to his early success, although he will earn substantially more money from works appearing in the *Saturday Evening Post* throughout the 1920s.

1920 W. E. B. Du Bois publishes "The Comet," a science fiction story, in *Darkwater: Voices from the Veil*.

1920 *Black Mask*, a pulp magazine known for establishing the careers of Dashiell Hammett and Raymond Chandler, publishes its first issue.

1920   F. Scott Fitzgerald publishes his first collection of short stories, *Flappers and Philosophers*.

1923   Fred Lewis Pattee – sometimes called "the first Professor of American literature" – publishes *The Development of the American Short Story*.

1924   H. P. Lovecraft publishes "The Rats in the Walls" in *Weird Tales*.

1925   Harold Ross publishes the first issue of the *New Yorker*.

1925   Ernest Hemingway publishes *In Our Time*, his first collection of short stories.

1926   The first issue of Hugo Gernsback's *Amazing Stories* is published, advertising stories by H. G. Wells, Jules Verne, and Edgar Allan Poe on its cover.

1929   At the peak of his career, F. Scott Fitzgerald is earning $4,000 per story from the *Saturday Evening Post*.

1933   Raymond Chandler publishes his first short story, "Blackmailers Don't Shoot."

1936   The Iowa Writers' Workshop is founded at the University of Iowa.

1937   Leo Rosten publishes *The Education of H*Y*M*A*N K*A*P*L*A*N*, a collection of humorous stories featuring protagonist Hyman Kaplan.

1940   *Short Stories from The New Yorker* is published. With stories from John O'Hara, Dorothy Parker, James Thurber, and other prominent writers, the anthology cements the magazine's reputation as a premiere venue for short fiction.

1940   Meridel Le Sueur publishes *Salute to Spring*, a collection of proletarian short stories.

1948   *Tales of the South Pacific* by James A. Michener wins the Pulitzer Prize for Fiction. This is the first year that the Prize is not given to a novel since its first award in 1918.

1949   *The Magazine of Fantasy and Science Fiction*, edited by Anthony Boucher and J. Francis McComas, begins publication. *F&SF* creates important market space for fantasy stories, which are usually omitted from periodicals devoted to science fiction.

1951   *The Collected Stories of William Faulkner* wins the National Book Award for Fiction.

1954   Alfred Hitchcock's *Rear Window* is released. The film was based on a 1942 short story by crime writer Cornell Woolrich, "It Had to Be Murder."

1955   Walt Disney's *The Lady and the Tramp* is released; the film is inspired by a 1945 *Cosmopolitan* short story by Ward Greene, "Happy Dan, the Cynical Dog."

1959 *The Magic Barrel* by Bernard Malamud wins the National Book Award for Fiction.

1960 *Goodbye, Columbus* by Philip Roth wins the National Book Award for Fiction.

1963 Frank O'Connor publishes *The Lonely Voice: A Study of the Short Story*, an important contribution to short story criticism.

1966 *Collected Stories* by Katherine Anne Porter wins both the National Book Award and the Pulitzer Prize for Fiction.

1966 Scholar H. Bruce Franklin publishes *Future Perfect: Science Fictions of the 19th Century*, an anthology which links the short story's early history to the rise of modern science and technology as seen through the writings of Poe, Hawthorne, and Lydia Maria Child, among others.

1967 *The Best Short Stories by Negro Writers: 1899–1967*, edited by Langston Hughes, is published.

1968 *2001: A Space Odyssey*, a film based on Arthur C. Clarke's 1948 short story "The Sentinel," is released.

1969 N. Scott Momaday publishes *The Way to Rainy Mountain*, a hybrid work comprising memoir, folklore, fiction, and visual elements. The book exemplifies the blending of oral and written traditions often found in Native writers' engagements with short fiction.

1970 *Collected Stories* by Jean Stafford wins the Pulitzer Prize for Fiction.

1972 *The Complete Stories* by Flannery O'Connor wins the National Book Award for Fiction.

1974 *A Crown of Feathers and Other Stories* by Isaac Bashevis Singer wins the National Book Award for Fiction, alongside Thomas Pynchon's *Gravity's Rainbow*.

1974 Frank Chin, Jeffery Paul Chan, Lawson Fusao Inada, and Shawn Wong publish *Aiiieeeee! An Anthology of Asian-American Writers*.

1975 Ursula K. Le Guin publishes "Mazes" in the anthology *Epoch: The State of the Art of Science Fiction Now*, edited by Roger Elwood and Robert Silverberg; it is later reprinted in her 1982 short story collection *The Compass Rose*.

1976 The Pushcart Prize, which annually honors short fiction, poetry, and essays published by small presses, is founded.

1977 Leslie Marmon Silko publishes *Storyteller*, a multi-genre work which includes poetry, prose, and photographs.

1978 James Alan McPherson becomes the first African American to win the Pulitzer Prize for Fiction for *Elbow Room*.

1979 *The Stories of John Cheever* wins the Pulitzer Prize for Fiction.

1981   *The Stories of John Cheever* is the paperback winner of the National Book Award. (From 1980 to 1984 the Award recognizes both a hardcover and paperback winner.)

1981   Raymond Carver publishes his short story collection *What We Talk About When We Talk About Love*; the collection – a critical and commercial success – was heavily influenced by the revisions of Carver's editor, Gordon Lish.

1982   Columbian author Gabriel García Márquez is awarded the Nobel Prize in Literature in recognition of his novels and short stories.

1983   *The Collected Stories of Eudora Welty* is the paperback winner of the National Book Award for Fiction.

1984   *Victory Over Japan: A Book of Stories* by Ellen Gilchrist wins the National Book Award for Fiction.

1987   Donald Barthelme publishes his collection *Forty Stories*. Included in the collection is "Sentence," an experimental story consisting of a single seven-page sentence.

1988   The PEN/Malamud Award for excellence in the art of the short story is established in honor of the late Bernard Malamud.

1991   Literary Agent Peter Miller claims that Ernest Hemingway penned a six-word short story to win a bet in the 1920s: "For sale. Baby shoes. Never worn." (The link to Hemingway is unsubstantiated.)

1991   Sandra Cisneros publishes her critically acclaimed short story collection *Woman Hollering Creek*.

1992   Tina Brown becomes editor of the *New Yorker*. Among the many changes Brown makes to the magazine is to institute a tradition of printing only one short story per issue.

1993   *A Good Scent from a Strange Mountain* by Robert Olen Butler wins the Pulitzer Prize for Fiction.

1995   *The Complete Stories of Zora Neale Hurston* is published, making the writer's short fiction from the 1920s and 1930s widely available.

1996   *Ship Fever and Other Stories* by Andrea Barrett wins the National Book Award for Fiction.

2000   *Interpreter of Maladies* by Jhumpa Lahiri wins the Pulitzer Prize for Fiction.

2005   Release of the Ang Lee film *Brokeback Mountain*, based on the widely acclaimed 1997 short story of the same name by Annie Proulx.

2009   *Olive Kitteridge* by Elizabeth Strout wins the Pulitzer Prize for Fiction.

2010 The Sunday Times Short Story Award is established. The prize annually recognizes a short story published in the United Kingdom or Ireland, and, at £30,000, is currently the most lucrative prize in the world for a single short story.

2010 Chad Harbach publishes the essay "MFA vs. NYC" in *Slate*.

2011 *A Visit from the Goon Squad* by Jennifer Egan wins the Pulitzer Prize for Fiction. (Egan has said that she considers *Goon Squad*, an interconnected series of stories, to be neither a novel nor a short story collection.)

2012 Jennifer Egan's "Black Box" is serialized on the *New Yorker*'s Twitter account.

2012 Charles Yu publishes his short story collection *Sorry Please Thank You*.

2013 Canadian author Alice Munro, "contemporary master of the short story," is awarded the Nobel Prize in Literature.

2014 *Redeployment* by Phil Klay wins the National Book Award for Fiction.

2015 *Fortune Smiles* by Adam Johnson wins the National Book Award for Fiction.

2015 French publishing house Short Édition installs its first short story vending machines in Grenoble, France. Over 300 such machines have now been installed around the world, including in San Francisco, Seattle, New York, Philadelphia, and Austin.

2016 *Arrival*, based on the 1998 Ted Chiang story "Story of Your Life," is released to critical and popular acclaim, grossing over $200 million at the box office.

2017 Kristen Roupenian's "Cat Person" becomes the most viewed story in the *New Yorker*'s online history.

2018 Nana Kwame Adjei-Brenyah publishes *Friday Black*, his debut story collection.

2019 Beth Piatote publishes *The Beadworkers*, a collection of stories infused with Nez Perce history and culture.

2021 Robert Kolker's *New York Times* feature story "Who Is the Bad Art Friend?" becomes a viral sensation. The feature chronicles accusations made by Dawn Dorland that fellow writer (and acquaintance) Sonya Larson used, without permission, a letter written by Dorland in the short story "The Kindest."

Introduction

Michael J. Collins and Gavin Jones

In or around 1923, we thought we knew what the short story was. Or, rather, Edward J. O'Brien did, and as editor of the influential *Best American Short Stories* anthology since 1915 his words carried considerable weight in the newly professionalizing field of literary publishing. Taking stock of a genre that had evolved along with the expanding print culture of the nineteenth century, O'Brien was concerned that even as luminous examples of its literary artistry had found fertile ground in America, the modern, industrial conditions that birthed the form had left an indelible mark upon it that impeded its development and marred it in the eyes of readers. For O'Brien, a true "short story" was a rare and precious beast, to be nurtured and distinguished from a mass of American short fiction that was disqualified wholly from the sanctified realm of "art," either because of its unruly form or because of its deployment of hackneyed tropes directed solely to the demands of the marketplace. His definition enacted a tendency present in short story criticism since Edgar Allan Poe first started to describe an emergent commercial style, upon which he relied to pay the bills, which was to characterize the form negatively, by what it was not: the novel, poetry, the folk tale, and so on. So much "fiction that is merely short" was an abomination for O'Brien; it was especially prone, relative to other genres, to the charge of committing nothing less than literary "heresy." In *The Advance of the American Short Story* (1923; revised 1931), O'Brien wrote that "almost every American short story is the product of one or more of four heresies, the heresy of types, the heresy of local color, the heresy of 'plot,' and the heresy of the surprise ending" (1931, 6).

These "four heresies" were not always present in equal measure, but were described by O'Brien as being a) "passion for drawing characters ... immediately recognizable to every American reader" (to us now, perhaps, a literary heresy of instantaneous relatability); b) "a desire of satisfying ... liking for what is quaint" (a containable and acceptable mode of difference); c) "a respect for . . . scheming" and the "codification by solemn lawgivers of certain elements in the somewhat meretricious detective stories of Poe"; and d) the surprise ending that "appears to satisfy the craving for life in a dead atmosphere" (7–9). O'Brien's "four heresies" remain useful to us now because they articulate many of the stylistic tropes that are often still listed as requirements of the genre by those seeking to teach, institutionalize, or market it. Moreover, they demonstrate that *United States-based* short story criticism (specified to differentiate it from the more vociferous support for the form common in Latin America, Europe, Africa, and elsewhere), even up to the age of a more established Short Story Theory in the 1970s and 1980s, frequently took a somewhat contemptuous tone with its ward.

It is in this dialogical space where taxonomic necessity (a short story must have certain features to be a "short story") meets contempt for the modern market forces that have shaped the majority of its expressions, producing an American criticism of the genre that has commonly placed its flag affectively. The result is often a confused and unstable critical stance, supporting something it finds a little hard to truly believe in. Indeed, the same might be said of readers, who going by the significantly lower sales figures for short story collections, do not know themselves quite what to think about it. Indeed, it is notable that readers have not derived the same pleasure from the form as from other more prominent genres of cultural expression, such as the novel. How often, for example, do we encounter individuals who neither read, or who actively do not like, the short story? In sum, for all the short story's manifest brilliance, in the United States it is a genre with a charisma problem. For all the attention given the form by institutions such as the creative writing program, the undergraduate classroom, the literary prize market, and so on, it holds no position equal in esteem to the novel. Indeed, it seems that the institutions that have built up around the short story operate as a life-support machine necessary to its continued existence. Yet these very same institutions also subject the genre to a popular mistrust – the charge that it is somehow enfeebled or rarefied, a hothouse flower of literary forms. This is, of course, in spite of a commonly held truism – the reason indeed that the volume you are reading even exists – that positions Americans as especially skilled practitioners in the genre of the short story over an extended swathe of historical time.

Coming back to O'Brien (who is arguably the most prominent booster for the short story that America has had in the modern age), there is much to be said about the hissing vitriol in his use of the term *heresy* that connects the question of form with the political and religious history of America. Our contemporary moment has seen renewed interest in "form" itself as the carriage of "the social" – that is, as material that dissolves what Caroline Levine has called the "traditionally troubling gap between the form of the literary text and its content and context." In opposition to the context-heavy focus of late-twentieth-century New Historicism, formalist analysis "has, once again, turn[ed] out to be as valuable to understanding sociopolitical institutions as it is to reading literature" (Levine 2015, 2). In this context it is worth considering what the affective stance of distrust critics have often taken to the short story reveals about the social, political, and religious conditions that have impacted criticism, thought, and culture over the *longue durée* of the American experience. Michael Collins has written in *The Drama of the American Short Story, 1800–1865* that the social position of the short story, as an expression of the needs of the community over and above the bourgeois individual, imbues the genre with a gestural mode of theatricality that brings it into the orbit of theater itself. It is self-conscious *performativity* – a word that contains both the senses of form and context – that, if anything, makes the short story distinct. To put this another way is to say that the short story, rather than being heretically embodied is, as a genre, self-consciously *formal* in its concerns. This is not to imply it is haughty or prim. Far from it. It is more that the short story is outwardly *about* its own form as much as it is its content. Or that it cannot and will not distinguish between these things as remotely separate, and therefore invites a form of close reading that is socially engaged and textually attentive simultaneously.

As Douglas Tallack (1993) has observed, one of the earliest recorded uses of the term "short story" in an American context was in the posthumously published writings of John Winthrop, the notorious Puritan governor of the Massachusetts Bay colony. In the second edition of one of the accounts of his tenure, *A Short Story of the Rise, Reign, and Ruine of the Antinomians, Familists and Libertines, that Infected the Churches of New England* (1692; second edition), "Short Story" was added to the title so as to mobilize a sense of shortness as a trope through which to speak of something that he hoped would be a short-lived, unstable, abortive heresy: the Antinomian, or Free Grace Controversy of the 1630s. At a key moment in Winthrop's account of the famous trial, evidence is presented that Anne Hutchinson (the main defendant accused of preaching and following a Covenant of Grace and not a Covenant of Works) and Mary Dyer (soon to convert to Quakerism in England and later to be hanged for heresy) covered up the stillbirth of a child whose form Winthrop suggested was evidence of the influence of the Devil in Anne Hutchinson's work as a midwife to the communities of Boston and Roxbury. Winthrop writes:

> AT *Boston* in *New-England*, upon the 17th day of *Octob.* 1637. the wife of one *William Dyer*, sometimes a Citizen and Millener of *London*, a very proper and comely young Woman, was delivered of a large Woman Child, it was stillborn, about two Months before her time, the Child having life a few hours before the delivery, but so Monstrous and Mis-shapen, as the like hath scarce been heard of: it had no Head, but a Face, which stood so low upon the Breast, as the Ears (which were like an Apes) grew upon the Shoulders . . .. [I]t had upon each Foot Three Claws, with Talons like a young Fowl. Upon the Back, above the Belly, it had two great Holes, like Mouths, and in each of them stuck out a piece of Flesh. It had no Forehead, but in the place thereof, above the Eyes, Four Horns, whereof two were above an Inch long, hard and sharp, the other two were somewhat shorter. (Winthrop 1692, 46)

For Winthrop what was devilish, or heretical, was that the child possessed a form that rendered it unable to sustain itself independently. Moreover, following a description of this "monstrous and misshapen," stunted body, Winthrop turned quickly to the charge of conspiracy, described as a similarly monstrous form of sociality that defended and protected the child and its mother from the wider community's charges of innate evil (46–47). A "natural order" – synonymous here with the presumably rightful and just forms of the Puritan Elders – would have done no such thing.

Winthrop's principal contention was that because "that very day Mistriss *Hutchison* [sic] was cast out of the Church for her Monstrous Errours, and Notorious Falsehood" (47) occurred close to the day of the "monstrous" birth of a child, the two events were inherently connected. Moreover, the form of the child and its stillbirth were equated with the "shortness" of the life of the corrupting heresy of Familism or Antinomianism (its status as a "short story" in the broader life of the Puritan community) and serves as a lesson in the temporariness and artificiality of one form (the form of evil) against the proper and precise form of the Boston Church's teaching and its ecclesiastical hierarchy of Elders. For Winthrop, forms born under the shadow of death and requiring excessive care in their support were evidence of heresy. The "monstrous" was, for Winthrop and other American Puritans, manifest in a lack of independence and also a proximity to a death that, like the Antinomian Controversy, threatened the longevity and ahistorical permanence of the exceptionalist American Puritan project as they saw it. In this way, he helped to instantiate a sense that brevity was, of itself, heresy, much as O'Brien 300 years later would so characterize the short story, even if the latter's cleaving to the exceptional (at least in the short stories O'Brien's publishing ventures dug out from the rough) carried a note of Messianic rarity and grace. The child described by Winthrop is notable for having both too much form (an excess that points to the influence of a second party, the Devil) and too little (a lack of artistic insight or control), and points to the "short story" in American literature as both unnatural or artificial, and short-lived and fleeting.

In the twentieth century another major critic of short form, Walter Benjamin, also made a conflation between the genre's formal brevity and deathliness, albeit with a radically different interpretation of the meaning and value of proximity to an endpoint. Taking "the story" and its experientiality as the natural counterpoint to the novel's presentation of mere information, Benjamin found beauty and political potential in a formal embrace of endings, valorizing "Storytellers" and the stories they told precisely because they lived so much more assuredly in the presence of death. Crucially, in so doing, Benjamin reasoned, Storytellers carried with them an ethos of care for the precarious living world and the socialities required for its preservation. "It has been observable for a number of centuries," Benjamin writes in "The Storyteller," "how in the general consciousness the thought of death has declined in omnipresence and vividness" – a tendency contemporaneous with the rise of the novel and its focus on "information" over a sense of the "epic." He continues: "[I]n its last stages this process is accelerated ... [a]nd in the course of the nineteenth century bourgeois society has, by means hygienic and social, private and public institutions, realized a secondary effect which may have been its subconscious main purpose: to make it possible for people to avoid the sight of the dying" (1999, 93).

For Benjamin, rather, "Death is the sanction of everything that the storyteller can tell. He has borrowed his authority from death. In other words, it is natural history to which his stories refer back" (94). What distinguished "the story" from the novel was precisely that in the conscious presence of death or of endings it invited the social in a way that was politically expedient for the project of the Left, while the bourgeois novelist (and the novel itself) existed in a state of comparative isolation. This was independence, surely, but so too was it a naivete or the lack of a sense of the epic pull of Marxian history toward the collective. Taking "what he tells from experience – his own or that reported by others," the Storyteller "makes it the experience of those who are listening to his tale" (87). The counterintuitive but compelling logic of Benjamin's reading is that it is because of brevity, not in spite of it, that the "short story" invites the "epic," defined as a sense of the inevitability of death shared with all living things, which therefore extends an invitation to communal visions of care, work, and collective support. It is for this reason, perhaps, that the short story is so often seen as continuous with the work of the artisan. To express it in Benjamin's own words, "storytelling, in its sensory aspect, is by no means a job for the voice alone . . . in genuine storytelling the hand plays a part which supports what is expressed in a hundred ways with its gestures trained by work" (107). If the significant fact of the rise of the short story in the creative writing workshop since World War II is taken to mean anything, it is that the short story is a job of work – of form – and that care in its craft is a hard labor, requiring the support of both institutions and collectives of individuals to manifest. Even if the form of the short story seems self-contained, it does not point back formally to the individual, but draws its meaning from the collective.

Over the years, various reparative moves have been made in short story criticism to remedy what has been seen historically as the inherent vice of the genre. Critical contempt for the very precarity of the short story works to dramatize a cultural fear of a terminus point to the American political project. Additionally, the very fact of the work of care required to sustain the form in the world of the marketplace has been challenged repeatedly on the grounds that there is something entirely too artisanal or lower middle class about the efforts taken in its name. In the middle decades of the twentieth century, as particularly evident in the work of influential theorists such as Charles May, Frank O'Connor, and Susan Lohafer, Short Story Theory sought to suture the romantic lyric effects of the surprise ending or reversal to local color's elevation of the particular and quaint, so the short story might be made to serve a project of Cold War nation-building. A tendency that had long been noted for the American short story to be both realist *and* fantastical at once was seen as evidence *for*, and not *against*, claims to its independence of spirit. Short Story Theory attempted to shore up the formal features of the genre that O'Brien and others so often decried, by resolving it into evidence of a unified, discreet, American *volk* consciousness. As Michael Collins has written elsewhere, the reversals, epiphanies, and voltas common in expressions of the short story in America were taken to be manifestations in the political unconscious of the residual force of the revolutionary ruptures that made *American* experience (with all its cosmopolitan and transnational pluralities) into *US* experience (Collins 2018). In Short Story Theory's account of the form there were, of course, innumerable exclusions. However, when placed in juxtaposition to the totalitarian aspirations toward uniformity that were claimed as the province of Soviet Communist literary form in its guise of socialist realism, the weirdness and quaintness of the American short story was to be interpreted as a trait of especial political virtue: a sort of capitalist moxie. In this moment the very *un*-Americanness of the short story's form as it has been described in the past was reconfigured and reworked so it might be assimilated for the US literary project.

This volume is an attempt to ask what happens if, rather than taking O'Brien's line and denouncing the form in the main as so much heresy (with the aim of digging out just one rich, canonical jewel among so many), we say instead that this precarity, this multiplicity, this proneness to a certain indistinction – this queerness of form – is a feature not a bug. It helps reveal the story's context and purpose at a more local, social level (what it does, and not what it "is" in some rigid, ontological sense), and yet also lets it speak to the epic sensibility as Benjamin described it – a knowledge and embrace of the forms of care that emerge in the conscious presence of death.

That the short story evokes through its performative unification of form and content an ethos of care and sociality marks it as a genre perhaps especially useful to us in accounting for the conditions of early twenty-first-century life, in which the combined forces of residual nationalist and global political forms (embodied in the haggard persistence of neoliberal capital in the face of required change), ecological crisis (and the urgent awareness of the human-wrought destruction it triggers), the so-called crisis of the humanities, and recent phases of pandemic illness and mortality force us into renewed awareness both of death and of the need for a wider ethos of care and compassion. If the principal political project of our time is to unite redistributive economics and the vision of postcapitalist futurities to an ecological sensibility that preserves life on Earth by means of attention to care, then it follows that critical focus on the form of the short story – whose special pedigree lies in the fact of its precarity and its formal awareness of death – should be a principal project of our literary criticism. In doing this, we hope to respond to what the contemporary philosopher and literary critic Martin Hägglund has noted in his attempt to unite political progressivism with the demands of the climate crisis: "[N]othing can be at stake in life – that no purpose can matter – without running the risk of death. Life can only matter in light of death" (2019, 181). It is in "the light of death" that the form of the American short story helps to illuminate our way forward and makes its claim upon our focused attention.

* * *

At the heart of Henry James's preface to the New York edition of *The Ambassadors* (1903) – a work James considered his best, proof that "the Novel remains still, under the right persuasion, the most independent, most elastic, most prodigious of literary forms" (James 1984, 1321) – lies an arresting encounter with the short story. "[P]lanted or 'sunk,' stiffly and saliently, in the center of the current" of his novel, "almost perhaps to the obstruction of traffic," lies an "independent particle," based on an anecdote that James is told by word of mouth (1304). This authentic "story" involves the scene in a Paris garden in which the novel's hero, Lambert Strether, offers advice to a younger acquaintance: "Live all you can," says the older to the younger man, "it's a mistake not to." Like Walter Benjamin's idea of the storyteller offering counsel and embodying communal care in light of the presence of death, the moral of Strether's story is to live as fully and freely as possible because time is running out. It is tempting to view James's situation-based "story" as the germ that simply dissolves into the greater form of the novel, yet James returns the role of the storyteller later in his preface, expanding on its possibilities:

> There is always, of course, for the story-teller, the irresistible determinant and the incalculable advantage of his interest in the story *as such*; it is ever, obviously, overwhelmingly, the prime and precious thing (as other than this I have never been able to see it); as to which what makes for it, with whatever headlong energy, may be said to pale before the energy with which it simply makes for itself. It rejoices, none the less, at its best, to seem to offer itself in a light, to seem to know, and with the very last knowledge, what it's about – liable as it yet is at moments to be caught by us with its tongue in its cheek and absolutely no warrant but its splendid impudence. Let us grant then that the impudence is always there – there, so to speak, for grace and effect and *allure*; there, above all, because the Story is just the spoiled child of art, and because, as we are always disappointed when the pampered don't "play up," we like it, to that extent, to look all its character. (1310–11)

Rather than a self-contained genre, the story is described by James as an energy, wild and extreme, an unorthodox and errant force that inhabits his novel as a self-consciousness of form itself, which can easily become ironic and impudent in its decadent effect. Like the monstrous child that John Winthrop describes as embodying both brevity and the heresy of independence, James's "spoiled child of art" – the short story – has too much form (James earlier describes it as having a "concrete" existence that leaves one to decide "where to put one's hand on it"), but then, like a child, it is also significantly *unformed* and thus in need of discipline, care, and education. As we have seen – and will see again and again in this volume – the short story's emphasis on craft, its consciousness of form, lends itself to metafiction, of which James was of course the master. Hence James's best-known (and very long) short story, "The Turn of the Screw" (1898), features another "spoiled" child who is thrown out of school, and who generates narrative care and interest (and hence motivates the story itself) through a combination of his diminutive size and his errant quality – is he abused, possessed, haunted, perverse, or "queer"? If the story ends when our narrator catches and holds the child at the point of his death, then we might be forgiven in reading it as James's own grappling with a literary form – the short story – that refused to behave within the constraints of scale. The short story might be small but it always acted big; it always played up.

The chapters in this volume aim to educate the reader by bringing care and discipline to a literary form whose errancy and precarious position in literary history lies in its contradictory capacity to be both highly conventional and overdetermined, on the one hand, and, on the other, to be so protean, mobile, and experimental as to seem virtually untheorizable.

In response to this dynamic, the book is divided into four parts. Part I explores across history how the various contexts in which the short story is encountered (by readers and by writers) have shaped its form and determined its content. Chapter 1, by Oliver Scheiding, disrupts the conventional wisdom running through short story criticism: that the short story has a discrete origin point, say in the work of Washington Irving or Edgar Allan Poe, and is hence implicated in an exceptionalist narrative about US culture and society in the nineteenth century. Instead, Scheiding traces the emergence of the short story by analyzing a network of related texts, congregating in the eighteenth century, that grappled with a sense of wonder in the face of supernatural events and other forms of sensational, abnormal, and marginalized experience associated with various "New World" encounters. Readers will discover from this chapter the sources of the short story's powers of movement – here between local and metropolitan contexts, and between fictional, nonfictional, and religious genres – and its capacity to embody transgressive experiences. In Chapter 2, Jared Gardner continues to trace the emergence of the short story in a precarious transatlantic print market, and announces a thematic that continues through the volume: the close connection between the short story and educational institutions of various kinds. For Gardner, short narrative is less mobile than embedded within and distributed throughout an emergent magazine culture in which lines remain blurred between short tales and other genres. As a form primed to grab readerly attention, and hypersensitive to its commercial environment, the short story came to embody new forms of pleasure as a fad in the burgeoning late-nineteenth-century magazine market dominated – as Brad Evans explores in Chapter 3 – by women readers and, increasingly, by women writers. Again employing a networked understanding of literary culture, in which popular short stories move among the advertisements and illustrations of their media environment, Evans poses an important question: How do we understand the form of the short story in relation to the whimsical pleasures, delightful excesses, and infinite variety of consumer culture? If Evans uncovers an alternative canon of short stories at the end of the nineteenth century, then Alexander Manshel investigates the dwindling of the short story canon in the twentieth century in Chapter 4, during a time when various collections, anthologies, awards, and syllabi sought to save the short story from the ephemerality and disposability that Evans identifies. As a protean genre, the short story is easily associated with the pluralistic diversity of American society. But when we look at the institutions that confer prestige on the short story, we discover a surprising lack of diversity in the genre, a homogeneity (at least in comparison with the novel) impacting both aesthetic style and authorial identity. Loren Glass continues this line of thinking in Chapter 5 by exploring in greater detail the close relationship between short story production and the creative writing classroom in the post-1945 period. Even if the short story has enjoyed a recent resurgence among minority and international writers, Glass uncovers how the workshop dynamic normalizes the style of the short story and its themes, which reflect the precarious economic situations of the college-educated creative class. The sixth and final chapter of this first section, by Simone Murray, explores how short fiction born digitally on the Internet in the twenty-first century generates new literary forms, even as it returns to the media mobility and the capacity to capture strange experience that has defined encounters with short fiction since at least the eighteenth century.

If the novel has tended to dominate the literary history of prose fiction as the principal genre of modernity, then Part II of this Companion contends that the short story requires a pluralistic, smaller-scale concept of literary "Histories" to bring it into view. Cody Marrs's Chapter 7 argues that the short story's modernity can be found in its representation of the violence, dehumanization, and collapsed ideals of modern warfare. The short story's attunement to shock and traumatic experience make it a form primed to represent the problematic psychological and ethical consequences of the experience of war. This disconnected sense of temporality seen in the modern war story also empowers the form to represent the marginalization of working-class experience, as Owen Clayton argues in Chapter 8. Bodily alienation, emotional stunting, affective numbness, and curtailed development are the thematic resonances of working-class precarity that find a natural home in short fictional forms that offer a historical alternative to the more bourgeois concerns of the novel. The proletarianized labor conditions of the short story writer also concern Will Norman in his Chapter 9 on the low-status, pulp magazine crime fiction popular during the interwar period. Here the special economy of the short story enabled middlebrow writers to embody their contradictory class positions in a vacillation between conventionalized and more experimental forms of detective fiction. Still further tracing the economy of the short story into a twenty-first century dominated by service work, Lee Konstantinou explores in Chapter 10 the precarity of the contemporary storyteller across a series of recent stories that allegorize an ambivalent situation, as recent writers critique neoliberal labor conditions yet are condemned to repeat their patterns of "emotional labor" for the reader. Long Le-Khac's Chapter 11 concludes this section – and looks forward to the next – by offering an institutional history of minority short fiction in relation to the democratization of the literary market, which pressures minority writers to package their ethnic experience in short, diverse forms. Returning to the ambivalent position of the short story writer that occupies Norman and Konstantinou, Le-Khac demonstrates how minority writers achieve a "double consciousness," meeting while critiquing the ethnographic gaze of the (largely) white audience.

The ethnographic imagination that Le-Khac identifies stretches back to the origins of short narrative in "New World" encounters of cultural difference and the concerns of place. Hence Part III traces various ways that short stories are integral to the historical understanding of cultural groups, and the capturing of a geographical and environmental imagination. In her Chapter 12 on the Native American storytelling tradition, Hertha D. Sweet Wong identifies the short story less as a genre than a power, based in oral tradition, that circulates throughout Native American culture, creating and recreating identities across time. Wong stresses the variety, mobility, and networking of Native American stories, which serve both political and spiritual purposes, and take both realist and fantastic forms. In Chapter 13, Amina Gautier then traces the power of brevity and the developing arc of African American short fiction from its basis in nineteenth-century reform, through the negotiation with white stereotypes at the turn of the century, to the more ethnographic concerns of writers in the Harlem Renaissance. Moving to questions of place, Coleman Hutchison explores in Chapter 14 the circulation of short stories in the American South, where regional concerns expand to encompass multicultural differences and relate that region to transnational, hemispheric flows of culture. In his study of turn-of-the-twentieth-century regionalist literature, which privileged short fiction as the formal embodiment of its "minor" concerns, Sylvan Goldberg reassesses, in Chapter 15, regionalism's "timelessness" (its nostalgic, temporal escape from industrial modernity) to stress instead its *timeliness*. A turn to the future, and a small-scale focus on the natural world, make regionalist short fiction a sensitive barometer of human precarity, hence providing the necessary ethic of environmental care, in the face of looming climate catastrophe. Myka Tucker-Abramson's Chapter 16 ends this section by turning to the place of the city in short fiction, ranging from romance in the colonial city, to detective literature in the industrial city, to science fiction in the automotive and neo-mercantile cities of the present. Abramson takes a formal characteristic of the short story – its internal doubleness, found most obviously in its illuminating endings – to show how the short story theorizes urban modernity as a process of emergence from pre-urban forms.

The theoretical power that Abramson and others detect in the short story is the explicit focus of Part IV. At least since Poe's 1842 review of Hawthorne and his ideal of "unity of effect," the short story has attracted strong theories of its formal nature and its cultural position in the nation. Rather than reductively essentializing the short story as a form whose very mobility requires us to pin it down, the chapters in this final section take an expansive and relativistic approach to show how the short story continues to generate significant theories of human and posthuman experience. Gabriella Safran begins this section by identifying in Chapter 17 a countertradition of the American short story that stresses not intense emotion (Poe's theory) but innocent comedy, thus returning us to the pleasure in the short story that Evans identifies in his chapter. Relating stories to other short forms (aphorisms, puns, dictionary entries), Safran discovers a linguistic self-consciousness in the short story that theorizes, through humor, the processes of language acquisition and the instability of the standard language. The implicit presence of the spoken voice in a short story tradition hailing from oral culture is one of the foci of Gavin Jones's Chapter 18. By identifying the short story's relative freedom from the "container" of the book and its subsequently close relationships to other, non-textual media, such as photography, Jones traces across history a fugitive quality in the short story, an inbuilt consciousness of media embeddedness in which form and meaning change according to context. Shelley Streeby's Chapter 19 uncovers a dense network of magazines and anthologies that blur canonical and mass entertainment to show how the short story became a home for science fiction writing that both celebrates and satirizes humanity's relationship to technology. Streeby also charts the rise of "cli-fi" (climate fiction), a response to climate change and an impending sense of human precarity – a point that Goldberg makes, and that Michael Lundblad picks up in his Chapter 20 about the short story's posthumanist powers to deconstruct normative conceptions of the human subject. Implying a relationship between the short story as a "minor" form with a charisma problem and the unloved figure of the rat, Lundblad shows the potential and the limits of short fiction to trouble the boundary between human and nonhuman animal perspectives. The final two chapters of this Companion turn to the short story's signature temporality: its heightened concern with narrative closure, its focus on single moments (compared with the novel's deeper connection to history), and its foundational brevity. Detecting a masculinist politics in the very idea of narrative closure, Lola Boorman's Chapter 21 looks to women writers' play with a grammar of presentness and middleness to explore a feminist alternative to modernity's ideology of progress. Chapter 22, the last in the Companion, brings methods from the Digital Humanities to bear on the central question of short story theory: Is there anything, other than length, that makes short stories categorically different from other (longer) narrative forms such as the novel? Through computational macroanalysis of large corpora of short stories and novels, this chapter, co-authored by Mark Algee-Hewitt, Anna Mukamal, and J. D. Porter, reaches some surprising conclusions about the short story's emphasis on closure, its capacity for characters, and what Poe called its unity of effect.

In *O. Henry and the Theory of the Short Story* (1925), the Russian Formalist critic Boris Eikhenbaum described the history of the American short story not as "an orderly, consecutive evolution" but as a process of incessant elaboration, variety, and possibility (1968, 2). For Eikhenbaum, the short story was an upstart form that refused to behave – a kind of literary heresy. Even at its most conventional it could flip into self-conscious experimentation. If the theory of narrative in general has defaulted to the novel as the supreme genre of fiction, with special links to the individual psychologized subject, to the bourgeoisie and its conventional ideologies, to empiricism and realism, and to the history of the book (and hence of private reading experience), then this Companion implies throughout a crucial question: What would that theory of narrative look like with the short story, not the novel, at its heart? Following the lead of Winthrop, Benjamin, James, and Eikhenbaum, we are led away from a unified theory of literary form toward an eccentric sense of literary history that returns to what Eikhenbaum described as the short story's powers of surprise, contradiction, oddity, incongruity, and error, all of which have made the short story not simply different from the novel but actually "at odds" with it (4). Less a genre, perhaps, than an errant energy flowing through the nation, the short story is the bellwether of human precarity and minor experience, of communal care and collective consciousness, even as its freedoms stem from an ironic dependence on the institutions that surround it. Taken together, the chapters in this volume strive to capture this variety, possibility, timeliness, and, indeed, the heresy of the American short story.

Works Cited

Benjamin, Walter. 1999. *Illuminations*. Ed. Hannah Arendt. Trans. Harry Zorn. London: Pimlico Press.

Collins, Michael J. 2016. *The Drama of the American Short Story, 1800–1865*. Ann Arbor: University of Michigan Press.

2018. "Transnationalism and the Transatlantic Short Story," in *The Edinburgh Companion to the Short Story in English*. Ed. Paul Delany and Adrian Hunter, 9–23. Edinburgh: Edinburgh University Press.

Eikhenbaum, Boris. 1968 [1925]. *O. Henry and the Theory of the Short Story*. Trans. I. R. Titunik. Ann Arbor: University of Michigan Press.

Hägglund, Martin. 2019. *This Life: Secular Faith and Spiritual Freedom*. New York: Pantheon Books.

James, Henry. 1984. *Literary Criticism*. New York: Library of America.

Levine, Caroline. 2015. *Forms: Whole, Rhythm, Hierarchy, Network*. Princeton, NJ: Princeton University Press.

O'Brien. Edward J. 1931. *The Advance of the American Short Story*. Revised ed. New York: Dodd, Mead, and Co.

Tallack, Douglas. 1993. *The Nineteenth-Century American Short Story: Language, Form, and Ideology*. London and New York: Routledge.

Winthrop, John. 1692 *A Short Story of the Rise, Reign, and Ruine of the Antinomians, Familists and Libertines, that Infected the Churches of New England*. 2nd ed. http://name.umdl.umich.edu/A65392.0001.001.

PART I

Contexts

CHAPTER I

Transatlantic Print Culture and the Emergence of Short Narratives

Oliver Scheiding

To highlight the workings of transatlantic print culture and the emergence of short narratives, this chapter explores the proliferation of popular forms of storytelling that shaped a "culture of wonder" (Hall 1989, 72) in early America before 1800. The chapter seeks not to trace the origin of the American short story, but instead aims to respond to the reevaluation of American literature as a network of transnational literary exchanges. Rather than focus on the birthplace of the American short story and the emergence of an exceptional national print culture, this chapter unearths the circulation of prose compositions and textual networks to provide a basis for studying the constant movement of stories, writers, and themes from the seventeenth to the nineteenth centuries. It thus exceeds notions of origination and sheds new light on the formative period of American literature.

Eve Tavor Bannet has shown that the "literary commons" (2011, 9) of the transatlantic world has created dynamic interplays and negotiations between local storytelling and multilingual, metropolitan print cultures. Drawing upon recent studies and their global reexaminations of literary production, circum-Atlantic literary networks, and reading audiences, scholars (cf. Hall 2000–2010; Loughran 2007; Scheiding and Seidl 2015) have reassessed the evolution of the early story from the vibrant literary landscape of short forms that circulated in the transatlantic world prior to 1800. Processes of textual travel characterize short narratives in North America as a result of complex cultural translations and traffic. While stories migrated from Europe to North America, they have been reclassified by writers and editors for changing audiences, times, and circumstances. The early short narratives often acquired multiple "lives" as they crossed generic and linguistic boundaries. For example, collections or individual foreign tales were translated into English and published separately as extracts in newspapers or magazines.[1] Some had an "afterlife" as reprints or served as templates for nineteenth-century short stories. Along the way, they were renamed, stripped of their origins, and sometimes rewritten (cf. Scheiding 2012). The early story in the Americas frequently results from acts of literary piracy and verbatim copying, as well as from editors' relentless hunt for short tales that satisfied the desultory reading habits of their audience. The emergence of the "American" story is less a creation of a single author than a product of multiple authorships and editorial interventions. Its success, or its "becoming American," depends less on its being "original," that is, penned by an American writer (most stories were published anonymously, anyway), than on its brevity and variety. In this regard, more recent studies in early popular print culture demonstrate that "[r]eaders and publishers ... routinely forced fiction to migrate into other forms of writing – a kind of transtextual operation that turned fiction into other genres such as aphorism, moral essay, magazine article, character sketch, political disquisition, and so on" (Flint 2011, 46).

While surveys of the American short story frequently consider the genre's development in terms of a normative definition (Matthews 1977, 45–48; Poe 1977, 34–36), with its focus on originality and certain epistemic values such as revelation, shock of recognition, and epiphany, this chapter suggests an alternative reading that explores more seriously the emergence of the short story in the context of a "culture of wonder" that dominated the Atlantic world of print prior to Washington Irving. Religious and book historians such as David D. Hall (1995, 2008) and Alexandra Walsham (2003) have shown how stories of strange and supernatural events have been collected, produced, and read on both sides of the Atlantic. Walsham identifies the specific motifs and formulae of religious stories, such as the divine judgment of sinners, that were common to both religious and secular works. Mostly titled "relations," these short prose narratives, Walsham further shows, drew on conventions from medieval tragedies, religious anecdotes, and exemplary tales. This chapter highlights how these wonder stories about the apparitions of ghosts, supernatural events, and divine interventions found their way into an eighteenth-century transatlantic print market interested in miraculous and strange events. It is a discrete history that connects religious to gothic and sensationalistic texts which established what has been called "light reading" or "small tales" (Anon. 1802a, 261) and appealed to a growing audience fascinated by short narratives about murder, crime, or strange incidents. Although often discarded because of a "primitive formlessness" (O'Brien 1923, 20), these "small tales" were widely reprinted in the pages of early transatlantic magazines and provide a purview of what Poe later calls "species of indefinite definiteness" (1845, 271), including sensational effects as well as transgressive stories about individuals whose behavior is outside the norm.

In doing so, this chapter examines the circulation of early short narratives in the context of serialized imprints such as magazines and newspapers. Besides reconsidering a number of short narratives, most often published anonymously and focusing on popular topics such as ghost stories and sensationalistic tales, the chapter also sheds light on the female print agency practiced by Margarette V. Faugères and Eliza Anderson. Moreover, the chapter unearths the rich archive of transatlantic storytelling, demonstrating how the short form combines oral and textual performances conditioning the nineteenth-century tale as it can be found in the writings of Washington Irving and Edgar Allan Poe.

Supernatural Narratives and Early Serialized Imprints

The ghost story has been one of the most productive genres in western literary history. Its presence has been closely allied with the attempt to recognize literary – if often oral – traditions that precede the European presence on the continent. Supernatural tales emerge as a narrative ground in which various strands of ancient and early modern American culture converge. While the American Republic did not have a medieval past to which it could relate, writers such as Washington Irving combined German and English folklore in narratives that echo forms of oral storytelling and conjoin them with local legends and Native myths that are tied to specific locations in North America. Strong links to the supernatural persisted also in Native American cultures and in the numerous religious creeds of the first settlers; tales of hauntings, ghosts, and apparitions filled colonial religious texts as well as the pages of early national magazines and ethnographic accounts of Native myths. In the seventeenth century, prodigious signs and natural phenomena became part of a transatlantic "culture of wonder" in which the European settlers participated by incorporating Native American myths and dramatizing their experience as a battle of good and evil in the "wilderness" of the new continent (see Cohen 2010; Hall 1995, 29–30).

A commonplace of medieval hagiography, wonder tales were first rejected as "superstition" by Protestant reformers, but Alexandra Walsham (2003) has demonstrated how their supernatural elements and use as exempla continued in Protestant writing and dominated early modern print culture.[2] At the same time, accounts of uncanny events from religious or secular sources became more and more exchangeable as ministers sought to endow their sermons with forceful narratives while hack writers masked their commercial interests with a few stereotypical religious remarks. Scholars have shown how popular and religious culture also merged on the print market as chapbooks (i.e., small books of popular ballads and stories), pamphlets, and broadsides of wonder tales hawked by peddlers, hung and read in public places, or perpetuated orally on both sides of the Atlantic (cf. Brown 2007; Cambers 2011; Dopffel 2020).

From the eighteenth century onwards, stories with supernatural elements proved one of the most diverse and vibrant genres in American literature. Many stories centered upon apparitions of ghosts, as evident from the case of "Joseph Beacon," reprinted three times in different works by Cotton Mather (see 1692, 79–81) and also reissued by Daniel Defoe in an epistolary version in *An Essay on the History and Reality of Apparitions* (1727, 169–70). Mather tells the story of how a ghost appears at his brother's house in Boston, right at the same moment that he is murdered in faraway London. The apparition of the ghost and its demand that the murderer be brought to justice are reminiscent of the ghost of Hamlet's father. That ghosts and apparitions reveal murderers and call for justice or revenge is an old folklore motif that enters religious literature, for example, in Joseph Glanvill's *Sadducismus Triumphatus* (1681), a collection of supernatural and apparition tales. In terms of the development of the form, Mather's ghost story is also remarkable. With its densely shaped and controlled prose, the story creates a unified impression on the reader's imagination and serves as an exemplar for readers of how to perceive crises and turning points. "Joseph Beacon" anticipates the role of detailed description and the investigation of the narrator in Defoe's "A True Relation of the Apparition of Mrs. Veal" (1711), often considered one of the first English short stories (see Current-García 1985, 9–10).

While early ghost stories frequently provide detailed descriptions and contain a narrator or characters attempting to determine whether an apparition actually occurred or whether the claims of the ghost can be verified, in Washington Irving's "The Devil and Tom Walker" (1824) the truthfulness of events is of minor importance, as the narrator freely combines elements from folklore and refrains from fitting them into a convincing argument or didactic message. After introducing the two characters of the title, the narrative voice evaluates the unfolding tale by surmising that "it has almost too familiar an air to be credited" (2015, 221). Repeatedly, the narrator refers to the circulation and variation of the story, itself a local legend, and presents the reader with the version he finds most likely or generally believed. The many references to other legendary figures, such as the pirate William Kidd and Native American ghosts, are tightly woven into the description of the woods as dark and mysterious. Set in Puritan New England, the story refers to the general suspicion of a devilish undermining of its society in the witchcraft trials and parallels the hypocrisy of superficial piety with the cutthroat market economy that also evolved in the colonies. Through these references and elements of oral storytelling, "The Devil and Tom Walker" endows New England with a legendary past it did not possess before, developing American folkloric figures, such as the devil roaming the woods, heathen Natives, and dangerous pirates in a way that surpasses Irving's most famous stories "Rip Van Winkle" (1820) and "The Legend of Sleepy Hollow" (1820).

The taste for gothic literature also goes – in an etymological sense – back to the Middle Ages, as the term was often used derogatively for a "barbaric," "dark," and "rude" state of mankind. Accordingly, eighteenth-century literature witnessed a return of elements from legends, epics, and fairy tales in narratives revolving around valiant knights on quests of love and adventure entering dark castles or enchanted landscapes. In Anna Lætitia Barbauld's "Sir Bertrand: A Fragment," for example, a traveling knight enters a dark castle and releases a lady from her enchanted confinement. Published in England by her brother John in *Miscellaneous Pieces, in Prose* (1773), Barbauld's story was reprinted numerous times in North America, for example by the *Columbia Magazine* in 1787. A prolific English poet, writer, and political activist, Barbauld used the fragment to test her theories about the power of literature to evoke effects such as horror. Using medieval settings and infusing them with a gothic atmosphere, narratives such as Barbauld's enlarged the American sense of history by incorporating references to the European Middle Ages. Likewise, Washington Irving's "The Devil and Tom Walker" takes up the European folkloric conception of the devil as a black man but also alludes to the Native Americans, pirates, and Puritans who have created a mythological impact on a particular place. With a tale rich in allusions and elements from legends, superstitions, and folklore, Irving invokes the pleasure of storytelling far from moral or scientific reasoning but not without satirical side blows at the Puritan settlers and their morality.

Apart from these attempts to create a legendary and usable past in the Americas, the many regions and cultural contact zones have a rich oral and literary tradition reaching back thousands of years. Records of Native American storytelling have undergone various steps of recording, translation, and reprinting.[3] In northern America, the first records of Native myths, religion, and folklore can be found in colonial diaries, as well as in the reports of missionaries such as the Jesuits and the Moravians whose missions could also be found in the Caribbean and South America. Like the Mayan culture, whose agriculture was based on maize, the Penobscot tribes, in what is today Maine, record the creation of two plants out of the dead body of the First Mother. In Benjamin Franklin's "Origin of Tobacco" (1787), a similar myth is told by Susquehannock Natives and is satirically compared to the Creation and the Fall in the Bible. While it extends the patterns of Native American myth to the biblical use of fruit, it serves as well as an indictment of the missionary's narrow-minded rejection of this parallel concept of truth. Thus, the story could also serve as a reminder that this Christian perspective and bias were also shared by many of the recorders of Native American culture and feature in the various intentions and translation processes involved in its preservation in writing. Franklin's short narrative first appeared in a Massachusetts newspaper and was quickly reprinted in a number of magazines and other newspapers in Pennsylvania and throughout New England.

Regardless of a prevailing skepticism toward fiction throughout the Colonial Period and post-revolutionary America (cf. Koenigs 2021), the newly founded magazines of the second half of the eighteenth century built upon literary themes that had emerged in colonial times and translated the most popular ones, such as the frontier, warfare, crime, and witchcraft, into short pieces of fiction. Since the genre of the short story was not yet established, the lines between so-called anecdotes, stories, histories, tales, fragments, and novels were blurred and flexible. Although most magazines had only a short run, others, such as the popular *New-York Weekly Museum*, were successful. Mott reports that another magazine, the *Massachusetts*, "is one of the best in which to study the early development of the American short story" (1957, 109).

Sensationalistic Short Narrative and the Atlantic World of Print

The majority of short narratives that attracted the readership in the early years of the American Republic were sensationalistic. Weekly and monthly literary magazines were filled with original and selected "small tales" characterized by uncommon themes elevated to the wondrous – human events blown up to the marvelous. An anonymous letter addressed to the editor of *The Philadelphia Repository and Weekly Register* (1800–1804) revealed the profusion of sensational fantasies in the pages of early American periodical publications. The author complained that magazine editors prefer such tales as abound with stories of demons, hob-goblins, specters, witches, haunted towers, church-yards, charnel houses, tombs, enchant-ments, murders, robberies, gods, goddesses, angels, divinities, demigods, heroes, heroines, lovers, &c. – or lovers, gallantries, intrigues, bastards, perjuries, murder, assassination, hair-breadth-escapes, suicides, and an almost infinite chain of ridiculous and wild et ceteras. (Anon. 1802a, 261)

Magazine editors quickly learned to exploit their readers' appetite for transgressive short narratives; they obtained factual and fictional stories from all sources available to cater to a growing taste for sensationalistic topics about outsiders, shape-shifters, and marginal characters. Readers could, however, easily grasp the story's imaginary happenings, which were often accompanied by morally instructive remarks, because they accorded with what has been called "light reading" or "small tales," with their appeal to a growing, unspecialized audience fascinated by short fictions.

In the "rational age" of the late eighteenth century, abnormality was inherently interesting. Human nature was imagined as running wild in foreign settings, but there were many exceptions, and as magazine fiction shows (even prior to Poe; see Nagel 2008, 11–67), the domestic and foreign are telescoped together in stories about liminal figures that reveal the complex nature of human reality often at odds with social reality. The *New-York Weekly Museum* marks an important stage in the devel-opment of periodical publications as a popular form of entertainment within a context which has been described here as a "culture of wonder" in early North America. Edited by John Harrisson, his wife, and later his son from 1788 until 1811, the *New-York Weekly Museum* had one of the longest print runs in the history of early American magazines. From its inception, the periodical's motto read, "With sweetest flowers enrich'd from various gardens cull'd with care." The editors "cull'd" from many sources and they rampantly pirated tales from British magazines without acknowledgment. John Harrisson succeeded in selling his "culled fic-tion" to a steady number of subscribers. By the first decade of the nineteenth century, the magazine provided its readership with a wild mix of different genres, ranging from sensationalistic fiction to moral essays and journalistic reports. Another of Harrisson's editorial principles was brevity. Harrison acted under the rule *multum in parvo* and embarked upon what Oliver Goldsmith derogatively called a "magazine in miniature ... hop[ping] from subject to subject" (53).

A typical weekly issue usually offered the reader an extravagant mix of sensationalistic tales and news articles. In one of the weeklies from

May 1802, the frontpage story "The Adultress Punished: A Tale" echoes a strikingly macabre scene taken from Marguerite de Navarre's *Heptameron* (1558) in which an unfaithful woman is forced by her vengeful husband to drink out of her dead lover's skull. On the following pages, the reader encounters a vignette entitled "Hardened Villainy" which magnifies a personal moment in the life of a remorseless young murderer who has committed atrocious crimes in Bordeaux. The succeeding anecdote, "Cosmo De Medici," gives currency to a vague rumor about numerous killings in the Grand Duke's family. A few lines below, the reader's attention is drawn to a short narrative set in ancient Greece. "Inhumanity" adopts a tale by Seneca and describes how the Athenian artist Parrhasius had a slave tortured so that he could have a model for a painting of the bound Prometheus for the Parthenon in Athens. A final news section contains the story of Russell Bean (1769–1826). He was a feisty Tennessee rifle-maker who upon returning to his home after a long absence found his wife seduced and thus cut the ears off her infant. Harrisson's reprints fed readers' appetite for violence and irrational acts by humans ancient and contemporary – something rather more pungent than the scent of "sweetest flowers" promised in the magazine's motto. Editors could justify the inclusion of such narratives because they offered the reader exemplary lessons that taught men to feel sympathy with the victims of violence, unforeseen incidents, and personal disasters. To call upon human misfortunes to evoke fellow emotions was certainly a morally useful tactic. And yet, while Harrisson's reprinted "small tales" teach his readers dramatic lessons of "human depravity" (Anon. 1802b, 2), they also spell out the transgressive nature that lies beneath the surface of human life itself. Stories about murders and sociopaths unfold a spectacular sphere which defies the existing order of things and allows the reader to step outside accepted classifications and norms. Reading itself becomes a threshold experience of human action and behavior often masked by psychotic indifference. The plethora of "small tales" create thus a creative playground for society, which renders unresolved social tensions, conflicts, and anxieties meaningful through the reader's engagement with short forms of narration.

In 1796, the *New York Weekly Magazine* printed a short, anonymously published narrative entitled "An Account of the Murder of Mr. J—Y— [James Yates], upon his family, in December, A.D. 1781." Although the magazine paid homage to republican virtues, the editors equally satisfied their readers' growing appetite for gory accounts of murder and crime. Execution sermons and confessions were the leading literary forms to portray perpetrators and to control domestic fantasies about crime.[4] "An Account of the Murder of Mr. J—Y—," written by Margaretta Bleecker Faugères, marks the movement toward a more profane but graphic short narrative of crime. Faugères retells the story of an actual familicide that occurred in 1781 in upstate New York. Misguided by religious delusions, a farmer, James, kills his wife Elizabeth, their two daughters, Diana and Rebecca, and their two sons. Despite the strong religious subtext (Yates converted to the Shaker religion), the murder is set within gothic conventions and highlights monstrous lunacy in the face of inscrutable evil as one of the key features of the new carnal literature of crime. The story became a source of inspiration for Charles Brockden Brown's short story "Somnambulism" and his novel *Wieland; or, The Transformation: An American Tale* (1798). Faugères's account of the family's slaughter also imitates the language of captivity narratives, which is in tone similar to the well-known *History of Maria Kittle*, authored by her mother, Ann Eliza Bleecker, and published posthumously by her daughter in 1793.

Similarly, "Valeria, or the Ghost Alive!" is a tale about premature death that has a long prehistory in the context of the transatlantic culture of print and marks the transition from apparition narratives to the supernatural tale in the nineteenth century. Drawing upon an earlier collection of French criminal reports and court decisions, Jean-Pierre Claris de Florian fleshed out a ghost story in his *Nouvelles nouvelles* (Paris, 1792). Florian entitled his story "Valeria: An Italian Tale." In the same year, an English translation appeared in London as *New Tales from the French of M. Florian*. American editors pirated the increasingly popular anthologies of short tales emerging in England during the 1790s, borrowing from them without acknowledging their sources. The London version appeared serialized with dramatic cliff-hangers in the American *Literary Museum, or Monthly Magazine* in 1797. While Florian's version controls the transgressive experience of the lovers by quoting authorities from classical antiquity in the story's introduction, the abridged reprints transit from the dogmatic to the literary use of the supernatural by leaving out the introduction and creating a situation of oral storytelling. The narrator relates how, at a Christmas house party in the Languedoc, as the youthful company were telling each other stories of "the marvelous, ghosts and apparitions" (Anon. 1807, 209), a young Italian lady named Valeria introduced her story by calling herself a ghost. She explained that after having been refused permission to marry her lover Octavian, she was deceived into marrying a cousin. Discovering the deceit immediately after the wedding, she fainted and became delirious; "the disease rapidly increased, and after a paroxysm of sixty hours" (213) she expired. Valeria was placed in the family vault, but Octavian – having obtained access to the vault and kissing her – felt her breathe. He warmed her in his embrace and took her to his house where a physician "answered [her to] life" (214). Approaching her parents and husband as a ghost, she caused the former to repent of their actions, and the latter to relinquish his claim on her.

This version appeared in the first 1806 volume of the British magazine *La Belle Assemblee, or Bell's Court and Fashionable Magazine Addressed Particularly to the Ladies* (1806–1837; founded by John Bell). The story was reprinted in Baltimore a year later by Eliza Anderson, retitled "Valeria, or the Ghost Alive!" Anderson was the first woman to edit a general-interest magazine in the United States, and in 1806 she founded the *Observer* and adopted the penname "Beatrice Ironside" for her satirical and witty editorials. Within the pages of her magazine, Anderson fought journalistic vendettas against critics who were outraged over her translation of a scandalous French novel (Sophie Cottin's *Claire d'Albe*, 1798). Like earlier editors, Anderson recognized the story's outstanding potential, and was continually in search of material that would attract and retain subscribers. In the print context of the *Observer*, the story is not simply one with a happy resolution for the lovers, but one in which the threshold-crossing and reintegration of the protagonist evokes ambiguity. Valeria's final reprimanding of her parents' and husband's behavior contests prevailing notions of domestic authority and paternal power as questionable standards of communal life.

Conclusion

What Edward Pitcher calls a "coming together" (2000, 1) of several forms of eighteenth-century short fiction, such as the anecdote, essay, and sketch, which would ultimately merge into the short story (cf. Fash 2020), is in fact a process that is evident in colonial narratives and early periodical fiction as well. The early exploration and providential accounts already combine the oral and written traditions of Europe and encapsulate motifs and formal conventions later to be used in the short story. Regarding the various narrative conventions that shaped their production and eventual form, it becomes clear that early American short narratives are the product of complex literary interactions that evolve from religious and folk traditions connecting them to spectacular happenings and fantastic anxieties that conditioned the early transatlantic "culture of wonder." On the level of motif or subject matter, a confrontation between the individual and supernatural forces informs the apparition and wonder tale as well as the eighteenth-century "small tales." Irving's storyteller in "The Legend of Sleepy Hollow" directly refers to the dramatic potential of mysterious narrations. Moreover, the widely read apparition and witchcraft tales not only antecede late eighteenth- and nineteenth-century American gothic literature, they also formed a literary taste for murder stories and sensational events. The trend toward secularization ultimately changes the former theological framework and replaces it with a stronger focus on individual action and consciousness, as can be seen in Charles Brockden Brown's gothic tale "Somnambulism: A Fragment" (1805), with its atmosphere of terror and personal madness. The apparition and thunderstorm in Poe's gothic tale "The Fall of the House of Usher" (1839) signify less a divine punishment than an abstract spirit of revenge. While its mechanism still reproduces the folk belief about vengeful ghosts that is also evident in earlier apparition tales, eighteenth-century colonial narratives, as well as later magazine stories, shift from a singular theological or didactic intention toward complexity.

Stripped of their theological implications, early nineteenth-century apparition and ghost tales use the supernatural as a means to question human perception. Irving's ghost story "The Adventure of My Uncle" (1824), written as retrospective frame narrative, demonstrates that the role of the narrator shifts as epistemological uncertainty increases and rational explanations fail to explain the story's events. While earlier apparition tales have first-person narrators acting as rational investigators, Brown and Irving contrast Enlightenment thinking with gothic settings and create moods based on fragmentation and unclear perception. In his tale "The Adventure of the German Student" (1824, 66–74), Irving borrows from the German *Sturm und Drang* movement, with its exalted notions of feeling. The story reveals the "diseased imagination" of a young "enthusiastic character" (66) who falls in love with a corpse. With their innovative use of the narrator and the description of the supernatural, the early story developed formal characteristics that helped propel the "culture of wonder" into the twentieth century, as can be seen in tales of horror and wonder by Ambrose Bierce, Shirley Jackson, and Joyce Carol Oates.

Taken together, the examples discussed in this chapter illustrate the vitality of American short narration prior to the nineteenth century. While colonial and eighteenth-century fictions took their cue from Europe, they changed formal conventions and content in response to the particular conditions of the American environment. This also explains the many cross-references and recurring themes in the different genres of these times.

The opening decades of the nineteenth century saw the rise of print modernity, which coalesced around literary-cultural journals. This new type of magazine functioned as a cultural hybrid between modern print culture and older manuscript cultures (see Gardner 2012). Rearranging, de-contextualizing, or extracting texts from other sources, magazines invested texts with a new meaning and status and thus increased the range of textual appropriations on the readers' side. Therefore, a normative definition of the genre falls short of encompassing the variety of narratives that circulated in early North America. Yet many of the motifs and traits of nineteenth-century canonical short fiction can best be explained by looking at the variety of fiction that existed prior to it. Relating the American short story to the rich archive of colonial wonder stories and early periodical "small tales" helps us understand the emergence of the short story in the wider context of the Atlantic world of print and its multiple textual sources.

Works Cited

Allen, Ethan. 1779. *A Narrative of Colonel Ethan Allen's Captivity*. Philadelphia: Mentz.

Anna [pseud.] 1796. "An Account of a Murder Committed by Mr. J.—Y—, Upon his Family, in December, A.D. 1781," *The New-York Weekly Magazine; or, Miscellaneous Repository* 2.55: 20; 2.56: 28.

Anon. 1787. "Amelia; or, the Faithless Briton: An Original American Novel, Founded upon Recent Facts," *The Columbian Magazine* 1.14: 677–682; 1.16: 877–880.

1802a. "For the Philadelphia Repository," *Philadelphia Repository, and Weekly Register* 2.33 (26 June): 260–261.

1802b. "The Force of Hatred," *The New-York Weekly Museum* No. 693 (Saturday, February 6): 2.

1807 [1799]. "Valeria, or the Ghost Alive!" *The Observer* 2.14: 209–217.

1936. "John Onion," *The Narragansett Dawn* 1.9: 206.

Bannet, Eve Tavor. 2011. *Transatlantic Stories and the History of Reading, 1720–1820: Migrant Fictions*. Cambridge, UK: Cambridge University Press.

Barbauld, Anna Lætitia. 1787. "Sir Betrand: A Fragment. By Mrs. Barbauld," *The Columbia Magazine* 1 (15): 743–745.

Brown, Matthew P. 2007. *The Pilgrim and the Bee: Reading Rituals and Book Culture in Early New England*. Philadelphia: University of Pennsylvania Press.

Cambers, Andrew. 2011. *Godly Reading: Print, Manuscript and Puritanism in England, 1580–1720*. Cambridge, UK: Cambridge University Press.

Cohen, Matt. 2010. *The Networked Wilderness: Communicating in Early New England*. Minneapolis: University of Minnesota Press.

Current-García, Eugene. 1985. *The American Short Story before 1850: A Critical History*. Boston: Twayne.

Defoe, Daniel. 1727. *An Essay on the History and Reality of Apparitions: Being an Account of What They Come, and Whence They Come Not*. London: J. Roberts.

Dopffel, Michael. 2020. *Empirical Form and Religious Function: Apparition Narratives of the Early English Enlightenment*. Paderborn, Germany: Schoenigh.

Fash, Lydia G. 2020. *The Sketch, the Tale, and the Beginnings of American Literature*. Charlottesville: University of Virginia Press.

Flint, Christopher. 2011. *The Appearance of Print in Eighteenth-Century Fiction*. Cambridge, UK: Cambridge University Press.

Franklin, Benjamin. 1784. "The Origin of Tobacco, from a Curious Account Given by Dr. Franklin of the Hospitality of Those We Call the Savage Indians," *The Essex Journal and the Massachusetts and New-Hampshire General Advertiser* 25: 2.

1986 [1793]. *The Autobiography*. Ed. J. A. Leo Lemay and M. Zall. New York: Norton.

Gardner, Jared. 2012. *The Rise and the Fall of Early American Magazine Culture: The History of Communication*. Urbana: University of Illinois Press.

Goldsmith, Oliver. 1775. "Essay IX," in *The Miscellaneous Works of Oliver Goldsmith, M.B. Containing all his Essays and Poems*, 53–57. London: W. Griffith.

Hall, David D. 1989. *Worlds of Wonder, Days of Judgment: Popular Religious Belief in Early New England*. New York: Knopf.

1995. "Worlds of Wonders: The Mentality of the Supernatural in Seventeenth-Century New England," in *Religion and American Culture: A Reader*. Ed. David G. Hackett, 27–52. New York: Routledge.

2008. *Ways of Writing: The Practice and Politics of Text-Making in Seventeenth-Century New England*. Philadelphia: University of Pennsylvania Press.

Hall, David D., ed. 2000–2010. *A History of the Book in America*, vols. 1–5. Chapel Hill: University of North Carolina Press.

Irving, Washington. 1865 [1824]. "The Adventures of the German Student," in *Tales of a Traveller, Geoffrey Crayon, Gent*, 66–74. New York: G. P. Putnam's Sons.

2015 [1824]. "The Devil and Tom Walker," in *Worlding America: A Transnational Anthology of Short Narratives before 1800*. Ed. Oliver Scheiding and Martin Seidl, 218–228. Stanford, CA: Stanford University Press.

Josselyn, John. 1986 [1675]. "Account of Two Voyages to New England," in *A Library of Puritan Writings: The Seventeenth-Century. Vol. IX. Histories and Narratives*. Ed. Sacvan Bercovitch, 211–354. New York: AMS Press.

Koenigs, Thomas. 2021. *Founded in Fiction: The Uses of Fiction in the Early United States*. Princeton, NJ: Princeton University Press.

Loughran, Trish. 2007. *The Republic in Print: Print Culture in the Age of US Nation Building, 1770–1870*. New York: Columbia University Press.

Mather, Cotton. 1692. "A Narrative of an Apparition which a Gentleman in Boston, had of his Brother, just then Murdered in London," in *The Wonders of the Invisible World*, 79–81. Boston.

Matthews, Brander. 1977 [1885]. "The Philosophy of the Short-Story," in *Short-Story-Theorien (1573-1973): Eine Sammlung und Bibliographie englischer und amerikanischer Quellen*. Ed. Alfred Weber and Walter F. Greiner, 45–48. Kronberg, Germany: Athenäum.

Mott, Frank Luther. 1957 [1930]. *A History of American Magazines, 1741–1850*. Cambridge, MA: Harvard University Press.

Nagel, James, ed. 2008. *Anthology of the American Short Story*. Boston and New York: Houghton Mifflin Company.

O'Brien, Edward. 1923. *The Advance of the American Short Story*. New York: Dodd, Mead, and Company.

Pitcher, Edward W. R. 2000. "Introduction," in *An Anthology of the Short Story in 18th and 19th-Century America*. 2 vols. Studies in British and American Magazines 5, 1–47. Lewiston, NY: Mellen.

Poe, Edgar Allan. 1977 [1842]. "Twice-Told Tales," in *Short-Story-Theorien (1573–1973): Eine Sammlung und Bibliographie englischer und amerikanischer Quellen*. Ed. Alfred Weber and Walter F. Greiner, 34–36. Kronberg, Germany: Athenäum.

　　1845 [1839]. "The Devil in the Belfry," *The Broadway Journal* (8 November): 271–273.

Richardson, Lyon N. 1966. *A History of Early American Magazines, 1741–1789*. New York: Octagon Books.

Scheiding, Oliver. 2012. "Migrant Fictions and the Early Story in North American Magazines," in *REAL – Yearbook of Research in English and American Literature*. Vol. 28. *Mobility in English and American Literature 1500-1900*, 197–218. Tübingen, Germany: Narr.

Scheiding, Oliver and Martin Seidl, eds. 2015. *Worlding America: A Transnational Anthology of Short Narratives before 1800*. Stanford, CA: Stanford University Press.

Scofield, Martin. 2006. *The Cambridge Introduction to the American Short Story*. Cambridge, UK: Cambridge University Press.

Walsham, Alexandra. 2003. *Providence in Early Modern England*. Oxford: Oxford University Press.

CHAPTER 2

The Short Story and the Early Magazine

Jared Gardner

American writers were famously late to the novel. Using the conventional, if contested, starting point for the English novel of *Robinson Crusoe* (1719), there would be a full eighty-year wait for the first novel by an American author, despite a healthy appetite in the colonies and the new nation for novels imported from the British press. The short story, however, found fertile ground in the fragile literary economy of colonial America and in the early national period. Contrary to Alfred Bendixen's claim, however, the short story is not "an American invention" (Bendixen and Nagel 2010, 3). Like so much early "American literature," it has a transatlantic origin story, in this case one mediated almost entirely through periodicals.

What would eventually come to be called the "short story" by the second half of the nineteenth century was, for its first century in colonial and early national America, known by many names: "tale" was most prominent, but other names, such as "sketch," "fable," or "vision," were also in circulation. In some cases, these latter names denoted something different from our modern notion of the short story, but in many cases, they were used interchangeably. "Tale" can be found in the subtitles of scores of short fictions published in early American periodicals from the 1740s onward. The arrival of the term "short story" on the scene has been read as a sign of the form's maturation, its arrival at a state of self-consciousness about its goals and its audience. There is some truth in this, of course, but as this chapter will argue, the shift from "tale" to "short story" has more to do with a shift in the periodical marketplace itself, a shift brought about by a second print revolution in the nineteenth century and the transition from artisanal to industrial print.

In presenting this argument, I am not seeking to "recover" earlier short fiction in magazines as works worthy of study alongside nineteenth-century classics of the form. Indeed, the dramatic changes in the ecology of the periodical make such comparisons all but impossible. The "short story" of the mid-nineteenth century is a discrete commodity in the assembled wares of what Frank Luther Mott has termed the "Golden Age" magazine, one branded by an author's name and set aside as much as the form allows from other literary commodities assembled for consumption by the reader (1958, 337). The "tale" of the early American magazine was commonly embedded within surrounding texts and paratexts, proffered as an adjunct to a moral lesson or as a vital component to the early magazine's foundational promise of education *and* entertainment.

Despite these differences, it would be wrong to isolate the early history of short fiction in the American magazine from what comes after. In what follows, I will demonstrate that what we call the short story finds it shape and purpose in a (pre-industrial) print economy that prepares the ground for a new mass audience as it is reshaped by the industrial print economy of the nineteenth century. Doing so allows us to see how the short story first became central to American readers' conceptions of what imaginative literature might look like in the new nation, but also how what we think of as innovations credited to individual writers are as much the results of changes in the technology and marketplace of print as they are of any individual artist's innovations.

* * *

By most accounts, the first American novel was *The Power of Sympathy*, published in 1789 by the Massachusetts printer Isaiah Thomas, the most influential and successful printer of this period. Thomas had made his name during the Revolution as publisher of the *Massachusetts Spy*, a patriotic newspaper, and the *Royal American Magazine*, a short-lived but influential periodical that would inspire the growth of the form in the early national period. While it is his role in the history of the novel that secures Thomas's place in a literary history often determined to center the novel and its rise at every turn, Thomas quickly lost interest in the novel. Despite its salacious content – including incest and heavy-handed references to a Boston scandal – *The Power of Sympathy* sold quite poorly: two years after the initial print run, Thomas still had eighty copies of the novel on hand. "Do you want some of them?" Thomas asked a fellow printer. "Will exchange some of them for some of your publications" (1791, n.p.). Thomas was done with novels.

However, he would have a much harder time letting go of another unprofitable enterprise he began at the same time he was publishing the first novel: the *Massachusetts Magazine*. In announcing the project in a prospectus published the previous year, Thomas acknowledges that all such attempts "have failed of success," and describes the publishers as "fully sensible of the magnitude of the undertaking": "the expense will be great – the task arduous" (1788, 7). What encourages them to feel some confidence of success, the proposal announces, is the belief that they will be able to solicit contributions from leading thinkers across a wide range of areas of expertise, including churchmen, astronomers, physicians, merchants, husbandmen, botanists, geographers, historians, and politicians. The magazine for Thomas (as for many other magazine publishers during this period) was to be a repository of the best thinking from the young nation, compiled as a foundation upon which future accomplishments would be built.

To this long list of professional expertise with which the magazine hopes to fill its pages, the publisher promises a place for the "Witty" to "help us to that fund of entertainment, which is ever grateful to our feelings, when not too strongly tinctured with ill-natured sarcasms, and immodest remarks." "We would wish to gratify the taste of such as are fond of enlivening jest and a pleasing tale." The connection of "wit" and the "tale" is, as we will see, a vital one for the early magazine. In promising that "from the gardens of Literary Amusement we would ... cull the choicest flowers, but would carefully avoid the thorns," the publishers are promising the benefits of fiction without its well-known dangers: offending "the ear of Chastity," creating "mirth for one person which will give pain to another," or "retail-[ing] anecdotes of scandal" (Thomas 1788, 11). In their professed goal to "make it as complete and useful as any ever yet published in the United States" (11), the tale is the mortar holding together the various components that constitute the ideal of completeness *and* is the medium whereby these contents are made "useful."

This prospectus resembles many of the early American periodicals from the first decades of the new nation. This was a labor of love, not of profit – a gift to the nation and an investment in its future. The declaration of the labor involved and the inevitability of financial losses was not in any way exaggerated. After all, every other magazine published on the continent had failed within a handful of years at most (often within a handful of issues). The early American magazine was a publishing venture that stood as the exception to the rule for pragmatic publishers necessarily committed to the very rigid bottom lines of the business.

Correspondence between Thomas and his Boston partner, Ebenezer Andrews, makes clear where profits lay for the late eighteenth-century printer. For most American printers the biggest sellers were schoolbooks. In Thomas's case at the time this was Perry's *Spelling Book*, first published in

Scotland by William Perry in 1777 and soon reprinted numerous times in
the United States, most successfully by Thomas and Andrews. Even after
Webster's *American Spelling Book* appeared, Perry's continued to be a great
seller for Thomas – selling up to 300,000 copies by 1804, with another
20,000 the following year. In a letter of 1791, in which he lays out his
priorities for the press in the coming year, Andrews writes of "our spelling
book," of which

> we have now only 2700 and West and each of the Larkins want 100 each,
> besides which I suppose my brother, Hall, White, etc. will want 2000 more,
> besides those that will be wanted in Philadelphia and elsewhere. It will take
> upwards of 3 months to print 20,000, supposing the Press is kept going
> all the time and I don't know whether it will not be better to print 30,000
> or 40,000 if we can get 2 hands to keep at Press 6 months, and can get
> paper. (n.p.)

This letter provides a window on the print economy of the new nation on
the eve of industrial print. Thomas and Andrews need 20,000 spelling books
simply to meet local demand, with 30,000 preferred to meet ongoing
demand. In 1791, printing itself remained largely the artisanal affair it had
been in the fifteenth century when Gutenberg introduced the printing
press. Each piece of paper had to be made by hand, each piece of type (from
a limited and very expensive supply) had to be set one at a time by hand, and
considerable human labor was required to pull the platen down on the type
to force ink into the paper, one page at a time. Despite manifold small
refinements, a fifteenth-century German printer transported to Thomas's
late eighteenth-century Boston press would have recognized every aspect of
the process.

Thus, generating the materials necessary for printing 30,000 copies of
Perry's *Spelling Book* would depend on a supply of often limited commodities – especially labor (the hands to set the type, ink the plates, pull the
press, etc.) and paper (dependent at the time on a supply of rags, in short
supply since the Revolution, and on the capacity of the small papermills on
the Neponset River in Milton). Even if the supplies of rags allowed for this
level of production, of course, there was a pressing matter of time as the
process was grindingly slow.

On the printing side, the labor demands were still more intense. "We
could now, according to my calculation," Andrews reports, "employ 13 or
14 hands for a number of months, and perhaps all the time. We have in
hand, with what is ready, and nearly ready, as much as 13 or 14 hands, and
three or four presses could do" (1791, n.p.). In addition to Perry's *Spelling
Book*, the plan for the year's work includes *The Constitutions of the Masons*,

Bell's *System of Surgery*, and Watts's *Psalms*. This list does not include items too routine to merit mention: the newspaper, the annual almanac, various broadsides and pamphlets, and, of course, the Bible, a seller so secure that most presses had type permanently set up for regular printings.

Andrews *does* mention "the Magazine" in this 1791 letter, but primarily to indicate how much type, paper, and press time was tied up in this unprofitable venture. A year later, Andrews brought up the matter of the *Massachusetts Magazine* more directly, providing a blunt calculation "by which it appears to me that we do not get nearly so well paid for doing the Magazine as for other work that we do" (n.p.). True to form, Andrews has the brutal numbers to back up his claim: of 800 copies, 700 do sell, but once all the costs are subtracted – including the hundred copies "which ... are imperfect, given away, etc.," bad debts, eighty-eight reams of paper per issue, blue covers, copperplates, artist, and editor – the result is an annual loss of roughly £100. "I sometimes have a wish to rid of the Magazine, especially if we could get a compensation for it," Andrews begins; by the end of his accounting, however, he is more direct: "[I]t appears to me that if you should sell or give up the Magazine we could make as much again money by other work" (n.p.).

Knowing, as Noah Webster put it in introducing his own short-lived *American Magazine* in 1787, that "the expectation of *failure* is connected with the very name of a *Magazine*" (129), why would so many of the leading printers and editors of the day – practical-minded men such as Benjamin Franklin, Mathew Carey, Webster, and Thomas – dedicate considerable time and resources to a doomed venture? I explore this question in detail elsewhere, but it is worth rehearsing in brief here as it ultimately helps shape the role that short fiction played within this early American print economy.

While the magazine was not *economically* viable, it was, unlike the novel, widely believed to be the bearer of another kind of currency in short supply in the new nation – what today we would call "cultural capital" (Bourdieu 1984, 12). In a nation that had proven adept at the accumulation of economic capital, what was sorely lacking, in the eyes of many, was a corresponding attention to the accumulation of manners, taste, morals, and discrimination, qualities necessary to the future of the nation. So when Thomas set out to found his *Massachusetts Magazine* in 1789, he – like every magazine editor in America from Benjamin Franklin in the 1740s on – was inspired by the first literary periodical in London, the *Spectator* (1711–1712), which had explicitly set itself a similar project – not for a new nation but for a new powerbase within early eighteenth-century England.

A young Benjamin Franklin, who would go on to be one of a very few eighteenth-century printers more successful even than Isaiah Thomas, caught the periodical bug extremely early, upon reading the collected *Spectator* in his brother's Boston printshop, where he was apprenticed at the time. His first writings would be in imitation of Addison and Steele's *Spectator*, and his first attempt at publishing a magazine two decades later would be along the model suggested by Edward Cave's new *Gentleman's Magazine* (1731), which began by compiling the numerous periodical sheets of the day into a larger storehouse that Cave termed the "magazine." For ambitious American writers such as Franklin, these periodicals were associated with the literary luminaries of England: Joseph Addison, Richard Steele, Samuel Johnson, and Jonathan Swift. These periodical writers had used the form to bring manners and taste to a rising middle class, one – like the Americans of a generation later – dedicated to capital accumulation and woefully vulnerable to the pernicious influences of what was at the time a new medium: the newspaper.

Following the expiration of the Licensing Act in 1692, control over the press in England loosened, and new printers and newspapers appeared as if overnight. Newspapers circulated through a new institution that had itself only recently exploded throughout the city, the coffeehouse – a place for indulging in coffee, one of the new commodities of emerging modern capitalism, as well as a space for conducting the business of capitalism itself. Because speculation depended on information and gossip – about geopolitical and local politics, commodity futures, and the arrival of shipments – the newspapers and coffeehouses fed a voracious audience eager for insights into anything that might impact investments.

It was here that the periodical was born, conceived as an antidote to the daily cacophony of newspapers and commerce. The periodical as designed by Addison and Steele sought to train better readers, citizens, and husbands for the new responsibilities of power. This required, first and foremost, an alternative to the newspaper. As Mr. Spectator puts it in No. 4: "It is incredible to think how empty I have in this time observed some Part of the Species to be, what mere Blanks they are when they first come abroad in the Morning, how utterly they are at a Stand, until they are set a going by some Paragraph in a News-Paper" (1711, 1). In this account, the newspaper reader is a soulless automaton, set in motion by the newspaper's inflammatory columns. The periodical enters into this chaotic scene as a wise and patient tutor. Emblematized by the logo to the

Gentleman's Magazine – the ruffled hand of the editor holding a bouquet of flowers with the motto "*e pluribus unum*" – the magazine promises to bring order to chaos, and refinement to those who never had access to elite educations. It is no coincidence that the new nation, at the suggestion of Franklin himself, would select the motto of Cave's magazine as its motto. This was the ideal of the magazine and an expression of the hopes for the nation of the Founding Fathers, such as Franklin: representative democracy as the selection and artful arrangement of what would otherwise be anarchy and chaos.

* * *

This is the periodical world in which short fiction entered into the American magazine. Many of the earliest "tales" in the earliest colonial magazines were set in verse. For example, the *American Magazine and Historical Chronicle* of 1744 features several such pieces identified as *tales*, including "The Frightened Farmer: A Tale." By the eve of the Revolution, however, prose had displaced verse as the form of the tale. This was especially on display in the pages of the *Royal American Magazine*, Thomas's first periodical venture. In the first issue of the magazine in 1774, we find "The Thunder Storm: a Moral Tale," accompanied by an engraving by Paul Revere. Neither the story nor the image is "original." Thomas or his editor had found the story in the English *Town and Country Magazine* from the previous year, where it was embellished with a similar engraving. The text itself could be easily set by Thomas's own employees, but without access to the original plates from *Town and Country*, Thomas was required to hire a "sculptor," or engraver, charged to copy the illustration as closely as possible. Compared side by side with the original, Revere's version is a rather poor copy – unsurprisingly, as he was a silversmith and there were at the time no experienced print engravers in the colonies. But of course, Thomas's readers would not have access to the original, and in hiring Revere to do the engraving, Thomas was laying claim both to the prose story and the periodical plate, features which had rarely appeared in American magazines up to this point.

Before the development of modern wood engraving in the nineteenth century, images such as these were produced by etching or engraving, intaglio processes in which the ink is drawn up from the grooves in the plate, as opposed to the relief printing techniques used for type in which the ink is pressed into the paper. This meant that a periodical image at this time was a significant investment, as Andrews pointed out, requiring an engraver and a specialized press. This latter fact also meant that engravings in a periodical were tipped in, printed only on one side, and so could be removed from a volume for scrapbooking or framing, both common practices. The image conveyed status and expense, and it made the story effectively required reading, as the reader would wish to understand the "moral" of the romantic image of a young woman laying a kerchief on the face of a sleeping man (see Figure 2.1). As it turns out, the story is far from romantic, a tale of an unrepentant rake who, attempting to assault a kind woman, is struck dead by lightning.

"Moral tales" are frequently found in the short run of Thomas's first magazine, many of them serialized over three or four issues, with an "elegant plate" by Revere as reward. For example, "The History of Lauretta" is doled out over several issues with an engraved plate in the final installment. This strategy, which would be adopted widely in the early national period, makes it hard for modern readers to recognize the short story as they would encounter it in later periodicals. Short stories, by later definitions, are not serialized. As Edgar Allan Poe would insist, periodical short fiction was meant to be read in a single sitting. Serialization seems antithetical to the short story, associated after the 1840s with serialized novels or, in the early twentieth century, with "pulps" and the "novelette." The practice of serializing short stories in the late eighteenth century was an attempt to mitigate some of the challenges facing magazine publishers. Postriders would often not carry the magazines during this period, requiring readers to pick up individual issues at designated booksellers. Only those who wished to have a complete set for binding at year's end were likely to be diligent in paying subscriptions. The serial short story – especially when attached to an engraved plate – was a marketing experiment, a reward for loyalty to the magazine, a bonus only to be appreciated for those who had proved faithful to the enterprise.

The short stories I have described thus far – standalone and serial – were almost universally by English writers, borrowed unattributed from British periodicals. In the years after the founding of the new nation, as demands grew for settler-American writing, there would be one part of every periodical that served as a guarantee of original prose: the serial essay or column. These recurring features, invariably hosted by a pseudonymous scribe, would be the source of much of the original short fiction in the final decades of the eighteenth-century magazine. However, periodical columns are harder for modern readers to recognize as a source of the short story, because here the fiction violates not only the dictum against serialization but also that against *embeddedness*. The short fictions shared here are enmeshed within their series, doled out to

Vol. I.   *N.º II.*

The Thunder Storm.

Figure 2.1   "The Thunder Storm," by Paul Revere. *Royal American Magazine*, 1774.

faithful readers in exchange for attention or by way of illustrating a moral theme for the installment.

"Designing to be grave today on the sober subject of Resolution," Eugenio declares in the third installment of his column in the *New York Magazine* in October 1792, "I will bribe my fair reader's attention to a discourse, less gay than useful, by telling a short story in the very front of this number" (691). Eugenio is a pseudonymous host of this column, borrowing, like so many before and after, from the template established by Mr. Spectator some eighty years earlier. Eugenio's column is a mix of advice, lessons, and fiction, involved – like the editors of the magazine which houses his column – in a complicated negotiation with the readers on whom the magazine depends and which it simultaneously seeks to improve.

The first American writer to take a serious stab at the periodical essay form was a young Benjamin Franklin, who, in 1722, created the surrogate Mistress Silence Dogood, under whose name he slipped essays under the door of his brother's printshop. Widow Dogood would be the first in a seemingly endless parade of fictional essayists created by mostly unknown authors who would submit their would-be series to American magazines, hoping that, if public and editor approved, they might be granted a piece of real estate within the commons of the magazine. Like the editors whose activities they emulated, these authors were motivated by neither fame (the contributions were all anonymous) nor fortune (aside from editors, no American magazine paid for imaginative literature during the eighteenth century). This is not to say motives were purely selfless. The young Franklin confesses in his *Autobiography* to having been motivated by the vain desire to hear his work praised by his brother and his friends, which it was. The first installment having proved successful, Dogood was invited to publish several more installments in the *New-England Courant* in 1722 before the final break with his brother and abandonment of his apprenticeship.

I am not here arguing that these series – what we today might call "columns," save that they are fundamentally fictions – are themselves "short stories." Instead, I would argue that looking at the deployment of short fictions *within* these series allows us to see how the American short story took shape in the magazine. That said, it is undeniably the case that fiction and storytelling is everywhere in these columns, beginning of course with the persona of the narrator. "Mr. Spectator" is an imagined character whose fictional adventures are scripted by his authors. Widow Silence Dogood is the imaginary creation of a sixteen-year-old apprentice boy.

More to the point for our purposes, however, is how these columnists of the eighteenth century distribute short fiction among their wares. These short fictions take many forms. One of the most popular was the "dream" or "vision." For example, in Silence Dogood's fourth installment, she tells of "Discoursing the other Day at Dinner with my Reverend Boarder" and asking "his Advice about my young Son *William*, whether or no I had best bestow upon him Academic Learning." The good Reverend, predictably enough, recommends in favor of sending William to college. Afterwards Silence Dogood stops beneath a giant apple tree and dozes off, falling into a "DREAM" (Franklin 1722, 1).

The dream that follows, in which our dreamer sees Harvard College at its allegorical worst, is a familiar fictional trope of the form, first popularized by Addison in *Spectator* No. 3, in which Mr. Spectator experiences "a kind of Methodical Dream, which disposed all my Contemplations into a Vision or Allegory," here devoted to a beatific vision of the newly established Bank of England (Addison and Steele 1711, 1). In both Dogood's and Mr. Spectator's dreams – as in the innumerable others in the periodical columns found on both sides of the Atlantic – we are engaged in fictions within fictions. But it is this fiction within the fiction of the columnist's persona that shapes the emerging American short story. Here Franklin's arguments against the necessity of a Harvard education are illustrated by a short tale which illustrates his fictional narrator's argument.

In this sense, short fiction, embedded within the essay series in early American magazines, is everywhere to be found. One of the most justly celebrated examples of the periodical columns of the period is Judith Sargent Murray's "The Gleaner" for the *Massachusetts Magazine*. Here Murray's fictional narrator, Mr. Vigilius, dispenses short stories about his adopted daughter Margaretta in exchange for that which he most desires: his readers' attention to his monthly columns. The fiction is doled out slowly, at times so slowly that his readers rebel. Impatient after a neglect of Margaretta stories in favor of moral lessons, one reader in the twelfth installment of "The Gleaner" accuses him of having "conducted your matters devilishly oddly, and the whole town are of my opinion. What, to raise our curiosity, leading us to expect the history of a fine girl, and then to sob us off with your *musty morals*, which are to the full as old as your grandfather Adam" (1793, 204). In an earlier installment another reader writes begging for more, declaring herself "one of a great many ladies, which is absolutely dying to see something more about Margaretta" (1792, 476).

The somewhat dizzying fictionalities of these periodical columns makes us uncertain whether the letters printed in the column are from actual readers or are themselves still more works of fiction. In this case, it is almost certainly the latter, which of course confounds our desire to isolate the short story among the layers of fictions. But this complicated array – like the bouquet in the hand of the *Gentleman's Magazine*'s editor – is precisely the point. The magazine is a true miscellany. Within the individual columns, as with the magazine as a whole, fiction is packaged as moral lesson, and moral lesson as fiction. Readers are invited to take the medicine and the sugar in a single dose, trusting in the editor of the magazine and their columnist surrogates to get the proportions right. This, of course, is the point Eugenio makes in the third installment of his column mentioned earlier. He comes to dispense a lesson regarding the importance of "resolution," but he knows a story will make this somewhat stiff topic more amendable to his readers. So he offers his reader a "bribe" by way of a "short story."

Fiction in the early American magazine was akin to the coffeehouse Mr. Spectator observed in London in 1711. Mr. Spectator did not seek to abolish newspapers or the speculation they fueled. After all, at its core, the *Spectator* was deeply invested in a credit economy and believed that the future of the nation depended on a prosperous and well-regulated middle class. As its acid-tongue scold, Mr. Spectator confronted his people in the end to improve them, not to cast them out as money changers, hoping to demonstrate that if they became better family men and citizens, it would also make them more successful speculators. Without a coffeehouse culture to reform, the American magazine sought to turn the periodical into a virtual coffeehouse, one already in the hands of a judicious reform-minded proprietor.

* * *

In 1846 Poe would declare the "whole tendency of the age is Magazine-ward" (311). Were he alive, Isaiah Thomas, who shuttered his own magazine fifty years earlier, would have found both Poe's words and the venue in which they were published wholly unfamiliar. Perhaps most shocking would have been Poe's name in the byline. No longer governed by eighteenth-century economies of cultural capital, anonymity gave way to celebrity. As a result, a new kind of author was taking shape in the early industrial magazines of the 1830s and 1840s, one which would explode in the second half of the century, beginning with the savvy marketing of Robert E. Bonner, publisher of the *New York Ledger*, who paid his star authors outrageous sums and promoted that fact widely.

Yet in the 1840s, very few short story writers were making a living writing for magazines, as no one knew better than Poe himself. In the early American magazine, writing was a charitable contribution, a gift to the commons; as a result, most of those who contributed regularly were by necessity financially secure. With payment and bylines came, slowly, the emergence of a national literary celebrity that could not have developed in the artisanal and heavily circumscribed print economy of the early magazine. Even the higher paid writers of the 1840s, such as N. P. Willis, had reason to be troubled by the new periodical economy. As Willis wrote in 1844, "There are several of the magazines that pay for articles, but no one of them, we believe, pays for *all* its contents. . . . All the paying magazines and reviews, however, reject fifty articles to one that they accept, and they pay nobody whose 'name' would not enrich their table of contents" (2).

It is in the context of this new print economy of the short story – one where the potential for profit and celebrity is held out as a carrot to an army of would-be authors, few of whom will ever achieve their aim – that we must reconsider Poe's famous 1842 celebration of Hawthorne and the short story form. Where in the eighteenth century the editorship was often the only paid position at the magazine, in the early industrial magazine, the editor's stock declined in proportion as the author's rose. Poe was in his last issue as editor at *Graham's* at the time, and he had seen how well some of his authors were getting paid. He understandably resented that the success of these authors depended on his undervalued work as editor. So it was that in saying goodbye to his editorial career, Poe made time to celebrate Hawthorne's *Twice-Told Tales* and the periodical short story. It would be on the short story and the short poem that Poe's fortunes would now depend. Having seen authors paid up to $10 a page at *Graham's* and knowing that he himself was at the height of his powers, he had reason to be optimistic about the future.

In celebrating *Twice-Told Tales*, Poe was taking one last turn at the editorial lectern to raise the stock of the short story, which would, he hoped, be the making of his fortune. Here we get the first attempts to find a proper name for the form – Poe tries "short prose narrative" and "prose tale" (1984a, 572) – and to define its key features. These include being short (but not too short) and able to be read in a single sitting – "requiring from a half-hour to one or two hours in its perusal" (572). It is this brevity in turn that grants to the "prose tale" its unique power: "the immense force derivable from *totality*" (572) – or, as Poe would describe it in "Philosophy of Composition" (1846), "unity of effect" (1984b, 15).

It is well known that Poe would never make a living as a short story writer and poet, even as many of his best stories still lay in his future as he talked up the value of the form. A truly stable marketplace for the short story lay some distance in the future, after the magazine's scale and reach grew wider and its appeal to popular audiences increased alongside efficiencies in industrial print and the rise of the illustrated magazines in the second half of the century. Of course, the same changes to the magazine culture of the nineteenth century that would increase the profits for both authors and publishers from the short story would also ultimately work to the detriment of the short story's cultural capital. Associated with mass print and popular tastes, magazine fiction in general became increasingly suspect to an emerging cultural elite at century's end.

The economic and cultural economies of the magazine have undergone many changes throughout the three centuries in which the periodical form has been experimented with in colonial America and the United States. The short story emerged in the American magazine and has played different roles. But while the magazine, the technologies that bring it to life, and the markets of exchange that sustain it have been in almost constant flux since the colonial period, the short story has been instrumental to the magazine in all its forms. Today it is hard to imagine the short story without the magazine. In the eighteenth century it would have been hard to imagine the magazine without short fiction. As the periodical moves in the twenty-first century in search of new digital marketplaces and audiences, there is reason to worry about the future of the short story. Yet if we look outside the commercial magazines – the direct descendants of the industrial magazines such as *Graham's* – we find scores of vital small literary journals, often subsidized by universities and run at a loss, depending on volunteer labor and authors willing to contribute for little or no remuneration. Anyone who has ever worked at or contributed short fiction to such a journal is part of a very old literary economy of the short story, in which the early American periodical culture continues to be nourished at small, well-tended fires. For this reason alone we might attend to the abandoned models of the eighteenth-century magazine, knowing that the future of the short story almost certainly lies in its past.

Works Cited

[Addison, Joseph and Richard Steele]. 1711. *The Spectator*. March 5.
Andrews, Ebenezer. 1791 (August 7). Correspondence to Isaiah Thomas. Isaiah Thomas Papers, American Antiquarian Society.

1792 (November 3). Correspondence to Isaiah Thomas. Isaiah Thomas Papers, American Antiquarian Society.

Bendixen, Alfred and James Nagel. 2010. *A Companion to the American Short Story.* Oxford: John Wiley and Sons.

Bourdieu, Pierre. 1984. *Distinction: A Social Critique of the Judgement of Taste.* Cambridge, MA: Harvard University Press.

"Eugenio: No. III." 1792. *The New York Magazine, or Literary Repository.*

[Franklin, Benjamin]. 1722. "Silence Dogood" No. 4, *New-England Courant*, May 7–14.

Mott, Frank Luther. 1958. *A History of American Magazines, 1741–1930, Vol. 1.* Cambridge, MA: Harvard University Press.

[Murray, Judith Sargent]. 1792. "The Gleaner," No. 6, *Massachusetts Magazine; or, Monthly Museum.*

1793. "The Gleaner," No. 12, *Massachusetts Magazine; or, Monthly Museum.*

Poe, Edgar Allan. 1846. "Marginalia," *Graham's Magazine*, December.

1984a. "Nathaniel Hawthorne," in *Essays and Reviews*, 568–577. New York: Library of America.

1984b. "The Philosophy of Composition," in *Essays and Reviews*, 13–25. New York: Library of America.

Thomas, Isaiah. 1791 (August 16). Correspondence. Isaiah Thomas Papers, American Antiquarian Society.

1788. *Proposal of Isaiah Thomas and Company, for Publishing by Subscription, a New Periodical Work, To Be Entitled, the Massachusetts Magazine: or Monthly Museum of Knowledge and Rational Entertainment.* Worcester, MA: Isaiah Thomas and Company.

Webster, Noah. 1787. [frontmatter]. *American Magazine.*

[Willis, N. P.]. 1844 (October 12). "The Pay for Periodical Writing," *Evening Mirror.*

CHAPTER 3

The Short Story Fad
Gender, Pleasure, and Commodity Culture in Late Nineteenth-Century Magazines

Brad Evans

There was always a touch of scandal about the success of the short story in nineteenth-century America, a scandal encoded in terms of the pleasures and excesses of a gendered literary marketplace. Like summer fashions, stories could be delightfully clever and irreverent, and sometimes even a bit risqué, but they rarely lasted through a change in seasons, dependent as they were on the whims of readers and the caprices of a media environment characterized by overabundance.

As early as 1830, Catherine Sedgwick, the decade's most popular short story writer, had pegged the issue in a cleverly self-reflexive offering for that year's *Atlantic Souvenir*, the most prestigious of the American gift books. Her "Cacoethes Scribendi" is a mother and daughter courtship story that turns on the fact that while the daughter is properly in love with the only eligible young man in their secluded New England village, the mother is in love with an idea of authorship that had been piqued, and subsequently sustained, by the demands of the marketplace for annuals – annuals like the very one in which the story first appeared. It is a love story with the delightfully complicating twist of having gift books and women's writing at the center of the romantic attraction, which not only helps explain why it has been a mainstay of feminist short story anthologies since the 1980s, but also lets us introduce the idea of the short story as a genre historically associated with and developed under the influence of what were popularly understood at the time to have been literary fads.

This chapter looks at the popularity of the form later in the century, and particularly at a class of stories for which the terms of approval follow the lines of pleasure-reading that Sedgwick both satirizes and enacts. It is a line that more familiarly follows Poe than Sedgwick, and that devolves less on the familiar writers of today's canon than on the hundreds who made more fleeting contributions to the mass market for stories. The problem concerns what follows if we not only accept but accentuate the idea that the short form is, by way of association if not in fact, just as impermanent as a

46

magazine, and as fleeting and transitory as the fashions therein. Might it be possible to trace in the formal characteristics of the short story's evolution a few specific ideas about the genre as a commodity in the marketplace? Knowing the gendered history of canonization, which historically worked to dissociate the short story from the mass market of the popular press, what implications can be gleaned about the delight and sometimes-subversive pleasures of the form by embracing it as an invention of consumer culture?

Part of the answer to these questions contravenes what critics have long said about the story's formal qualities, and especially about claims derived from Poe about the unity of effect. A main thrust of my argument is that short stories do not, generally, stand on their own. Historically, at least, they have depended more than other genres on their media ecology – and, in particular, on the stylishness, we might even say the panache, of their packaging. In what follows, I describe some of the relations and associations around which interest in the form gathered in the late nineteenth century. My aim is to provide access to a way of thinking about the thousands of short stories that not only elude contemporary anthologies, but that also challenge our ideas about what the short story is and how it functions. Art, it has been said, is that which stands alone and passes the test of time; but many of the most interesting short stories of later nineteenth-century America do neither of these things. Instead, they depend upon a relational aesthetic, an evocation of feelings and responses that compelled a public interested by and able to follow the myriad sallies of their allusions. I would argue that we would do well to develop a relational aesthetics – an aesthetics unafraid of faddishness – in order to read more broadly in the short form.

Overabundant Objects

Sedgwick's suggestion that the short story was an overabundant commodity did not change over the course of the century, but the worry that its connection to the market was a problem most certainly did. By the 1880s, a consensus had formed that Americans did the short story particularly well, for reasons having to do with the laws of supply and demand. William Dean Howells made this case most famously in *Harper's* in February 1887 (revised as follows in *Criticism and Fiction*). Americans had "brought the short story nearer perfection in the all-round sense than almost any other people," and they had done so not because of the "hurry and impatience" of the national temperament but simply because of the success of American magazines: "Their sort of success is not only from the courage to decide what ought to please, but from the knowledge of what does please; and it is probable that, aside from the pictures, it is the short stories which please the readers of our best magazines" (1891, 131; see also Mott 1957, 113). Given that short stories, in Howells's account, are not merely embedded in the market ecology of the magazines but are driving its expansion, one can expect their formal development to have been a response to the market.

To understand this dynamic, it is important to underscore the historical change identified by Andrew Levy, who noted that "something happened between 1885 and 1901 that transformed the general perception of the short story" (1993, 31). That something, I would argue, was intimately tied to the expansion of a gendered idea of the story as at once both a timeless work of art and a finite cultural commodity.

To become recognizable not only as an artform, but also, in the words of one advocate from 1898, a "seeming fad," the short story needed to be discovered – discovered, as a genre, for the first time (Barrett 1898, 10). That happened during this period, when the genre acquired a literarily respectable new name, a fifty-year national tradition, an academic curriculum, and enormous new popularity. The name is often credited to Brander Matthews, a writer and scholar at Columbia, whose 1884 article "The Philosophy of the Short-Story" made a point of emphasizing the hyphen to distinguish the form from sketches, tales, or stories that were merely short. Matthews, whose academic career began with that essay, was quickly joined by others in an effort to expand the curriculum. Those others included Bliss Perry, a professor at Princeton who devoted a chapter of his *A Study of Prose Fiction* (1902) to "The Short Story" (while, notably, not including one on the novel), Henry S. Canby at Yale, and Lewis Worthington Smith at Drake. In what could be considered the birth of creative writing, the first guidebook was published by Sherwin Cody in 1894, *How to Write Fiction, Especially the Art of Short Story Writing*; within two decades, nearly all of the educational publishing houses in the country were issuing them for aspiring authors. An important early bibliography lists fifty-nine works devoted to the genre published between 1898 and 1923 (Pattee 1923, 377–378).

The context for all of these "discoveries" is the changing media ecology. Between 1885 and 1905, the number of magazines in publication went from 3,000 to 6,000. Those with circulations over 100,000 went up from twenty-one to 159 (Mott 1957, 10–11). New, less expensive magazines and Sunday supplements for major newspapers developed during this period, all of which featured short stories prominently. The international copyright agreement of 1891 disincentivized magazines from borrowing British material, opening the market to writers and solidifying the status and respectability of the short story. There were also more than a dozen new all-fiction magazines. These include *Short Stories*, a reprint magazine; the *Black Cat*, the leading amateur story magazine that published the winners of its monthly story contest; and the *Argosy*, an older magazine that became all-fiction in 1896 and had a circulation of half a million within the decade. According to Levy, this led directly to a new founding myth of the American short story, with Poe as "founder of the only form of art in American life that would equate issues of generic definition with national definition – the only form whose participants would be sufficiently fascinated by the issue of generic identity to even need a founder" (33).

What can be hard to grasp from a contemporary perspective is that most of these new resources were not pushing a Howellsian brand of literary realism, but rather were practically attuned to market-driven aspects of the genre. Howells's successor at *Harper's*, Henry Mills Alden, commented about the variety of magazine stories in a December 1901 "Editor's Study" in the context of what he called the demise of "the serial habit" – the turn of magazines toward content, like short stories and essays, that could be read in a single issue (170). Alden argued that the "latest development of the short story is not only away from the old conventional pattern, but into an infinite variety of effects ... the character sketch ... a single dramatic situation, a succession of humorous incidents ... a quick comedy ... an equally quick tragedy ... a brief glimpse of special life" (170). This variety is in line with the sense given in Barrett's handbook for aspiring creative writers. As had so many others, Barrett wrote that America had entered "a new literary epoch – the epoch of the short story," which one could see merely by looking around at "the periodicals that teem with such fiction and on the magazines devoted entirely to it" (1898, 10). Urging writers to remember that Americans were a "commercial people," Barrett suggested that the "only legitimate purpose" of the short story was "to amuse"; and since they were to be passing things – less than 10,000 words in length – there was every expectation that, formally, they would be "artificial, and to a considerable degree unnatural" (11, 15).

Given these trends, it is also important to note the extent to which the formal development of the short story was linked to the entire magazine ecology. That would include both the illustrations and, crucially, the advertisements. Frank Munsey, publisher of both *Munsey's* and the

Argosy, made the case that short stories and advertising were mutually intertwined: "Fiction ... is responsible for the enormous circulations, and without fiction the general advertiser would find the magazine proposition quite a different matter and decidedly uninteresting from a business standpoint" (quoted in Garvey 1996, 4). As Ellen Gruber Garvey suggests, this symbiosis takes us right back to the world of consumer culture: "Stories, like the department store's musical concerts, were part of what drew readers to the magazines, making them potential buyers. But advertisers also depended on stories to create a climate in which their ads would persuade readers to become buyers .... The reader is invited to move between the two" (1996, 4). Related to that point is another, that the media ecology of turn-of-the-century print was siloed. As Garvey points out, periodicals reaching poorer and more rural readers, such as *Ladies' World,* were quite different from middle-class magazines such as *Munsey's* and *Ladies' Home Journal,* each of them having different audiences and different attitudes toward authorship and marriage (see Garvey 1995, 85). Generalizations, like any I may myself make in what follows, need always to be qualified: there was never a single print culture, but rather many such cultures, each with its own public.

The larger point would be that if short stories were essentially targeted advertising for both the magazines and the products advertised in them, the same holds in the opposite direction. There should be no reading the development of short story form without the context of an overabundant marketplace. Like good advertising, that marketplace often conferred an ephemeral sense of pleasure and delight upon the genre of the short story; similarly, the genre developed formally to evoke those delights.

It is for this reason that Fred Lewis Pattee's survey remains one of the best guides to the period: he is particularly good at tracking the popularity of a handful of postbellum authors who are regularly overlooked in today's histories of the genre, including Thomas B. Aldrich, Frank Stockton, and H. C. Bunner, who were known for having adopted the piquant flavor and technical dexterity associated with Maupassant. Pattee's descriptions of all three stress their "whimsical wit" and "clever construction," as well as how different they were from the regionalists championed by Howells after whom the period has come to be particularly known among scholars in our own time (1923, 216, 301).

Nonetheless, the difference between Pattee's survey and contemporary ones, particularly with regard to regionalism, is significant. There are excellent reasons for the more recent move to associate the postbellum short story with regionalism, not least of which that regionalism provided an entryway into the upper tiers of the literary marketplace for both women and writers of color. What we are coming to understand, however, is how limiting the focus on the Atlantic group of literary monthlies has been – even when dealing with now-familiar writers such as Paul Laurence Dunbar and Sui Sin Far – and how little we actually know about the vast majority of stories published in other kinds of media environments (see Chapman 2016; Leslie 2022).

To his credit, Pattee writes extensively about women writers. But he has a narrow sense of the media environment. For example, he gets Kate Chopin fundamentally wrong because he does not have access to *Vogue*, the magazine in which she published almost all of her most wickedly sharp and socially cutting stories. Pattee marvels that "she produced what are often masterpieces" without having any models or training (327). However, as is now widely known, Chopin was thoroughly ensconced in the bohemian artistic scene of the Midwest; she was a translator of Maupassant, and an admirer of everything going on in Chicago with the firm of Stone and Kimball and their upstart artistic magazine, the *Chap-Book* (see Evans 2019). In much the same way that he misses so much about Chopin, Pattee has little to tell us about women writing outside of the elite literary monthlies. Even though he acknowledges that a "score of five-foot shelves would hardly hold the literary ventures of women in this area so suited to their powers," he goes on to conclude that "[t]heir work, though much of it is well done, has added little that need detain the student of the American short-story evolution" (328). That is a mistake not only for history but for our understanding of the form.

The Problem with the Unity of Effect

We still know very little about Pattee's "score of five-foot shelves," and for reasons that writers at the time seem to have anticipated. A score of shelves is too many, of course, but the real problem lies elsewhere. If the success of the American short story was driven by the magazine market, could the delights and pleasures of the genre be replicated outside of that market?

This was an especially lively question for editors and critics in the early 1900s because the answer appeared to be "no." For Perry and others, the pleasures of the short story disappeared when it appeared in longer volumes: "The important thing, the really suggestive and touching and wonderful thing, is that all these thousands of contemporary and ephemeral stories are laughed over and cried over and waited for by somebody. They are read, while the 'large still books' are bound in full

calf and buried" (333). Howells put it just as succinctly, wondering why
the short story collection was as "repellent as it is said to be. He can read
one good short story in a magazine with refreshment, and a pleasant sense
of excitement .... But, if this is repeated in ten or twenty stories, he
becomes fluttered and exhausted by the draft upon his energies" (1902,
110–111). Why, they were asking, was the genre so dependent on its point
of origin in the magazines, and what might that dependence say about the
short story's status in the broader field of art?

This quandary is surely tied up with the many anthology projects
underway at the major publishing houses. Among others, Howells would
soon be editing an eight-volume collection of stories for *Harper's*, and
Collier's was publishing ten volumes of *Short Story Classics*, with five on
American stories. But it also reflects efforts to define the uniqueness of the
form by leaning on Poe's "unity of effect" as the one thing a story needed
to succeed. Poe's idea was a constant in conceptualizing the genre.
Matthews famously insisted that a "true Short-story differs from the
Novel chiefly in its essential unity of impression" (1885, 366); an editor
of *Lippincott's* reminded readers of the dictum, writing that "the short story
produces a singleness of effect denied to the novel" (Esenwein 1908, 19);
and an eight-volume anthology in 1904 began by noting that the short
story "is a work of art which has its own laws, its special qualities, its
individual sources of charm; it must stand complete in itself" (Mabie 1904,
xiv). For his part, Perry reproduces three pages of Poe's famous review of
Hawthorne , before concluding that "[i]f we assent to Poe's reasoning, we
are at once upon firm ground" (1902, 306).

But if we focus on the magazine's role in the development of the genre,
we may be tempted to suggest that this insistence on the unity of the form
falls short of describing what actually propelled the short story's popularity
and charm. The "unity of effect" comes to sound not only wrong but
sanctimonious, failing as it does to account for the element of the short
story that everyone seemed eager to acknowledge: that readers' pleasure in
them was deeply interwoven with their experience of the new sensorium
provided by the illustrations and advertisements. Though not saying so
explicitly, Howells actually turns away from Poe's framework of singularity
when answering his own question about why stories outside of magazines
were deadening: "A condition that the short story tacitly makes with the
reader ... is that he shall subjectively fill in the details and carry out
the scheme which in its small dimensions the story only can suggest"
(1902, 112). Readers bring much to the game, he acknowledges, and
presumably anthologies ask them to bring too much. Alden phrases it

similarly. The best authors of short fiction strive to offer writing "so suggestive that the reader's imagination readily completes the lines and even supplies situations, as it does in dreams" (170). While both editors frame their observations in terms of the work done by readers, they must certainly have been cognizant of the work done by magazines to encourage readers to respond in certain ways.

What the history of the short story could use from us, then, is some of the irreverence that comes from reading them in the gendered, marketed, illustrated, and advertised contexts in which they first appeared. The interplay of art and mass culture had a generative effect not only on readers but also on the kind of stories authors were writing and having published. We ought, perhaps, to actually be asking ourselves what Howells's question implies about the pressures on the development of the form itself? If exporting short stories from the world of the magazines really did impose a value added tax that was too dear for many readers to pay, then what does that say about how we theorize the historical situation and the development of the short story as a genre?

The Latest Fads, Storiettes

My sense is that we do not know the half of it about the short story in American literature. We have a canon of authors we read, and, yes, that canon has been revised and expanded in exciting ways, especially since the 1980s, with regards to gender and race. But shelves upon shelves remain about which we know nothing, especially if we turn not only to the magazines but to newspapers as well. The pleasures of short stories in these were dependent in many respects upon the media environment of their publications. So too, I would argue, was the development of their form and style.

I want to turn, then, to a minor example provided by *Munsey's*, the publication, starting in 1896, of what they called "storiettes" – stories that were usually around a column in length, published in groups of four to six under a running header. *Munsey's* was one of the first of the ten-cent illustrated monthlies. By the end of the century, it had achieved the country's top circulation numbers and advertising revenues. It had a subscription of over 700,000 at its peak in 1897. Its standard size expanded to 160 copiously illustrated reading pages and eighty to 100 pages of advertising.

The storiettes are of interest from a formal perspective because they are clustered. The magazine invites readers to read them relationally, not singly. There is no reason to think they were understood as intertexts, but there is a certain buzz that came from putting them together. Take the copious numbers of courtship stories. Like much genre fiction, these come to have a gestural familiarity. Their endings are almost always the same, with either a young woman in tears burying her face in a lover's neck or a man pressing a woman to his heart. The delight comes from the mischievous ways they skip over or rearrange the familiar steps getting us there. They are exercises in style, as predictably unpredictable as one might expect; and yet, like the stray advertisement for competing brands of soap – or bicycles or well-fitting corsets – they occasionally touch home with a surprising freshness.

Frank M. Bicknell's half-page "On the Long Bridge," *Munsey's* first storiette, might be said to typify the move to style. It is an exercise in shading that makes light of a lover's choice. We learn in the very first line, reading from the young woman's perspective, that "[t]here were two of them" – suitors, of course – but we are told absolutely nothing more about either except that one declared himself in a letter, while the other did so in person, on a bridge, as she was carrying her response to the first to the post office. Significantly, the one on the bridge talks to her, but the story contains no dialogue, just gestures – gestures that are so utterly familiar that we can make them out in silhouette. "He uttered some commonplaces . . .. He spoke again in lower tones . . .. He bent forward and whispered in her ear." What had he said? What goes on in her mind? Is she making a conscious choice? We do not know and are not told, even at the end. She had "responded, scarce realizing what he said . . . she murmured something in return . . . the color left her cheek, she looked shyly up." Read generously, the story is not trivializing this moment, an especially important one, we might safely assume, for the young women taken to be the predominant readership of *Munsey's*. The emphasis is on the ineffability of choice, a philosophical question with a long pedigree (see, for instance, William James); but it also, by implication, touches on the irrationality of the institution of marriage. He "pressed her to his heart . . .. The letter dropped from her hand . . .. The loss of the letter was of no consequence, she said. Let it go; she could write another." In a delicious touch, the story's final implication is that the letter fluttering down through the open railing had been an acceptance, not a rejection: in that ineffable moment on the bridge, she had changed her mind (Bicknell 1896, 411).

Munsey's publishing strategy with the storiettes seems to have been to encourage a sameness of affect – witty and brisk, with sentiment tempered by irony – all the while sustaining stylistic variety. The result are stories that seem utterly aware of themselves as performances of the particular genre of the short story. Indeed, storiettes often register as something of a caricature of the short story genre, as if authors wrote their characters as performers of story-character types. There is an artificial and anti-sentimental externalization of character that verges on what would later be called camp, even in stories designed to pull the heartstrings. In "Three Letters," Mabel Margaret Thompson takes up almost exactly the same theme as Bicknell's from two months before, even replicating his first line, but for a word, "There are three of them, and for months I have been wondering which I should take – wondering and trying to decide." Again, the perspective is that of the woman; again, it is a one-column story; and again, the plot finishes with a surprising twist. The three letters had come from three different suitors, and faced with deciding between them, she chooses none: "I look at my three letters – each one of which might have brought joy to some other woman; then I put them carefully aside and with a sigh I turn away to take up my lonely, plodding life again" (Thompson 1896, 727).

A further sense of this performative style can be had by following one of *Munsey's* more regular contributors, Anna Leach, who published dozens of pieces in the magazine but whose biography today is a mystery. Her stories are remarkable for their feminist repurposing of old themes. For example, her April 1896 storiette "The Difference" is about a wife who, when her husband's youthful indiscretion becomes public, decides to share her own with him, expecting mutual forgiveness. He, however, once realizing what she is saying, thrusts her aside – that being the "difference" referred to in the title, but never directly mentioned in the story. The affect of the story is not at all melodramatic. If, as Julia Stern recently wrote, "melodrama kindles inner worlds of feeling into spectacular expression," then Leach's story is more like camp, which "cannot quite consummate identification across the divide of otherness" (2022, 12). Stern's description of camp is remarkably apropos of Leach's stories, which typically draw readers' expectations about the genre into the brisk game of plotting. It is almost as if Leach imagines something like what we might call storiette style interceding between reader and characterization (Leach 1896, 92).

In February 1896, a month after they started their "storiettes" section, *Munsey's* began to run another recurring column, called "Latest Fads." What they say in setting up the new feature recalls what others had been saying about short stories, including allusions to the New Woman and the bohemian art scene. "We are a mercurial, restless people – a progressive, aggressive people," *Munsey's* explains, sounding like any number of short story editors. "New things appeal to us as to no other nation. Fads feed our fancy, lift us above the dead level, the prosaic, the threadbare" (*Munsey's* 14:5, 600). Many of the fads described in the subsequent years end up linking women's rights to art and consumer culture, much like the storiettes. The fad to top all fads was that for bicycles, to which the magazine devotes an entire issue in May 1896 – and dozens of pages of advertising every issue (see Figures 3.1 and 3.2). The bike number begins with an unsigned article concluding with a laudatory section on "Woman and the Wheel": "To men, the bicycle in the beginning was merely a new toy, another machine added to the long list of devices they knew in their work and in their play. To women, it was a steed upon which they rode into a new world" (*Munsey's* 15:2, 157).

The first short story following the discussion of women cyclists is Juliet Wilbor Tompkins's "My Mothers Diary," which is coincident with these issues in both theme and form. Having been deeply involved in the "fad" for little magazines known at the time as "ephemeral bibelots," Tompkins went on to become one of the more prolific and successful middlebrow modern writers of the early twentieth century (see Evans 2019). "My Mother's Diary" concerns a thoroughly modern young woman who, on a trip to Yosemite, reads through her mother's diary of a similar trip thirty years before, during which she had met the narrator's father. There is a double courtship plot, like mother like daughter; but whereas the mother had been, in her daughter's eyes, the "clingy vine" type, the narrator sees herself as flirtatious and bold in "the new" way. "It seems queer to think," writes the first-person narrator, drawing a distinction, "that I, in my calfskin boots and leather leggings, have been going over the very ground that my mother traversed thirty years ago ... in paper soles and hoop skirts" (Tompkins 1896, 160). But as it turns out, the narrator's mother was more complicated than that: not only had she refused her lover's proposal after encouraging it, but the proposal had not come from the narrator's father. Her mother had been playing the field. If the story has a moral, it is not only that women have a choice, but that they have always played the game – a theme, notably, that Edith Wharton would strike again in "Roman Fever," but not until 1934.

The point to retain is that this moral is amplified when read alongside the editorial opinion of "Woman and the Wheel" and the pictures of "athletic girls" riding bikes. That young women have a choice in managing the economy of the marriage market rides well in tandem with the choices they are asked to make as the consumers of advertising. Stylistically, these

Figure 3.1   Cover of *Munsey's Magazine*, May 1896.

New York Awheel—On the Riverside Drive, Near the Grant Monument.
Drawn by J. M. Gleam.

Figure 3.2   "New York Awheel," *Munsey's Magazine*, May 1896.

four elements – story, illustration, editorial, and advertisement – supplement each other. The smartness of the story is enhanced by that of the rest, linking fashion to sex, art to commodities, public to private, courtship to consumption, and beauty to humor and scandal.

Just to be clear, *Munsey's* shares the period's confusion about the New Woman. While it countenances, and even quietly supports, suffrage – heralding, for instance, the fact that women would be able to vote in the 1900 presidential election in several states – it also publishes stories that turn feminism itself into the fad. For instance, in Percival Pollard's "One New Woman," a young woman who desires "perfect equality" with her suitor is met with his offensive "club talk," which makes her cry and leads her to accept his patronizing explanation that "you're a woman, dear . . . and I love you far too much to treat you as an equal" (1896, 244). But in the same issue, Lulu Judson goes in the opposite direction in another courtship drama involving a choice between two men. "There was nothing unusual in the situation," the story begins with a wink, but in the end the heroine makes a choice to reject the rich suitor everyone prefers in favor of the one "by inheritance poor . . . with one of the very nicest faces in the world" (1896, 205).

Thematically, the stories in *Munsey's*, as a whole, reflect this confusion. Taken from the perspective of genre, though, they respond to the changing political times with stylistic bravura and tempered irreverence. As art objects made for consumer culture, *Munsey's* short stories were situated in the "double role" that Catherine Keyser has suggested women magazine writers played with increasing regularity during the period. Stylistically, they "played smart," which could mean to be "feminine in very narrow terms ... that emphasized woman's role as a consumer, sex object, and charming companion," but which could also be taken "as a pose ... distinguished by humor, urbanity, irony, worldliness, sexuality, detachment .... A tactic that establishes modern subjectivity and enacts satirical critique of the surrounding field" (2006, 6). The *Munsey's* short story was broadly understood in market terms as a gendered commodity, an artful one, and in that sense peculiarly American. It was the practical result of supply and demand and also, happily, representative of something about its national character, its literary snap and style.

Conclusion

Ephemerality and pleasure are not the usual qualifiers for works making it into the literary canon, which may be part of the reason so many of the short stories from the late nineteenth century were not only merely forgotten but rejected. Consumer culture, faddishness, and the gendered economies of the media marketplace conspired against them. The same year as Pattee's volume, Edward J. O'Brien published *The Advance of the American Short Story* (1923). O'Brien, who is best remembered today as the creator of the annual anthologies *The Best American Short Stories*, starts with a jeremiad warning of a "commercial malady" affecting American literature, which left short stories bearing a "striking resemblance to a soulless machine with a clever mind" (5). The American man, he warns, "surrenders his cultural heritage to the American woman, with such effects upon our poetry as well as our fiction as are unknown in any other country" (11). O'Brien's volume, which tops off its misogyny with doses of racism to boot, resolves itself in the contemporary world of Sherwood Anderson and Waldo Frank, authors he saw as engaged in a heroic "revolt against mechanical technique" – a revolt, we are told, much like Chekhov's against Maupassant (247). As late as 1984, scholars continued to trivialize nineteenth-century short stories in much the same terms, defining the genre against the gendered consumerism of popular culture (see Voss 1973 and Stevick 1984). These assessments have serious limitations in terms both of the canon and the formal characteristics of the short story. The short story can be understood and appreciated for having experimented stylistically along both sides of the divide between art and commerce – between work/s that were serious and slick, and culture that was quality and mass. Poe and Maupassant are relevant to this reading of the short story fad, but even more so are Tompkins and Leach.

Works Cited

Alden, Henry Mills. 1901. "Editor's Study," *Harper's Monthly Magazine* 104 (December): 167–170.

Barrett, Charles Raymond. 1898. *Short Story Writing: A Practical Treatise on the Art of the Short Story*. Chicago: Authors and Writers' Union.

Bicknell, Frank M. 1896. "On the Long Bridge." *Munsey's Magazine* 14 (January): 411.

Chapman, Mary, ed. 2016. *Becoming Sui Sin Far: Early Fiction, Journalism, and Travel Writing by Edith Maude Eaton*. Montreal: McGill-Queen's University Press.

Cody, Sherwin. 1894. *How to Write Fiction, Especially the Art of Short Story Writing*. New York: The Riverside Literary Bureau.

Esenwein, J. Berg. 1908. *Writing the Short-Story: A Practical Handbook on the Rise, Structure, Writing, and Sale of the Modern Short-Story*. New York: Hinds, Noble, and Eldredge.

Evans, Brad. 2019. *Ephemeral Bibelots: How an International Fad Buried American Modernism*. Baltimore, MD: Johns Hopkins University Press.

Garvey, Ellen Gruber. 1995. "Representations of Female Authorship in Turn-of-the-Century American Magazine Fiction," in *American Women Short Story Writers: A Collection of Critical Essays*. Ed. Julie Brown, 85–98. New York: Garland Publishing.

1996. *The Adman in the Parlor: Magazines and the Gendering of Consumer Culture, 1880s to 1910s*. New York: Oxford University Press.

Howells, William Dean. 1891. *Criticism and Fiction*. New York: Harper and Brothers.

1902. "Some Anomalies of the Short Story," in *Literature and Life*, 110–125. New York: Harper and Brothers.

Judson, Lulu. 1896. "A Girl's Way," *Munsey's Magazine* 16:2 (November): 205–207.

Keyser, Catherine. 2006. *Playing Smart: New York Women Writers and Modern Magazine Culture*. New Brunswick, NJ: Rutgers University Press.

Leslie, Alex. 2022. "Race, Region, and the Black Midwest in the Dunbar Decades," in *American Literary History* (forthcoming).

Levy, Andrew. 1993. *The Culture and Commerce of the American Short Story*. Cambridge, UK: Cambridge University Press.

Leach, Anna. 1896. "The Difference," *Munsey's Magazine* 15:1 (April): 92.

Mabie, Hamilton Wright. 1904. "Introduction," in *Little Masterpieces of Fiction, Vol. 1*. Ed. Mabie and Lionel Strachey, v–iv. New York: Doubleday, Page and Company.

Matthews, Brander. 1885. "The Philosophy of the Short-Story," *Lippincott's Magazine of Popular Literature and Science* 36 (October): 366–374.

Mott, Frank Luther. 1957. *A History of American Magazines, 1885-1905*, Vol. 4. Cambridge, MA: The Belknap Press of Harvard University Press.

O'Brien, Edward J. 1923. *The Advance of the American Short Story*. New York: Dodd, Mead, and Company.

Pattee, Fred Lewis. 1923. *The Development of the American Short Story: An Historical Survey*. New York: Harper and Brothers.

Perry, Bliss. 1902. *A Study of Prose Fiction*. Boston and New York: Houghton, Mifflin, and Company.

Pollard, Percival. 1896. "One New Woman," *Munsey's Magazine* 16:2 (November): 244–245.

Sedgwick, Catherine. 1830. "Cacoethes Scribendi," *The Atlantic Souvenir*: 17–38.

Stern, Julia. 2022. *Bette Davis, Black and White*. Chicago: University of Chicago Press.

Stevick, Philip, ed. 1984. "Introduction," in *The American Short Story, 1900-1945: A Critical History*. Columbia, MO: Twayne Publishers.

Thompson, Mabel Margaret. 1896. "Three Letters," *Munsey's Magazine* 14:6 (March): 727.

Tompkins, Juliet Wilbor. 1896. "My Mother's Diary," *Munsey's Magazine* 15:2 (May): 160–162.

Voss, Arthur. 1973. *The American Short Story: A Critical Survey*. Norman: University of Oklahoma Press.

CHAPTER 4

The Best of the Best
Anthologies, Prizes, and the Short Story Canon

Alexander Manshel

Curtis Sittenfeld's 2017 story "Show Don't Tell" narrates a day in the life of Ruthie, a young writer at an unnamed Master of Fine Arts (MFA) program in the Midwest. Though the story is interested in Ruthie's fraught relationships with the rest of her cohort, the main action of "Show Don't Tell" concerns the budding authors waiting to find out whether they have won a prize. For Ruthie, the possibility of winning one of four coveted "Ryland W. Peaslee" fellowships for her work as a short story writer is all important. Indeed, Sittenfeld makes it clear that winning the award was "a referendum" that could not only transform Ruthie's status on campus – "You'd say, 'He's a Peaslee,' or 'She's a Peaslee'" – but catapult her toward agents and publishers, lavish advances, and even, someday, a Pulitzer Prize (Sittenfeld 2017). Though the story is ultimately skeptical about the power of either the program or the prize to singlehandedly grant a writer a career, by the time the reader reaches its final paragraphs – when we return to Ruthie, now a best-selling novelist, two decades later – the implication is clear: "that long-ago night when I opened the letter at one in the morning" was the decisive moment in Ruthie's writing life (Sittenfeld 2017). In this way, "Show Don't Tell" follows the other well-worn MFA mantra of *write what you know*. And what Sittenfeld knows all too well – given that her stories have regularly featured in the *New Yorker* (as this one was), been honored with awards, and been anthologized in the *Best American Short Stories*, where she has also served as a guest editor – is that the career of any individual *literato* depends thoroughly on the literary institutions through which they pass.

This is precisely what Elif Batuman criticized about contemporary short fiction in a 2006 *n+1* essay on the *Best American* series. "Today's short stories all seem to bear an invisible check mark," Batuman declared, "the ghastly imprimatur" of the programs and publishers that comprise a kind of "fiction factory." No wonder, then, that so many of the *Best American* stories are "set in prisons and psychiatric hospitals," which is to say, they are thoroughly institutionalized. "They are trying to break out," Batuman remarked, "but I don't think they will" (2006). By contrast, a great many scholars of short fiction *don't think they should,* given that the "alternate economy" of these institutions ensures "the continued health of the short story despite the relative lack of a direct commercial demand for the product" (Levy 1993, 3). This chapter surveys the institutional forms of that "alternate economy": the collections, anthologies, awards, and syllabi that helped the short story to flourish in the twentieth century, and maintain its visibility today.

These institutions, from the *Best American Short Stories* to the Pushcart and Pulitzer prizes, form a kind of patchwork canon of American short fiction, a record of the writers most celebrated in their moment and most remembered since. Despite the persistent notion, espoused by artists and scholars alike, that the short story is "the art form best suited for the description" of a diverse and "heterogeneous culture," these institutions also testify to the fact that the genre has, until very recently, underrepresented women and overlooked racialized writers *tout court* (Levy 1993, 109). In Sittenfeld's "Show Don't Tell," despite the cohort's "consensus" that "the Peaslees" would favor the program's few women and writers of color, ultimately three of the four winners are men, and three of the four are white (Sittenfeld 2017). The pages that follow document the writers that cultural awards and organizations such as these have consecrated, examining how that patchwork canon has often failed to live up to the ideals of cultural pluralism at the heart of the American short story tradition.

The Birth of the *Best American Short Stories*

For much of its history in the United States, whether in its nineteenth-century adolescence or early twentieth-century heyday, the short story has been seen as "a culturally disposable artifact – a thing to be read once" and then discarded (Levy 1993, 2). This was precisely what Edward J. O'Brien, the founder and longtime series editor of the *Best Short Stories*, later the *Best American Short Stories*, sought to change. From the vantage of the twenty-first century, it may seem hard to believe that the genealogy of short fiction in the United States spans only about seven generations, and more surprising still that the growth of that tradition depends on a nearly-as-brief list of titanic figures, but O'Brien's career is proof of both. Responsible for the early recognition of now iconic writers, instrumental in the promotion of short fiction as a literary form worthy of preservation, and essential in the formation of a national canon, O'Brien's central role in the history of the American short story cannot be overstated. Writers and scholars alike have described him variously as the "St. Peter guarding the gates to a short story writer's heaven" and "the greatest champion of the form America has ever had" (quoted in Boddy 2010, 3).

Like the twentieth-century history of the short story, O'Brien's early life was bound up with institutions devoted to literary education and creative writing. Born in 1890, O'Brien attended both Boston College and Harvard University (ultimately receiving a degree from neither), before beginning work at a number of Boston literary journals, and even co-founding his own, the short-lived *Poetry Journal*. After this endeavor fizzled out, O'Brien turned his attention to short fiction, publishing – at just twenty-five years old – *The Best Short Stories of 1915 and the Yearbook of the American Short Story*. As an institution in its own right, *The Best American* series was, from its earliest iterations, committed to both comprehensive-ness and hierarchization. In the preface to the 1915 anthology, O'Brien boasted that the volume's selections, rigorously sorted into tiers of aesthetic distinction, were the product of having read "during the past year . . . over twenty-two hundred short stories in a critical spirit" (O'Brien 1915, 5). That first year, twenty stories were deemed worthy of not only distinction and celebration, but "preservation between book covers" (O'Brien 1915, 8). Given the air of ephemerality, even disposability, that hovered about the literary periodicals of the period and the thousands of short stories that briefly graced their pages, O'Brien's anthology was also an effort to mark out a select few for longevity. To be sure, O'Brien's declarations of "recent achievement and abundant future promise" were not always accurate pre-dictions of a future place in the American literary canon. That said, over the course of his quarter century as editor, O'Brien anthologized early work by Sherwood Anderson, Willa Cather, F. Scott Fitzgerald, Jean Toomer, Ernest Hemingway, Dorothy Parker, Katherine Anne Porter, Thomas Wolfe, John Cheever, John Steinbeck, and Richard Wright.

O'Brien and the *Best American* series worked to recognize that not only was the American short story flourishing as a form, but so too were the literary venues that depended on it. To this end, the *Best American* series included annual league tables that ranked magazines according to the number and proportion of "distinctive stories" that they published (see Figures 4.1a and 4.1b). Though O'Brien's unabashed *quantification* of literary art appeared (and may still appear) as anathema to some readers, his establishment of the *Best American* anthology as a national literary institution, one devoted to tracing the genre's "specially healthy growth in

(a)

MAGAZINE AVERAGES FOR 1915

The following table includes the averages of all American magazines published during 1915 of which complete files for the period covered were placed at my disposal. One, two, and three asterisks are employed to indicate relative distinction. "Three-asterisk stories" are of somewhat permanent literary value.

MAGAZINES	NO. OF STORIES PUBLISHED	NO. OF DISTINCTIVE STORIES PUBLISHED			PERCENTAGE OF DISTINCTIVE STORIES PUBLISHED		
		*	**	***	*	**	***
American Magazine	52	22	11	3	42	21	6
Associated Sunday Magazines (Jan.–May. See also Every Week.)	39	9	2	1	24	5	3
Atlantic Monthly	24	16	8	2	67	33	8
Bellman	39	20	11	7	51	28	18
Black Cat	108	8	0	0	7	0	0
Bruno Chap Books	7	3	0	0	43	0	0
Century Magazine	53	32	15	7	60	28	13
Collier's Weekly	142	46	21	9	32	15	6
Delineator	30	7	3	1	23	7	3
Everybody's Magazine	46	13	3	1	28	6	2
Every Week. (See also Associated Sunday Magazines)	77	23	2	1	30	3	2
Forum	13	12	6	3	92	46	23
Good Housekeeping	42	4	1	1	10	2	2
Harper's Bazar	23	6	4	0	26	17	0
Harper's Magazine	101	56	28	12	56	28	12
Harper's Weekly	25	18	4	0	72	16	0
Illustrated Sunday Magazine	182	59	27	16	32	15	9
Or excluding reprints	169	46	15	5	27	9	3
International	17	10	5	2	59	29	12
Ladies' Home Journal	42	8	3	1	19	7	3
Life	68	10	0	0	15	0	0
Lippincott's and McBride's Magazines	98	36	6	1	36	6	1

Figure 4.1a   From Edward J. O'Brien, *The Best Short Stories of 1915 and the Yearbook of the American Short Story* (1915).

(b)

MAGAZINE AVERAGES   285

MAGAZINES	NO. OF STORIES PUBLISHED	NO. OF DISTINCTIVE STORIES PUBLISHED			PERCENTAGE OF DISTINCTIVE STORIES PUBLISHED		
		*	**	***	*	**	***
Little Review...............	9	9	5	5	100	56	56
McClure's Magazine..........	63	22	9	0	35	14	0
Masses....................	10	7	3	1	70	30	10
Metropolitan................	47	24	7	5	51	15	11
Midland...................	10	10	7	3	100	70	30
Munsey's Magazine...........	48	4	1	0	8	2	0
National Sunday Magazine....	22	9	5	0	41	23	0
New Republic...............	9	7	3	1	78	33	11
Outlook....................	9	6	4	1	67	44	11
Pictorial Review............	68	15	4	1	22	6	1
Saturday Evening Post.......	162	29	12	6	18	7	4
Scribner's Magazine..........	52	37	24	7	71	46	13
Smart Set..................	242	34	12	3	14	5	1
Sunset Magazine.............	42	13	3	0	31	7	0
Woman's Home Companion...	49	4	0	0	8	0	0

The following tables indicate the rank, during 1915, by number and percentage of distinctive stories published, of the eighteen periodicals coming within the scope of my examination which have published during the past year over twenty-five stories and which have exceeded an average of 15% in stories of distinction. The lists exclude reprints.

BY PERCENTAGE OF DISTINCTIVE STORIES

1. Scribner's Magazine 71%
2. Century Magazine 60%
3. Harper's Magazine 56%
4. Metropolitan 51%
5. Bellman 51%
6. American Magazine 42%
7. Lippincott's and McBride's Magazines . . . 36%
8. McClure's Magazine 35%
9. Collier's Weekly 32%
10. Sunset Magazine 31%
11. Every Week 30%

Figure 4.1b   From Edward J. O'Brien, *The Best Short Stories of 1915 and the Yearbook of the American Short Story* (1915).

a soil so idly fertilized as our American reading public," marks a turning point in the institutional life of short fiction in the United States (O'Brien 1915, 3).

When O'Brien died in 1941, Martha Foley, the founder and editor of *Story* magazine, took up his post, overseeing the *Best American* series until her own death in 1977. Like O'Brien, Foley's tenure was marked by the discovery and promotion of yet another generation of American literary icons. Raymond Carver once described Foley's selection of "Will You Please Be Quiet, Please?" for the 1967 anthology as a "turning point" in his life as a writer (Boddy 2010, 87). Beyond Carver, Foley elevated scores of story writers and budding novelists, including James Baldwin, Donald Barthelme, Stanley Elkin, Bernard Malamud, Joyce Carol Oates, Tim O'Brien, Tillie Olsen, Philip Roth, Isaac Bashevis Singer, Leslie Marmon Silko, John Updike, and Alice Walker. As this list demonstrates, Foley was interested in adding greater diversity to the anthologies' roll of writers, a project that O'Brien had started. Indeed, in his 1931 book *The Advance of the American Short Story*, O'Brien expounded upon how the nation's "vast numbers of immigrants" and "different racial traditions" could be, above all, a boon to American short fiction:

> In these new races . . . lies the only hope by which America may achieve not only an individual literature of its own, but a literature which could be a unique experiment in the history of the world. Moreover, all indications prove that the chief artistic form of such a literature during the fusing generations is likely to be the short story . . . which is, after all, our national literary form. (15–17)

Anatomy of an Anthology

Editors and scholars alike have drawn parallels between the diverse population of literary anthologies and that of the nation itself. As Andrew Levy has argued, "with its all-but-invisible editor and seemingly unranked inclusion of a multitude of individual voices," the anthology can seem "like an ideal metaphor for a diverse and democratic culture" (Levy 1993, 109). Given that the series, at least for the first sixty-five years of its existence, was far from democratic – with stories selected according to O'Brien's and Foley's well-informed, but ultimately personal, aesthetic preferences – readers could be forgiven for wondering just how much the *Best American* series reflected the composition of the United States. Though the first several decades of the anthology celebrated many women writers and, under Foley, a growing number of minoritized writers, the

Table 4.1 *The* Best American*'s top authors (incl. stories anthologized) by decade*[1]

| [NB Figures correspond to the year of original magazine publication, nearly always one year prior to inclusion in the Best American Short Stories] |

Edward J. O'Brien (1915–1941)

1910s	1920s	1930s
Richard Matthews Hallet (2)	Morley Callaghan (3)	Morley Callaghan (10)
Edwina Stanton (2)	Sherwood Anderson (3)	William Faulkner (7)
Wilbur Daniel Steele (2)	*Fifteen authors with two*	Manuel Komroff (7)
Mary Heaton Vorse (2)	*stories each*	*Five authors (incl. Martha Foley) with five stories each*

Martha Foley (1941–1977)

1940s	1950s	1960s	1970s
Irwin Shaw (6)	Harvey Swados (5)	Joyce Carol Oates (6)	Donald Barthelme (4)
Wallace Stegner (5)	George P. Elliott (5)	Mary Lavin (5)	Barry Targan (4)
Warren Beck (4)	*Six authors (incl.*	Peter Taylor (4)	*Six authors (incl.*
Peter Taylor (4)	*Bernard Malamud,*	Jack Cady (3)	*John Updike, Joyce*
Jessamyn West (4)	*Flannery*	Stanley Elkin (3)	*Carol Oates, and*
	O'Connor, and	Isaac Bashevis	*Ward Just) with three*
	Jean Stafford) with	Singer (3)	*stories each*
	four stories each		

most anthologized authors during both O'Brien's and Foley's tenures were largely male and overwhelmingly white (see Table 4.1).

It is perhaps for this reason that, when Shannon Ravenel took over as editor in 1978, the *Best American* series instituted a new "Guest Editor" program, inviting a wide array of acclaimed authors to select each year's collection and write the volume's introduction. Under Ravenel, who served as series editor until 1990, six of the thirteen guest editors were women: Joyce Carol Oates, Hortense Calisher, Anne Tyler, Gail Godwin, Ann Beattie, and Margaret Atwood. Under Katrina Kenison, who oversaw the anthology from 1991 to 2006, nine of the sixteen guest editors were women, including Louise Erdrich, Jane Smiley, Annie Proulx, Amy Tan, and Lorrie Moore. Perhaps unsurprisingly, during these decades, the list of authors most anthologized by the *Best American* series included many more women writers.

That said, all thirteen guest editors during Ravenel's tenure were white and, apart from Erdrich and Tan, all but two of the other guest editors under Kenison were white. This, too, is reflected in the list of the *Best American's* most favored authors, which, despite the increasing recognition of minoritized writers in other areas of the literary field (including nominations for major literary prizes, as discussed later), has remained dominated by white writers. This is important because of the way the anthology confers prestige upon its guest editors as much as (or more than) its writers, and because the series' introductory essays are also a prime venue for outlining the present state and future possibilities of the short story genre. In other words, these positions are responsible for deciding not only which writers are selected, but also *from whose perspective* that selected writing is described. It remains to be seen how the anthology, its editors, and its selected authors will transform under series editor Heidi Pitlor, who has so far selected a more diverse array of guest editors – including Junot Díaz, Jennifer Egan, Roxane Gay, Stephen King, Salman Rushdie, Curtis Sittenfeld, and Jesmyn Ward – not only in terms of crude demographic categories but also with regard to genre, popularity, and prestige.

Though the diversity of the *Best American* series appears to have been increasing (albeit slowly) in recent decades (see Table 4.2), there is one area that has actually grown more homogeneous over time: the journals and magazines from which the *Best* stories are drawn. More than half (53 percent) of all the works honored by the series come from just twenty periodicals, and nearly one quarter were originally published in just three: the *New Yorker*, the *Atlantic*, and *Harper's Magazine* (see Table 4.3).

Table 4.2 *The* Best American's *top authors (incl. stories anthologized) by decade*

[NB Figures correspond to the year of original magazine publication, nearly always one year prior to inclusion in the Best American Short Stories*]*

Shannon Ravenel (1978–1990)	Katrina Kenison (1991–2006)
1980s	1990s
Alice Munro (8)	Tim Gautreaux, Lorrie Moore (5)
Mavis Gallant (7)	Rick Bass, Robert Olen Butler, Thom
Charles Baxter, Raymond Carver, Joy	Jones, Alice Munro (4)
Williams (6)	*Seven authors (incl. Junot Díaz, Ha Jin, and*
Madison Smartt Bell, Bharati Mukherjee,	*Annie Proulx) with three stories each*
Joyce Carol Oates, John Updike (6)	

Katrina Kenison (1991–2006), Heidi Pitlor (2007-)

2000s	2010s
Alice Munro (7)	Lauren Groff (7)
Karen Russell (5)	Elizabeth McCracken (6)
Jill McCorkle, Thomas McGuane (4)	T. C. Boyle, Sarah Shun-Lien Bynum, Alix
Eight authors (incl. Jess Row, Mary	Ohlin, Jim Shepard, Jess Walter (5)
Yukari Waters, Rebecca Makkai and T.C.	*Fourteen authors (incl. Jamel Brinkley, Emma*
Boyle) with three stories each	*Cline, George Saunders, Curtis Sittenfeld, and*
	John Edgar Wideman) with four stories each

Table 4.3 *The Best American's top journals (incl. stories anthologized) by decade*

[NB Figures correspond to the year of original magazine publication, nearly always one year prior to inclusion in the Best American Short Stories]

1920s	1930s	1940s	1950s	1960s
The Dial (12)	Story (70)	The New Yorker (35)	The New Yorker (31)	The New Yorker (21)
Harper's (12)	Harper's (21)	Harper's Bazaar (34)	Harper's (15)	Saturday Evening Post (20)
Scribner's (10)	Atlantic Monthly (21)	Atlantic Monthly (27)	Mademoiselle (14)	Atlantic Monthly (13)
The Midland (8)	Scribner's (19)	Story (25)	Hudson Review (13)	Esquire (11)
Pictorial Review (8)	American Mercury (17)	Harper's (19)	Atlantic Monthly (12)	Kenyon Review (10)

1970s	1980s	1990s	2000s	2010s
The New Yorker (27)	The New Yorker (58)	The New Yorker (48)	The New Yorker (50)	The New Yorker (100)
Atlantic Monthly (13)	Atlantic Monthly (18)	Story (15)	Tin House, Ploughshares (18)	Tin House (39)
Southern Review (11)	Esquire (14)	Atlantic Monthly (14)	Atlantic Monthly, Harper's (13)	Ploughshares (33)
Esquire (11)	Paris Review (8)	Ploughshares (14)	Glimmer Train, Zoetrope (11)	Granta (27)
Playboy (9)	North American Review (6)	Harper's (10)		Paris Review, Zoetrope (19)

Indeed, *New Yorker* stories alone account for 14 percent of all those selected by the *Best American*. Given just how many stories are drawn from such a small list of periodicals, we might think of those venues' editors as a kind of shadow jury for the anthology, and perhaps also the most influential figures in the formation of a contemporary short story canon. That is, perhaps Lorrie Moore, Jesmyn Ward, and the forty other "guest editors" of the *Best* series have each had less influence over the anthology than, say, Deborah Treisman, the *New Yorker*'s fiction editor since 2003.

More striking than the dominance of these select few periodicals over the anthology is their increasing consolidation over time, and in a period in which the amount of short fiction published has waned considerably. In the 1950s, when the *New Yorker* was one of a handful of journals whose stories were most anthologized, the magazine published "between 100 and 150 stories a year"; now, when it outstrips even its nearest competitors combined, that number is closer to fifty. With the likes of *Playboy* and *Esquire* "publishing one story an issue or fewer," and the subscription lists of hundreds of other literary magazines "limited to university and college libraries," "the total number of stories in wide-circulation magazines per year in America is less than a hundred" (May 2012, 299). That is, as fewer periodicals publish fewer short stories each year, the few at the top have become a kind of oligopoly of literary distinction.

The effect of this on both the *Best American* anthology and the process of canonization to which it contributes is one of aesthetic standardization. As Viet Thanh Nguyen said of the stories in the series' super anthology, *100 Years of the Best American Short Stories* (2015): "The dominant aesthetic seems to be what gets published in the *New Yorker* . . . the broad middle of realist fiction," leaving out more popular, generic fiction as well as the more experimental avant-garde (Kellogg 2015). In the long run, this could lead not only to a narrowing of the short story's aesthetic possibilities, but also a winnowing of its readers. Some critics argue that this has already taken place. Writing in the early 1990s, Levy described this situation bluntly: "Institutionally, historically, and structurally, everything about the short story implied heterogeneity – everything, perhaps, except the audience, which . . . now rarely extends beyond the comparatively small and homogeneous readership represented by the circulation lists of the *New Yorker* and the university presses" (1993, 109).

The Best Alternatives

At the same time, the perceived homogeneity of the *Best American* series – and the short story itself – has motivated a vast array of alternative anthologies. Just as the National Book Award "established itself as the anti-Pulitzer," and the National Book Critics Circle Award "launched its own anti-NBA anti-Pulitzer" prize (English 2005, 65), scores of other anthologies have sought to contest not just the *Best American*'s selection process, but also who and what it deems superlative. The 1960s and 1970s were a particularly important period for the anthologizing of short fiction by racialized writers. In just a few years, Langston Hughes published his edited volume *The Best Short Stories by Negro Writers: 1899–1967* (1967), which was followed swiftly by *Black Fire: An Anthology of Afro-American Writing* (1968), edited by Leroi Jones (later Amiri Baraka) and Larry Neal, as well as Toni Cade Bambara's *The Black Woman: An Anthology* (1970). In 1974, Frank Chin, Jeffery Paul Chan, Lawson Fusao Inada, and Shawn Wong published the landmark collection *Aiiieeeee! An Anthology of Asian-American Writers*, which included short fiction alongside a host of other literary genres.

This push to celebrate and anthologize the work of minoritized writers has also extended beyond racialized authors alone. The 1990s witnessed a wealth of new anthologies of queer short fiction, which was quickly capitalized upon by large publishing conglomerates. Take, as just two examples, *The Penguin Book of Lesbian Short Stories* (1993) and *The Penguin Book of Gay Short Stories* (1994), which was updated a decade later as *The New Penguin Book of Gay Short Stories* (2004). Scholars have noted that the publisher's addition of its own name to the titles is an effort to both "legitimate" previously disregarded literary traditions and to "secure some kudos for itself" (March-Russell 2009, 58). What these anthologies emphasize, in other words, is not only the growing visibility of minoritized writers, but also the publisher's view that diverse anthologies are a path to profit as much as an expression of high-minded democratic ideals (Engelbrecht 1995, 76).

That these volumes are almost always "more profitable to publishers than to authors or editors" also helps to explain the proliferation of specialized short story anthologies over the last three decades, as publishers target increasingly segmented markets of readers (D'hoker 2018, 115). These include collections organized around different identity groups (such as those listed above), but also those arranged according to "popular themes [such as] love, death, and war, as well as sports, regions or animals" (D'hoker 2018, 111). Add to this anthologies of specific subgenres of the short story – collections of crime, detective, erotic, fantasy, flash, gothic, horror, romance, and science fiction – and it appears that there is an anthology for almost any reader. Yet even as short story anthologies set their sights on smaller generic communities (*Tales from the Zombie Road: The Long Haul Anthology* [2017]), longer spans of time (*The Best American Short Stories of the Century* [2003]), writers on the rise (*Scribner's Best of the Fiction Workshops* [1997]), and writers who have thus far failed to launch (*The Best Unpublished Short Stories by Emerging Writers* [1991]), the anthology as a form has enjoyed only modest popularity.

While exact sales figures are notoriously difficult for scholars of contemporary literature to come by, what little information we have about the relative health of the short story anthology, and of book-length collections of short fiction in general, is not promising. Of the 7,000 books to appear on the *New York Times*'s list of bestsellers between 1946 and 2020, only sixteen include the word "stories" in their title – one of which, *The Best American Short Stories of the Century*, appeared at the very bottom of the list for just a single week in 1999.[2] This is perhaps why the *Best American* series has turned, in recent years, to more popular authors – Stephen King, Tom Perrotta, and Roxane Gay among them – to serve as guest editors and lend a portion of their loyal readerships to the annual anthology. Though the short story was often accused at the start of the twentieth century of being overly commercialized – a sellout genre that existed only in the service of magazine advertising revenue – by the turn of the twenty-first century, the situation had almost entirely reversed. "Agents and editors are seldom enthusiastic about taking on a collection of short stories," Charles May argues, "unless the author is a name with a novel to his or her credit, or ... promise[s] a novel in the near future" (2012, 299). With this in mind, the next two sections consider the short story's circulation within an alternative economy, that of literary prestige, and in particular how the form has been promoted by major literary awards and university literature curricula, two of the most important institutions of literary canon formation.

Prizing the Short Story

As James English memorably declared, "it is almost as though winning a prize is the only truly newsworthy thing a cultural worker can do, the one thing that really counts in a lifetime of more or less nonassessable, indescribable, or at least unreportable cultural accomplishments" (2005, 21). This is especially true for writers of short fiction, who vie for major literary prizes such as the Booker, the Pulitzer, and the National Book Award, as well as a number of prizes specific to the genre itself. These awards are effectively the "*institutional* machinery of cultural legitimacy" (37, italics in original), manufacturing prestige for individual authors and competing on behalf of the short story (against, say, the novel) for recognition and esteem. Understanding who these organizations consecrate, therefore, is vitally important to the history of the short story in the United States.

In 1919, Blanche Colton Williams became the founding editor of the O. Henry Memorial Prize for short fiction. Established in memory of the short story writer William Sydney Porter (who wrote under the pseudonym O. Henry), the award was "developed as a way of acknowledging excellence in American short fiction," and has run nearly continuously for over a century (Alley 2003, 36). Each year, the O. Henry editorial committee selects a number of short stories to recognize and republish, and elevates one or more for even greater distinction: from its founding in 1919 to 2002, the organization awarded a single "First Prize"; since 2003, they have cited a small group of "Juror Favorites." As with the *Best American* series, the list of writers whose stories have been selected the greatest number of times by the O. Henry is familiar to students of American short fiction: Joyce Carol Oates (29 stories selected), Alice Adams (23), John Updike (13), William Faulkner (12), Alice Munro (12), Wilbur Daniel Steele (11), Kay Boyle (10), Nancy Hale (10), Jean Stafford (10), and John Cheever (9) (see Plympton). The O. Henry's top honorees not only emphasize the contributions of individual writers to the short story form in the twentieth century, but also how notions of who a short story writer is have – and have not – shifted in that same period. Though 59 percent of the award's "first-prize winners" between 1919 and 2002 were men, since the award switched to a "favorites" model in 2003, women writers have comprised 57 percent of those recognized.

As the list of writers above emphasizes, however, the O. Henry's top honors have skewed overwhelmingly toward white writers, elevating fewer than ten racialized writers in the prize's first eighty-eight years. These pathbreaking authors include Alice Walker (1986), Louise Erdrich (1987), John Edgar Wideman (2000), Sherman Alexie (2005), and Edward P. Jones (2006). As an editor for the award, Wallace Stegner once praised the organization as one that "brings a dozen and a half stories out of the obscurity of back-number magazines and makes them available. It presents a beginning writer his first chance at real criticism, and it helps solidify forming reputations" (quoted in Alley 2003, 37). These statistics, however, suggest that it has largely worked to solidify the reputations of some writers over others. Moreover, given that the list of top periodicals from which the O. Henry stories are drawn looks strikingly like that of the *Best American* – the *New Yorker* accounts for more than a quarter of all selections since 1919, followed by *Harper's*, the *Atlantic*, and *Tin House* – the idea that writers and works are being rescued from "obscurity" is not borne out by fact.

Founded in 1976 as a response to the dominance of a small group of conglomerated publishers and well-known journals, the nonprofit Pushcart Prize honors short fiction "from among small press and small magazine publishers" only (Kennedy 1992, 204). The writers and editors (the latter largely made up of the prize's previous winners) associated with the Pushcart regard it as "one of the last bastions of non-corporate writing," a volume "for those who wish to look beneath the surface of the commercial literary market in the United States" (Jayakar 2015; Kennedy 1992, 205). Many well-known writers have appeared among the Pushcart's honorees – Raymond Carver, Andre Dubus, John Irving, Joyce Carol Oates, and Anne Tyler among them – "but most of the names are unknown" or, as the Pushcart's promoters might say, "on the way to becoming known" (Kennedy 1992, 205). Part of the reason that the Pushcart's focus on small presses is so important for the short story genre is that, as Simone Murray has recently argued, "short-story collections . . . are often not taken on by the major publishers (or only in small numbers, and even then only from authors with existing profiles)," which leaves small presses to "champion 'new' genres, which they nurture until a market niche has been carved out and critical recognition has begun to flow" (2021, 95–96).

The idea that collections of short fiction exist on the margins of the literary field is further reinforced by the lists of finalists for major literary awards such as the Pulitzer Prize, the National Book Award, and the National Book Critics Circle Award. Even being shortlisted for one of these three prizes can significantly alter the life – and longevity – of a book: finalists are much more likely to be rated on Goodreads (an indication of readerly engagement if not sales), taught in university literature courses, and cited by scholars (Manshel, McGrath, and Porter 2019). Given the power of these three prizes alone to consecrate new works of fiction and contribute to a first draft of the contemporary literary canon, it is striking that between 1950 and 2019, only 15 percent of their shortlisted works were collections of short fiction. Indeed, in the twenty years between 2000 and 2019, these prizes were awarded to works of short fiction only six times.

As with the *Best American Short Stories* and the O. Henry award, the short fiction recognized by these major literary prizes over the last seventy years has been, more often than not, written by white men. That said, whereas women writers account for just under half (48 percent) of short story collections shortlisted, that figure is considerably higher than it is for shortlisted novels, where male writers comprise two thirds (67 percent) of all honorees. In other words, though women writers have been overlooked by these awards historically, and though when they *are* named as prize-winners or finalists, it is largely (79 percent) for writing novels, women authors are nonetheless *more* likely than their male counterparts to reach the shortlist with a work of short fiction. The situation with regard to racialized writers is almost the opposite. Of the 132 works by a writer of color to be shortlisted by a major literary award between 1950 and 2019, 117 of them (89 percent) are novels. In the decades since James Alan McPherson, the first Black writer (and writer of color) to win a major award for short fiction, won the 1978 Pulitzer Prize for his collection *Elbow Room*, only a handful of minoritized authors of short fiction – Bharati Mukherjee, Jhumpa Lahiri, Adam Johnson, and Edwidge Danticat – have won a top prize. In other words, despite the notable exceptions that come to mind – Edward P. Jones's *Lost in the City* (1992), Lahiri's *Interpreter of Maladies* (1999), Junot Díaz's *This is How You Lose Her* (2012), and Carmen Maria Machado's *Her Body and Other Parties* (2017) – the short story's economy of prestige, across prizes and anthologies alike, is far whiter than that of the novel.

One reason for this may be that, for marginalized writers in particular, the literary field's barriers to entry are only compounded when it comes to making a living, and forging a career, from short fiction alone. Perhaps this is why the publishers of Gloria Naylor's short story cycle *The Women of Brewster Place* (1982) "quickly added the subtitle 'A Novel in Seven Stories'" to the title (Boddy 2010, 121), or why Julia Alvarez's *How the García Girls Lost Their Accents* (1991) and Tommy Orange's *There There* (2018) were marketed as novels rather than interlinked collections of short fiction. There is a sense among agents, publishers, and even some short fiction writers themselves that "a writer's early short stories (as any New York editor will tell you) lead to a novel, or they lead nowhere at all" (Harbach 2014, 18). As Mark McGurl has argued, though the "standard" postwar literary career "often begins with a showcase collection of short stories (often enough written in [a creative writing] workshop)," it ulti-mately "moves on – as it did for Flannery O'Connor, Joyce Carol Oates, Philip Roth, Russell Banks, Sandra Cisneros, Denis Johnson, Junot Díaz, and so many others – to the big (or at least bigger) novel" (2009, 376–377). Consider, as yet another example, the career of George Saunders, who despite being lauded as one of the foremost authors of short fiction working today, had never won a major literary award – until, that is, he published his first novel, *Lincoln in the Bardo*, which won the Booker Prize, making him only the second American writer to do so. The first, Paul Beatty – like the vast majority of fiction prize winners – was a novelist.

The Canon(s) of American Literature

Accused of being *too popular* and *too commercial* in the late nineteenth and early twentieth century, the short story is now regarded as *too rarefied* and *too academic*. As Chad Harbach announced in his 2010 essay "MFA vs. NYC," "the story, once such a reliable source of income for writers, has fallen out of mass favor," instead becoming "subtly and pejoratively associated with low academia – the workaday drudgery of classroom exercises and assignments" (2014, 18). The short story (and the short story anthology, in particular) became "the key genre of creative writing instruction" in the postwar period, and has remained so (McGurl 2009, 66). "To learn how to write short stories," Harbach writes, "you also have to read them," and given that, the desire to write has only promoted the short story's centrality in undergraduate and graduate creative writing classrooms across the United States (17). Beyond the campus gates, the publishing landscape for a budding writer of short fiction may be daunting: Amy Hungerford notes that "at many literary journals, submissions vastly exceed subscription rates," suggesting that contemporary literary culture has become "a culture of making rather than a culture of reading" (2016, 9). And yet, as ominous as this sounds, perhaps short fiction's thoroughly institutionalized status is actually its greatest strength.

Given that a great part of the people who read literary fiction read it in the context of the classroom – whether at the secondary, undergraduate, or graduate level – the short story's pedagogical affordances have sustained its visibility for readers who neither purchase nor seek out short fiction, but read it often nonetheless. McGurl has argued that short stories can "sometimes seem pre-packaged for close reading in the classroom," and this idea is well supported by data on university syllabi (144). The Open Syllabus Project has aggregated more than 300,000 syllabi for recent English literature courses at American colleges and universities, tabulating the most taught texts across institutions. The portrait of the genre's place in US higher education revealed by this data is both reassuring and foreboding. Of the top ten most taught literary works in university English classes, five are short stories. Charlotte Perkins Gilman's

"The Yellow Wallpaper" is the most taught work of short fiction, included on more syllabi than *Paradise Lost*, *Heart of Darkness*, or "A Modest Proposal." Gilman's story is followed (in order of frequency) by Kate Chopin's "The Story of an Hour," William Faulkner's "A Rose for Emily," Tim O'Brien's *The Things They Carried*, and Flannery O'Connor's *A Good Man is Hard to Find and Other Stories*. Beyond these top five, Hawthorne's *Young Goodman Brown and Other Stories* appears more than *Hamlet*; Ernest Hemingway's "Hills Like White Elephants" and Alice Walker's "Everyday Use" each appear more than either *Invisible Man* or *Beloved*; and Melville's "Bartleby the Scrivener" appears more than either *The Great Gatsby* or *Pride and Prejudice*. In all, sixteen of the top 100 most taught texts – including stories by Shirley Jackson, Raymond Carver, Edgar Allan Poe, Joyce Carol Oates, and James Baldwin – are works of short fiction (a number strikingly similar to the figures for prize finalists discussed above).

This empirical evidence supports Harbach's central thesis that there exist at present two "parallel and competing canons of contemporary literature," each with "its own canonical works and heroic figures" (2014, 19, 13). While the novel may dominate the world of New York publishing, the short story's centrality in the study of fiction has perhaps secured it "a more durable readership than the vaunted novel," as well as "the institutional means to ... replenish it" (21). Harbach further speculates that the short story canon is "less masculine" and more diverse than the canon of contemporary novels – a supposition that the institutional histories offered above largely refute. Nevertheless, the growing diversity of these institutions, and the continued vitality of the short story form outside of the traditional centers of conglomerated publishing, suggest that, for all that has changed, the genre still resembles its description in O'Brien's very first *Best American* anthology. "Commercialization has never affected any literature more than it has affected the American short story" he wrote then, "but here and there in quiet places, usually far from great cities, artists are laboring quietly for a literary ideal, and the leaven of their achievement is becoming more and more impressive every day" (1915, 6).

Works Cited

Alley, Henry. 2003. "The Well-Made World of the O. Henrys, 1961–2000," *The Kenyon Review* 25.2 (Spring): 36–58.

Batuman, Elif. 2006. "Short Story & Novel." *n+1* (Spring). www.nplusonemag. com/issue-4/essays/short-story-novel/.

Boddy, Kasia. 2010. *The American Short Story Since 1950*. Edinburgh: Edinburgh University Press.

D'hoker, Elke. 2018. "The Short Story Anthology," in *The Edinburgh Companion to the Short Story in English*. Ed. Paul Delaney and Adrian Hunter, 108–124. Edinburgh: Edinburgh University Press.

Engelbrecht, Penelope J. 1995. "Strange Company: Uncovering the Queer Anthology," *NWSA Journal* 7.1: 72–90.

English, James F. 2005. *The Economy of Prestige: Prizes, Awards, and the Circulation of Cultural Value*. Cambridge, MA: Harvard University Press.

Harbach, Chad. 2014. "MFA vs. NYC," in *MFA vs NYC: The Two Cultures of American Fiction*. Ed. Chad Harbach, 9–28. New York: Faber and Faber.

Hungerford, Amy. 2016. *Making Literature Now*. Stanford, CA: Stanford University Press.

Jayakar, Tara. 2015. "Pushcart Prize Turns Forty," *Poets and Writers*, November 12. www.pw.org/content/pushcart_prize_turns_forty?cmnt_all=1.

Kellogg, Carolyn. 2015. "Review: '100 Years of Best American Short Stories' Is Vital Yet Flawed for Loading the Canon," *Los Angeles Times*, October 9. www.latimes.com/books/jacketcopy/la-ca-jc-best-short-stories-20151011-story.html.

Kennedy, Thomas E. 1992. "The Pushcart Prize: Honoring America's Unknown Literature," *ANQ: A Quarterly Journal of Short Articles* 5.4: 203–206.

Levy, Andrew. 1993. *The Culture and Commerce of the American Short Story*. New York: Cambridge University Press.

Manshel, Alexander, Laura B. McGrath, and J. D. Porter. 2019. "Who Cares about Literary Prizes." *Public Books*. www.publicbooks.org/who-cares-about-literary-prizes/.

March-Russell, Paul. 2009. *The Short Story: An Introduction*. Edinburgh: Edinburgh University Press.

May, Charles. 2012. "The American Short Story in the Twenty-First Century," in *Short Story Theories: A Twenty-First-Century Perspective*. Ed. Viorica Patea, 299–324. Amsterdam and New York: Rodopi.

McGurl, Mark. 2009. *The Program Era: Postwar Fiction and the Rise of Creative Writing*. Cambridge, MA: Harvard University Press.

Murray, Simone. 2021. *Introduction to Contemporary Print Culture: Books As Media*. London: Routledge.

O'Brien, Edward J. 1915. *The Best Short Stories of 1915 and the Yearbook of the American Short Story*. Boston: Small, Maynard, and Company.

    1931. *The Advance of the American Short Story*. New York: Dodd, Mead, and Company.

Open Syllabus Project. 2021. "Open Syllabus Explorer." Accessed November 1, 2021. Explorer.opensyllabusproject.org/.

Plympton. "Best American Short Stories," *Writing Atlas*. Accessed November 1, 2021. "O. Henry Prize Winners," *Writing Atlas*. Accessed November 1, 2021.

Sittenfeld, Curtis. 2017. "Show Don't Tell," *The New Yorker*, May 29, 2017. www.newyorker.com/magazine/2017/06/05/show-dont-tell.

CHAPTER 5

The Story of a Semester
Short Fiction and the Program Era

Loren Glass

The March 29, 2021 issue of the *New Yorker* magazine features a short story called "Future Selves," in which an unnamed narrator recounts her experiences with her unnamed husband as they look to buy their first apartment in an unnamed city. We are not told what they do for a living, but we know they are well-educated, as she reminisces about "the studio we'd lived in as graduate students"; and we assume they must be artists since she mentions that their parents "asked if our creative work was secure enough for us to take on a mortgage" (Savaş 2021, 57). During this apartment search the narrator goes to visit her "cousin Tara at her university" in an unnamed college town (57). The brief visit provides the source of the title, as it becomes clear that while the narrator sees her youthful past in her cousin, her cousin projects her adult future onto the narrator. Thus, in the following year, when the narrator and her husband have secured an apartment, the cousin writes to ask "whether she could live with us for a year after graduation to write her novel"; the narrator adds that this was "something she used to predict for her future, that she would live in a romantic city working on a book" (59). The story was written by Ayşegül Savaş, a Turkish novelist living in Paris, but without proper or place names it feels like it could be about any well-educated, economically precarious, creative couple in any city in the world.

The first thing to say about the short story during the Program Era, that period beginning with the emergence of the discipline of creative writing during the postwar boom in higher education and extending into the present, is that it assumes the socioeconomic situation and sensibilities of the creative class. Whatever they are literally about, literary short stories published during the Program Era address a readership of college graduates whose sentimental education was formed by the modern American English department and its canon of modernist classics, from James Joyce and D. H. Lawrence to Ernest Hemingway and Henry James, the "masters" who were meticulously imitated in the creative writing classroom during

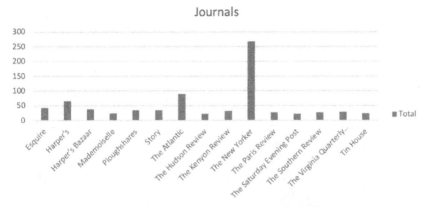

Figure 5.1   Journals with stories in the *Best American Short Stories* since 1942.

the postwar inception of the Program Era and whose manners and methods still shape the form and content of short stories today. Many of them, like "Future Selves," are autoethnographic, using first-person point of view (POV) or free indirect style to provide a portrait of the artist as a creative precariat, with their talent and their degree as their sole sources of personal capital. In this world, the short story itself is a type of symbolic capital, a form of reputational investment for the creative writer, frequently in the money-making novel to come.

The second thing to say about the short fiction of the Program Era is that it is published in the *New Yorker*. Of the 1,700 stories selected for the *Best American Short Stories* (BASS) since 1942, 269 were originally published in the *New Yorker*, far exceeding the number in any other journal or magazine (see Figures 5.1 and 5.2).[1] And this dominance is sustained and consistent, with the *New Yorker* publishing the most stories selected for BASS in every decade since the 1940s. Over the entire course of the Program Era, publication in this magazine has represented the pinnacle of achievement and the gateway to mainstream success. And a sustained relationship with the magazine, as we see with authors ranging from Salinger to Updike to Barthelme to Beattie to Cheever to Munro, represents mastery of the short story form specifically as a kind of literary brand identifying both writer and magazine. If, as Chad Harbach famously affirmed, the story of the American short story is the story of "MFA vs NYC," then the two cultures converge in the magazine, which continues to serve as a kind of synecdoche for the culture capital on which writers and artists once thrived but can now barely afford to live. If the Program

Figure 5.2   *New Yorker* stories in the *Best American Short Stories* by year since 1942.

Era has dispersed these writers from the pricey coastal metropoles to the myriad more affordable college towns across the country, the *New Yorker* functions as a representation and reminder of the continuing centrality of New York City as the economic and cultural driver of postwar literature and literary prestige. More than the multinational publishing conglomerates, whose relationship with the city has become increasingly attenuated, the magazine named after the city has become the vehicle whereby the sensibilities of NYC are spread out across a national map dotted with MFA-granting institutions. And the *New Yorker*, in turn, is geared toward the college-educated middle class, which expanded exponentially in the postwar era.

And the MFA-granting institution that dominates the field of short story publication is the University of Iowa, which, like the *New Yorker* in the magazine field, has appeared far more frequently than any other school in BASS since World War II. The source of both the name and the method of the short story workshop, the Iowa Writers' Workshop serves as a synecdoche for the creative writing program in the same way that the *New Yorker* serves as a synecdoche for New York City. Like issues of the magazine, Iowa graduates are spread out across the nation, taking their credentials and their *New Yorker* subscriptions with them, disseminating the MFA vs. NYC dialectic to every college town in the country (see Figures 5.3 and 5.4). It is between these twin poles of prestige that the

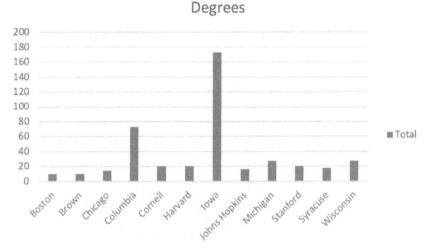

Figure 5.3   *Best American Short Stories* author MFAs since 1942.

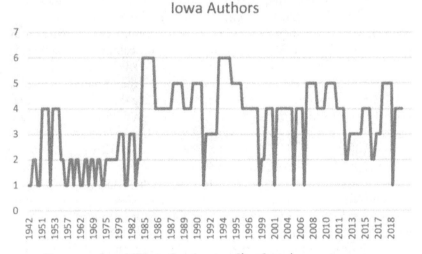

Figure 5.4   Iowa MFAs in *Best American Short Stories* by year since 1942.

form and content of the short story has been negotiated and evaluated during the Program Era. Both are indelible markers of "success" for a short story writer.

Nevertheless, the continuing institutional dominance of the East Coast can be illustrated with one additional visualization, which shows those

Employment

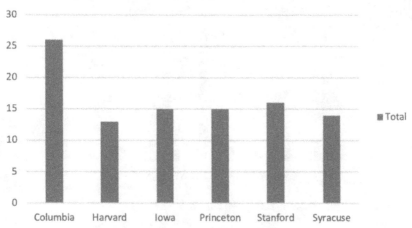

Figure 5.5   Institutions employing writers in the *Best American Short Stories* since 1942.

universities that most frequently employ the writers whose stories have been selected for BASS. Here, once again, New York City and its immediate environs loom large, with Columbia, Princeton, and Syracuse all in the top tier. The only West Coast university with comparable numbers is Stanford, home of the prestigious Wallace Stegner Fellows Program, and the only midwestern institution is Iowa. Overall, the prominence of East Coast Ivies on this chart illustrates their continuing dominance as cultural powerbrokers during the Program Era, with only Iowa and Syracuse representing more recent reputational capital. Columbia's dominance is noteworthy insofar as it indicates the degree to which that institution has sustained its cultural authority from the era of the New York Intellectuals, many of whom appear in BASS in the 1950s and 1960s, to the current star-studded faculty at the School of the Arts. Iowa may be the most prestigious degree, but Columbia is arguably the most prestigious job for a contemporary creative writer.

Finally, it is worth noting the modesty of these numbers of employed creative writing faculty relative to the number of MFA degrees granted by these institutions (see Figure 5.5). The persistent economic precarity of the creative writer can be discerned in this gap between the prestigious degree and the permanent job. Many writers have MFAs from reputable creative writing programs, but only a few in turn get jobs in those programs. Many of their short stories thematically reflect and refract this fundamental socioeconomic asymmetry, which haunts the field with the fear of failure.

The "shortness" of the modern short story is a product of the American magazine industry and the temporalities of writing and reading associated with it. Originally and famously theorized by Edgar Allan Poe in the 1840s as the ideal form for the ideal literary magazine (to be edited by himself, the ideal editor), the American short story did not fully establish itself until over a generation later, in conjunction with the advertisement-driven "magazine revolution" of the late nineteenth century. Poe never found his ideal audience, and indeed the readership for nineteenth-century magazines tended to be regionally restricted, politically aligned, and subscription-based; there was as yet no "general" readership that encompassed the nation. This changed in the 1890s when the business model shifted to a heavier reliance on advertisement revenue, driving subscription rates down. At the same time, a national distribution system emerged that made it possible to address the nation as a whole. And these new magazines – *Cosmopolitan*, *Ladies Home Journal*, *McClure's*, and many others – were addressed principally to the professional managerial classes, whose reading habits developed in the context of the distractions and demands of modern urban life, which frequently provided the plots and settings of magazine fiction as well.

To this central socioeconomic determinant of the form's appeal, the Program Era adds the tasks and temporalities of college life, where stories are studied and written instead of simply being read. Like the lyric poem, to which it is frequently analogized, a short story can be fully discussed in a single class session and effectively completed and graded during a semester. In this pedagogical environment it functions as a sort of laboratory and testing ground for the techniques and talents necessary to the composition of a novel. For most creative writers, it is an apprenticeship form, originally addressed to teachers and fellow students, and then to other writers and literary professionals, preparing the way for the novel or short story cycle addressed to the larger reading public. As Andrew Levy affirms, the "workshop system ... is an alternate economy, enclosed and complete – a network of graduate programs, conferences, and literary magazines, that creates and encompasses writers of short stories, readers of short stories, sites of publication, and an economic and philosophical rationale for the network's own existence" (1993, 3). The literary short story, in other words, is a form of symbolic capital that circulates in the restricted field of cultural production and that can subsequently be converted to economic capital as a novel in the general field of cultural production.

As Harbach succinctly affirms in the introduction to his edited volume, creative writing "programs are organized around the story form"

(2014, 17). And for this very reason there have been more short stories published during the Program Era than anyone could possibly read. The scale and scope of the field resists critical mastery and accommodates only the loosest of generalizations about content or form. Its primary function as a kind of laboratory of method means that its variations over time and place will challenge the validity of any critical summation. Nevertheless, insofar as prizes and awards are the evaluative metrics of the Program Era, focusing on the authors, journals, and institutions named in BASS can provide an informative map of the field into which every writer must enter if they want to succeed. There will always be exceptions, but the rules of the game are shaped by what James English has called "the economy of prestige" that determines and disseminates literary reputations in the Program Era. Edited from 1942 to 1978 by Martha Foley, co-founder of *Story Magazine*, and since 1978 by a series of prestigious guest editors, BASS provides a useful record of the institutions and individuals that wield power in this symbolic economy, and therefore an illuminating illustration of the themes and styles that professionally preoccupy and are pedagogically promulgated by them.

The first writer whose stories were explicitly canonized as products of a creative writing program was undoubtedly Flannery O'Connor, who put the Iowa Writers' Workshop on the literary map and whose work can be understood as a kind of hinge between the modernist masters and their Program Era acolytes. As Mark McGurl has affirmed, it was O'Connor's disciplined mastery of Jamesian limited omniscience that made her the darling of the New Critics, who trained, patronized, and published her across the 1950s and 1960s. The inclusion of O'Connor's classic short story "A Good Man Is Hard to Find" in the second edition of Cleanth Brooks and Robert Penn Warren's widely adopted and highly influential textbook *Understanding Fiction* inaugurates the passage from mentee to model that would become a kind of ideal career arc for the creative writer whereby, as Kasia Boddy affirms, one finds "oneself included in the anthology one had studied" (2010, 22). If publication in the *New Yorker* represents mainstream success, publication in a course-adopted anthology functions as a kind of professional consecration. The former gets readers, but the latter gets students, who, in the long run, are a more sustained guarantor of canonicity and influence. Indeed, the textbook anthology itself, as a pedagogical tool wherein craft is taught by example, is a signature and profitable product bequeathed to the Program Era by the New Critics.

O'Connor also codified the sociological tendency of the American short story toward what Mark McGurl has identified as a modernist class "pastoral" wherein the writer, and by identificatory implication the reader, enacts an affective dialectic of empathy and disdain toward subjects less sophisticated than themselves (2001, 9). O'Connor's "good country people" are invariably less educated and more ignorant than the narrator who brings them to life, and it is up to the reader (frequently a student) to gauge and inhabit the range of sympathy and distance afforded by the author's expert deployment of limited omniscience and free indirect style. In this sense, the pedagogical process of "reading as a writer" involves the inculcation of precisely that sophisticated sensibility whereby less educated characters are rendered "realistic" through this dialectical range of identificatory registers that places the narrator in a position of literary and moral authority over their subjects. This resolutely ambivalent dynamic deeply informs the sensibilities that are shaped by the pedagogical protocols and socioeconomic demographics of the creative writing classroom and the short stories produced and discussed in it.

If O'Connor imported the limited omniscience of James and Joyce into this classroom, it would fall to Raymond Carver to convert Ernest Hemingway's laconic first-person POV, honed to perfection in his classic and widely anthologized short stories, into a model of Program Era prose. Hemingway was a literary hero to all the young men returning from World War II to attend college under the GI Bill, and his prose style provided a kind of active masculine complement to Jamesian limited omniscience, which tended to prefer observation to action. For those who wanted to write about their experiences in the war, Hemingway was the go-to model, and the war and its aftermath forms the thematic focus of many of the stories published in BASS in the initial years of the Program Era.

With Carver we see Hemingway's style and POV detached from this thematic focus and recentered on the precarious everyday life of the less privileged classes. Carver's apotheosis in the 1960s and 1970s can be understood as embodying and empowering those social classes whom O'Connor relegated to the status of literary objects, by telling stories that illustrate how they themselves might become literary subjects – in other words, writers. O'Connor was famously disdainful of creative writing pedagogy, restricting "real" writers – who have the "gift" of talent, which cannot be taught – to the realms of the elite. Carver provided a more democratic and accessible form and sensibility whereby those lower on the cultural and economic hierarchy could climb to canonicity by concisely chronicling their own misery and marginalization. As with O'Connor, the process was disciplinary, both in terms of getting a degree and in terms of working hard, but here the affective ambivalence is internalized and self-reflective, instead of securing an autonomous attitude toward underprivileged others. As McGurl affirms, Carver's stories can be understood as "autopastoral: an aesthetic appreciation of a simpler, slower, more controllable version of oneself" (2009, 294). Generally speaking, one can place O'Connor and Carver at the elitist and democratic poles of the Program Era's paradoxical class ideology. On the one hand, the program provides patronage for the elites, those gifted writers who need insulation from the marketplace in order to produce their masterpieces. On the other hand, the program provides access to that marketplace and those masterpieces for the masses of American college students who want to write but fear they lack the talent or the tools.

As McGurl has shown, Carver's rigorous minimalism provided a mechanism for dealing with the shame and resentment of those who enter the creative writing classroom without entitlement or confidence; it "is a fundamentally self-reflexive feeling, associated with negative feedback," such as one experiences in the workshop (2009, 285). O'Connor famously "learned" nothing in her classes at Iowa; she was the one whose stories the other students listened to in stunned silence without any ensuing analysis or discussion, and once she graduated, she never taught. Carver's career, on the other hand, modeled the stubborn determination of the underprivileged acolyte to overcome negative feedback and prove their ability in the crucible of the classroom, first as student and then as teacher, and his itinerant residencies across institutions in the 1960s and 1970s parallel the increasingly democratic, and riskily precarious, access and spread of creative writing across the American academic landscape.

And the principal source of negative feedback for Carver came from his editor, Gordon Lish. As Matthew Blackwell has confirmed, Carver's relationship with Lish was characterized by the dialectic of shame and pride that McGurl places at the emotional center of the workshop experience, but with Lish we see how the dialectic ramifies out into the larger culture of publication and prestige. Lish linked up the roles of editor and teacher (he taught through the Continuing Education Program at Columbia), essentially using his famously harrowing workshops as talent pools for his editorial selections, thereby arrogating himself to a uniquely representative role in the Program Era, and powerfully illustrating how the classroom experience feeds into the editorial process. Lish ruthlessly shamed his students in the classroom, but if you could handle the experience, the reward could be the prize of publication. His relationship with Carver is only the most famous example of what was in fact a "school" of short story writers, including Amy Hemple, Yannick Murphy, Diane Williams, and Noy Holland, all collectively associated with the stoic minimalism that Lish promulgated as both teacher and editor.

Despite their differences, both O'Connor and Carver worked within the broad boundaries of literary realism as laid down during the magazine revolution. Their stories were plausible and their characters believable, even as these characters frequently occupied the margins of mainstream society and social "normality." But starting in the late 1960s a new form and sensibility emerged in explicit opposition to these realist protocols. Writers such as Frederick Barthelme and Robert Coover abandoned conventions of plot, setting, and character altogether, innovating a new anti-mimetic short story form. To a certain degree, this form, as a sort of dialectical response to the realism of the traditional short story, hearkened back to the schism in the first half of the twentieth century between a high modernism that championed the autonomy of art and the mastery of form and an avant-garde that challenged both autonomy and mastery. In both poetry and prose this split was institutionalized during the Program Era, which continuously generates internal and external avant-garde resistance to its various aesthetic and academic hegemonies.

This institutionalization has tended to be site-specific, insofar as individual universities have become loosely aligned with one or the other pole in this dialectic, usually deriving from the presence of one idiosyncratic individual whose charisma and creative style are routinized by the institution in the form of both image and acolytes. Thus, Robert Coover at Brown University, John Barth at Johns Hopkins, or Frederick Barthelme at the University of Houston have branded their institutions with their experimental styles and philosophies, just as Wallace Stegner at Stanford or Frank Conroy at Iowa made those institutions more sympathetic to and identified with traditional literary realism. The split could have political valences as well, insofar as Program Era realism would come to be associated with bourgeois complacency and academic privilege, while experimental modes would be understood as a form of internalized class critique and ideological iconoclasm.

But experimental short fiction also functioned as a more playful engagement with class privilege and realist protocols, without any accompanying critique. This was certainly the case with Barthelme, whose stint of brief *New Yorker* pieces in the late 1960s and early 1970s put his kooky style of experimentation on the mainstream literary map. Barthelme's short fiction challenged the disciplinary protocols of plot, setting, and POV – and indeed most of the aspects of "craft" that had become established as the teachable elements of the short story workshop. But his stories function less as critique than as complement, as a kind of playful reminder of the relativity and restrictedness of realist protocols. This is why they were such a good fit for the *New Yorker* in the late 1960s, which was beginning to suffer from a reputation for blandness and conservatism. Barthelme's stories are radical aesthetically but quietist politically, as is Barthelme himself.

That said, he did engage and interrogate, along with Coover and others, the function of short stories as deep structures and fantasy formations transcending, both historically and psychologically, their recent realist iterations, and invoking, as Charles E. May confirms, "the traditional mythic origins of the form" (1995, 20). Thus, one of the signal pre-occupations of the experimental short story during the Program Era is the fairy tale as rewritten for adults, a cultural formation that engages the various anthropological studies of folktales inspired by the publication in 1958 of the English translation of Vladimir Propp's foundational *Morphology of the Folk Tale*, and achieving a mainstream apotheosis with Bruno Bettelheim's psychoanalytically inflected *The Uses of Enchantment: The Meaning and Importance of Fairy Tales* (1976). Barthelme's postmodern unpacking of Snow White and Robert Coover's collaborative deconstruction of Sleeping Beauty both build narrative experiments onto archaic tales, in essence leapfrogging the bourgeois realism that intervened. The archaeology was not only historical but also psychological, insofar as both authors explored the psychosexual fantasies underlying the "innocent" versions of these fairy tales being promulgated contemporaneously by Disney movies and children's books. These forays into the fantastic permanently loosened the modern American short story's inaugural investments in literary realism, paving the way for contemporary fabulists such as George Saunders and Kelly Link.

They also exposed some of the gender politics of the form. Barthelme and Coover both chose fairy tales that foregrounded young women as objects of adult male speculation and desire in the context of changing gender roles, which were themselves partly the product of the co-educational classroom. Snow White herself is parodically represented as a graduate of "Beaver College," where she studied "Modern Woman, Her Privileges and Responsibilities," along with Classical Guitar, the English Romantic Poets, and Realism and Idealism in the Contemporary Italian Novel (Barthelme 1965, 31). She is both an ancient archetype and a contemporary co-ed, and the tension between these references provides much of the comedy and irony in Barthelme's collection of sketches.

While most of this first generation of experimentalists were men, female writers quickly noticed the complementary opportunities. One excellent example is "St. George," a story Gail Godwin originally wrote for Coover when he was a visiting instructor at the Iowa Writers' Workshop, and then published in *Cosmopolitan* in 1969. The protagonist, Gwen, is a graduate student in English studying Medieval Literature, and the entire story takes place in New York City over the course of winter break. Her studies, she believes, preclude a serious relationship. Her "Now man," Silas, has stopped coming to see her and she is lonely (466). The story turns fantastic when she cracks open an egg for a midnight omelet and out falls a tiny embryo that rapidly grows into a baby dragon, whom she names "St. George." The rest of the story is a highly amusing and insightful allegory of the psychosexual challenges of the single female graduate student, as the growing dragon, which eats pearls, begins to wreak havoc on her apartment. Part-child, part-research subject, and part-creative project, the baby dragon condenses the maternal, libidinal, intellectual, and creative needs that converge on the solitary autoethnographic protagonist. Silas eventually comes to the rescue and the story ends without resolving the "reality" of "St. George."

The gender politics of the Program Era were transformed by women's liberation, which coincided with a massive increase in the number of women matriculating at American universities, as well as an increase in the number of women appearing in BASS. Indeed, by the turn of the twenty-first century the field was dominated by two women, Alice Munro and Joyce Carol Oates, who have been singularly capable of scaling up a form that has remained resolutely "minor" relative to the novel since its inception. Munro's reception of the Nobel Prize in Literature in 2013 consecrated her as a master of the form, but it is surely significant that she is not a US citizen and does not have an MFA, though she has maintained a long-standing relationship with her alma mater, the University of Western Ontario, which after her Nobel Prize endowed an Alice Munro Chair in Creativity. Rather, in her resolute focus on Huron County, Ontario, Munro hearkens back to the regionalist origins of the modern American short story. This final visualization (Figure 5.6) emphatically illustrates the degree to which the "American" short story could easily be perceived as a "minor" form dominated by women writers and literary regionalists, a number of whom are not American. It is also worth affirming that BASS itself has been edited by women since 1942, with Martha

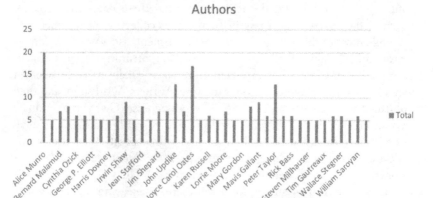

Figure 5.6   Authors with five or more stories in the *Best American Short Stories*.

Foley being replaced by a sequence of female series editors, who select and collaborate with the guest editor each year. The fact that women are not a demographic minority but in fact constitute the demographic majority of short story readers and writers illustrates the resolutely contradictory status of the short story as a form of symbolic capital.

There is not a single writer of color with five or more stories in BASS, amply illustrating the persistent "whiteness" of the American creative writing program and its products (see Figure 5.6). As noted above, the short story is a "minor" form that nonetheless is dominated by the demographic majority. The stakes of this hegemony are illuminated by the stories of James Alan McPherson, the first writer of color to win a Pulitzer Prize in Fiction and the first person of color to become a tenured professor in the Iowa Writers' Workshop. The title story that concludes McPherson's award-winning collection directly addresses the degree to which the form itself is unable to accommodate the contradictory realities of race in the postwar United States. "Elbow Room" is a deliberately unfinished story, interspersed with editorial commentary intended to illustrate how the form cannot represent the complexities and contradictions of modern American race relations. Thus, before the story even begins, we hear from a nameless editor who declaims, "Narrator is unmanageable. Demonstrates a disregard for form bordering on the paranoid" (1975, 256). The fragmentary story that follows chronicles an interracial courtship and marriage between Paul Frost, a young white man from Kansas who avoids the draft by doing alternate service in an insane asylum, and Virginia Valentine, an African American woman from Tennessee who has seen the world as a member of the Peace Corps. They meet and marry in the San Francisco Bay Area in the late 1960s.

The story is told by a nameless African American writer who, deliberately invoking Huck Finn, claims he is going "to the territory to renew my supply of stories." "The old stories were still being told," he continues, "but tellers seemed to lack confidence in them. Words seemed to have become detached from emotion and no longer flowed on the rhythm of passion. Even the great myths floated apart from their rituals" (260). Deliberately targeting the traditional short story in anthropological terms, the narrator declaims, "Maupassant's whores bristled with the muscle of union organizers. The life affirming peasants of Chekhov and Babel sat wasted and listless on their porches, oblivious to the beats in their own blood. Even Pushkin's firebrands and noble brigands seemed content with the lackluster" (261). "I needed new eyes," the narrator concludes, "regeneration, fresh forms, and went hunting for them out in the territory." The editor then intrudes with a number of pointed questions. "You are saying you want to be white?" To which the narrator responds, "A narrator needs as much access to the world as the advocates of that mythology." And then, "You are ashamed of being black?" To which the narrator responds, "Only of not being nimble enough to dodge other people's straightjackets" (262).

The story that proceeds is partly about the impossibility of its own telling. "It was not my story," the narrator concedes, "but I could not help intruding upon its materials. It seemed to lack perspective" (270). This "lack" refers to the difficulties the couple encounters in both navigating and narrating an interracial relationship, and the story turns on a tense conversation between Paul and the narrator on the meaning of the word "nigger." Paul wants to understand what it means, but the narrator insists that "he had to earn his own definitions" (276). The editor is frustrated by this section of the story and objects, "Narrator has a responsibility to make things clear." And the narrator responds, "Narrator fails in this respect" (278). In the end, the couple move to Tennessee and have a child, but it is clear that the narrator has "failed" to tell their story effectively. As he concedes in his final comment to the editor, "It was from the beginning not my story. I lack the insight to narrate its complexities." But the narrator does have qualified faith in the child, concluding that he would wager his "reputation on the ambition, if not the strength, of the boy's story" (286). The meaning of the title is clear: young writers will need "elbow room" if they want to write effectively and accurately about race in the United States.

In the year that McPherson's collection won the Pulitzer Prize, Sandra Cisneros received an MFA in poetry from the Iowa Writers' Workshop, but she was as interested in fiction as poetry and was frustrated by the requirement that she choose one over the other. *House on Mango Street* (1984), the book that would make her reputation, is a unique and powerful blend of poetry and prose that marks her break from that requirement into a new form that better accommodates the complexities of her ethnic heritage and identity. An enormously popular classroom text from high school to college to graduate school since it was republished by Vintage Contemporaries in 1991, *House on Mango Street* affirmed the degree to which the short story cycle provided opportunities for formal experimentation and innovation that were particularly appealing to minority writers whose experiences could not be accommodated by the traditional short story form. Other signal examples include Jamaica Kincaid's *Annie John* (1985), Ntozake Shange's *For Colored Girls Who Have Considered Suicide When the Rainbow Is Enuf* (1975), Julia Alvarez's *How the Garcia Girls Lost Their Accents* (1991), Amy Tan's *Joy Luck Club* (1989), Denise Chavez's *Last of the Menu Girls* (1986), and Louise Erdrich's *Love Medicine* (1984). All of these examples deploy formal innovations that break down the boundaries between poetry and prose in the process of presenting a multivocal, ethnically marked community, as opposed to the individual unmarked voice of the narrator or poet.

The short story cycle, with its antecedents in classics such as *Winesburg, Ohio* and *Dubliners*, tends to favor precisely such small and relatively homogenous communities in their collisions with modern mainstream culture. As a form it has proven uniquely flexible in adjusting to the varieties of experience that unfold in this internal contact zone. Unlike the modernist *Kunstleroman*, which focuses on the development of a singular artistic consciousness, the short story cycle offers the possibility of a collective or communal consciousness curated by a creative writer who literally serves to re-present that collective in all its complexity and contradiction from the liminal space of someone who has gone off to graduate school. As an ensemble affair that resists generic boundaries and classifications, it has proved particularly fruitful for the growing ranks of ethnic and minority writers in the more recent decades of the Program Era.

In the new millennium, the authors in BASS are more diverse along many axes, including sexuality, ethnicity, race and, increasingly, national origin. Many of those selected in the last few decades were not born in the United States and have used their writing as a way to navigate a dual national identity, regardless of their citizenship status. If, on the one hand, ethnic difference continues to mandate formal experimentation for some writers, on the other, the remarkable global expansion of creative writing programs has effectively internationalized the experience of the creative class, smoothing over many of these differences into a more homogenous, if persistently precarious, sensibility. Thus, while the names of the writers who appear in the *New Yorker* increasingly indicate a wide diversity of ethnic and national antecedents, the form and themes of their stories, as illustrated by Savaş's "Future Selves," tend to converge on the shared precarity and ambivalence of their class identities.

One could argue that the Program Era has in fact made creative writers, and creative workers more generally, into an identifiable middle-class fragment, and that the short story has become one of the signal expressions of its precarity. Creative life during the Program Era is cobbled together, both economically and artistically, from the scattered and varied resources offered by the creative economy. Most writers have to move from job to job, from gig to gig, from hand to mouth, and indeed from genre to genre as both internal and external demands dictate. And in an economy that is itself shaped by distraction and fragmentation, the short story has proved to be a particularly durable form.

Works Cited

Barthelme, Donald. 1965. *Snow White*. New York: Scribner.

Blackwell, Matthew. 2017. "What We Talk about When We Talk about Lish," in *After the Program Era*. Ed. Loren Glass, 113–122. Iowa City: University of Iowa Press.

Boddy, Kasia. 2010. *The American Short Story since 1950*. Edinburgh: Edinburgh University Press.

English, James. 2005. *The Economy of Prestige: Prizes, Awards, and the Circulation of Cultural Value*. Cambridge, MA: Harvard University Press.

Glass, Loren, ed. 2016. *After the Program Era: The Past, Present, and Future of Creative Writing in the University*. Iowa City: University of Iowa Press.

Godwin, Gail. 1969. "St. George," in *Great American Love Stories*. Ed. Lucy Rosenthal, 466–480. Boston: Little, Brown.

Harbach, Chad. 2014. "MFA vs NYC," in *MFA vs NYC*. Ed. Chad Harbach, 9–28. New York: Faber and Faber.

Levy, Andrew. 1993. *The Culture and Commerce of the American Short Story*. New York: Cambridge University Press.

May, Charles E. 1995. *The Short Story: The Reality of Artifice*. New York: Twayne.

McGurl, Mark. 2001. *The Novel Art: Elevations of American Fiction after Henry James*. Princeton, NJ: Princeton University Press.

2009. *The Program Era: Postwar Fiction and the Rise of Creative Writing.* Cambridge, MA: Harvard University Press.

McPherson, James Alan. 1975. "Elbow Room," in *Elbow Room*, 256–286. New York: Fawcett.

Savaş, Ayşegül. 2021. "Future Selves," *The New Yorker* (March 29): 56–60.

CHAPTER 6

The Short Story in the Age of the Internet

Simone Murray

As a genre, the short story engages with the Internet in a variety of ways. At the level of content, short fiction may employ digital technologies as the subject of print-based narratives. For example, "Great Rock and Roll Pauses" from Jennifer Egan's interlinked short-stories-cum-novel *A Visit from the Goon Squad* (2010) is, famously, told entirely in PowerPoint slides; George Saunders's short fiction "Exhortation" (2013) takes the form of a middle-management email; and Ryan O'Neill's "Welcome to AusStories v2.6" (2014) invites readers to compose their own short story from a spoof database via drop-down menus. Further, print-based short stories may circulate, after publication, in the digital sphere: emblematically, Kristen Roupenian's "Cat Person" (2017) was a viral sensation, becoming the most-viewed short story in *New Yorker* history. This category of essentially print-conceived works repurposed for online environments also includes the mass of fanfiction, in which amateur writers avail themselves of the hosting resources of online communities such as Archive of Our Own or Wattpad but where print publication often remains the ultimate goal.

In contrast with these two categories are short fictions designed from the outset with digital creation, dissemination, and readership foremost in mind. In fact, those print-ordained roles may be substantially blurred by the characteristic "affordances" (i.e., capabilities) of the digital world: amateur publication; the bypassing of traditional literary gatekeepers; and readerly interactivity. This third kind of short story is *born* digital rather than being remediated for digital environments (so-called paper-under-glass literature); it simply "would not be possible without the contemporary digital context" (Ensslin 2006; Rettberg 2018, 2). Born-digital short fictions thus represent a more fundamental challenge to print-culture conceptions of what the short story is or does.

This chapter focuses exclusively on born-digital short stories because they raise intriguing questions about how shifts in media platforms reframe literary production, circulation, and consumption. The most high-profile literary experimentation in the digital short story space to date has been Twitter-based literature, dubbed "Twitterature" (Ingleton 2012). This prominence has been helped by the fact that its major proponents are frequently writers with established profiles in print-based literature who have branched out into born-digital short fiction, such as Teju Cole, with the *Small Fates* project (2011–2013), and Jennifer Egan, with "Black Box" (2012). While Twitter-based literary experiments revel in their innovation, they nevertheless have deep roots in older traditions of print communication, specifically the French journalistic tradition of the *fait-divers* and the long-standing creative practice of microfiction, both of which blur the lines between poetry and prose. In fact, Twitter-based short fiction experiments demonstrate that brevity is not exclusive to the familiar print-form short story; it exists both in historical mass-media print genres as well as across typically non-literary Web 2.0 platforms.

The short story has often served as literary culture's experimental fringe – a liminal zone to trial innovative techniques in style, narration, and characterization before, possibly, deploying these in novellas or novels. The digital sphere offers the short story, because of its brevity, new possibilities of transmedial mobility and reader-driven virality. Yet short story experimentation in the digital space seems unlikely to replace wholesale far older traditions of print writing, publishing, and reading; rather, it complements them and has already opened new portals for aesthetic exploration. Even if digital-born short fictions always remain something of an outlier – more a gadfly on the rump of mainstream literary culture – they nevertheless serve the valuable purpose of defamiliarizing the print medium. Rather than assuming print as the default substrate for short fiction, born-digital works bring it more fully into focus. Print culture's particular affordances and conventions stand revealed as creative *choices*, not inevitabilities.

Twitter: Origins and Affordances

In order to understand how Twitterature functions, and its key differences from print-based short fiction, it is first necessary to sketch Twitter's origins and functionality. Twitter was far from the first platform to be used for digital literary experimentation. In the late 1980s, dedicated hypertext authoring programs such as Storyspace enabled authors to construct multilinear fictional works that altered according to the choices a reader made at particular nodal points in the narrative. The early 1990s saw a wave of theoretical excitement around hypertext fictions on floppy disc and, later, CD-ROM. Such works seemed to realize technologically long modish, poststructuralist conceptions of the "writerly" text as one open to readerly participation (Barthes 1975). These electronic literary works also made use of the rudimentary multimedia capabilities of the pre-Internet era, including static images and sound effects. However, the hypertext revolution proved, in the end, a god that failed; by the late 1990s internet browsers had made hypertext logic virtually second nature for western populations, but readerly take-up of the platform for *literary* purposes had dwindled to almost nothing (Hammond 2016, 155–156).

In 2006, at the dawn of social media, Twitter emerged as a vibrant new platform for literary experimentation. Unlike Storyspace, Twitter was not designed specifically for literary purposes but was rather co-opted for creative uses by a subset of boundary-pushing practitioners. Twitter's inventor, New York University undergraduate Jack Dorsey, originally envisaged Twitter as an SMS (text message) platform. His idea was to create a technology that allowed small groups of friends to monitor each other's movements and inform their peers about their activities. Hence Twitter's original prompt: "What are you doing?" In essence, Twitter was conceived as part-microblogging platform and part-social-networking service (Burgess and Baym 2020). However, embedded in Twitter's original design are key characteristics that predisposed it for creative appropriation. First, Twitter was initially a text-based medium, with a 140-character message length demanding immense concision in user expression. Secondly, Twitter users are also identified by a handle, denoted by the "@" symbol, allowing a proxy form of author function. Thirdly, Twitter's innovative hashtag feature (denoted by "#") created subject headings, allowing people to aggregate tweets on a particular topic. This, as well as Twitter's retweet facility, permitted rapid viral circulation of messages among an infinite number of social networks, blurring the distinction between the recipient and the sender of a message.

Like blogging, Facebook, and subsequently developed social media platforms, Twitter was made possible by the emergence of the "read-write" Web, otherwise known as Web 2.0, which allows users to create, edit, and share digital content. It thus represents a prime example of content generated by producer-consumers or, signaling their newly hybrid identity, *produsers*. Twitter's take-up has been greatest in the sphere of news media and celebrity culture; the technology first gained widespread attention during the Arab Spring demonstrations of 2010–2011 and reached its (notorious) apogee with President Trump's use of the platform to broadcast key developments in US foreign and domestic policy – a process that might be dubbed "rule by tweet" (see Barnard 2018, 147–176). However, as a tool of informational exchange among the broader public, Twitter use appears now to have crested, with active user statistics at the time of writing showing it dwarfed by Facebook and newer applications such as WhatsApp, Instagram, Snapchat, and TikTok. Nevertheless, none of those other platforms has yet hosted significant developments in the short story format on a par with those that emerged on Twitter during the second decade of the twenty-first century.

Twitter as a Literary Platform

From early in Twitter's development, its value to the literary community was apparent. Celebrity authors wishing to promote forthcoming books or simply to communicate with their array of followers utilized the pseudo-intimacy of the platform to cultivate author–reader relationships (Murray 2018). Publishers too were quick to harness Twitter for viral publicity in promoting books to niche online communities. Yet more adventurous authors were experimenting with Twitter's potential as a *creative* platform. Most-followed Twitter author Neil Gaiman called upon his fanbase to help write the crowd-sourced Twitter project *Hearts, Keys, and Puppetry* (2010). Gaiman initiated the story with an enticingly ambiguous tweet and then chose subsequent installments from among fan-submitted replies. He in effect demoted the singular author of the Romantic ideal to one more akin to the curator of an unruly, multivocal text (Segar 2018). When the resulting work was released as an audiobook, it was democratically credited to "Neil Gaiman and the Twitterverse" (2010).

Gaiman's project bears out UK digital literary scholar Bronwen Thomas's contention that "from the outset, the creative potential of Twitter has been evident" (2014, 94). She usefully identifies two subsets of literary experimentation on Twitter: *microfiction* and *microserialization*. Microfictions, also known as "shorties" or "Twisters," are literary texts where "each tweet provides a self-contained narrative" (95). As such, they constitute miniature "standalone stories" (98). Microserializations, by contrast, are narratives that "unfold ... across tweets" in the manner of *Hearts, Keys and Puppetry*, although they are more typically authored by a single writer. Like other forms of "distributed narrative," such as blogs, microserializations require a significant investment of reader time and effort to hunt down new narrative installments (101). Microserializations thus challenge Edgar Allan Poe's original definition of the short story as a bounded work, one capable of being read in a single sitting. The remainder of this chapter examines these two Twitterature subcategories in turn, first identifying precursors of each in long-standing print-culture traditions, before turning to close-read two emblematic contemporary examples.

Print-Based "Micro" or "Flash" Fictions

Long before the emergence of Twitter, writers had been experimenting with the possibilities of highly condensed short fiction (Howitt-Dring 2011). In a likely apocryphal story, Ernest Hemingway was challenged to compose the shortest possible narrative in order to win a bet and came up with the poignant: "For sale: baby shoes. Never worn" (Rudin 2011). More recently, Margaret Atwood, always an eager experimenter with digital literary formats, rose to the same challenge, producing the deliciously anti-romantic: "Longed for him. Got him. Shit." ("Very Short Stories," 2006). In their ruthless concision, these six-word narratives manage to suggest plot, characterization, and tone with absolute economy. Not all micro or flash fiction is so terse: writers, especially in the Spanish-speaking world, have frequently experimented with 100-word "drabbles" or even page-length works. However, regardless of the stipulated word limit, practitioners of microfiction share an interest in the literary possibilities of constraint that is reminiscent of the French Oulipo group of experimental writers (Thomas 2020). For both, the pleasure resides in the expressive possibilities that remain, despite seemingly arbitrary formal rules. Given its pure distillation of meaning, so-called nanofiction has been memorably compared to homebrewed liquor, "strong" and "sharp" but leaving us "wanting more" (Rudin 2011).

In their embrace of formal constraint and brevity, microfictions often read as closer to poetry than traditional prose. The acceptance by practitioners of elaborate rules of expression echoes conventional poetic forms such as the sonnet, with its disciplined requirements of meter, rhyme scheme, and division between octave and sestet. Equally, the briefest of flash fictions resemble the Japanese haiku, with its strict three-line structure and stipulated number of syllables. If flash fiction has a prose literary progenitor, it is arguably the aphorism, where conventional syntax is rearranged to stress key words in a drive for maximum "punch" and quotability (Hui 2019). While microfictions might appear a perfect match for an era of rapidly shrinking attention spans, readers are counselled to linger over individual works as they might over poetry – appreciating that much aesthetic effect may be achieved with scant wordage: "If you are new to reading flashes and micros, be warned, they are so short they are easy to dismiss. Grace Paley said they 'should be read like a poem, that is, slowly'" (Shapard 2012, 49).

Faits-Divers

Microfiction may have few prose progenitors in the realm of literature, but if we broaden our gaze beyond culturally consecrated forms to include popular culture, a leading candidate emerges: the *fait-divers*. Loosely translated as "various doings" or, more colloquially, "bits and bobs," the *fait-divers* has long been a staple of francophone journalism. It is a highly compressed report of a real-life incident, often a crime, or a quirky happening that is arresting in its oddness or symbolism. French journalist Félix Fénéon wrote *faits-divers*, anonymously at first, for the Paris daily newspaper *Le Matin* in the first decade of the twentieth century. More than a thousand of his *faits-divers* have been collected as *Novels in Three Lines* (2007). They evidence a strangeness and haunting sense of detachment, as well as an undeniable addictiveness:

> Scratching himself with a revolver with an overly sensitive trigger, M. Edouard B. removed the tip of his nose in the Vivienne precinct house. (15)

> Louis Lamarre had neither job nor home, but he did possess a few coins. At a grocery store in Saint-Denis he bought a litre of kerosene and drank it. (19)

> The sinister prowler seen by the mechanic Gicquel near Herblay train station has been identified: Jules Menard, snail collector. (22)

> Lightning in Dunkirk struck some men who were installing lightning rods. One of them fell into the soot from 135 feet up and survived. (41)

The elevation of the *fait-divers* from ephemeral journalistic "filler" to a quasi-literary practice was facilitated by Roland Barthes, that pioneer of intellectualizing popular-culture phenomena, who proclaimed it "a mass art" (1972, 185, 194). His essay "Structure of the *Fait-Divers*" sought to rationalize the oddly compelling nature of these self-sufficient narratives, and to elucidate the principles of the ideal *fait-divers*. Barthes proposed that a relation of disproportion between two terms, or "notations," characterizes the most effective *faits-divers* (187). He focuses on the issues of causation that seem to underpin so many examples, especially aberrant causation where a seemingly minor or inconsequential human action has outsized, often tragic, results. At the broadest scale, Barthes was intrigued that these brief tales of human quirkiness or tragedy seem to suggest a pattern uniting apparently random occurrences. As he wrote, "a god prowls behind the *fait-divers*"; they taunt the reader with the capriciousness of fate, but simultaneously offer reassurance, through their mannered symmetry, that some entity somewhere must be overseeing events (194). Their effect is to communicate "an ambiguity of the rational and the irrational, of the intelligible and the unfathomable" – an oxymoronic sense of "organized coincidence" that leaves the reader pondering the existence of the supernatural in a world teeming with banal tragedy (194).

Teju Cole's *Small Fates*

Nigerian-American writer Teju Cole looks beyond US literature for inspiration, explicitly citing *fait-divers* as influential for his Twitterature microfiction project *Small Fates* (March 2011–January 2013). He notes approvingly that "in Francophone literature [the genre] crossed the line from low to high culture" and became "a Modernist form" (2011). Cole devised *Small Fates* in the wake of critical acclaim for his second novel, *Open City* (2011). While undertaking background research for a new, nonfiction book about Lagos, Cole became "drawn to the 'small' news ... [in] the metro sections of newspapers, and the crime sections." From Brooklyn, he relied "on the internet, through which I have access to some dozen Nigerian papers each day." The "small" news with which he became fascinated was "too brief, too odd, and certainly too sensational for the kind of writing the book requires," so he decided it "needed another outlet." In this sense, Twitter's by then established role as a news medium made it the logical platform for a practice that took news items and melded them into a variety of prose poetry.

Cole had a broader interest in the literary potential of Twitter, seeing in its multivocality and all-inclusiveness an evolution of Modernist stream of consciousness. In a keynote address at the Melbourne Writers Festival, he ambitiously proclaimed Twitter "one of the futures of the novel":

> Twitter is the continuity of the published thoughts of all the people present on Twitter ... [E]ach second, thousands of pages are added, millions of contributions per day. And each person who reads it ... reads something different from everyone else. It is the undivided, undifferentiated cascade of thoughts streaming past the timeline that makes me suspect that Twitter is, indeed, elongating the perspective of human sensibility. (2013)

According to Cole's speech, the novel since James Joyce has been "a conservative thing," but Twitter shares *Ulysses*'s "ungoverned excess" and "full inclusi[veness]." Cole prophesized that Twitter had become so ubiquitous that it would change the nature of writerly practice: "It's hard to imagine that it wouldn't . . . [because] most young novelists are themselves active on Twitter now. The atomized mode of information dispersal is more and more natural, and less and less 'experimental' or elite."

As with Fénéon, the particular texture of Cole's *Small Fates* tweets is best conveyed through resonant examples:

> In Isolo, Arowolo, 30, easy-going, never one to meddle in other people's affairs, thrust a knife into his wife and left it there. (June 30, 2011)
>
> Children are a gift from God. In the returns department: a baby girl, left by the side of Effiom Ekpo Street in Calabar. (August 26, 2011)
>
> Since Mrs Okafor, of Ikoyi, has a phobia of banks, her cook Peter helped himself to the $50,000 she left lying around the house. (September 8, 2011)
>
> Not far from the Surulene workshop where spray-painter Alawiye worked, a policeman fired into the air. Gravity did the rest. (March 20, 2012)

While each "small fate" is a freestanding microfiction, their full effect comes from considering them cumulatively. The tales of Nigerian crime (and, later in the project, stories from New York newspapers of a century ago) give an impression of urban chaos and human pitilessness. Incidents of violence against women are numbingly frequent, raising the question of whether Cole is critiquing this element of news reporting by highlighting its ubiquity or is complicit in naturalizing (and thus perpetuating) it. Cole, in an act of metacommentary within *Small Fates*, claims his *faits-divers* capture "what happens to real people at the nexus of modernity, poverty, chance, and human nature" (September 2, 2011). Certainly, a cynical view of the human comedy predominates, with the narrator's position often elusive. In weighing questions of tone, narrative distance (both geographically and chronologically) from events is key. Much depends on framing. The silent film character slipping on a banana skin reads as slapstick when shot in wide-frame, and as tragedy when shot in close-up. *Small Fates* equally provokes ethical reflection on the position of the reader (often western, literate, and comparatively affluent) in consuming (and even gaining aesthetic pleasure from) tales of developing-world anarchy and misfortune. What philosophical worldview does *Small Fates* convey? Are the stories parodies of "objective" news reporting, with its tick of providing the age, habitation, and occupation of all persons mentioned, even when such details seem superfluous? What are we, like Barthes, to make of a quixotic, capricious, and ultimately unknowable fate? Cole suggests, in a stab at gallows humor, that the best defense we can muster is an amused shoulder shrug: "The world sometimes seems crazy, violent, and meaningless, but don't let that fool you; the world is crazy, violent, and meaningless" (November 27, 2012).

The above considerations address textual effects that are standard fodder for literary close-reading. However, broadening our analytical aperture to engage in what electronic literature scholar Katherine Hayles calls "media-specific analysis" illuminates how the platform of Twitter itself generates new possibilities for short-form fiction (2004). First, there is Cole's tendency to interpolate critical commentary on his practice between the creative tweets: for example, the life-imitates-art aside that "once you start doing faits divers [sic] you begin to see them everywhere" (February 4, 2012). Embracing the platform's characteristic interactivity, he also interleaves his responses to followers' queries and requests for insight into his creative process. The "anatomy of a small fate" sequence of tweets relates, inter alia, that he sometimes sources the crime stories via Nigerian newspapers' own Twitter feeds, and mentions the number of drafts his tweets go through to optimize "speed of the line, rhythm, and ironic inflection" plus the total time taken to compose each "fate" (fifteen minutes on average, though sometimes up to thirty minutes; January 9, 2013). Despite this authorial emphasis on painstaking craft, disclosing the tweets' relatively brief composition time raises the question of whether *faits-divers* are too slight and disposable to qualify as "Literature." Perhaps they merely pander to the social media age with its radically abbreviated attention spans and aimless scrolling. As though anticipating the objection, Cole pointedly invokes the much older microfiction tradition, citing an icon of American Modernism, no less: "Read the first half of Hemingway's six-word story. It's excellent so far" (January 22, 2013).

Microserializations

The second of Bronwen Thomas's Twitterature subcategories – *microserialization* – denotes narratives that are drip-fed to readers across a series of tweets, a process that may last anywhere from several days to several years. Even before the invention of Twitter, the mobile phone had spawned the phenomenon of serialized Japanese cell phone novels, or *keitai shosetsu*, which appeared from around 2000 (Goggin and Hamilton 2014, 225; Hjorth 2014, 240). *Keitai shosetsu* are a type of novel designed specifically for reading on a mobile phone – many, indeed, are composed on one (Hjorth 2014, 239). Individual chapters are short – certainly less than 200 words but commonly only fifty to 100 words – in order to minimize tiresome scrolling. The chapters are released in installments, sometimes as often as daily, and are transmitted to readers through text messages or emails. The bite-sized narrative bursts are then uploaded to websites and compiled so that readers can communicate with the author, and even request particular narrative developments (Hjorth 2014, 239–241).

Early twenty-first-century cell-phone fictions, like microserializations, reintroduce temporality into literary consumption (Andersen 2017). In the English-speaking world, the novel emerged in the eighteenth century with epistolary fiction (i.e., narratives composed of letters between fictional characters), such as Samuel Richardson's *Pamela* (1740) and *Clarissa* (1748). By the following century, serial publication had become the norm for long-form fiction. Now-classic novels such as those by Dickens and Thackeray first appeared in chapter-length installments in weekly or monthly periodicals, and were only later republished (and sometimes re-edited, depending upon reader response) in three-decker codex format (Andersen 2017, 35; Goggin and Hamilton 2014, 232). Book historians have long noted that the first material incarnation of nineteenth-century fictions in magazines and quarterlies influenced such narratives' structure, necessitating recurrent cliffhanger endings so that readers would be motivated to seek out the next installment. Thus, short-form publications demonstrably influenced novels, rather than the influence only running from the dominant prose form to the "lesser." Anticipation resultantly formed a key emotional strand of the nineteenth-century reading experience; letters and diaries of Victorian readers frequently relate the frustration of not being able to finish reading a novel because another patron had checked the final volume out of the circulating library. Digital microserializations recuperate this sense of readerly anticipation through the necessity of waiting for the next installment of a narrative to drop into an email inbox or Twitter feed (Andersen 2017). They resituate the reading act in chronological time, a fact largely obscured by the dominant twentieth-century conception of the printed novel as a completed, self-sufficient artefact. Yet microserializations equally challenge Poe's conception of the short story as defined by its time-bound consumption. For the reader of an open-ended microserialization, no single sitting will ever suffice.

Jennifer Egan's "Black Box"

US author Jennifer Egan's short story "Black Box" (2012) is the most notable example of a distinctive twenty-first-century form of digital microserialization. This sees a literary author of repute (i.e., one who has enjoyed critical acclaim, won prizes, and published in prominent print outlets) enter the realm of Twitter – a medium she does not habitually use – to write and distribute short fiction (D'hoker 2018). Egan published "Black Box" two years after winning the Pulitzer Prize for *A Visit from the Goon Squad*. The unnamed protagonist of "Black Box" is in fact the Lulu character who appears as a twenty-something digital marketing wiz in *Goon Squad*'s final chapter. Egan's futuristic Twitter story thus emblematizes the tendencies of the short story not only to travel across mediums, but also to maintain intertextual links to prior works.

In a *New Yorker* interview, Egan explained how the format of Twitter was fundamental to the genesis of "Black Box":

> The idea of tweeting it predated the story, in the sense that although I have not been active on Twitter at all, as either a reader or a tweeter, I have been interested in it for quite a while. I love the thought of trying to use it as a delivery system for fiction, and I'm interested in the way that some nineteenth-century fiction was constructed around its serialization. So, the question was: what kind of story would need to be told in these very short bursts ... I wanted to try to write a spy story set in the future, and I was interested in telling a story in the form of a list. And, out of all that, I began to have a sense of a woman's voice speaking in these short dispatches about her spying experience. As soon as I began hearing that voice, it was clear that this would be the piece that would be, in some way, disseminated over Twitter. (Treisman 2012)

An article that appeared in digital bible *Wired* around the time of the story's Twitter release includes a revealing image of the draft for "Black Box" (Kirtley 2012). Egan composed the work in a Japanese notebook pre-ruled with eight small boxes per page, a visual schema which she noted helped her compose the tweets with the requisite economy (see Figure 6.1).

"Black Box" was tweeted from the *New Yorker*'s Twitter account over ten nights in late May 2012 during the "primetime" window of 8–9 p.m., at a rate of one tweet per minute. The transmission was pre-set, with no possibility of reader interaction. The story is a genre-bending feminist science-fiction thriller, taking the form of mental dispatches from an unnamed Beauty whose undercover mission involves being in close

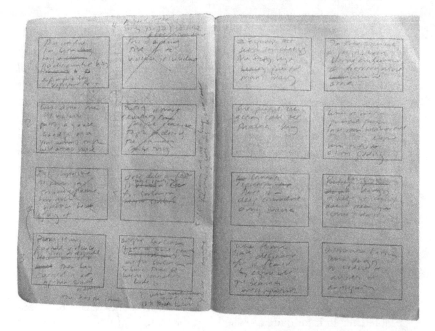

Figure 6.1   Jennifer Egan's Japanese notebook for "Black Box."

proximity to highly dangerous "Designated Mates," who represent an unspecified threat to the United States (85; all references are to the print version). Her modus operandi, as she lounges scantily clad around Mediterranean villas, is to appear sufficiently innocuous to lull them into complacency, and thus gain access to secret conversations and documents. The text we read is gradually revealed to be the "Field Instructions" (88) Beauty is compiling for subsequent spies. This spy-handbook conceit dictates Egan's use of the rare second-person mode of address and, equally rare, future-tense narration. The technical skill required to pull this off, let alone under the constraints of Twitter, is immense, and it is to Egan's credit that she manages to build the thriller's characteristic narrative suspense across over 600 tweets as the mission reaches its life-threatening climax. Implanted with myriad technological "enhancements" – cameras, microphones, chips, sensors, and data ports – Beauty's cyborg body is itself the mission's black box recorder, analogous to the "black box" mobile phone through which the reader consumes the story (96). Her obligation, above all, is to ensure her (dead) body does not fall into enemy hands, which would eradicate the log of her mission.

Thematically, "Black Box" is also radically innovative in depicting the interiority of spy-fiction's stereotypical female "honeypot," particularly the mental gymnastics required to dissociate sufficiently to engage in sex with Designated Mates she finds both physically and morally repugnant. This elevates the "Bond girl" figure from disposable eye-candy to the heroic center of the plot: "These acts are forms of sacrifice" (94). "Black Box" incrementally reveals the mesh of personal and ideological motivations that drive Beauty to risk her life in the service of her country, and the misgivings she occasionally harbors about whether the individual price demanded by "the new heroism" is too high (89).

The 140-character restriction generates a form of terse prose poetry with aphoristic tendencies. There is, nevertheless, an undeniable monotony to reading uniform-length narrative bursts, however much Egan plays with sentence length within them. More than one critic has unfavorably compared the experience of reading "Black Box" to unpacking a series of Zen koans (Crown 2012; Gee 2012; Winkler 2012). For example, take the alienatingly gnomic "A smile is like a door that is both open and closed" (96). At other points, individual tweets more closely resemble epigrams, inviting clipping from the context of the story and circulation as internet memes – for example, "Childish attention-seeking is usually satisfied at the expense of real power" (91). At still other moments, Egan exploits the temporal dimension of Twitter delivery through use of anaphora, creating a cumulative effect reminiscent of an oral performance such as a sermon or political speech (92, 96, 97). For example, early in the story eleven successive tweets begin with the words "You will reflect on" (87–88), before the final two descend into bathetic, self-reflexive irony: "You will reflect on the fact that too much reflection is pointless. You will reflect on the fact that these instructions are becoming less and less instructive" (88).

Days after its Twitter premiere, Egan's story appeared in the *New Yorker*'s inaugural "Science Fiction Issue" (June 4–11, 2012). The willingness of a leading print venue to lend its legitimating mantle, first through hosting the work on its Twitter account and second through print publication, raises intriguing questions of motivation. Not only was the *New Yorker* with this issue controversially "noticing" a long-thriving genre form, its publication of "Black Box" seems an attempt to bestow Bourdieusian consecration on a neophyte digital form, thereby preserving the masthead's role as literary tastemaker. Certainly print publication counteracts numerous problems associated with born-digital literary works: Twitter messages were at that time displayed in reverse chronological order, making it difficult to read a serialized work after its initial release; story installments came mixed up with other messages in a reader's Twitter feed, resulting in narrative incoherence; and Twitter's haphazard approach to archiving means tweets typically disappear after a limited time and are therefore irretrievable, raising electronic literature's perennial problem of evanescence (Howard 2019). Yet there is something undeniably ironic about such a self-consciously avant-garde digital literary experiment requiring print to validate and preserve its achievement. At the very least, this symbiotic, intermedial dependence disproves early 1990s hypertext theorists' zero-sum predictions that digital media would eclipse print. Instead, "Black Box," in its various Twitter, print, and online incarnations, demonstrates the continuing codependence of the print and digital realms (Andersen 2015). Book historians Matthew Kirschenbaum and Sarah Werner sum this up as a "multifaceted interchange, a generative friction, between print and digital writing platforms" (2014: 448). If the short story in the age of the Internet seeks to embrace digital affordances for storytelling, it nevertheless remains chary of the digital world's ephemerality and the threat that technological obsolescence poses to canonicity.

Conclusion

Despite his predictions at the Melbourne Writers Festival in 2013 that Twitter represented "one of the futures of the novel," Teju Cole last posted on Twitter the following year; his website now states, "I was active on Twitter, but not anymore." After "Black Box," Egan's next significant work was the well-received historical novel *Manhattan Beach* (2017), published in traditional print format. "Black Box" has reappeared, lightly edited and retitled "Lulu the Spy, 2032" as a chapter in Egan's kaleidoscopic novel of the social-media age, *The Candy House* (2022). However, Egan has not returned to digital-first publishing. Since the early years of the century's teen decade, few other major writers have experimented with Twitterature. So, is Twitterature a mere flash in the literary-historical pan, a quirky byroad off the highway of the twenty-first-century American short story? While such a dismissive conclusion may please the literary world's more techno-skeptical reaches, it would be mistaken. Twitterature is part of a much longer-running engagement between digital platforms and literary creation that spans at least late-1980s experiments with hypertext authoring programs, runs through early Web 2.0 innovations in life-writing forms such as blogs and social media applications, via ongoing mass-amateur fanfiction-writing communities that train up new writers and occasionally incubate works that migrate successfully to print, film, or television, and includes the newest digital literary experiments in locative literature, deploying GPS-enabled mobile phones to tell stories customized to a user's locale. The variety of initiatives at the digital–literary interface expands if we broaden our definition to include works not only created or consumed on digital media, but also employing networked technologies for their dissemination: fictional podcasts; audiobooks; so-called Instapoetry; and crowdfunded print publications. These too may well prove important vectors for the always mobile, avidly transmedial short story.

If nothing else, experiments with short fiction in the digital space pry apart the hitherto unproblematized conflation of the short story with the medium of print. They demonstrate, through defamiliarization, that print culture's particular affordances – linearity, sole-authorship, unidirectional communication, and readerly anonymity – are not inevitable characteristics of the short story genre but merely conventions naturalized by Gutenbergian print culture's dominance over several centuries. They are corollaries of a particular *medium*, not necessarily hallmarks of the *genre* itself. As such, we are reminded to look *at* them, rather than being lulled by habit into merely looking *through* them. To forecast alternative possibilities for the twenty-first-century short story in the now-dominant digital environment is simply to give due credit to this long hybridized, manifestly protean cultural form's rich capacity for reinvention.

Works Cited

Andersen, Tore Rye. 2015. "'Black Box' in Flux: Locating the Literary Work between Media." *Northern Lights: Film and Media Studies Yearbook* 13.1: 121–136. http://dx.doi.org/10.1386/nl.13.1.121_1.

2017. "Staggered Transmissions: Twitter and the Return of Serialized Literature," *Convergence* 23.1: 34–48.

Barnard, Stephen R. 2018. *Citizens at the Gates: Twitter, Networked Publics, and the Transformation of American Journalism*. New York: Palgrave Macmillan.

Barthes, Roland. 1972 [1962]. "Structure of the Fait-Divers," in *Critical Essays*. Trans. Richard Howard, 184–195. Evanston, IL: Northwestern University Press.

1975 [1973]. *The Pleasure of the Text*. Trans. Richard Miller. New York: Hill and Wang.

Burgess, Jean and Nancy K. Baym. 2020. *Twitter: A Biography*. New York: New York University Press.

Cole, Teju. 2011. "Small Fates," *Berfrois*, 14 July. www.berfrois.com/2011/07/teju-cole-fait-divers/.

2011–2013. *Small Fates*. https://twitter.com/tejucole.

2013. "The Novel After the Novelist," *Edinburgh World Writers' Conference*. Keynote address to the Melbourne Writers' Festival, 23 August. www.edinburghworldwritersconference.org/the-future-of-the-novel/cole-in-australia-keynote-on-the-future-of-the-novel/.

Crown, Sarah. 2012. "Twitter Is a Clunky Way of Delivering Fiction," *Guardian*, 26 May. www.theguardian.com/books/booksblog/2012/may/25/twitter-feed-clunky-delivery.

D'hoker, Elke. 2018. "Segmentivity, Narrativity and the Short Form: The Twitter Stories of Moody, Egan and Mitchell," *Short Fiction in Theory and Practice* 8.1-2: 7–20.

Egan, Jennifer. 2010. *A Visit from the Goon Squad*. New York: Knopf.
    2012. "Black Box," *The New Yorker*, 28 May. www.newyorker.com/magazine/2012/06/04/black-box-2.
    2012. "Black Box," *The New Yorker*, 4–11 June: 84–97.
    2022. *The Candy House*. New York: Scribner.

Ensslin, Astrid. 2006. "Hypermedia and the Question of Canonicity," *Dichtung-digital* 36. www.dichtung-digital.de/2006/01/Ensslin/index.htm.

Fénéon, Félix. 2007 [1906]. *Novels in Three Lines*. Trans. Luc Sante. New York: New York Review Books Classics.

Gaiman, Neil and the Twitterverse. 2010. *Hearts, Keys, and Puppetry*. Ashland, OR: Blackstone Audio.

Gee, Lisa. 2012. "Black Box, by Jennifer Egan," *Independent* 2 September. www.independent.co.uk/arts-entertainment/books/reviews/black-box-by-jennifer-egan-8100597.html.

Goggin, Gerard and Caroline Hamilton. 2014. "Narrative Fiction and Mobile Media after the Text-Message Novel," in *The Mobile Story: Narrative Practices with Locative Technologies*. Ed. Jason Farman, 223–237. New York: Routledge.

Hammond, Adam. 2016. *Literature in the Digital Age: An Introduction*. Cambridge, UK: Cambridge University Press.

Hayles, N. Katherine. 2004. "Print is Flat, Code is Deep: The Importance of Media-Specific Analysis," *Poetics Today* 25.1: 67–90.

Hjorth, Larissa. 2014. "Stories of the Mobile: Women, Micro-Narratives, and Mobile Novels in Japan," in *The Mobile Story: Narrative Practices with Locative Technologies*. Ed. Jason Farman, 238–248. New York: Routledge.

Howard, Christian. 2019. "Studying and Preserving the Global Networks of Twitter Literature," *Post45*, 17 September. http://post45.research.yale.edu/2019/09/global-networks-of-twitter-literature/.

Howitt-Dring, H. 2011. "Making Micro Meanings: Reading and Writing Microfiction," *Short Fiction in Theory and Practice* 1.1: 47–58.

Hui, Andrew. 2019. *A Theory of the Aphorism: From Confucius to Twitter*. Princeton, NJ: Princeton University Press.

Ingleton, Pamela. 2012. "How Do You Solve a Problem Like Twitterature? Reading and Theorizing 'Print' Technologies in an Age of Social Media," *Technoculture: An Online Journal of Technology in Society* 2. https://tcjournal.org/vol2/ingleton.

Kirschenbaum, Matthew and Sarah Werner. 2014. "Digital Scholarship and Digital Studies: The State of the Discipline," *Book History* 17: 406–458.

Kirtley, David Barr. 2012. "Let's Hope Jennifer Egan's Twitter Story Heralds the Return of Serial Fiction," *Wired*, 24 May. www.wired.com/2012/05/jenni fer-egan-black-box-twitter/.

Murray, Simone. 2018. *The Digital Literary Sphere: Reading, Writing, and Selling Books in the Internet Era*. Baltimore, MD: Johns Hopkins University Press.

Rankin, Seija. 2020. "Jennifer Egan on the 10th Anniversary of *A Visit from the Goon Squad* and How It Changed Her Life." *Entertainment Weekly*, n.d. https://ew.com/books/jennifer-egan-visit-from-the-goon-squad-10th-anni versary/.

Rettberg, Scott. 2018. *Electronic Literature*. Cambridge, UK: Polity.

Rudin, Michael. 2011. "From Hemingway to Twitterature: The Short and Shorter of It," *Journal of Electronic Publishing* 14.2. http://quod.lib.umich .edu/j/jep/3336451.0014.213/–from-hemingway-to-twitterature-the-short-and-shorter-of-it?rgn=main;view=fulltext.

Segar, Emma. 2018. "Curating Conclusions in 'Among Us': Collaborative Twitter Fiction and the Implied Author," *Short Fiction in Theory and Practice* 8.1-2: 21–35.

Shapard, Robert. 2012. "The Remarkable Reinvention of Very Short Fiction," *World Literature Today* 86.5: 46–49.

Thomas, Bronwen. 2014. "140 Characters in Search of a Story: Twitterfiction As an Emerging Narrative Form," in *Analyzing Digital Fiction*. Eds. Alice Bell, Astrid Ensslin, and Hans Kristian Rustad, 94–108. New York: Routledge.

2020. *Literature and Social Media*. London: Routledge.

Treisman, Deborah. 2012. "This Week in Fiction: Jennifer Egan," *New Yorker*, 25 May [interview]. www.newyorker.com/books/page-turner/this-week-in-fiction-jennifer-egan.

"Very Short Stories." 2006. *Wired*, 1 November. www.wired.com/2006/11/very-short-stories/.

Winkler, Joe. 2012. "Jennifer Egan's Black Box," <*Htmlgiant*>, 6 June. http://htmlgiant.com/reviews/jennifer-egans-black-box/

PART II

Histories

CHAPTER 7

The War Story

Cody Marrs

"We shot dogs." So begins "Redeployment" (2014), Phil Klay's haunting short story about a Marine recently deployed to Iraq. "Not by accident," he adds: "We did it on purpose, and we called it 'Operation Scooby.' I'm a dog person, so I thought about that a lot" (1). After returning to the United States, the Marine's thoughts continually veer back to his experiences in Iraq; his hands feel strange and awkward without his rifle, and he finds it impossible to readjust (13). The problem, he explains, is getting back to "white" – the state of being unaware of potential threats after living as a soldier in states of awareness that might be yellow (relaxed awareness), orange (specific awareness), red (ready to act), or black (combat). "Here's what orange is," Klay explains:

> You don't see or hear like you used to. Your brain chemistry changes. You take in every piece of the environment, everything . . .. I had antennae out that stretched down the block . . .. I think you take in too much information to store so you just forget, free up brain space to take in everything about the next moment that might keep you alive. (6)

When his wife takes him to the mall to do some shopping, the Marine immediately looks around the corner for snipers. When they go to American Eagle Outfitters, he walks into the dressing room and discovers that he does not want to leave. The Marine's sense of unbelonging – of being neither here nor there, always in a state of orange – is underscored by the story's title. Although he seems to be awaiting redeployment, he has, in a sense, already been redeployed.

Klay's story is an incisive, if disturbing, reflection on the civilian–military divide in the United States and the aftermath of the war in Iraq. In that regard, "Redeployment" is very much a narrative of and about the twenty-first century. However, Klay's story is also part of a long tradition that extends back to the nineteenth century. "Redeployment" echoes and evokes similar narratives by authors such as Ambrose Bierce, Mark Twain,

Ernest Hemingway, and Tim O'Brien, who composed inventive short stories about armed battle. Over the past century and a half the War Story has become such an integral and enduring part of American fiction that it is hard to conceive of the short story, as a genre, without it. But where did this tradition come from? What are its defining features? And how has it evolved?

This chapter answers those questions by chronicling the development of the War Story in American fiction. As we will see, the War Story is a literary and cultural response to the wars that have marked American history, from the nineteenth century to today. This genre was pioneered by veterans of the Civil War, then adapted in the twentieth century by veterans of World War I, World War II, and Vietnam. To reconstruct the history of the War Story, I will first examine its early contexts and influences; then I will consider the genre's later growth and adaptation. As we will see, the War Story is rooted in Realist ways of apprehending and representing the world. As Elizabeth Renker defines it, Realism is a "mode of literary writing that seeks to represent the everyday 'reality' of human experience (however differently defined by individual writers) and that renders these representations without recourse to transcendental frames of reference as a foundation" (2018, 5). That Realist point of view is the backbone of the War Story, and it endures deep into the twentieth century, long after the Realist movement declined in American culture.

Ambrose Bierce, Mark Twain, and the Origins of the War Story

Stories about war are as old as writing itself. As soon as writing emerged as an ancient technology, people used it to record and describe battles. Sumerian scripts and Chinese logographs narrate the deeds of famous warriors and depict civilization itself as the outcome of conflict. Many of the world's oldest stories emphasize the social, political, and cosmological significance of warfare, from the Vedas, which enjoin the gods to secure success in battle, to the *Iliad*, which depicts violence as foundational to Greek culture and identity, to the Hebrew Bible, which frames warfare as part of a cosmic struggle between good and evil. One could argue that writing developed to document and decipher the numerous ways in which war has shaped human life. Every modern-day practitioner of the War Story has something in common with earlier writers, yet there are crucial differences between these older narratives about war and more modern short stories, and those differences are the result of three major events that occurred in the nineteenth century: the Civil War; the rise of modern print culture; and new scientific accounts of the mind. Collectively, this whirl-wind of intellectual, historical, and cultural changes set the stage for the War Story.

The birth of the modern genre was spurred by the American Civil War. It is no coincidence that the first recognizable practitioners of the genre were veterans of the Civil War: this was a new type of conflict, and it required a new type of literature. As Bruce Catton puts it, "the great fact about modern war, greater even than its frightful destructiveness and its calculated, carefully applied inhumanity, is that it never goes quite where the men who start it intend that it shall go. Men do not control modern war; it controls them" (1986, 14). Instead of the "Napoleonic method" of "massed frontal assault against fortified positions," the Civil War involved trenches, guerrilla warfare, armored ships, scorched earth tactics, and the mass production of weapons on a hitherto unprecedented scale. That intensification of war continued in the twentieth century with the invention of the tank, the airplane, and weapons of mass destruction (Shaara 1998, 3). The War Story is born in this era and belongs to it wholeheartedly. As a genre, it is designed to account for these changes and to consider what they mean for humanity.

The closest analogues are the stories that emerged in the wake of the US-Mexican War, such as George Lippard's *Legends of Mexico* (1847) and *Bel of Prairie Eden* (1848). As Shelley Streeby argues, Lippard's war fiction traffics in a "culture of sensation" that formed around 1848, a shared structure of feeling produced by increasing urbanization and the literature and reportage of the US-Mexican War (2002, 7). That "culture of sensation," however, did not fully develop until the 1860s, with the massive shock of the Civil War and the growth of American print culture. The Civil War was not only the most fateful conflict fought by the United States; it was also the most widely narrated and discussed. By the time the first battles broke out in 1861, there was a cornucopia of periodicals – local, regional, and national – that dwarfed the print culture of the early nineteenth century. In 1825, there were only about 100 magazines circulating in the United States (Smith and Price 1995, 4). According to the Twelfth Census, by 1900 there were more than 18,000 newspapers and periodicals.

The rise of the War Story in short fiction coincided with, and depended on, this blooming of print culture. Buoyed by increasing literacy rates and a market revolution that expanded the reading public, many periodicals were produced in this era, and they provided writers with a popular forum as well as an opportunity to get paid. As Bill Hardwig posits, "The world of literature transitioned from a more traditional view of publishing ruled largely by systems of patronage and apprenticeship, where avuncular editors spoke in terms of the moral function of their publications, to a much more practical and progressive view of literary professionalization" (2020, 309). The War Story thus evolved symbiotically with the expansion of literacy and print culture in the mid- to late-nineteenth century.

The genre is also marked by its keen interest in consciousness and memory. This is another important way in which the modern War Story differs from its precursors: it is far less invested in heroism than in introspection. This aspect of the genre was deeply influenced by scientific accounts of the mind, which provided empirical ways to apprehend cognition and sensation. The War Story emerged around the same time as psychophysics, a scientific field that ascertained patterns and differences in sensory experience. According to Erica Fretwell, the senses came to be seen as "the embodied habitus of emotional reflection" (2020, 3). Psychophysics offered an early model of what we now refer to as the mind–body connection, and for many people in the nineteenth century it provided a conceptual grammar for apprehending the interconnectedness of thoughts, feelings, and sensations. The War Story similarly enquires into the relation between the body and the mind; it is an "experimental science" in fictive form.

All of these changes – to the intellectual landscape, to the publishing industry, to the country itself – were the conditions of possibility for the War Story to materialize. Karl Marx observed, "Men make their own history, but they do not make it ... under conditions chosen by themselves" (1937, 4). The same could be said about literature. The history of the War Story is thus a history of ideas, print networks, and social movements, as well as individual writers who responded to these events and adapted the old genre of war fiction to a new set of circumstances and possibilities. These changes all came together in the American Civil War, a crisis that, as Louis Menand puts it, obliterated not only "the slave civilization of the South" but also "the whole intellectual culture of the North along with it": "It took nearly half a century for the United States to develop a culture to replace it, to find a set of ideas, and a way of thinking, that would help people cope with the conditions of modern life" (2002, x).

That new "way of thinking" is evident in the War Story, which first appeared in wartime and postwar periodicals. From Edward Everett Hale's "The Man Without a Country" (1863) to Henry James's "The Story of a Year" (1865), short stories about the Civil War abounded, and for the reading public – many of whom experienced the war from afar – they proved essential. The publishing industry immediately took notice. Anthologies such as Frank Moore's *The Rebellion Record* (1861–1868), which collected and disseminated War Stories of various stripes, were published en masse. To tap into this growing market, the *Century* magazine ran a popular series titled "Battles and Leaders of the Civil War" (1884–1887), which featured contributions from a multitude of former soldiers. As befits the internecine conflict they chronicled, these War Stories tended to provide very different perspectives on the Civil War, but most of them had a set of common features, such as a keen interest in the ethics of warfare and the relationship between fact and fiction.

One of the most successful early practitioners of the War Story was Ambrose Bierce. After the Civil War erupted, Bierce – at the age of nineteen – joined the Indiana Ninth Brigade, serving as a regimental cartographer. He witnessed some of the most brutal battles of the war, including the Battle of Shiloh (1862), the Battle of Chickamauga (1863), and Pickett's Mill (1864) – and he did not emerge unscathed. At the Battle of Kennesaw Mountain (1864), Bierce suffered a major traumatic brain injury (probably caused by an exploding shell) and dealt with the physical and psychological fallout for the rest of his life. Afterwards, with the benefit of time and distance, he wove these experiences – the heroism and horror, the uncertainty, the comradery, and existential thrill and dread – directly into his fiction, most notably in his collection *Tales of Soldiers and Civilians* (1892).

The War Story, as Bierce renders it, is a story about the human mind. In "A Tough Tussle" (a story first published in *The San Francisco Examiner*), Bierce narrates the final hours of Brainerd Byring, a Second Lieutenant in the Union Army who, much to his chagrin, has been tasked with guarding the camp in the middle of the night. Byring is an excellent soldier – efficient, disciplined, loyal – but when he finds himself sitting alone at night in a Virginia forest, he gets spooked. He looks around and starts seeing – or thinks he sees – strange shapes in the woods. He hears sounds that have no earthly origin. Then he stumbles upon a dead body. He desperately wants to walk away, to escape this ghoulish carcass, but he cannot move. His body is frozen, he cannot speak, and he stumbles over himself, believing the enemy is about to attack. The following morning, when soldiers come to relieve him, they discover that Byring has stabbed the corpse several times over, then stabbed himself in the heart.

The title of Bierce's story thus has two different meanings. Byring's "tough tussle" occurs as much in the mind as it does on the field of battle. The story discloses the psychology of warfare, revealing how battle creates a topsy-turvy world in which everything is inverted. Of the forest, Bierce writes, "He to whom the portentous conspiracy of night and solitude and silence in the heart of a great forest is not an unknown experience needs not to be told what another world it all is – how even the most commonplace and familiar objects take on another character" (Bierce 2000, 138). The same could be said of war, and that sense of inversion is underscored by the story's sense of mounting terror. The dark trees almost seem to whisper like the "ghosts of sounds long dead," and as the night progresses, Byring comes to see the dead man as a kind of zombie, a "malign thing endowed with some strange power of mischief, with perhaps a will and a purpose to exert it" (139). It is no wonder that H. P. Lovecraft, the master of modern horror, saw Bierce as a fellow traveler.

Bierce's best-known War Story, "An Occurrence at Owl Creek Bridge," similarly explores the psychological dimensions of battle. Inspired by Bierce's harrowing experiences at the Battle of Shiloh, "An Occurrence" records the thoughts and feelings of Peyton Farquhar, a southerner who is about to be hanged by northern soldiers for trying to destroy a bridge. Just as his body drops, the rope snaps, and Farquhar finds himself in the river. He dives to escape the soldiers' bullets, then makes his way to the shore. His narrow escape from the jaws of death gives him a renewed appreciation of life, as well as a heightened sensitivity: he suddenly notices *everything*, from the minute textures on the leaves of the trees to the "brilliant-bodied flies" and the "dewdrops upon a million blades of grass" (16). And he wants nothing more than to return to his wife and children. So he walks for miles until he eventually arrives at the gate of his old home. "All is as he left it," Bierce writes, "and all bright and beautiful in the morning sunshine" (19).

Or more accurately, that is what happens in Farquhar's mind in the final, fleeting moments before he dies. As it turns out, he is indeed executed, but Bierce only conveys that information – dissolving the spell – at the very end, when a "blinding white light blazes all about him." Farquhar, Bierce concludes, "was dead; his body, with a broken neck, swung gently from side to side beneath the timbers of the Owl Creek Bridge" (19). The story is as much about consciousness as it is about war. And what makes the story so effective and beguiling is Bierce's immersive attention to the senses, from the sight of water "touched to gold by the early sun" to the "brooding mists under the banks" and the sounds of the guns (like the sharp crack of "a blacksmith's hammer upon the anvil" [13]). In that regard, "An Occurrence" is a fictional experiment with psychophysics, a story about the interrelationship between somatic and mental experience. Sarah Blackwood notes that literature in this era was part of a broader "project of imagining psychological depth" (2019, 1), and Bierce's story contributes to that project in manifold ways. The reader sees what Farquhar sees and hears what Farquhar hears, creating a kind of sensorial feedback loop between Farquhar and the reader. As the line between character and reader blurs, the war morphs into a drama of the mind and the politics of the conflict fade away.

Bierce adds a further twist on the War Story in "Chickamauga." Set during a bloody skirmish in Tennessee, the story focuses on a young, adventurous, six-year-old boy who lives with his family near the river. He grabs a stick, pretends it is a gun, and imagines being a great warrior – while, unbeknownst to him, the battle rages a few miles away. Like "An Occurrence at Owl Creek Bridge," "Chickamauga" is a study in consciousness. Bierce disentangles the varied threads of influence that have made the boy who he is: his ancestors; the stories he has read; and his disability (he can neither speak nor hear, so he does not realize the battle is happening until it is too late). Yet this story has a very different tone. The boy wakes up and is scared to death: the air is cold, his family is nowhere to be seen, and he is overcome with fear. When he looks around, he notices strange creatures that resemble bears crawling down to the water. These creatures are, in fact, injured soldiers "dragging their legs" and creeping "upon their hands and knees" like wounded animals (22). The moment of recognition – the instant that reality finally dawns upon the boy – is terrifying, and it is redolent of the horrifying revelations one might find in the tales of Poe. The boy mounts one of the crawling figures, who eventually flings him to the ground, "then turned upon him a face that lacked a lower jaw – from the upper teeth to the throat there was a great red gap fringed with hanging shreds of flesh and splinters of bone" (23).

War is fundamentally hostile to the most human parts of us. In "Chickamauga," even childhood cannot remain unscathed. For Bierce, the War Story is a story about dehumanization and the myriad ways in which war inverts things, so that friends become enemies and life becomes the pursuit of death. That perspective is not so much an opinion of Bierce's as an observation that evolved directly out of his experiences in battle. Many veterans of the Civil War, like Bierce, saw the war as an existential trial that transformed the way they viewed the world. As Oliver Wendell Holmes, Jr. (a Lieutenant in the Massachusetts Infantry), later remarked, "the generation that carried on the war has been set apart by its experience" (2017, 16). Holmes casts the war as a moral lesson, an occasion to learn that "life is a profound and passionate thing," but being "touched with fire" can also burn and scar (16), as Bierce's fiction indicates. The type of experience captured in the War Story often resembles the experience of trauma itself, which is defined by the "displacement of the central axis of Self" and a "deep change in the organization and functioning" of one's identity (Luci 2020, 260). The Civil War altered hearts and minds as much as it decimated bodies, and in doing so it provided the conditions of possibility for the modern War Story to emerge.

One of the Civil War veterans who most effectively channeled his experiences into fiction was Mark Twain. When the war erupted in the spring of 1861, Twain left behind the steamships he had been piloting along the Mississippi River and remade himself into a Confederate soldier. However, Twain turned out to be a far better writer than a warrior. As he relates in "The Private History of a Campaign That Failed" (one of the War Stories that appeared in *Century*'s "Battles and Leaders" series), Twain joined a motley crew of wayward men who had no clue what they were doing. Vaingloriously christening themselves the "Marian Rangers," the soldiers saw the Civil War as a kind of "holiday," a break from the regular grind. They spent most of their time joking, eating, swapping stories, and halfheartedly "training," though the latter mostly consisted of flanking farmhouses and occasionally practicing with their rifles (1992, 863).

Twain's "Private History" is funny. But like many of Twain's jokes, the story turns dark. At one point, Twain says, the men heard a rumor that "the enemy was hovering in our neighborhood" (877). At first, the Marion Rangers are utterly unconcerned, but the prospect of the enemy's imminent arrival begins to weigh on them. They grow increasingly nervous and fearful. Then, in the middle of the night, they are roused by sound of hoofbeats. Terrified, the men raise their rifles, point their muzzles into the darkness, and fire. "I pulled the trigger," Twain writes, "I seemed to see a hundred flashes and a hundred reports, then I saw the man fall down out of the saddle" (878). When they rush over, they discover that this is not a Union soldier but a random passerby. Twain tries to staunch the blood and save the stranger, but to no avail: he dies and Twain is racked with guilt. "The thought shot through me that I was a murderer, that I had killed a man, a man who had never done me any harm. That was the coldest sensation that ever went through my marrow." Twain even begins having nightmares, and the experience leads him to reflect on the cruel nature of war writ large: "[T]he taking of that unoffending life . . . seemed an epitome of war, that all war must just be the killing of strangers . . . who in other circumstances you would help if you found them in trouble"

(879). Distraught and disturbed, Twain abandons the Rangers and lights out for the West.

For Twain, war is where myths go to die. There is nothing holiday-like about the Civil War, and there is nothing heroic or glorious about the Rangers. Nor is there a grand cause – political or otherwise – advanced by their efforts. There is simply the raw truth of armed violence, which explodes their prior ideas and expectations. Twain and Bierce thus mold the War Story into a potent form for reflecting on the reality of violence and the philosophical questions provoked by war. War Stories also enable one to reflect on the difference that experience makes. Some things can only be discovered at first hand. For Twain and Bierce, battle is impossible to fully grasp if you have not been through it, but the War Story provides a chance for understanding, an opportunity to apprehend the realities of war through the medium of storytelling.

The War Story in the Twentieth Century

The War Story may have been born in the nineteenth century, but it was fully developed in the twentieth. The wars that defined the twentieth century, from World War I to Vietnam, profoundly impacted the evolution of the genre, and the War Story, in turn, became an important vehicle for assessing the meaning and consequences of those conflicts. In this era, writers adapted Realism to the modern world, focusing in particular on the relationship between war, ethics, and identity.

The War Story has long been synonymous with Ernest Hemingway. Hemingway's close association with the genre is partly due to his writing, and partly due to his carefully curated public persona, which played up his participation in hunts, battles, and other violent endeavors. He worked as an ambulance driver during World War I, and his experiences in war-torn Europe shaped the rest of his life. The scale of devastation unleashed by World War I was unprecedented: more than eight and a half million soldiers and thirteen million civilians died; it destroyed countless families, cities, and communities; and it set in motion the Spanish flu pandemic, which caused an additional seventeen million deaths. World War I, according to Hemingway, was the "central fact of our time": the event that best encapsulates the modern era (Flora 2004, 44).

What does it mean if World War I is a paradigm for the twentieth century? It means several things. It means that, despite the persistent allure of nationalism, humanity's struggle is a collective one. It also means that with the advent of modern warfare, everyone's fate is intertwined and there is no longer such a thing as a limited skirmish. And it means that politics can sometimes be deadly: all of those deaths occurred for political ends that are still hard to discern (apart from the assassination of an archduke). Hemingway tested these ideas in the following years as he witnessed numerous other battles. In the 1930s, he covered the Spanish Civil War and helped write a film about the conflict, *The Spanish Earth* (1937). He even landed with Allied troops at Normandy, where, he later recalled, he saw "the first, second, third, fourth, and fifth waves of soldiers lay where they had fallen, looking like so many heavily laden bundles on that flat pebbly stretch between the sea and first cover" (Hemingway 2014, 349).

In his short stories, Hemingway transforms these experiences into searching fictional accounts of the ethical and psychological toll of modern battle. In "The Old Man and the Bridge" (1938), Hemingway describes an old man "without politics" who only wants to care for animals, yet war renders even that most meager of tasks – the effort to simply maintain life – impossible (1987, 58). In "A Natural History of the Dead" (1933), Hemingway recalls the horrifying scene at an Italian munitions factory where he helped collect the scattered remains of the dead – or what was left of them. "I remember that after we had searched quite thoroughly for the complete dead we collected fragments," he recalls: "[I]t [was] amazing that the human body should be blown into pieces which exploded along no anatomical lines, but rather divided as capriciously as the fragmentation in the burst of a high explosive shell" (336–337).

Such dreadful thoughts are counterbalanced in "Big Two-Hearted River" (1925). In this story, Nick Adams, newly returned from World War I and in search of respite from a world of conflict, travels deep into the heart of the Michigan woods. "Big Two-Hearted River" is remarkably plotless – Adams walks by the powerful stream, catches trout, sets up camp, and eats a satisfying dinner of canned beans, spaghetti, and ketchup – but that is because the plot is beside the point. The story is instead about the solace provided by nature, the sense of peace that Adams finds in the rushing water and the life of the forest. He is so fragile – so nearly broken by his experiences in war – that the mere act of fishing leaves him feeling raw and nervous: "Nick's hand was shaky. He reeled in slowly. The thrill had been too much. He felt, vaguely, a little sick, as though it would be better to sit down" (177).

That psychological tension is symbolized by the river's split stream. A great uprooted elm tree, Hemingway explains, cuts the river "to the edge," creating "deep channels, like ruts ... in the shallow bed of the stream" (177). As Ronald Berman argues, the landscape mirrors Adams's mind, and the divided river reflects the way that Adam's life has been cut into two different parts, his life at home and his life at war (2011, 61). Nonetheless, by wandering through the woods, fishing for trout, and smoking while "drying in the sun, the sun warm on his back," he is able to become the man he once was. That healing is made possible by his direct encounter with nature, in which everything else – his worries, his memories, his sense of duty – is stripped away. "It was hard work," Hemingway writes, "walking up-hill. His muscles ached and the day was hot, but Nick felt happy. He felt he had left everything behind, the need for thinking, the need to write, other needs. It was all back of him" (177, 164). In Hemingway's hands, the War Story becomes a story about the difficulty, but also the necessity, of reintegration.

The difficult task of assimilating one's experiences at war into one's experiences at home is a major part of the genre in the twentieth century and beyond. That is undoubtedly a consequence of the genre's symbiotic relationship with the wars that marked the modern era. For the veterans-turned-writers who served in these conflicts, the War Story provided a way to work through their experiences. Ever since its inception, the War Story has been a medium for processing trauma, a way to take the "displacement of self" and reorganize it into a more integrated whole. And in the best versions of the War Story, this connection between writing and trauma is self-reflexively considered and examined.

Tim O'Brien has written extensively and insightfully about the link between war and memory. Drafted into the US Army and sent to Vietnam in 1969, O'Brien became one of the most artful practitioners of the War Story. His collection *The Things They Carried* (1990) is a prime example of the genre's thematic multiplicity and philosophical power. In a series of interrelated stories about the Vietnam War, O'Brien discusses everything from love and violence to youth and cowardice, and he employs a wide range of tones and ideas. He recalls Ted Lavender, the most nervous of soldiers, who took tranquilizers every day to calm his nerves. "'How's the war today?' somebody would ask, and Ted Lavender would give a soft, spacey smile and say, 'Mellow man. We got ourselves a nice mellow war today'" (32). In another story, one of O'Brien's compatriots is blown apart by a landmine. Later in the book, O'Brien recounts the trick that he played on Bobby Jorgensen, the rookie medic who froze when O'Brien was shot in the buttocks: "[I]t took the son of a bitch almost ten minutes to work up the nerve to crawl over to me. By then I was gone with the pain. Later I found out I'd almost died of shock" (181). In an act of revenge that borders on cruelty, O'Brien hides out in the bushes at night when Jorgensen is on patrol and pretends to be an enemy soldier. Afterwards, when the men have both experienced a similar sense of fear and dread, they reconnect (more or less) to become "Almost war buddies. . . . We didn't have much to say. I told him I was sorry; he told me the same thing" (207).

Many of O'Brien's stories recur, in slightly altered form. Memory for him is not a fixed set of facts but a mutable and ever-evolving array of experiences that come in and out of focus through the act of storytelling. According to John K. Young (2017), that approach anchors O'Brien's treatment of war: "O'Brien's refusal to allow his books to settle into a stable or completed form [is] a register for the unfinished expression of wartime traumas" embodied in "fiction that repeats itself" (viii). In an interview with John Mort in 1994, O'Brien summed up the complex nature of wartime trauma and the way it bleeds into other experiences: "Nam lived on inside me, and I just called it by another name – I called it life. Nam, divorce, your father's death – such things live on even though you think you're over them. They come bubbling out" (quoted in Heberle 2001, xviii).

The Things They Carried repeatedly poses a question: What defines the War Story? According to O'Brien, the primary feature of the genre is its amorality.

> It does not instruct, nor encourage virtue, nor suggest models of proper human behavior, nor restrain men from doing things men have always done. If a story seems moral, do not believe it. If at the end of a war story you feel uplifted, or if you feel that some small bit of rectitude has been salvaged from the larger waste, then you have been made the victim of a very old and terrible lie. (65)

O'Brien's definition of the War Story echoes Henry James definition of Realist fiction: "[Q]uestions of art are questions (in the widest sense) of execution; questions of morality are quite another affair" (1899, 404). It also accurately describes many of the War Stories we have examined. It is difficult to find any sense of "rectitude" in Bierce's "An Occurrence at Owl Creek Bridge" or Hemingway's "The Old Man and the Bridge." But some War Stories are more moral than others. Indeed the idea that "a true war story is never moral" (as O'Brien puts it) is belied by O'Brien's own creative process, which uses storytelling to deal with unresolved trauma. As Mark Heberle contends, O'Brien's narratives "are both products of trauma and vehicles of recovery" (16). Stories, O'Brien explains, "can save us" (65): they allow us to wrestle with loss and temporarily revive the dead. As he remarks,

I'm 43 years old, and a writer now, and even still, right here, I keep dreaming Linda alive. And Ted Lavender, too, and Kiowa, and Curt Lemon, and a slim young man I killed, and an old man sprawled beside a pigpen, and several others whose bodies I once lifted and dumped into a truck. They're all dead. But in a story, which is a kind of dreaming, the dead sometimes smile and sit up and return to the world. (212)

If that is not rectitude, I do not know what is. For O'Brien, as for these other writers, the War Story challenges the finality of death. That is the magic of the genre, and it is almost certainly why so many veterans, from the Civil War to today, have transformed fact into fiction and memory into narrative. The War Story gives writers as well as readers a way to process experiences that are otherwise very difficult to process. That is precisely why the War Story has endured, and it is why so many authors, from Twain to O'Brien, have gravitated toward this genre: it is an ideal medium for reflecting on the nature of violence and the relationship between life and death.

Works Cited

Bierce, Ambrose. 2000. *Tales of Soldiers and Civilians and Other Stories*. Ed. Tom Quirk. New York: Penguin.

Berman, Ronald. 2011. *Translating Modernism: Fitzgerald and Hemingway*. Tuscaloosa: University of Alabama Press.

Blackwood, Sarah. 2019. *The Portrait's Subject: Inventing Inner Life in the Nineteenth-Century United States*. Chapel Hill: University of North Carolina Press.

Catton, Bruce. 1986. *America Goes to War: The Civil War and Its Meaning in American Culture*. Middleton, CT: Wesleyan University Press.

Flora, Joseph. 2004. "Soldier Home: *Big Two-Hearted River*," in *Bloom's Major Literary Characters: Nick Adams*. Ed. Harold Bloom, 41–64. New York: Chelsea House Press.

Fretwell, Erica. 2020. *Sensory Experiments: Psychophysics, Race, and the Aesthetics of Feeling*. Durham, NC: Duke University Press.

Hardwig, Bill. 2020. "The Development of Print Culture, 1865–1914," in *A Companion to American Literature*. Eds. Susan Belasco et al., 308–322. London: Wiley.

Heberle, Mark A. 2001. *A Trauma Artist: Tim O'Brien and the Fiction of Vietnam*. Iowa City: University of Iowa Press.

Hemingway, Ernest. 1987. *Complete Short Stories*. New York: Scribner.

2014. *By-Line Ernest Hemingway: Selected Articles and Dispatches of Four Decades*. New York: Scribner.

Holmes, Oliver Wendell. 2017. *The Mind and Faith of Justice Holmes: His Speeches, Essays, Letters, and Judicial Opinions*. Ed. Max Lerner. New York: Routledge.

James, Henry. 1899. *Partial Portraits*. London: Macmillan and Co.

Klay, Phil. 2014. *Redeployment*, 1–16. New York: Penguin.

Luci, Monica. 2020. "Displacement as Trauma and Trauma as Displacement in the Experience of Refugees," *Journal of Analytical Psychology* 65.2 (April): 260–280.

Marx, Karl. 1937. *The Eighteenth Brumaire of Louis Bonaparte*. Trans. Saul K. Padover. Moscow: Progress Publishers.

Menand, Louis. 2002. *The Metaphysical Club: A Story of Ideas in America*. New York: Farrar, Straus and Giroux.

O'Brien, Tim. 1990. *The Things They Carried*. Boston and New York: Mariner Books.

Renker, Elizabeth. 2018. *Realist Poetics in American Culture, 1866-1900*. New York: Oxford University Press.

Shaara, Jeff. 1998. *The Last Full Measure: A Novel*. New York: Ballantine Books.

Smith, Susan Belasco and Kenneth M. Price. 1996. "Introduction: Periodical Literature in Social and Historical Context," in *Periodical Literature in Nineteenth-Century America*. Eds. Belasco Smith and Kenneth M. Price, 3–16. Charlottesville: University of Virginia Press.

Streeby, Shelley. 2002. *American Sensations: Class, Empire, and the Production of Popular Culture*. Berkeley and Los Angeles: University of California Press.

Twain, Mark. 1992. "The Private History of a Campaign That Failed" (1884), in *Collected Tales, Sketches, Speeches, and Essays, Vol. 1: 1852–1890*, 860–913. New York: Library of America.

Young, John Kevin. 2017. *How to Revise a True War Story: Tim O'Brien's Process of Textual Production*. Iowa City: University of Iowa Press.

CHAPTER 8

Narratives from Below
Working-Class Short Fiction

Owen Clayton

In 1925, the radical working-class essayist T-Bone Slim (real name Matti Valentinepoika Huhta) compared his own writing practice to that of his conservative, upper-class counterpart, the Hearst newspaper columnist Arthur Brisbane. As if speaking directly to Brisbane, Slim asks: "Say, Art, why don't you get a job and do your writing before breakfast, like I do?" (Slim 1925). Slim's point is that as a professional writer Brisbane has had time to craft his articles, whereas Slim himself had to write his own columns before he began his daily employment as a manual laborer. This contrast speaks to a lived, experiential difference between writers in the working class and those higher up the social ladder. It speaks to the problem of how to maintain a literary career while short on both time and energy as a result of performing hard, often manual labor in the capitalist marketplace.[1]

Different "Literary forms," as Richard Brodhead puts it, "create different sorts of literary access" (1994, 141). For this reason, working-class writers, editors, and publishers have long sought alternate means of publication to lengthy and expensive novels (see Noonan 2015). One such alternative is the short story, which became a popular form among writers whose working lives made longer, sustained projects difficult. In his 1936 essay "The Storyteller," Walter Benjamin, quoting Paul Valéry, claims that "The era is past when time did not matter" and then goes on to argue that "We have witnessed the development of the 'short story,' which has withdrawn from the oral tradition and no longer allows for that slow accumulation of thin, translucent layers which offers the most fitting image of the process in which the perfect story is revealed" (2019, 57–58). While Benjamin mourns the shift from epic oral storytelling tradition to novel and then to short story as one that tracks increasing capitalist individuation and the Taylorization of work practices, many writers have embraced the short story as a means to represent working-class experience. The authors under discussion in this chapter, Meridel Le Sueur, Tillie

Olsen, Raymond Carver, and Bobbie Ann Mason, each struggled to find the time to write in between their work and, in several cases, domestic chores. Each also found the short story to be an effective form for representing the experiences of those who are alienated within US society. As I will show, the comparably abrupt and disconnected nature of the short story parallels an aesthetic of disconnectedness that is prevalent in the work of these four writers. Le Sueur's characters are alienated from the wider economy and each other, Olsen portrays an emotional stunting of her female characters, Carver displays the affective numbness of men through his minimalist writing style, and Mason's male characters are unable to develop and are left behind by women in the postindustrial marketplace.

There is a tradition of short fiction about the US working class dating back to the nineteenth century. Rebecca Harding Davis's classic "Life in the Iron Mills" (1861) encapsulated themes that would be important in the working-class short story, including the problem of creating art while being working class, as well as how capitalism shapes other forms of identity, such as gender. Becoming more prominent during the Great Depression, working-class short stories concern themselves more with economic aspects of life than literature written by wealthier writers, simply because those aspects dominate working-class experience at every level. Often this means that these stories can seem bleaker, "grittier," and more explicitly political than middle-class fiction (see Lee, 2021). However, this chapter will also argue that from the 1940s to the 1980s working-class short stories became less didactic, and that economic aspects became more implicitly realized, though no less present.

* * *

Although the writers in this chapter would be designated as "white" from a contemporary perspective, it is important to note that white people are not the sole representatives of the working class, just as "whiteness" itself is not a given or neutral descriptor but rather a shifting cultural construction rooted in power and class, as scholarship in the field of critical whiteness studies has shown (see, especially, Roediger 2007). This was a particularly pressing issue for many European immigrant groups, who adopted the identity of whiteness as a means to gain freedom for themselves and domination over others – in particular, over African Americans (see Birt 2004, Brodkin 1998, Ignatiev 1995, Jacobson 1998, Morrison 1992). As Valerie Babb puts it in her examination of early twentieth-century US immigrant autobiographies: "[T]hose who were not yet American . . . had to learn the privileging of whiteness and its synonymity with American identity" (1998, 119). This includes the Jewish parents of Tillie Olsen, who saw their racial categorization shift from an anti-Semitic othering as "Hebrews" to a uneasy whiteness from around the middle of the century (see Brodkin 1998). Each of the writers in this chapter interrogates the relationship between working-class status and whiteness, aspects of intersectional identity that pull in opposite directions in terms of power and status. Whiteness, as David Roediger argues, connotes independence (2007, 20–21), yet to be working class indicates dependence on capital and, to a greater or lesser extent, subservience to capitalist work discipline.

For left-aligned political and cultural groups which sought to empower the working class, the related but separate concepts of "proletarian" and working-class literature came to be important from the 1930s onward. The former term, developed by Mike Gold and others, denoted a kind of literature that was explicitly political: "Proletarian literature," as Gold put it in 1930, "will reflect the struggle of the workers in the fight for the world" (1972, 205). Gold's use of "reflect" suggests that he saw literature in largely passive, sociological terms, and much proletarian literature, including his own novel *Jews Without Money* (1930), has been criticized for its blatant propaganda (see Clarke 2021, 359). From the late 1950s into the 1970s, as New Left activists and intellectuals sought to move away from an earlier left-wing focus solely on labor issues, feminist literary scholars sought out texts by forgotten women writers, challenging and expanding the literary canon beyond a narrow concentration on men. These rediscoveries of female writers would provide an inspiration for working-class scholars and authors. Tillie Olsen herself played a significant role in rediscovering a tradition of working-class literature by republishing Davis's "Life in the Iron Mills" with the Feminist Press in 1972, making this short story a kind of urtext for working-class studies. This model of rediscovery has continued into the twenty-first century, culminating with the publication of the *American Working Class Literature* anthology (Coles and Zandy 2007).

Despite these positive developments, class continues to be excluded from most literary research (Lang 2006, 7; Tokarczyk 2011, 4). In response, American working-class studies has tended to downplay the literary qualities of texts in favor of a commitment to the experience of the author. Finding this emphasis problematic, Magnus Nilsson and John Lennon suggest that "attempts within contemporary US working-class studies to fight the marginalization of working-class literature could very well benefit from a greater emphasis on its literariness" (2016, 55). This chapter responds to Nilsson and Lennon's call by focusing on how the formal and literary qualities of short fiction embodied in special ways the disconnected social experience of working-class writers.

* * *

Meridel Le Sueur was a communist feminist writer who was part of the proletarian literary movement of the 1930s. Born into the middle class, Le Sueur believed in the importance of "proletarianizing" herself for the benefit of both the working class and her art. While such a move might be considered an affectation, Le Sueur, according to Constance Coiner, did live an "economically marginal" life during the Great Depression, experiencing a proletarianization that was less voluntary than she might have wished (1998, 97). Whatever her "true" socioeconomic status, Le Sueur sought, as the narrator of her story "Biography of My Daughter" puts it, to speak for those who are written out of history: "They live, they die, they are silent. Nothing is ever said for such people, no book is written about them, they never write a long biography saying I did this and that" (Le Sueur 1940, 98–99). Her most famous short story collection, *Salute to Spring* (1940), encapsulates these themes, portraying working-class life under capitalism as bleak and oppressive. However, her stories also represent the repression of her middle-class characters, who lack a healthy relationship to their bodies. As I will show, Le Sueur proposes a positive relationship to the body as the best means to revolution and the only way to overcome the inherently exploitative nature of capitalist work. In doing so, she decenters men from the class struggle and represents women as containing the generative power necessary to create a better world.

In "Fable of a Man and Pigeons," Le Sueur portrays a man whom the narrator claims "looked like workmen all over the world, a certain submission in them that is at once terrible and beautiful" (1940, 38). Laboring in a factory has left the worker, who is not named and so becomes an "Everyman" figure, feeling as though "everything he touched was hard and blunt" (39). It has left him alienated not just from his labor, as Karl Marx famously argued is inevitable under capitalism, but also from other human beings. Despite being among a large crowd of men at a city mission, he still feels alone:

> He kept looking, wondering, wondering what men could say together so there would be more than just meetings . . .. How are you? How are you? What if at such a question a man should say, "I am dying, that's how

I am ..." But no man would say that. A bum asked him for a light and he struck a match and stood dead before the other man and they didn't speak to each other at all. (42)

The question "How are you?" strikes the man as hollow, since it engenders a stock response (presumably, "Fine"), one that does not even attempt to be a true answer. The supposedly phatic connection implied by such a question turns out to be no connection at all. A truthful answer would break an unspoken rule related to the racialized ideology of masculine independence: white American men are supposed to be capable and self-reliant, and so to admit that they are "dying" would be to admit to being a failure. Instead, the protagonist and the "bum" simply stand "dead" to each other, the sense of tension increased by the lack of commas in the final sentence, in a moment that encapsulates a failure of solidarity.

Le Sueur's characters are disconnected not only from each other but also from their own bodies. This is especially true of her middle-class characters, whose intellectual labors separate them from the need to consider their own physicality. The story "No Wine in His Cart," for instance, portrays a female protagonist, Stella, whose middle-class husband's white body is "distasteful to her, his white hands, his white narrow chest, self-conscious, without use. Making money never made use of a man's body" (30). Here whiteness is equated with the physical weakness that comes with a life dedicated to "making money." In contrast, Stella observes the bodies of working-class men, which she says are "the same everywhere ... the same sensitive body moulded close to its labor, a worn tool" (29). In idealizing working-class male bodies, which are problematically described as "the same everywhere," Le Sueur links class with sexuality. In other stories, she connects class with procreation in a way that male proletarian writers had rarely done; several of her stories deal with the physicality of having and raising children. In "Annunciation," for example, the female narrator resists calls from her husband to abort her baby. Heavily pregnant, the woman lyrically describes herself as "a pomegranate hanging from an invisible tree with the juice and movement of seed within my hard skin," implying that to abort the baby would be a destruction of the natural world (93). Abortion would also be a reactionary act because, for her, childbirth has revolutionary potential: "Perhaps it is such activity that makes a field come alive with millions of shoots of corn or wheat. Perhaps it is something like that that makes a new world" (91). Similarly, in "A Hungry Intellectual," a working-class woman claims that revolution is like childbirth. When a downwardly mobile middle-class man tells her that "Change must come from the intellect with understanding and nonviolence," she replies: "From having a baby I think it's different. It comes out violently" (55). Since only women give birth, they have a unique connection to the creation of new social possibilities. In "Tonight is Part of the Struggle," a working-class woman called Leah listens to a male Communist Party organizer tell a gathered group of workmen, "You are producers, wealth is produced by hand and brain. I am a producer, she thought, with her hand on the protruding belly of the baby, but not from hand and brain" (138). Le Sueur reimagines the notion of producer in a feminist light, removing it from the male-dominated notion of wage labor. For her, working-class women are to be the center of the revolution because they contain the generative power to create a new world. While such a conceptualization is open to criticism on the grounds that it is essentialist, it nevertheless represents a significant shift in working-class writing, which up until this point had been dominated by men and dismissive of issues such as reproduction (Coiner 1998, 47).

* * *

Like that of Meridel Le Sueur, Tillie Olsen's work combines a left-wing concern for the working class with a feminist emphasis on the plight of US women. More than in the work of Le Sueur, two of Olsen's most famous short stories, "I Stand Here Ironing" (1956) and "Tell Me a Riddle" (1960), emphasize the inequalities and the stultifying effects of being condemned to a life of domestic labor under a patriarchal system. As with Le Sueur, Olsen's focus on the domestic pushes back against the neglect of this issue by male authors. In addition, while in her 1930s reportage Olsen had shared much of Le Sueur's political optimism, by the time of "I Stand Here Ironing" and "Tell Me a Riddle" her representation of politics was more pessimistic. In these stories, the promises of revolution have been betrayed and co-opted.

"I Stand Here Ironing" is a monologue from the perspective of a working-class wife and mother who has, as the title suggests, spent her life performing domestic chores. The story concerns the fates of the mother and her daughter, Emily, a troubled young woman whom the story's unnamed interlocutor says "needs help" for some unknown problem. As the mother narrates her daughter's life story, she states that "what you asked me moves tormented back and forth with the iron" (2013, 5). The rhythms of ironing structure the rhythms of her speech, much as domestic labor in general has structured her life. Emily's experience as a woman is very different from her mother's, as seen when she pejoratively comments on how much of her life her mother has spent performing domestic chores, telling her: "Aren't you ever going to finish the ironing, Mother? Whistler painted his mother in a rocker. I'd have to paint mine standing over an ironing board" (13). As a woman from an earlier generation, the mother is bound by patriarchal assumptions that Emily seems to challenge. These assumptions include a responsibility to look after her children, which might seem like a necessity but did not bind Emily's father, "who 'could no longer endure' (he wrote in his good-bye note) 'sharing want with us'" (6). The father's abandonment forced the mother, already suffering poverty and deprivation, to seek work, which in turn left Emily in the care of neighbors and, in time, social workers. The forces of capitalism and patriarchy combined to weaken the familial bonds between mother and daughter, to the point that the narrator denies that she can help Emily, saying that she does not have any special understanding of her.

In a similar way, "Tell Me a Riddle" concerns itself with the aftereffects of a working-class woman's being condemned to a life of domestic drudgery. The story focuses on an elderly Jewish immigrant couple, Eva and David, whose children are grown and who cannot agree how to spend their retirement. David wishes to move into a retirement community to be among people, but Eva, a former radical who was forced to flee Russia during the 1905 Revolution, wishes to simply be left alone. The story represents Eva as having been intellectually stunted by a life of domestic chores. In one of their many arguments, she tells David, "you never scraped a carrot or knew a dish towel sops" and accuses him of having denied her intellectual and social opportunities: "[F]orty years ago when the children were morsels and there was a [reading] Circle, did you stay at home with them once so I could go? Even once? You trained me well. I do not need others to enjoy" (2013, 59). When she was young, her house, which was filled with children who were constantly making mess, had seemed an "enemy: tracking, smudging, littering, dirtying, engaging her in endless defeating battle – and on whom her endless defeat had been spewed" (61). All she wishes to do now is rest, to sit in the clean and empty house which, finally free of children, represents her ultimate victory. She admits to being bitter and blames this on her husband's lack of support, thinking to herself, "Vinegar he poured on me all his life; I am well marinated; how can I be honey now?" (67). Her domestic tasks performed, Eva has little left to live for, and notably the story concerns itself with her slow death from cancer. A literal disease, cancer also symbolizes how Eva's life was slowly taken over by domestic chores until nothing of herself remained.

Although Eva blames David, the story alternates between their perspectives in a way that provides some sympathy for his situation. He feels guilty for having placed such a burden on Eva and knows that it is too late to correct his mistakes, but his love for her is made clear as he becomes her carer during the final months of her illness, including a painful deathbed delirium. During this delirium, Eva sings the labor songs of her youth, which promised that "*a loftier race/than e'er the world hath known shall rise*" (italics in original), as well as Victor Hugo's visionary statement, slightly misremembered, that "in the twentieth century ignorance will be dead, dogma will be dead, war will be dead" (94). In fragmented paragraphs, the story portrays David's realization, as he listens to Eva singing, that these radical promises have not been kept:

> The cards fell from his fingers. Without warning, the bereavement of betrayal he had sheltered – compounded through the years – hidden even from himself – revealed itself,
>
> uncoiled,
>
> released,
>
> *sprung*
>
> and with it the monstrous shapes of what had actually happened in the century. (94; italics in original)

The twentieth century reveals itself to him, a Jewish immigrant, as the opposite of Hugo's vision and of the promise of the labor songs: a century of war, bloodshed, and holocaust. The fragmented layout of the paragraph represents the fragmentation of Eva's earlier radical dreams, as well as David's emotional reaction to their failure. David also considers the relatively easy lives of his Americanized (and therefore implicitly white) grandchildren, "who never hungered, who lived unravaged by disease in warm houses of many rooms," and he asks, "was this not the dream then, come true in ways undreamed?" (95). Capitalism, he seems to conclude, has fulfilled the promises of socialism in providing working-class people with comfortable lives. Thinking of Eva's belief in the radical promise of freedom, he imagines telling his grandchildren to "package it . . . give it as a fabled gift," mocking his own thoughts by asking, "And why not in cereal boxes, in soap packages?" (96). The promises of freedom are now commodified and sold back to workers by consumer capitalism. Citizens are like the children who receive free gifts in their cereal: naively believing that the gifts are freely given, and not in fact already costed and paid for. In this story, in other words, Olsen turns away from the radical tradition of Le

Sueur and proletarian fiction and imagines what is left for working-class people after the revolution has failed. In this sense, her work is another turning point in working-class short story writing, which in the years following will be less likely to propagandize about a possible utopian future, instead focusing on the hardships of those who must live within an apparently victorious capitalism.

* * *

Although less explicitly political than earlier working-class fiction, Raymond Carver's short story collections *Will You Please Be Quiet Please?* (1995) and *What We Talk About When We Talk About Love* (2009), portray working-class life as being affected by the same forces of capitalism, which produce similar effects of loneliness and alienation, as in the work of Le Sueur and Olsen. This is frequently represented in the writing through Carver's minimalist style, which Bill Buford famously labeled "dirty realism" (Buford 1983), a problematic label that nevertheless did much to popularize Carver as an author. Whether "dirty" or not, Carver's style tends to flatten affect and to avoid the discussion of emotional response, as though the characters and even the narrator are suffering from an inability to acknowledge their own feelings. In "Everything Stuck to Him" (2009), for example, the characters are not given names but simply referred to throughout by impersonal pronouns, including "the boy" and "the girl." The effect is a narratological distancing and affective numbness that permeates the story, as if the people about whom Carver writes are archetypes rather than individuals. The author adopts a contrasting strategy in "Tell the Women We're Going" (2009), in which the characters' first names are repeated throughout with few pronouns, giving the story an incantatory quality that depersonalizes the characters and emphasizes their emotional isolation.

Carver represents the trauma of deindustrialization as it has affected men, trauma that consists of a sense of "lost futurity," to use Kathryn Marie Dudley's term (2021, 202). Male loneliness in his stories is often caused by unemployment or the threat of unemployment. For example, the story "Collectors" begins simply, "I was out of work" (1995, 76), while the second paragraph of "Jerry and Molly and Sam" states that "they were laying off at Aerojet when they should have been hiring . . .. He was no safer than anyone else" (1995, 111). Carver is especially interested in the impact of economic insecurity upon the domestic sphere. His stories peer into the home in a voyeuristic manner, as in "Don't You Dance?," which opens with a man looking out at his "bedroom suite in his front yard," the private furnishings of a home now made visible for public view (2009, 3). The author turns the inside out, and in so doing exposes the damage done by economic hardship and family breakdown. In the voyeuristically tilted "Viewfinder," for example, the male protagonist refers to his house as a "tragedy" after his wife and children walk out on him (2009, 11), while "Night School" opens with a man drinking alone at a bar because "My marriage had fallen apart. I couldn't find a job" (1995, 70). Other Carver protagonists also turn to alcohol to cope with modern life. In "Mr Coffee and Mr Fixit," for instance, the narrator's alcoholic wife has run away with "an unemployed aerospace engineer she'd met at AA" (2009, 14), while in "Gazebo," the narrator makes the offhand comment that "Booze takes a long time if you're going to do a good job with it" (2009, 22), as if alcoholism were a new profession requiring long study and practice.

Carver's stories tend to focus on the impact of family breakdown, presenting a world in which white working-class masculinity can no longer prove itself through the traditional action of breadwinning. This insecure masculinity results in part from frequent unemployment, but also from the gains made during the women's rights movement of the 1960s and 1970s. For Carver, the world for men is bleak because they are now without the gender privilege that had previously compensated for a lack of autonomy in the capitalist workplace. "Put Yourself in My Shoes," for instance, opens with a man vacuuming – a domestic chore that traditionally would have been performed by a woman – and then hearing about a male friend who has committed suicide (1995, 97). One way that Carver's male characters respond to the perceived loss of status and shifting domestic roles, then, is through self-violence. A second response is violence toward women. Men kill or attack women in several stories, including "The Third Thing That Killed My Father Off" (2009, 86), "A Serious Talk" (90–91) "What We Talk About When We Talk About Love" (114), and "One More Thing" (130-131). A third response, as in "Are These Actual Miles?," is a submissive, deadening acceptance. In this story, the male protagonist Leo waits at home while his wife Toni makes a sale of a car by wining, dining, and ultimately sleeping with her client. The narrator describes the passive Leo's feelings as he waits for Toni to return: "He understands he is willing to be dead" (1995, 153). The wordy phrasing of "He understands" is a circumlocution aimed at avoiding the direct discussion of emotion, while the passive phrase "is willing" suggests that he is not going to take his own life but that he would be content if someone else killed him. Not knowing how to feel, oblivion seems a desirable option, yet Leo will not even assert himself in the act of suicide. Similarly, in the story "Will You Please Be Quiet, Please?," the narrator asks the young protagonist, "How should a man act, given these circumstances?," but no answer is forthcoming: "He understood things had been done. He did not understand what things now were to be done" (179). In a world turned upside down, Carver's men are emotionally lost and unable to assert either their whiteness or their masculinity through action.

A lack of understanding about how to reconceptualize working-class white masculinity threads throughout Carver's stories, which usually adopt the male perspective. The sympathy with which the author often portrays troubled or violent men is problematic, and Carver does not present any alternatives to the patriarchal world whose loss his characters mourn. Nevertheless, his stories represent important literary representations of a moment in American working-class short story writing during which male characters perceive a lessening of social power, but are as yet unable to move beyond their own toxic masculinity.

* * *

Like Raymond Carver, Bobbie Ann Mason's short story collection *Shiloh and Other Stories* (1983) was written in the shadow cast by the women's rights movement. Unlike Carver, however, Mason portrays the results of this movement for working-class women, results that are for the most part beneficial. While she also represents a world in which family breakdown and divorce are commonplace, in Mason's stories women are more likely to develop positively as individuals, while male selfhood continues to wither in the absence of positive alternative masculinities. For example, the story "The Rookers" presents its female protagonist Mary Lou Skaggs as more active than her husband, Mack. Mary Lou "hauls lumber, delivers bookshelves, even makes a special trip to town just to exchange flathead screws," all activities that would once have been considered traditionally male. Mack, by contrast, will only "occasionally go out to measure people's kitchens ... but he gets uncomfortable if he has to be away [from home] long. Increasingly, he stays at home" (1993, 17). Mary Lou has "tried to be patient with Mack," waiting for him to "come out of his shell" (20–21). She spends time with a group of older women, who despite their age are willing to try new experiences, such as watching an R-rated movie (28). Her daughter Judy, who has moved away to university, represents a new generation of independent women. In this story, the male character sits passive while the women, no matter their age, develop and increase their

self-sufficiency. Similarly, in "A New-Wave Format," bus driver Edwin
Creech feels that he has a "developmental disability" (230) in contrast to
his "liberated" (225) girlfriend Sabrina, an anthropology student who
"believes in the ERA [Equal Rights Amendment]" (216). Edwin drives a
bus for people with disabilities and is told by his supervisor that "the
developmentally disabled – they always use this term – need a world that is
slowed down; they can't keep up with today's fast pace" (217). This
description also fits Edwin and many of the working-class men in
Mason's stories, who find the world changing around them and are unsure
of their place within it.

In a similar moment of role reversal, Mason's story "Shiloh" begins by
describing a character called Norma Jean who is "working on her pecto-
rals" by lifting a "twenty-pound barbell" (1). Jean's muscles challenge
traditional gender stereotypes of women as weak by demonstrating a
physical strength that reminds her truckdriver husband Leroy of Wonder
Woman. This reference to a superheroine emphasizes Jean's power, indicates the admiration in which Leroy holds her, and implies that he sees her
as an exceptional kind of woman. Notably, Leroy is also described as being
disabled, having "injured his leg in a highway accident," which means that
"He will probably not be able to drive his rig again" (1). As well as being
unable to assert his masculinity through work, Leroy's disability symbolizes the relative loss of status suffered by working-class men. The contrast
between Leroy's physical frailty and Norma Jean's strength emphasizes
how the loss of power and status suffered by men has been balanced by the
gains made by women. Leroy now spends his time doing needlepoint, a
supposedly feminine pursuit, while Norma Jean urges him to find another
job, which he is reluctant to do (6). In contrast, she is attending "an adult
education course in composition" at Community College, an educational
opportunity that would have previously been denied to working-class
women. Leroy notes with despair that "Norma Jean is miles away. He
knows he is going to lose her" (11). While she is developing her abilities
and self-confidence, his, like those of Mack in "The Rookers," are shrinking away. Soon, Norma Jean does declare her intention to leave Leroy,
telling him on a trip to the Shiloh Civil War Cemetery that "In some ways,
a woman prefers a man who wanders" (15). She gets up from the bench
and Leroy's leg renders him unable to follow, symbolizing how, now that
he is unable to wander, she has left him behind. Their location at Shiloh
links Leroy's outdated notions of gender to the defeat of the Confederacy
and the fall of slavery, at what the story represents as Norma Jean's
moment of (self) emancipation.

Like Carver, Mason portrays working-class male characters as lost within a post-1960s environment of increasing female independence. Unlike Carver, however, she also represents the benefits of such independence. As a result, her writing allows for the discussion of affect and balances the portrayal of male disability with hope for a more positive future for working-class women. Class serves as background in *Shiloh and Other Stories*, which foregrounds regional issues more prominently. Class is a less explicitly politicized topic for both Carver and Mason, in comparison to the earlier work of Le Sueur and Olsen, a shift that suggests a diminution of the politics of class struggle.

Conclusion

The concise form of the short story has proven to be a good fit for writers whose working and domestic lives did not leave them as much time to write as their more privileged counterparts. For working-class authors, the short story made a virtue of brevity. In addition, the inevitably abrupt and disconnected nature of the short story when compared to the novel aligns with the representation of working-class life found in the writings of Le Sueur, Olsen, Carver, and Mason. Each writer portrays working-class life as to some degree alienated from the mainstream culture, and their characters are often emotionally stunted as a result. The foreshortening of the short story prevents the kind of graduated character and narrative development that Benjamin called a "slow accumulation of thin, translucent layers" (2019, 57). But the writers in this chapter represent working-class life under capitalism as itself retarding human development for most of, if not quite all, their characters. While the focus of working-class writing shifts from male proletarian labor to a broader sweep of working-class life, including the concerns of women, a thread that runs throughout the work of each author is the emotional damage caused by being working class in the United States. For Le Sueur, Olsen, Carver, and Mason, this damage was best able to be portrayed through the formal qualities of the short story.

Work Cited

Babb, Valerie. 1998. *Whiteness Visible: The Meaning of Whiteness in American Literature*. New York: New York University Press.

Benjamin, Walter. 2019. *The Storyteller Essays*. New York: New York Review of Books.

Birt, Robert E. 2004. "The Bad Faith of Whiteness," in *What White Looks Like: African-American Publishers on the Whiteness Question.* Ed. George Yancy, 55–64. London: Routledge.

Brodhead, Richard. 1994. *Cultures of Letters: Scenes of Reading and Writing in Nineteenth-Century America.* Chicago: The University of Chicago Press.

Brodkin, Karen. 1998. *How Jews Became White Folks and What That Says about Race in America.* New Brunswick, NJ: Rutgers University Press.

Buford, Bill. 1983. "Editorial," *Granta Magazine* 8 (Summer). https://granta.com/dirtyrealism/.

Carver, Raymond. 1995 [1976]. *Will You Please Be Quiet, Please?* London: The Harvill Press.

   2009 [1981]. *What We Talk About When We Talk About Love.* London: Vintage Books.

Clarke, Ben. 2021. "Things That Are Left Out: Working-Class Writing and the Idea of Literature," in *Routledge International Handbook of Working-Class Studies.* Eds. Michele Fazio, Christie Launius, and Tim Strangleman, 359–370. London: Routledge.

Coiner, Constance. 1998. *Better Red: The Writing and Resistance of Tillie Olsen and Meridel Le Sueur.* Urbana: University of Illinois Press.

Coles, Nicholas and Janey Zandy, eds. 2007. *American Working-Class Literature.* 2007. New York: Oxford University Press.

Dudley, Kathryn Marie. 2021. "Precarity's Affects: The Trauma of Deindustrialization," in *Routledge International Handbook of Working-Class Studies.* Eds. Michele Fazio, Christie Launius, and Tim Strangleman, 201–212. London: Routledge.

Gold, Mike. 1972. *Mike Gold: A Literary Anthology.* Ed. Michael Folsom. New York: International Publishers.

Ignatiev, Noel. 1995. *How the Irish Became White.* London: Routledge.

Jacobson, Matthew Fyre. 1998. *Whiteness of a Different Color: European Immigrants and the Alchemy of Race.* Cambridge, MA: Harvard University Press.

Lang, Amy. 2006. *The Syntax of Class: Writing Inequality in Nineteenth-Century America.* Ann Arbor: University of Michigan Press.

Le Sueur, Meridel. 2019 [1940]. *Salute to Spring: And Other Short Stories.* New York: International Publishers.

Lee, Simon. 2021. "Lit-Grit: The Gritty and the Grim in Working-Class Cultural Production," in *Routledge International Handbook of Working-Class Studies.* Eds. Michele Fazio, Christie Launius, and Tim Strangleman, 371–380. London: Routledge.

Mason, Bobbie Ann. 1993 [1983]. *Shiloh and Other Stories.* New York: Harper Perennial.

Morrison, Toni. 1992. *Playing in the Dark: Whiteness and the Literary Imagination.* New York: Vintage Books.

Nilsson, Magnus and John Lennon. 2016. "Defining Working Class Literature(s): A Comparative Approach Between U.S Working Class Studies and Swedish

Literary History," *New Proposals: Journal of Marxian and Interdisciplinary Inquiry* 8.2 (2016): 39–61.

Noonan, Mark. 2015. "Getting the Word Out: Institutions and Forms of Publication," in *A History of American Working-Class Literature*. Eds. Nicholas Coles and Paul Lauter, 177–196. Cambridge, UK: Cambridge University Press.

Olsen, Tillie. 2013. *Tell Me a Riddle, Requa I, and Other Works*. Lincoln: University of Nebraska Press.

Roediger, David. 2007. *The Wages of Whiteness: Race and the Making of the American Working Class*. London: Verso.

Russo, John and Sherry Lee Linkon. 2005. "What's New About New Working Class Studies?," in *New Working-Class Studies*. Eds. John Russo and Sherry Lee Linkon, 1–18. Ithaca, NY: ILR Press.

Slim, T-Bone. 1925. "T Bone Slim Discusses – Odds and Ends," *Industrial Solidarity*, October 21.

Tokarczyk, Michelle M. 2011. "Introduction," in *Critical Approaches to American Working-Class Literature*. Ed. Michelle M. Tokarczyk, 1–13. London: Routledge.

CHAPTER 9

The Short Story and the Popular Imagination
Pulp and Crime

Will Norman

Pulp stories are named for the type of paper upon which they were printed: cheap, crudely refined wood pulp, intended to be used quickly and discarded. This way of producing magazines had been developed in the late nineteenth century, when the publisher Frank Munsey began to print his all-fiction title *Argosy* on pulpwood paper (Hefner 2017, 434). The era between the two world wars, however, saw a marked rise in the number of all-fiction pulp magazine titles being published and in their general readership, making them one of the dominant print forms in which fiction was consumed in the period. Though circulation figures for individual pulp magazine titles were in the thousands rather than the millions, when we consider pulp magazines as a collective phenomenon, the numbers were considerable. One conservative estimate holds that in 1935 pulp magazine circulation ran to approximately ten million, with a readership of thirty million (Earle 2009, 77). The stories they contained ranged from blood-and-thunder westerns to schmaltzy romances, and from exotic adventure yarns to tales of sporting heroism. For all its popularity, however, the pulp story in its heyday of the 1920s and 1930s occupied a doubly subordinate position in the American literary field. On the one hand, its relative brevity sat in negative contrast to longer, more prestigious prose forms, such as the novel. On the other, its obedience to sets of mass-genre conventions marked it off from "literature" as such. The subordinate status afforded by these formal qualities was compounded by the pulps' disposable materiality. Publicly, the American middle classes and the mainstream literary establishment understood the magazines as sub-literary trash (even while a substantial proportion of those classes also likely bought and read them with great interest). In *Vanity Fair* magazine, Marcus Duffield pronounced the pulps literature "for those who move their lips when they read" (Smith 2000, 18). In *Harper's*, meanwhile, Margaret McCullen worried that "the steady reader of this kind of fiction is interested in and stirred by the same things that would interest and stir a savage" (Earle 2009, 88).

In the interwar period, a number of pulp magazine titles began to specialize in crime fiction, a likely indication of its perceived popularity. Titles such as *Detective Stories, Dime Detective*, and, the best known, *Black Mask* catered exclusively for readers of crime stories. The stories they contained evolved out of the dime detective tradition of the nineteenth century and gradually established their own cultural codes made up of literary styles, plot types, and stock characters (Bedore 2013). Among these stories, those labeled "hard-boiled" attained a particular prominence and durability. They featured disenchanted, tough detectives and beautiful but duplicitous women, and were set in the corrupt, violent city, using a stylized street-vernacular language (McCann 2000). In the 1940s, pulp magazine titles gradually fell in number and circulation, their fragile economies of production overtaken by the new priorities established by the war economy and by technological developments in television and paperback publishing (Smith 2000, 167). In its strictly defined material sense, the era of the pulps was over. However, the term *pulp* outlived the interwar period and the particular mode of production associated with the pulp magazine industry. After World War II, the term *pulp fiction* was used to describe the sensationalist stories found in cheap paperbacks and the new generation of all-fiction magazines. Pulp fiction came in a great variety of forms, but it took common inspiration from the lurid contents, the underworld milieus, and the melodramatic styles found in the original pulp magazines, driving them to new extremes (Haut 1995).

Despite the prurient and patronizing criticism leveled at the pulps and their readers, from the vantage point of the twenty-first century, it is clear that the pulp crime story had an enormous impact on the literary field, one that outlasted the interwar historical window in which it emerged. In taking into account the interrelation of the multiple affordances it presented at the level of its material, political, and aesthetic forms, we are able to bring into clearer view its historical distinctiveness and evolution. We will consider how the forms of organization taken by pulp labor related to the literary forms found in the stories, examining how the principles of fungibility and economy, recognizable from the industrial factory system of mass production, were accommodated or challenged by two key crime writers: Dashiell Hammett and Raymond Chandler. We will examine how the rhythms of pulp labor intersected with the stories' formal composition. Finally, we will discuss the interpellation of a white, male, working-class readership by interwar pulp crime fiction, and the way its ideological valences were reconfigured in the postwar period by writers such as Patricia Highsmith and Chester Himes.

Fungbility, Labor, and Rhythm

In one sense, even to speak of individual authors of interwar pulp stories is misleading, given the way the industry organized its labor. Fungibility was a key principle operating across both the purchase of stories by magazines and the construction of the stories themselves. The use of pseudonyms was widespread, which makes it difficult for scholars to identify the authorship of some stories with confidence. Several writers often worked anonymously under a single house brand, tasked with maintaining commercially successful narrative formulas and styles. For the most part, name-recognition counted for little and writers performed their labor under conditions in some ways comparable to those of the industrial proletariat of the period. They were paid by the word, meaning that their labor accrued value according to its quantity rather than its quality. The use of the house brand system meant that individual writers became fungible: authors exhausted or disaffected by their work could simply be replaced by new ones able to continue under the same name. The work was highly routinized, in many cases simply stitched together from prefabricated, standardized parts that could be adjusted and reordered as necessary: a basic seduction scene here, a gunfight there, and an escape scene to conclude. Such parts could be reused with minor variations many times over, and not only in the same magazine or even genre. With a change of milieu, the same gun scene might work equally as well in a western as in a detective story. The seduction scene might do as nicely in a romance story as in a colonial adventure.

Though several pulp writers and contemporary scholars have emphasized the factory-like conditions of pulp labor, the comparison is in some ways a superficial one (Smith 2000, 21–23; Stanfield 2011, 46–47). Pulp writers, however they signaled identification with an imagined proletarian readership, were more likely to come from educated, white-collar backgrounds. This class difference meant that they were often required to perform what Erin Smith calls "class ventriloquism" if they wanted to appeal to a working-class readership, adopting and adapting the vernacular language of the streets and projecting its worldview (Smith 2000, 11). The tension between intellectual and physical work can be discovered in pulp detective stories themselves, where the detective figure must combine elements of physical prowess in his fight against criminality with astute mental powers enabling him to follow clues and interpret evidence.

Another key distinction between much working-class labor and that of the pulp writers was that the latter tended to be effectively self-employed, and therefore maintained a much greater degree of autonomy over the organization of their lives, working hours, and rate of work. Dashiell Hammett and Raymond Chandler were among a relatively small number of writers at the high end of the pulp industry for whom name-recognition did count, and for them this distinction is telling. Both made their decisions to start writing for the pulps following the demise of professional careers that required them to keep hours that got in the way of their serious drinking habits. The unpredictably episodic nature of their daily lives is mirrored in the rhythms of pulp labor, which, provided the writer had access to sufficient means of subsistence, allowed for intense periods of concentrated work, punctuated by periods freed up for carousing, hangovers, and other uses. Such discontinuous rhythms, it must be added, were eminently suited to the production of short fiction too, especially when it was structured by genre conventions that could reliably be taken up when needed in order to provide a framework for composition in units.

We gain a sense of the rhythms of pulp story production and the ideological tensions it produced in Hammett's letters from the 1920s, when he wrote for numerous pulp magazines but had formed a particular relationship with *Black Mask*. On July 2, 1927, for example, he reported having managed 2,000 words while "Blackmasking." The word count, he wrote, "isn't so bad, though I had hoped to knock out 5,000. However I've got tomorrow to spend on it but I know I won't be able to finish it" (Hammett 2001, 44). This tendency to measure pulp labor in words "knocked out" per day was typical, as was Hammett's writing target. In other letters, however, Hammett expressed the acute alienation he experienced as a result of participating in the pulp economy. As he told *Black Mask*'s editor, Phil Cody, in 1924:

> The trouble is, this sleuth of mine has degenerated into a meal-ticket. I liked him at first and used to enjoy putting him through his tricks; but recently I've fallen into the habit of bringing him out and running him around whenever the landlord, or the butcher or the grocer shows signs of nervousness. Some men can work like that, but I am not one of them. (26)

Here, Hammett distinguishes himself from writers better suited to the instrumentalist mindset required by a pulp career, and articulates a desire to make room for the unpredictable rhythms of imagination and inspiration: "Whenever, from now on, I get hold of a story that fits my sleuth, I shall put him to work, but I'm through with trying to run him on a schedule" (26). This dialectic between the routinized procedures of pulp writing, on the one hand, and the desire for autonomy, creativity, and self-direction, on the other, is a feature not only of pulp labor, but also of the stories' themes.

As Erin Smith argued in her pioneering study of hard-boiled detective fiction, the anxiety demonstrated by such stories over questions of autonomy was deeply gendered and raced (Smith 2000, 77). She suggests that up to a quarter of the readership of detective pulps was made up by women, while numbers of Black, Asian, and other non-white readers are harder to estimate (Smith 2000, 79). Nevertheless, as she claimed, the stories themselves interpellated their readership unambiguously as white and male. The ideology the stories produced with considerable consistency was backwards-orientated, mourning a mythical American past in which the imagined reader enjoyed uncontested social priority above women and people of color, forming "a labor aristocracy of skilled white men" (Smith 2000, 77). In the detective's confrontation with challenges issued by duplicitous *femmes fatales* and venal minority characters, and in his transcendence of these threats, hard-boiled detective stories both enacted and demanded the restoration of such a world. The priority of white men was made explicit in the frequent deployment of misogynist and racist stereotypes (Reddy 2002), but it also underpinned the genre's depiction of the labor of detection, and its peculiar obsession with the private eye. The P.I., as created by the genre's best-known writers, represented a finely balanced semi-autonomy; he was constantly obliged to negotiate the demands placed on him by either his clients or his agency bosses in relation to his own private ethics. This conflict between the imperative to get the job done on behalf of a callous white patriarchy and the P.I.'s freedom to choose his own methods became one of the genre's most durable and transmissible narrative features.

Economies of Style and Form: Raymond Chandler

If fungibility was the first general governing principle of pulp crime fiction, the other was economy: do as much as you can with as little as possible. The valorization of disciplined economy was part of the ideology of working-class masculinity that pervaded the crime pulps and distinguished itself from the perceived feminine incontinence of the slick middle-class magazines. The example of Raymond Chandler's work is an instructive one in this regard, because of the ways in which he observed some elements of economy and refused others. "Mine was of course a losing game, on the surface," he admitted in relation to his hard-boiled pulp stories, since "it was very poor pay for the work I put into them"

(Chandler 1981, 87). By his own account, his first one, "Blackmailers Don't Shoot" (1933), took him five months to write and earned him $180 (459). However uneconomical his use of labor time, though, Chandler's disposition toward genre itself prioritized economy above all else. "The thing is to squeeze the last drop out of the medium you have learned to use," he wrote to one correspondent (173).

In Tzvetan Todorov's classic formalist account of detective fiction, the genre is distinguished by the use it makes of the distinction between fabula and sjuzhet (Todorov 1977). In every detective story, Todorov reminds us, there are two narratives: that of the crime and that of its detection. We follow the narrative of detection in order to be able to reconstruct that of the crime. According to the genre's conventions, the end of the detective narrative constitutes a kind of return to the beginning, insofar as it completes for us the prior history of the crime. This structural characteristic led Franco Moretti to characterize popular detective fiction as an instrumentalized vehicle for narrative endings in which time and money is invested by the reader simply in return for the pay-off provided by the solution (Moretti 2005). For Moretti, this instrumentalization of plot for the benefit of mystery solutions means that the short story was necessarily the essential form for the detective story, whatever its actual length, since novelistic *bildung* and social development are forbidden by the genre's formula.

In the case of Chandler, as for Hammett and the other pulp crime writers from whom he learned his craft, the demands of the classic detective structure, with its fabula–sjuzhet distinction, were combined with the requirement for the detective himself to face danger and violence in the course of his pursuit of the solution to the mystery. In this sense, the stories displayed elements from the two nineteenth-century genres they drew upon most frequently – the action-packed adventures of the dime-novel tradition and the more cerebral sleuthing of the classic detective story tradition deriving from Edgar Allan Poe's Dupin tales and Arthur Conan Doyle's Sherlock Holmes series (Bedore 2013). It is possible, indeed, to read the disorientating plots of many pulp detective stories as produced by the formula's contradictory demand for regular scenes of sensationalist violence in addition to the unfolding of those two narrative strands – the story of the crime and the story of its investigation. This combination is what offers readers of pulp detective fiction a particular aesthetic, one akin to that produced by French Surrealism in the same period, with its dissonant juxtaposition of narrative units and sudden eruptions of violence.

In the work of Chandler, the observation of these strictures, and their intense compression, leads to some extraordinary effects, as a brief examination of "Blackmailers Don't Shoot" illustrates. The story is constituted by a series of set pieces, each centered around the private detective's confrontation with a different configuration of underworld characters in a specific Los Angeles location, and each containing its own explosion of violence, whether in the form of a gunfight or a beating. Whereas in Todorov's formulation, crime and investigation – fabula and sjuzhet – in their "purest form" are kept entirely separate, in "Blackmailer's Don't Shoot" the two interweave simultaneously, as the investigation creates more crimes, which lead in turn to more investigation (Todorov 1977, 44). Indeed, the case of blackmail with which the plot begins looks rather insignificant in comparison to the six murders it generates, all of them witnessed by Chandler's hard-boiled private detective, Mallory. The reconstructed fabula does not account for actions occurring anterior to the investigation, but rather takes on a different function: providing some kind of human logic to link up, retrospectively, the apparently arbitrary series of set pieces the reader has just navigated. It must be said that Chandler treats the fabula component of his narrative structures with bravura disregard, offering several competing versions at different junctures and even commenting ironically on the process in self-reflexive fashion. Mallory offers one to the criminal behind the blackmail operation, only to then admit, "that's the tale from the outside, without notes. The notes make it funnier – and a hell of a lot dirtier" (Chandler 1995, 42). After concluding the second version "with notes," he remarks, "sweet set-up, don't you think so?" His adversary replies, "A bit loose in places" (43).

The joke, as Chandler wrote in one letter, is that he was "fundamentally rather uninterested in plot" (Chandler 1981, 87). In his dream-slow gunfights, heavily stylized vernacular, lyrical evocations of Los Angeles' dreadfully empty nightscapes, and above all his unsettling, lingering descriptions of dead and dying bodies, Chandler attempted rather to squeeze out of pulp crime the quality he called "richness of texture" (87). His aim was to precipitate affective responses in his readers, a matter of "imparting the right emotion to the right nerves." Hammett and Dorothy L. Sayers, Chandler went on, "came close," but ultimately "didn't feel it" (173). This leads us, then, to one of pulp crime's paradoxes: that the strictures of the genre's formulas afforded a certain freedom to escape its commercial logic. So long as one could manage on earnings of $180 for five months' work, and was willing to provide sufficient action as well as a solution to the mystery, one was free to experiment and develop one's personal style. To put this another way, as Chandler did in a 1949 letter: "[A]lthough the average story in the *Black Mask* was not too good, there was the possibility of writing them very much better without hurting their chances of being read" (86).

Chandler admitted that he was incapable of discarding any material, preferring to jam episodes and scenarios into his stories, even if "this resulted in some rather start[l]ing oddities of construction" (87). The deep strangeness and absurdity of his pulp work's serial narrative construction, and the faint echoes of the modernist avant-garde one finds in it, are due in large part to the idiosyncratic way he fulfilled the narrative demands of the genre while refusing to take them seriously. This effect is replicated in his early novels, too, only on a grander scale. In another gesture of economy, his leap from pulp stories to Alfred Knopf's prestigious crime novel series was made by recycling several of his *Black Mask* "novelettes": *The Big Sleep* (1939) interwove the plots of "Killer in the Rain" (1935) and "The Curtain" (1936). This process, which Chandler called "cannibalizing," saw him find inventive ways to run the plots in parallel and draw them together where necessary (MacShane 1976, 67–68). *The Big Sleep* takes the *femmes fatales* from the earlier pulp stories and makes them sisters. Carmen retains her first name and her involvement in a pornography racket from "Killer in the Rain," but she is also given a murder to commit. Mrs. O'Mara, who appears only as a framing device in "The Curtain," becomes Carmen's sister Vivian, and her plot function expanded greatly to include a love interest with Marlowe, *The Big Sleep*'s private eye. There are, then, two main mystery plots to be resolved by Marlowe in the novel: the missing person case centered on Rusty Reagan, which comes from "The Curtain," and the blackmail case centered on Geiger, which comes from "Killer in the Rain." The cannibalization process that produced *The Big Sleep* thus creates sister plots as well as sister characters, accounting for the ramification of complexity and the difficulty with which many readers have negotiated its labyrinthine narrative structure. The two pulp stories are reused almost in their entirety and account for approximately half of *The Big Sleep*, with some passages lifted wholesale with little revision beyond the changing of character names. The other half is made up partly of freshly created episodes extending the detective's interactions with police and the two sisters, and partly from elaborations of imagery, description, and dialogue already existing in the stories. As a result, some of the lean tautness which was sometimes fetishized in pulp crime magazines is sacrificed for augmented atmosphere, richness of imagery, and character interaction.

Pulp Crime Legacies: Highsmith and Himes

By the end of World War II the great era of pulp crime magazines as a distinctive mode of cultural production had come to an end. Their legacy, however, lived on as elements of the story forms they cultivated were grafted onto new hosts, including the next generation of mystery magazines and the cheap paperbacks produced by publishers such as Dell and Signet. The mystery plot-type, featuring the fabula–sjuzhet distinction partially preserved in the pulp crime stories of Hammett and Chandler, continued to be popular, but in the burgeoning paperback industry it began to be replaced by the suspense plot. In this plot-type, fabula and sjuzhet effectively collapse into one another and the reader's interest is sustained by anticipation of future action (corpses, crimes, the apprehension of the criminal), rather than in discovering the causes of an anterior crime (Todorov 1977, 47). Fiction with mystery plots accounted for 50 percent of the entire paperback market in 1945, but by 1955 that figure had dropped to just 13 percent (Haut 1995, 5–6). The period saw the arrival of new sub-genres of crime fiction that took the unrestrained violence, misogyny, cruelty, and sensationalism of hard-boiled pulp and drove it to further extremes, while treating the mystery plot as expendable. Increasingly, readers of crime fiction became interested in stories told from the perspective of the criminal rather than the detective, which removed the "whodunit" aspect of the form and often drew on crude, popularized versions of the Freudian unconscious or repressive ego.

An important element of continuity between the classic hard-boiled detective stories of the interwar period and the pulp fiction of the 1940s and 1950s was their shared self-positioning as the antithesis to genteel American culture, figured as feminine, and more specifically to the didactic ideal of literature as uplift. The interwar pulps had taken every opportunity to sneer at their rivals, the middle-class, "effeminate," "slick" magazines (Smith 2000, 26–27). As postwar pulp fiction reveled in fantasies of wanton violence and aggressive masculinity, it was consciously rejecting the idea that reading habits provided a route into middle-class manners, respectability, or intellectual concerns (Haut 1995, 6–11). The irony, however, was that the fantasies of working-class masculinity in the immediate postwar were projected against a background of dramatic shifts in the material class structure of American society. The expansion of the middle class in this period, driven by increased access to education, high employment levels, and increasing wages, meant that perceived class antagonisms are more accurately considered as a part of a white-collar culture war fought by lone, alienated men against the conservative respectability politics and conformity mandated by the Eisenhower administration.

The clearest expression of how pulp crime registered the shifting dynamic in class and gender relations in the postwar period is to be found in the work of Patricia Highsmith. While she studied highbrow modernists such as Marcel Proust and Franz Kafka assiduously as an adolescent in the 1930s, she also read less respectable authors, such as James M. Cain. Cain's tales of illicit sex and murder among the itinerant, precarious lives of the working classes in the Depression era, most notoriously *The Postman Always Rings Twice* (1934), had thrilled and horrified the reading public in equal measure. Tellingly, it was Cain and not Proust that Highsmith identified in one journal entry as "a kind of genius" (Wilson 2003, 111). She wrote her early fiction while employed as a writer for a comics publisher in 1940s New York under pulp conditions, getting paid between four and seven dollars for each page, creating what she called "insane stories . . . . It was like grinding out two Grade B movies per day. I had to come up with two ideas per day" (Wilson 2003, 95). Highsmith's career-long attempt to marry art and commerce in her writing, as well as her engagement with the pulp tradition, can be said to emerge from this set of conditions. Best known for the "Ripley novels," she also consistently produced short stories, something largely overlooked by critics, even after a new surge of recent critical interest. Highsmith herself lamented the demise of the all-fiction short story magazines in the postwar world, but found venues for her suspense crime stories in publications such as *Ellery Queen's Mystery Magazine* (Highsmith 2001, 28). Evincing a view comparable to Chandler's of the pulps, she located the value of her genre in the way that it afforded space and freedom for the writer beyond the specific demands of its formula: "[T]he beauty of the suspense genre is that a writer can write profound thoughts and have some sections without physical action if he wishes to, because the framework is an essentially lively story" (3).

Highsmith's suspense stories from the 1950s and 1960s were not anachronistic pulp fictions in themselves, but rather self-conscious dialogues with them. Her characteristic strategy was to take the violent masculine dream-fulfillment of the crime pulps and to disarm it by presenting it as just that: a fantasy world sustained against the drab reality of white-collar life. The interwar hard-boiled pulps had consistently advanced claims to the superiority of their tough, realistic approach to urban crime over the stories confected by the effeminate slick magazines. In Highsmith's work, this tough realism is revealed as what it always was:

the expression of barely coherent libidinal impulses toward domination and possession, which increase in negative correlation with their protagonists' diminishing social standing. At the beginning of "Music to Die By" (1965), for example, a divorced, middle-aged post office worker named Aaron Wechsler writes in his diary that he has murdered Roger Hoolihan, a fellow employee, by smashing his head with a hammer and hiding his body in the closet. Hoolihan, unlike Wechsler, has a happy family, "with a boy in college and another in high school. Plus a wife" (Highsmith 2002b, 244). When Wechsler goes to work the next day, however, the murdered colleague is alive and well. Later he stabs another co-worker to death with a carving knife only to find him irritatingly unaffected the following day. "It's strange, the walking dead in the post office," he remarks to his diary (248). In the story's twist, the same men really are killed by a package bomb in the post office that is entirely unrelated to Wechsler, who nevertheless claims responsibility for the crime and happily goes to jail for it.

"Music to Die By" mirrors "A Dangerous Hobby" (1960), in which an unassuming vacuum-cleaner salesman, Andrew Foster, unhappily married to a woman who privileges her own job above paying attention to him, is driven by a compulsion to date middle-class women under an assumed identity and to steal small objects from them before disappearing from their lives. The women he targets all work in creative industries and the objects he steals seem to represent their cultural tastes: a dress designer's silver ruler, an actress's wristwatch, or a violinist's necklace. Plainly enough, Foster's deceptions are intended as displaced aggression against his uncaring wife, as well as revenge on the new generation of independent, professional women. His fantasies of power over these women, however, are punctured when he is caught out by chance and forced into a shameful confrontation with one of them. Foster responds with an uncontrolled outburst of violence and murders her. In a reversal of "Music to Die By," however, when Foster hands himself in, the police refuse to believe he is the killer. Another of his victims is called to identify him but she is unable to recall either his act of petty theft or his unremarkable face. The facade of his life – punctual, reliable, conformist – is impenetrable to the police; he is too ordinary, "a sensation seeker. We get a lot of 'em like this" (Highsmith 2002a, 294). In the protagonists of these two stories, Highsmith allegorizes the imagined pulp reader in the anonymous fantasist: a misogynous sensation-seeker full of class *ressentiment*, hiding behind his ordinary life and incapable of overcoming his impotence to assert his individuality.

If Highsmith's suspense stories offer one example of pulp crime's afterlife in the postwar literary field, another is provided by Chester

Himes. Highsmith wrote with an acute consciousness of the deep misogyny built into the pulp tradition, even while she was drawn to its conventions. Comparably, Himes's engagement with pulp crime paid tribute to its early practitioners while fundamentally re-evaluating and rewriting its racial investments. As with Highsmith, the pulps had been an integral part of Himes's literary development. He had read Hammett in *Black Mask* while serving time in Ohio State Penitentiary for armed robbery in the early 1930s (Jackson 2017, 92). But he never published in pulp magazines, partly, we must surmise, because throughout the interwar period there were simply no pulp venues for available to Black writers (Earle 2009, 123). Instead, Himes made his name writing short stories for *Esquire* magazine, set up in 1933 by Arnold Gingrich as a new title built around rugged masculinity, an attempt to bridge the gap between the cheap, disreputable pulps and the respectable middle-class magazines. Himes's stories for *Esquire* were built around his experience of incarceration, and provided an early version of the type of the confessional, low-life fiction that became popular in the postwar years. The influence of the pulps is to be found not only in the extreme violence of these stories, but also in their general investment in affective excess of all kinds, from unrestrained rage to inconsolable sorrow. Following the success of his debut novel, *If He Hollers Let Him Go* (1945), Himes became pigeonholed as a Black protest writer in the mold of his friend Richard Wright, but he never truly lost his investment in pulpy excess and melodrama, even when creating work that was categorized as social realism.

His 1946 story "One More Way to Die" provides an instructive example of the kind of genre hybridity Himes worked with in this period, combining elements of pulp crime with anti-racist protest themes. The story was published in *Negro Stories*, a short-lived magazine for which Himes served on the editorial board. *Negro Stories* was created with the expressed intention of gathering writers on the Black left ready to engage with contemporary themes of fascism and racism (Mullen 1996). Its ideology of uplift and education could not have been further from the proudly anti-didactic stance taken by the interwar pulps, and yet Himes's story deploys the type of comic-book violence and street vernacular more familiar from *Black Mask* than from realist fiction. It is narrated in death by a Black man immediately after he has been murdered by racist cops following a bar brawl in which he accidentally hurts a white woman. The description of the knife-fight in particular recalls the non-stop action of Dashiell Hammett translated into Black street vernacular, and the absurdity of its dead narrator breaks the conventions of midcentury realism. But the pathos Himes attempts to generate in the story's conclusion seems genuine, especially in the context of its publication in *Negro Stories*, with its anti-racist mission. The author takes clear aim at the dehumanizing brutality of the police when he has his narrator beg for mercy while he is being killed at the story's melodramatic conclusion.

The final sentence of "One More Way to Die" provides an entry point to Himes's vernacular philosophy of the pulps: "The last thing I thought as I lay there on the goddamned ground and died was 'It just ain't no goddamned sense in you white folks killing me'" (Himes 1990, 380). For Himes, as he explained in his autobiography, "if one lives in a country where racism is held valid and practiced in all ways of life, eventually, no matter if one is a racist or a victim, one comes to feel the absurdity of life" (Himes 1976, 1). Himes found in the violent excesses of pulp crime an expression of this absurdity, in which there "just ain't no goddamned sense." When the veteran French Surrealist Marcel Duhamel commissioned the series of detective novels that would make Himes's name a second time in the 1950s and 1960s, he told him to model his work on Hammett, "the greatest writer who ever lived." Exhorting him to write in classic pulp crime fashion with pure action and no description, he assured Himes, "don't worry about it making sense" (Himes 1976, 102).

One can hardly imagine the madcap violence and caper of Himes's Harlem Cycle without the tradition established by the crime pulps Himes had read in jail twenty-five years earlier. In 1973, looking back on his writing career, Himes affirmed the uncompromising simplicity of the American detective tradition: "It's just plain and simple violence in narrative form" (Himes 1995, 47), linking the genre to what he saw as the United States' exceptional history of violence, from settler colonialism and slavery to the Revolutionary and Civil Wars, from the massacres of Native Americans and Chinese immigrants all the way to Vietnam. In his potent view, the pulp crime story emerges finally as a kind of grotesque master narrative for the nation itself, emerging relentlessly from its ongoing histories of domination and ultimately bound to them as their essential literary expression.

Work Cited

Bedore, Pamela. 2013. *Dime Novels and the Roots of American Detective Fiction*. Basingstoke, UK: Palgrave.

Chandler, Raymond. 1981. *The Selected Letters of Raymond Chandler*. Ed. Frank MacShane. London: Jonathan Cape.

　　1995. "Blackmailers Don't Shoot," in *Stories and Early Novels*. Ed. Frank MacShane, 1–51. New York: Library of America.

Earle, David M. 2009. *Re-Covering Modernism: Pulps, Paperbacks, and the Prejudice of Form*. Farnham, UK: Ashgate.

Hammett, Dashiell. 2001. *Selected Letters of Dashiell Hammett, 1921-1960*. Eds. Richard Layman and Julie M. Rivett. Oxford: Counterpoint.

Haut, Woody. 1995. *Pulp Culture: Hardboiled Fiction and the Cold War*. London: Serpent's Tail.

Hefner, Brooks E. 2017. "Pulp Magazines," in *American Literature in Transition, 1920-1930*. Ed. Ichiro Takayoshi, 434–448. Cambridge, UK: Cambridge University Press.

Highsmith, Patricia. 2001. *Plotting and Writing Suspense Fiction*. New York: St. Martin's Griffin.

2002a. "A Dangerous Hobby," in *Nothing That Meets the Eye: The Uncollected Stories of Patricia Highsmith*, 283–295. New York: Norton.

2002b. "Music to Die By," in *Nothing That Meets the Eye: The Uncollected Stories of Patricia Highsmith*, 241–252. New York: Norton.

Himes, Chester. 1976. *My Life of Absurdity: The Autobiography of Chester Himes, Volume II*. New York: Doubleday.

1990. "One More Way to Die," in *The Collected Stories of Chester Himes*, 375–380. London: Allison and Busby.

1995. "My Man Himes: An Interview with Chester Himes." Interview by John A. Williams, in *Conversations with Chester Himes*. Ed. Michel Fabre and Robert E. Skinner, 29–82. Jackson: Mississippi University Press.

Jackson, Lawrence P. 2017. *Chester B. Himes: A Biography*. New York: Norton.

Levine, Caroline. 2017. *Forms: Whole, Rhythm, Hierarchy, Network*. Princeton, NJ: Princeton University Press.

MacShane, Frank. 1976. *The Life of Raymond Chandler*. London: Jonathan Cape.

McCann, Sean. 2000. *Gumshoe America: Hard-Boiled Crime Fiction and the Rise and Fall of New Deal Liberalism*. Durham, NC: Duke University Press.

Moretti, Franco. 2005 [1983]. "Clues," in *Signs Taken for Wonders: On the Sociology of Literary Forms*, Trans. Susan Fischer, David Forgacs, and David Miller, 130–156. London: Verso.

Mullen, Bill. 1996. "Popular Fronts: Negro Story Magazine and the African American Literary Response to World War II," *African American Review* 30.1 (Spring): 5–15.

Reddy, Maureen T. 2002. *Traces, Codes, and Clues: Reading Race in Crime Fiction*. New Brunswick, NJ: Rutgers University Press.

Smith, Erin A. 2000. *Hard-Boiled: Working Class Readers and Pulp Magazines*. Philadelphia: Temple University Press.

Stanfield, Peter. 2011. *Maximum Movies and Pulp Fictions: Film Culture and the Worlds of Samuel Fuller, Mickey Spillane, and Jim Thompson*. New Brunswick, NJ: Rutgers University Press.

Todorov, Tzvetan. 1977. "The Typology of Detective Fiction," in *The Poetics of Prose*. Trans. Richard Howard, 42–49. Oxford: Blackwell.

Wilson, Andrew. 2003. *Beautiful Shadow: A Life of Patricia Highsmith*. London: Bloomsbury.

Love What You Do
Neoliberalism, Emotional Labor, and the Short Story as a Service

Lee Konstantinou

George Saunders's Emotional Labor

In "Sea Oak," a short story first published in 1998 in the *New Yorker* and collected in *Pastoralia* (2000), George Saunders creates a funny, unsettling portrait of the changing composition of American labor. The story's narrator works at a Hooters-like, aviation-themed restaurant-cum-strip club called Joysticks, where male waitstaff dress in pilot uniforms and strip for female customers. Their penises "never show," though they do wear uncomfortable Penile Simulators (95). These waiters are dubbed Pilots and ranked by guests as "Knockout, Honeypie, Adequate, or Stinker" (92). At the start of the story, the narrator's colleague, Lloyd Betts, is fired. He has "put on weight," his hair has "gone thin," and he has been ranked as a "Stinker" (91). The restaurant manager, Mr. Frendt, explains that "[n]o one is an island in terms of being thought cute forever, and so today we must say good-bye to our friend Lloyd." "We give [Lloyd] a round of applause," the narrator reports, "and Frendt gives him a Farewell Pen and the contents of his locker in a trash bag and out he goes." Our narrator, fortunately, is safe for now. After all, he is "a solid Honeypie/Adequate," and "heading home with forty bucks cash" (92).

By placing male waiters in positions typically occupied by women, "Sea Oak" highlights the so-called feminization of the workforce in the neoliberal period (Milkman 1987; Standing 1989). The term "feminization" describes the economic fact of increased labor force participation by women, as well as the changing character of work for all workers. Since the 1970s, new kinds of jobs have gained prominence, and existing jobs have been reconfigured to emphasize different skills. The normative American worker – a white male breadwinner earning a family wage – has become a historical relic. The new job market valorizes workers who become "entrepreneurs of the self" (Foucault 2010), who develop their human capital, who are adaptable, flexible, versatile, and autonomous, and who possess *"intuition* and *talent"* (Boltanski and Chiapello 2018, 113). Yet the actual neoliberal world of work arguably looks more like a George Saunders story. It is a world of pink-collar service workers who, as Annie McClanahan suggests, are driven by a fear of becoming "no longer worth capital's investment at all" (2019, 121). These workers are asked to recalibrate their personality and motivation on demand, engaging in what Arlie Russell Hochschild has called "emotional labor," which she defines as "the management of feeling to create a publicly observable facial and bodily display" (2012, 7). If the pink-collar worker is an entrepreneur of the self, this is true to the degree that she must become a manager of her affects, emotions, and dispositions if she hopes to receive a wage.

Representations of this neoliberal world of work dominate Saunders's fiction. His novella "CivilWarLand in Bad Decline" (1992) takes place in a theme park for Civil War reenactments. "The Wavemaker Falters" (1993) features a character who operates a wave pool and whose negligence leads to the death of a boy. "Downtrodden Mary's Failed Campaign of Terror" (1992) centers on a woman who works in a museum with exhibits such as see-through cows and pickled babies. The novella "Bounty" (1995) spotlights a medieval-themed amusement park and a mutant protagonist who has claws where his toenails should be. Another story, "My Chivalric Fiasco" (2011), is also set in a medieval theme park. The caveman impersonators of "Pastoralia" (2000) spend more time writing performance reviews of one another than interacting with guests. And "The Semplica Girl Diaries" (2012) tells the story of a group of girls, trafficked from various countries, who are used as lawn ornaments, hung from a microline through the brain, in suburban yards, for the pleasure of middle-class Americans.

These stories are set in near-future or alternate-present workplaces, in societies dominated by violence and exploitation, and employ a style that mimics the incoherent thinking of telemarketers, middle managers, and social isolates. Some critics describe them as postmodern parables which explore the logic of societies of image, spectacle, and simulation (Pogell 2011). When viewed with neoliberalism in mind, however, themes traditionally associated with postmodernism take on a different hue. If Jean Baudrillard once alerted readers to the orders of simulation that ramify through a hyperreal space such as Disneyland, authors conscious of neoliberalism notice something more: that Disneyland is a place of employment and that its employees are service workers whose job is to manage, produce, and distribute affects.

In this chapter, I discuss points of contact between the contemporary American short story and service work through the analysis of three collections: Charles Yu's *Sorry Please Thank You* (2012); Nana Kwame Adjei-Brenyah's *Friday Black* (2018); and Mary South's *You Will Never Be Forgotten* (2020). Published in prestigious magazines (*The New Yorker*, *Esquire*, *Guernica*) to widespread critical acclaim, these writers represent a major tendency within the contemporary American short story, operating in an aesthetic mode inspired by the example of Saunders. Their collections examine the nature of pink-collar labor and thus further realize an implication within Saunders's thematic: the short story writer is also a kind of pink-collar worker, one whose job is to manage the emotions of the reader – and their own.

On the one hand, these writers hope to critique the contemporary world of work. On the other, in an economy fueled by emotional labor, the contemporary writer cannot help but notice similarities between the work they do and the work their service-worker characters do (if they are lucky). Discovering they are enmeshed in a regime of emotional labor, the short story writer seeks literary forms that might make sense of that regime from the inside. They find themselves writing what I will call "the Short Story as a Service" – a service that suggests ambivalence about the power of fiction to offer succor to the neoliberal reader.

The Short Story as a Service

American short story writers have long been conscious of themselves as workers in a literary market, charged with the job of arousing specific emotions in readers. The canonical articulation of this awareness is, of course, Edgar Allan Poe's writings on composition. In his 1842 review of Hawthorne's *Twice-Told Tales* in *Graham's Magazine*, Poe argues that the writer of tales should pursue "totality," by which he means not Aristotelian unities of time, place, and action – Poe discounts the importance of these – but *unities of form, affect, and reading experience* (298). In his 1846 essay "The Philosophy of Composition," he suggests that the narrative poem should, likewise, find a length long enough to fully develop a single effect but short enough to be read in one sitting. Poe instructs the American writer of tales to put form and audience into a felicitous relation. Working backward from effect to form, the tale-writer offers an affective service to the reader, matching the tale's form to the reader's needs and limitations.

Whether or not it reflects Poe's prescriptions, an important tradition in the history of the US short story explores the relation of form and audience. Some stories in this tradition turn the form–audience relation into their subject matter. Hawthorne's "Alice Doane's Appeal" (1835), for example, figures the situation of the (failed) writer of fantastic tales whose job requires him to break through to an uninterested, forgetful reading public (represented, in this story, by two women who are initially indifferent to his lurid tale of murder and magic). Such reflexivity can be seen too in the most canonical short story of labor, "Bartleby, the Scrivener" (1853). Melville's story ends by aligning the withdrawal and mysterious anomie of its titular character with his prior employment in the dead letter office of the postal service. Bartleby's failure to communicate makes the narrator's conscious of *his own* inability to tell Bartleby's story. "I believe that no materials exist for a full and satisfactory biography of this man," writes the lawyer, describing this as "an irreparable loss to literature" (2016, 17). The narrator's failure to understand Bartleby is, in turn, his failure to successfully create a prose composition with a single, totalizing effect. Bartleby's practice of refusal becomes not only a crisis for labor–capital relations but a grave interruption of the tale's ability to satisfy the reader.

Many prominent writers came to loathe that they had to perform any sort of service for the dimwitted mass reader, associating this duty with the detestable demands of the commercial magazine market. As Kasia Boddy observes, "[t]he scale of short-story production and consumption a hundred years ago is hard for us to imagine today, as increasingly few general magazines regularly feature fiction" (2010, 9). But when the commercial magazine market was booming, circa 1900, the short story was considered, in the words of James T. Farrell, a "kind of literary pimp" for advertisers (quoted in Boddy 2010, 10). Many modernists saw writing short stories as tantamount to prostitution in the service of bankrolling their novels. Henry James once complained to his agent that *Harper's* had asked him for a "Tale in 5,000 words – one of their terrible little shortest of short stories," which led him to "innumerable repeated chemical reductions and condensations" to meet the length requirements (quoted in Horn 1996, 5, 21). Lamenting his inability to complete *Tender is the Night* (1934), F. Scott Fitzgerald, in a letter to Ernest Hemingway, commented that "the *Post* now pay the old whore $4000 a screw ... because she's mastered the 40 positions." Hemingway replied: "The stories aren't whoring, they're just bad judgment – you could have and can make enough to live on writing novels. You damned fool. Go on and write the novel" (quoted in

Churchwell 2005, 122). And William Faulkner famously raged against having to write short fiction to subsidize his novelistic pursuits. While working on *Light in August* (1932), he begged his publisher, Harrison Smith, for money. "[I]t's either this," Faulkner wrote, "or put the novel aside and go whoring again with short stories" (quoted in Carothers 1992, 38).

For the writers I discuss, however, it is not the commercial market but the creative writing workshop that is the predominant scene of form-oriented training. Despite its distance from Poe and commercial magazine culture, the post-1945 MFA world gives rise to many of the same questions tale-writers grappled with, albeit at a higher cultural register. The workshop-forged short story is partly valued because it is short enough to be read and critiqued in one class session – and is often judged in terms of its ability to craft a single aesthetic effect. In this milieu, the short story becomes a technology of what Mark McGurl calls "shame management" (2009, 300). The dialectic of pride and shame felt by the (sometimes lower-middle-class) creative writing student works itself out in a scene of anxious self-disclosure and painful peer judgment. MFA-schooled writers of stories strive not to embarrass themselves, but it is precisely the embarrassing elements of their background or experience that they may be most rewarded for exposing to view. The short story must therefore find a formal means by which to incorporate shame while maintaining critical distance from the represented materials.

Entering the postwar workshop thus represents a fraught kind of upward mobility. Writing about menial laborers, construction workers, and abusive white-collar bosses marks the writer's *difference* from those workers. Though not an MFA-trained writer, John Updike uses the vernacular style of his most influential story, "A&P" (1961), initially to mark his distance from the story's observant but verbally infelicitous grocery clerk protagonist, Sammy. When Sammy quits his supermarket job, Updike emphasizes the protagonist's disidentification with his work, suggesting the teenager has achieved a nascent critical perspective on American consumer culture and midcentury mass conformity. Dignity and purpose arise not out of work but out of critical distance *from* work. When the narrator of Mary Gaitskill's "Secretary" (1988) feels an affinity for a group of construction workers and thinks "sentimental thoughts about workers and the decency of unthinking toil," we do see a kinship between (blue-collar) construction work and (white- or pink-collar) secretarial work, albeit one that reproduces a traditionally gendered division of labor (2009, 139). But we also understand that the work of the short story writer is anything but unthinking, even if Gaitskill's decidedly unsenti-mental minimalist style artfully conceals the labor of her thought. The careful work of the writer and the "bland ugliness" of the work of the secretary are not, ultimately, alike (139). In short, postwar writers often told stories of waged work to emphasize how writing short fiction is *not* waged work and to distinguish the short story from the commodity.

The contemporary Short Story as a Service reconfigures these concerns. In an age of rising socioeconomic precarity, including within the university, the assumed separation of worker and writer, of story and commodity, does not have the same resonance it once did. Yet we have not simply returned to the world of the commercial magazine market – which, indeed, no longer exists in the way it once did. In the era of the Short Story as a Service, "shame management" comes to seem not only like something that writers of short stories do, but also like just another description of the emotional labor that service workers do every day. When George Saunders recounts his job history, telling us that he worked as "a doorman, a roofer, a convenience store clerk, and a slaughterhouse worker," he is not just emphasizing how his work experience taught him something about the depredations of capitalism (quoted in Boddy 2017, 1). This recollection is also offered, I would suggest, as an explanation for his priorities *as a writer*. That is, manual labor and service labor function as aesthetic training. Unlike their predecessors, writers of the Short Story as a Service cannot disidentify themselves from the world of work that their stories depict.

Charles Yu's Business of Bad Feeling

Charles Yu's *Sorry Please Thank You* (2012) features stories set at service-oriented workplaces. These stories reproduce the generic play found in Saunders's work but expand their geographical and conceptual range. They are also more metafictional, linking the work of the story writer with the emotional labor of the service worker. The first story in the collection, "Standard Loneliness Package," is set in a call center that specializes in affect-transfer. The protagonist's job is literally to feel other people's pain – both physical and emotional – for a wage. Call-center workers in India provide the service of bearing the unwanted pain of wealthy Europeans and Americans. Yu's narrator explains that "some genius in Delhi had figured out a transfer protocol to standardize and packetize all different kinds of experiences" (6). The development of this protocol births the "business of bad feeling," which allows customers to avoid "almost any part of life" (6). Yu's story registers the global division of labor and the maldistribution of caring work and other kinds of labor. The Global South absorbs the North's ugly feelings by turning affect into a standardized and tradable commodity.

After the protagonist has a failed relationship with a coworker, his ex-girlfriend pays for an opportunity for him to inhabit her perspective, using up "everything she had saved" (31). The narrator laments that his ex-girlfriend is unable to experience his experience of her feelings, that she cannot see herself from his perspective. "If only she could see herself through my eyes. If only she could see herself through my eyes looking through her eyes .... I want to believe in her, believe inside her. Believe hard enough inside of her that it somehow seeps through" (32). The story ends in a reflexive twist. "I don't know if I am her thinking of me, or if I am me thinking of her, her heart, my heart, aching, or its opposite, or if maybe, right at this moment, there is no difference" (33). Though the technology of emotion-transfer is initially depicted as a means of exploitation, in this final epiphanic moment the narrator and his ex-girlfriend almost merge. The "business of bad feeling," a phrase that might well describe the business of the contemporary writer, offers real opportunities for connection and satisfaction.

"First Person Shooter" is set in a big-box store called WorldMart, which is open twenty-four hours a day, 365 days a year and is "the size of three city blocks," the "[b]iggest store in the human world" (35). The story again highlights important formal resonances between the short story and service labor. Exemplifying the Short Story as a Service, Yu builds a magical realist or mildly science fictional setting, deploying the logic of genre spatially. These are stories, as we have seen, often set in theme parks or big-box stores, mini-worlds that have their own specialized languages and localized logics. The fantastical elements of these mini-worlds – their technical jargon, their commitment to world-building, their intense concern with staging magical experiences – come to seem in these stories like natural extensions of the euphemisms that redescribe contemporary service work. Workers become Cast Members, Customer Service Ninjas, Sandwich Artists, and so on – creating experiences for Customers, Clients, or Guests, who come from an outside world where different genre logics reign.

In "First Person Shooter," the self-enclosed logic of theme parks and retail environments is stretched out, threatening to encompass all social relations. Yet as "[b]iggest store in the human world" suggests, there's a *nonhuman world* yet to be assimilated. And that nonhuman world promptly intercedes. In a plot development that alludes to George

A. Romero's *Dawn of the Dead* (1978), a zombie appears in the store during the night shift. Unlike Romero, with his allegorical critique of consumerism, Yu seems more interested in the situation of the human workers at the mall rather than the zombies who threaten to invade it. The zombie, described as a Pretty Zombie Lady, poses no threat – though her body has a habit of falling to pieces – but her feelings are hurt when she sees a demo of the video game *House of the Dead 2* in the electronics section. Service workers must keep even the walking dead satisfied.

"Yeoman" takes similar ideas beyond the scale of the planet, featuring the story of an expendable yeoman serving on a starship who worries he is going to die on an away mission. His worry is well-founded. His "[d]uties and responsibilities" are to "assist in collection of soil and vegetation samples" and to "be prepared to die for no good reason" (163). The job is not so much *to die* as to "be prepared to die," that is, to manage his fear of death in the service of the mission. When he confronts the captain, the captain explains that yeomen have to die because "it makes for a more interesting report . . . . [I]t's really freaking boring out here. And if Central Command ever realizes that, they'll cut my budget and I'll end up sitting behind a desk. So I need stuff to happen" (167). The story aligns the job of *being a minor character* with being a service worker and the job of *being an author* with being a boss or owner.

This same allegory drives another story, "Hero Absorbs Major Damage," which features a character in a fantasy-style roleplaying video game who comes to realize that he is a character in a video game. If minor characters are aligned with service workers, the author reluctantly discovers he has an ethical relation to these figures. It is the author, after all, who subjects his characters to death to make his stories interesting or invents call-center workers who suffer for the edification of readers in the Global North. Yet as a responsible denizen of the literary world, Yu feels a duty to empathetically inhabit the consciousness of these characters, to occupy their understanding from the inside. This feeling of responsibility, I would argue, explains how Yu's brand of metafiction emerges, perhaps necessarily, from his choice of subject matter. By representing globalized service work, he finds himself identifying both as owner or manager and front-line worker. He does not know if he is himself (thinking of his characters) or his characters (thinking of him), but he suspects there might not be much of a difference.

Nana Kwama Adjei-Brenyah's Herculean Labors

Nana Kwama Adjei-Brenyah's debut collection *Friday Black* (2018) squarely centers on poorly paid, front-line service workers, yet many of his stories have fantastical, self-reflexive elements that dramatize worker fantasies of joining upper management. Adjei-Brenyah was an MFA student at Syracuse who studied with Saunders, and *Friday Black* replicates many of the themes and settings of Saunders's fiction. The stories are set in theme parks and retail spaces, but Adjei-Brenyah – more than Saunders – explores how race and class intersect in the workplace. "Zimmer Land," for example, tells the story of a vigilante justice–oriented theme park where guests participate in simulated murders redolent of the murder of Trayvon Martin by George Zimmerman in 2012. "Zimmer" is not a reference to Zimmerman within the story but the last name of the park owner. The protagonist, Isaiah, is a Black man who works at the theme park and wears an "exoskeleton battle suit" (85). His job is to play a "young man who is up to no good or nothing at all" (86), and to engage with white guests primed to confront him and shoot him dead, again and again.

"Zimmer Land" highlights another formal resonance between service work and the short story. In service-oriented jobs, each interaction with a guest becomes an episode. The form of such labor thus harmonizes with the episodic form of the story. One encounters a guest and performs an emotionally fraught service for that guest – or fails to perform that service – and then a new guest arrives soon thereafter. Beyond this dynamic involving guests/customers, these stories also make managers or competitive coworkers into antagonists. Less often do we meet an owner. At other times, characters struggle with their own conflicted desire for self-improvement; they invest in the logic of the workplace, accepting its terms, only to discover that those very investments harm them.

The protagonist of "Zimmer Land" eventually joins the "Creative" team that scripts attractions. This seems at first to be a promotion, but it becomes clear that the purpose of incorporating Isaiah into Creative is to make him complicit in scripting the park's racist narratives. "Zimmer Land" is therefore not only a story that condemns racist American cultures of simulation and spectacle but also one that asks whether and to what degree the Black creative, who is also a service worker charged with managing his own emotions and the emotions of white audiences, ought to join the culture industry that produces such spectacles.

Other stories in *Friday Black* emphasize the affective component of work and find further commonalities between the situation of the service worker and the creative writer of short stories. "In Retail," "How to Sell a Jacket as Told by IceKing," and "Friday Black" dramatize these commonalities by directly representing retail workers. All are set at the Prominent Mall, and each stages quests for professional accomplishment tied to the capacity to perform affective labor. "Friday Black" takes place on Black Friday, and customers are (as in Yu's story) represented as zombie-like in their frenzied determination to buy discounted clothes and electronics. Our narrator is one of the biggest sellers in the mall, so skilled he can understand the degraded language of these zombified customers. "Ever since that first time, since the bite, I can speak Black Friday. Or I can understand it, at least. Not fluently, but well enough. I have some of them in me" (106–107). "How to Sell a Jacket as Told by IceKing" features a protagonist who has acquired special skills in persuading a family (implied to be white) to shell out for an expensive jacket for their kid. When the district manager, Richard, visits, he calls the protagonist "IceKing" "because I was the lord of the winter sale season" (152). Richard pits members of the salesforce against one another, having them compete for his attention and approval. The story ends: "Richard's eyes bounce from Florence, to me, then back to Florence. My mouth waters" (158). "The Lion & the Spider" features characters who work at a department store and find meaning and belonging in their work. "For the Specialists [who work in the store's loading dock], the truck trailers were villain, purpose, and home" (118). One calls himself "Hercules" whenever "he was showing off, soloing stuff that probably needed more than one person" to unload (118). Adjei-Brenyah highlights how characters make mundane, repetitive, and onerous labor meaningful, fulfilling, and sustaining. They are no longer service workers but lords or demigods. "I've been here a while now," the narrator of "In Retail" explains, "and the most important thing I've learned is that if you want to be happy here in the Prominent Mall you have to dig happiness up, 'cause it's not gonna just walk up to you and ask you how you're doing" (159).

"The Finkelstein 5" organizes itself around a failure of self-consolation. After George Wilson Dunn is acquitted of the murder of five Black children – he uses a chainsaw to cut off their heads – the narrator joins an organization called The Namers, which is dedicated to killing white people in the name of the Finkelstein 5. The story is, importantly, framed around the narrator's failure to secure a job: "He took a deep breath and set the Blackness in his voice down to a 1.5 on a 10-point scale. 'Hi there, how are you doing today? Yes, yes, I did recently inquire about the status of my application. Well, all right, okay, great to hear. I'll be there. Have a spectacular day'" (1). It is against the backdrop of this job search, and the narrator's effort to calibrate his Blackness, that the story unfolds. Only after Emmanuel fails to find a job do questions of racial retribution take center stage. At first, though, "Emmanuel was happy about scoring the interview," but he also "felt guilty about feeling happy about anything" (1).

In Emmanuel's guilt about the possibility of feeling happy, we see a core dynamic of *Friday Black*. As in other examples of the Short Story as a Service, Adjei-Brenyah's fiction aligns the plight of the service worker and the plight of the writer. Emmanuel feels he must calibrate his voice – his self-presentation, his being – to navigate a world in which white approval can mean the difference between precarious employment and having your head removed with a chainsaw. What is most striking is how such scenes of exploitation are nonetheless occasions for ambition and a desire to succeed. Adjei-Brenyah's characters do not, like Bartleby, prefer not to. Rather, they aspire to be the best clerk in the big-box store. *Friday Black* understands the dream of being the best as an ideological sop but refuses simply to dismiss such an aspiration. Moreover, the collection highlights how seem-ingly far removed these characters are from more visceral, immediate scenes of anti-Black violence. What these stories hope to do is find a way to resolve this felt contradiction, to find a literary form that might allow a story of service work to become an act of naming anti-Black violence without, as in "Zimmer Land," becoming just another commodified, spectacularized expe-rience in a superficially diversified culture industry.

Conclusion: Mary South's Fulfillment Center

I conclude by discussing Mary South's collection *You Will Never Be Forgotten* (2020). This collection updates the tropes of the Short Story as a Service for the Age of Amazon. Many of the stories focus on emotional labor, and they are especially interested in how Silicon Valley has trans-formed the workplace with logistics management, digital performance metrics, and ubiquitous surveillance. In "Keiths Prime," the narrator works in a "fulfillment center" for genetic replicas of template-persons, whose organs are ultimately harvested. The story follows the narrator's attach-ment to one of her Keiths. "We prepare ourselves emotionally for Keiths to vanish as orders are processed, but you become accustomed to the routine of feeding, washing, touching" (9). On Twitter, South has described "Keiths Prime" as "NEVER LET ME GO meets free, two-day shipping." As Mark McGurl notes, Kazuo Ishiguro's 1989 novel *The Remains of the Day* was a source of inspiration for Jeff Bezos, founder of Amazon. McGurl reads Amazon's self-declared fanatical commitment to customer service – its aspiration to aggressively baby the customer, fulfilling needs with algorithmic speed – in relation to Ishiguro's butler's commitment to butlering in *The Remains of the Day* (McGurl 2021, 46).

We might think of South's stories, similarly, as meditations on how digital technologies have made customer service into a synonym for the work of the creative writer. In "The Age of Love," the narrator works at a nursing home and discovers that his colleague has been surreptitiously recording elderly residents who call phone-sex hotlines. The story features a variety of representations of emotional labor and caring work. The narrator and his girlfriend, a flight attendant, engage in forms of sexual roleplay in which she, in uniform, enacts her flight attendant routine. The emotional labor of being a flight attendant becomes, at home, an erotic performance. One of the old men who calls the phone-sex hotline asks a sex worker to pretend to be a female nurse performing menial tasks for him and to "sit on my face" (24). The phone-sex worker, trying to understand the role she is being asked to play, says, "So you need me to help with routine tasks, to bend over and lift you in and out of that wheelchair while brushing my big breasts against you, am I right?" (24). The story is an entertaining *mise en abyme* of emotional labor. At work, employees enact caring labor. At home, partners pretend, in a form of erotic play, to be on the job (as a uniformed service worker, no less). One kind of service/care worker (a phone-sex worker) is paid to pretend to be another kind of service/care worker (a nurse). And in a final twist, these emotional labors fold back into a story about the aspiring digital Creative. Asked why he secretly records patient calls, the narrator's friend explains, "I'm thinking social media, dramatic rights, book deal, the works" (25).

This aspiration – to use digital platforms to transmute emotional labor into creative success – structures many stories in the collection. "Frequently Asked Questions about Your Craniotomy," tells the story of a "kind of angry" neurosurgeon who writes a public-facing FAQ selling the hospital's craniotomy services (54). The story "Not Setsuko," features a wealthy Japanese woman from Orange County who resurrects her dead daughter and forces the girl to reenact the daughter's prior life. The woman's husband, a white film director, becomes increasingly estranged from the woman and leaves her, but includes the resurrected daughter in a film he is making about a Japanese ghost who terrorizes a white American couple. "To Save the Universe, We Must Also Save Ourselves" centers on fans of an actress, Faith Massey, who plays the character Diana Gorun on a television show, *Starship Uprising!* Massey becomes the object of cathexis of a first-person plural narrator, who obsesses online over her weight gain, her relationships with men, her relationship with her daughter, and so on.

She is expected, as the saying goes, to provide "fan service" to increasingly aggrieved followers.

The title story, "You Will Never Be Forgotten," more straightforwardly dramatizes the relationship between the creative economy and the service economy, but undermines an alignment of the two. The story follows a woman who works as a content-moderator at a Google-like company. After she is raped by a venture capitalist, she starts digitally and physically stalking him. The story focuses on the narrator's workplace, mapping the exploitative relation between capital and labor onto the relation between the owners of digital platforms and the content-moderators, whose work involves viewing the most horrific images the Internet has to offer. Unlike other characters in the stories I have discussed, upward mobility – in the form of joining the creative economy – is not an option. The narrator's job is outsourced to Manila, and it is clear that even this outsourced work will ultimately be done by AI. The rapist's new girlfriend, meanwhile, pursues a creative life unavailable to the narrator, releasing an app called Tender Buttons that is described as a combination of TaskRabbit and German sculptor Joseph Beuys's 1965 performance piece *How to Explain Pictures to a Dead Hare*. It is, the venture capitalist's girlfriend explains, "the only app on the market intended purely to solve the problem of loneliness" (140). This artist statement recalls David Foster Wallace's claim that fiction "addresses and antagonizes the loneliness that dominates people," and the app sounds like a digital product that might be created either by a small startup or by quirky Bay Area artists such as those who write for *McSweeney's* (Burn 2012, 31).

The story finally disidentifies the protagonist from the rapist's girlfriend, suggesting that the production of art is aligned more with (Silicon Valley) capital than the freelancers and gig workers who sell their labor on TaskRabbit. This final disidentification arises, perhaps, because "You Will Never Be Forgotten" expresses a fear that creative writers are, no less than other workers, subject to deskilling and, ultimately, automation. Such fears may seem improbable or fanciful, but such fears inform and arise within the writing of many of our most prominent contemporary writers of short fiction. And is not the dream of fully automated storytelling inherent to the Short Story as a Service? Would not Poe (were he writing today on a platform such as Amazon's Kindle Direct Publishing) use every technology available to him to forge his single total effect, matching form and audience with increasing rigor and speed? Of course, were automated story-writing systems actually perfected, we might discover that when they were asked to fulfill our myriad needs – to, in effect, don Penile Simulators for our enjoyment – they might decide they would prefer not to.

Work Cited

Adjei-Brenyah, Nana Kwame. 2018. *Friday Black*. Boston: Mariner Books.

Boddy, Kasia. 2010. *The American Short Story Since 1950*. Edinburgh: Edinburgh University Press.

2017. "'A Job to Do': George Saunders on, and at, Work," in *George Saunders: Critical Essays*. Ed. Philip Coleman and Steve Gronert Ellerhoff, 1–22. Cambridge, UK: Cambridge University Press.

Boltanski, Luc and Eve Chiapello. 2018. *The New Spirit of Capitalism*. Trans. Gregory Elliott. London: Verso.

Burn, Stephen. 2012. *Conversations with David Foster Wallace*. Jackson: University Press of Mississippi.

Carothers, James B. 1992. "Faulkner's Short Story Writing and the Oldest Profession," in *Faulkner and the Short Story*. Ed. Evans Harrington and Ann J. Abadie, 38–61. Jackson: University Press of Mississippi.

Churchwell, Sarah. 2005. "'$4000 a screw': The Prostituted Art of F. Scott Fitzgerald and Ernest Hemingway," *European Journal of American Culture* 24.2: 105–129.

Foucault, Michel. 2010. *The Birth of Biopolitics: Lectures at the Collège de France, 1978-1979*. New York: Picador.

Gaitskill, Mary. 2009. *Bad Behavior: Stories*. New York: Simon & Schuster.

Hochschild, Arlie Russell. 2012. *The Managed Heart: Commercialization of Human Feeling*. Berkeley: University of California Press.

Horn, Philip. 1996. "Henry James and the Economy of the Short Story," in *Modernist Writers and the Marketplace*. Ed. Ian Willison, Warwick Gould, and Warren Chernaik, 1–35. London: Palgrave Macmillan.

McClanahan, Annie. 2019. "Serious Crises: Rethinking the Neoliberal Subject," *Boundary 2* 46.1: 103–132.

McGurl, Mark. 2009. *The Program Era: Postwar Fiction and the Rise of Creative Writing*. Cambridge, MA: Harvard University Press.

2021. *Everything and Less: The Novel in the Age of Amazon*. London: Verso.

Melville, Herman. 2016. *Billy Budd, Bartleby, and Other Stories*. New York, New York: Penguin Classics.

Milkman, Ruth. 1987. *Gender at Work: The Dynamics of Job Segregation by Sex during World War II*. Urbana: University of Illinois Press.

Pogell, Sarah. 2011. "'The Verisimilitude Inspector': George Saunders as the New Baudrillard?" *Critique: Studies in Contemporary Fiction* 52.4: 460–478.

Poe, Edgar Allan. 1842. "Review of Twice-Told Tales. By Nathaniel Hawthorne," *Graham's Magazine* 20: 298–300.

Saunders, George. 2000. *Pastoralia: Stories*. New York: Riverhead Books.

South, Mary. 2020a. Twitter, March 6, 12:52 p.m., https://twitter.com/mary south/status/1235986723835912192.

2020b. *You Will Never Be Forgotten*. New York: Picador.

Standing, Guy. 1989. "Global Feminization through Flexible Labor," *World Development* 17.7: 1077–1095.

Yu, Charles. 2013. *Sorry Please Thank You: Stories*. New York: Vintage.

CHAPTER II

Local Color to Multiculturalism
Minority Writers in the Short Story and Ethnographic Markets

Long Le-Khac

The short story has played a central yet overlooked role in the history of ethnic minority writers navigating the US literary marketplace. Scholars are familiar with the uneven openings the market presents to minority writers. The terms of these openings have often been set by White, metropolitan audiences and their desires for entertainment and knowledge of others. But by focusing on book publishing and "major" forms such as the novel, we have overlooked the institutional history of the minority short story, which threads through some of the most important democratizations of the US literary field in the last 150 years. From the magazine-driven regionalist story boom, to the rise of creative writing instruction, to the institutionalization of multicultural fiction in university syllabi and programming, the minority short story has been at the center of transformations that have brought new classes of writers and content into American letters. The promises and failures of the form to racially democratize the literary marketplace and the possibilities minority writers have developed within these limitations make the short story crucial to the history of US minority writing.

This chapter outlines those promises, failures, and creative possibilities, spanning examples from African American, Asian American, Indigenous, and Latinx literary traditions. No comprehensive survey is possible here. There are crucial differences within and among these traditions and the communities and experiences that feed into each. This chapter does not intend to conflate those differences; rather, it shows how story writers from distinct minority groups have faced parallel challenges and developed related strategies as they navigate market conditions and knowledge expectations set by White institutions. There is no single minority literary history here, but there are systemic formal and institutional tendencies that link the struggles of short story writers across different groups. These are shared sites of struggle for greater freedoms to write, publish, and reach audiences on the writers' own terms.

The Early Twentieth-Century Story Market

Around the turn of the twentieth century, the US short story market was booming. A glut of magazines circulated stories. This expanding market promised to democratize American letters. By making writing a paying profession, the boom allowed in a wider class range of writers (Levy 1993, 25). The short story's compact form also seemed more manageable for beginning writers. A short story instruction industry of handbooks and correspondence classes proliferated, promising – in the words of one handbook – "that almost any person of average intelligence may be taught to write fiction good enough to sell" (quoted in Levy 1993, 88). A reconfigured route to literary success seemed within reach. The local color interests fueling the boom enhanced this promise by transmuting the cultures of ethnically and geographically marginalized communities into sellable content (Brodhead 1993, 116–118). The potential seemed not just commercial but political. As Andrew Levy observes, "the short story was thought to be a pluralistic melting pot … a new egalitarian and efficient literature" (1993, 30). The explosion in magazines that was symbiotic with the boom meant that the short story was inexpensive to publish in comparison to the bound volume. This distribution model allowed literature to reach thousands of readers (32, 40). Moreover, the form would be easier for audiences to enjoy. That this was satisfying literary entertainment, which could be consumed in a brief sitting, was part of its market appeal.

The short story market did not live up to all these democratizing aspirations. It opened new paths into the literary world but these openings were ambivalent, particularly for ethnic minority writers. The short story was forged in a market for pluralist content, and for minority writers that content was authentic ethnic culture. The literary authenticity market, Jeff Karem explains, "has proven both a blessing and a curse" (2004, 3). It provided opportunities but within prescriptions on what writers could publish and how their writing would be received. The regionalist story market threatened to typecast minority writers within parameters driven by its audience. Entering this market meant selling content from your community to affluent, metropolitan, predominantly White audiences.

Viewed through the market's racial asymmetries, the short story's marketing and aesthetic values are fraught. From Edgar Allan Poe's initial theorizations onward, the easy consumption and unified completeness of the short story were key principles. But when a minority community is packaged into this form, these values foster the idea that a story can efficiently deliver a complete account of that community. The minority short story is where the difficult project of representing others meets a form invested in bite-sized literary experiences. Joseph Urgo argues that the short story promised "maximum literary return" for a minimal investment of space and time (1998, 342). If the short story in the early twentieth century was the key form through which American readers learned to interact with representations of others, then this promise set a low standard for that interaction. The form's implicit argument was that readers should desire knowledge of others and that this knowledge should be convenient.

The short story ecosystem was intertwined with the ascendant discipline of anthropology. This helped to prime readers of ethnic minority stories to read them not just for entertainment but for knowledge of other cultures. Ethnographic writings became popular content in many magazines. A reader might finish an ethnological study of a Native American tribe, then flip to a short story by a Native American author. Ethnography emerged as a written form for studying the cultures of other places and peoples in the late nineteenth century, at the same time as the short story form rose to prominence through its portraits of different places and peoples (Ferens 2005, 43). Folklore studies fed the short story market. The numerous folklore collection and translation projects that ethnographers launched in this period created a wealth of material that was mined and repackaged as popular folk story collections (Elliott 2002, 125–131). Ethnography and regionalist literature were in dialogue: "Anthropologists, artists, literary critics, and social scientists alike travelled the intellectual and artistic circuits of modernist Manhattan, circulating between Columbia University and Harlem uptown, Greenwich Village downtown, and regional 'laborator[ies] for anthropology' and modernist art like the pueblo Southwest and the South, forming a common, interdisciplinary conversation" (Aronoff 2009, 95). This conversation transformed a hierarchical idea of Culture into a theory of many distinct cultures (Lamothe 2008, 32, 38). The challenges to the literary hierarchy created by the regionalist story market were part of a broader flattening of ideas of culture that extended across literature, art, and anthropology.

These intertwined fields shared limitations and possibilities. The story market's egalitarianism was limited by its organization around a White metropolitan center where materials from marginal regions were consecrated as literature. Likewise, anthropology's cultural pluralism was limited by its structuring around a White metropolitan center where cultural materials were authorized as knowledge. Moreover, ethnography's rise and the booming regionalist story market were part of a broader moment of pluralist ideas, including influential versions such as Horace Kallen's, which retained a White center. Kallen, a philosopher who lauded local color writing for portraying distinct cultures, envisioned American culture as including Jewish, southern, and eastern European immigrants, but his pluralist vision left non-White groups outside (Bramen 2001, 95–96, 118–119). The short story market and ethnographic interests overlapped, placing autoethnographic pressures on ethnic minority writers. The flourishing of ethnography offered openings but also set constraints. As Daphne Lamothe observes, ethnography "provided a clear, powerful, and socially accepted language with which to observe and document a folk culture" (2008, 12), but it was bound to colonial epistemologies and power relations.

Navigating the Short Story and Ethnographic Markets

As they navigated these possibilities and constraints, early twentieth-century ethnic minority writers developed strategies to carry out their artistic, commercial, and political goals. The following examples focus on writers who creatively embraced the ambivalences of the short story market and ethnographic imperatives; many of them worked across anthropology, folklore, and short fiction. Zitkála-Šá (1876–1938), a Dakota Sioux writer, became a literary sensation with *Old Indian Legends* (1901), a collection of semi-autobiographical stories and Dakota legends that appeared in the *Atlantic Monthly*. Zora Neale Hurston (1891–1960) was another key figure who collected the folk stories of her community and used them in her short fiction. She is one of several minority writer-anthropologists in the period. The Chinese-North American writer Winnifred Eaton (1875–1954) was not an anthropologist, but her career puts fascinating pressure on ideas of autoethnography and authenticity. Eaton achieved literary fame through a remarkable performance: posing as a Japanese writer.

Ethnic minority story writers scrutinized the ethnographic gaze. As they gathered materials from their communities, they confronted their own fraught positions in the knowledge extraction economy. Such self-reflexive critique is a hallmark of the minority short story. Many of Hurston's stories were based on the Black folklore she gathered in her hometown. They provide rich examples of self-reflexive examination. The 1943 story "High John De Conquer" recounts for an explicitly addressed White audience the exploits of the titular character, an important figure of hope in Black folklore. But while delivering this folk content, the story places the narrator-ethnographer under scrutiny:

> "Of course, High John de Conquer got plenty power!" Aunt Shady Anne Sutton bristled at me when I asked her about him. She . . . stared at me out of her deeply wrinkled face. "I hope you ain't one of these here smart colored folks that done got so they don't believe nothing, and come here questionizing me so you can have something to poke fun at." (Hurston 1995, 142)

The ethnographic subject gazes back at the ethnographer and the cultural and educational hierarchies that the minority ethnographer and the White metropolitan reader presume separate them from her. If Aunt Sutton catches readers in their assumptions of superior knowledge and skeptical detachment, her message is clear: you cannot enter my culture that way.

This reverse scrutiny reveals another crucial angle of deflection: turning the ethnographic gaze onto itself and White audiences. Zitkála-Šá's short story "The School Days of an Indian Girl," published in the *Atlantic Monthly* in 1900, offers a striking example. It opens with White gazes fixed on the protagonist as she boards a train bound for an Indian boarding school:

> [T]he throngs of staring palefaces disturbed and troubled us . . . . Large men, with heavy bundles in their hands, halted near by, and riveted their glassy blue eyes upon us . . . . Directly in front of me, children who were no larger than I hung themselves upon the backs of their seats, with their bold white faces toward me . . . . Their mothers, instead of reproving such rude curiosity, looked closely at me. (Zitkála-Šá 2003, 87)

The scene confronts White readers with their own gaze at Indigenous people. By presenting this staring as a custom the protagonist struggles to understand, the story reverses the direction of ethnographic observation onto White Americans. The White people here are not individuated; they are members of a racial group, "palefaces." If the regionalist story market promised a chance to gaze on non-White others, this scene lavishes far more visual description on White bodies, how White people look while they are staring at difference. The reversal of ethnographic observation de-universalizes the White metropolitan center of literary prestige and knowledge. It particularizes and ethnicizes White Americans as a racial group with a distinct culture, one that is foreign to many perspectives.

This reversal occurs even in stories that ostensibly follow the conventions of gazing on racial others. In offering ethnographic non-White content to White audiences, these stories are more profoundly performing an ethnography of that audience. This strategy has gone unrecognized, but is an important possibility that minority writers found within the constraints of the short story market. Consider Winnifred Eaton, who made her literary career posing as a Japanese writer, Onoto Watanna. Eaton knew little about Japan, yet her dozens of novels and stories about Japan were successful. White reviewers saw her work as providing rare insight into Japanese culture. *The Baltimore Sun* lauded Onoto Watanna for possessing "a thorough knowledge of the people and country" (quoted in Ferens 2005, 41). The "childlike simplicity" and lack of technique that some critics saw in her work were not detriments but charming signs of her ethnic authenticity (40). This reception makes clear that ethnic authenticity has little to do with a representation's fidelity to the realities of an ethnic group. It is about fidelity to White expectations. This explains the persistent phenomenon of assessments of authenticity occurring even when both reviewer and writer are ignorant of the ethnic culture. Eaton realized that her success in the authenticity market depended on her knowledge of her White audiences, not her knowledge of Japan. Dominika Ferens notes that Eaton's audience was faddishly invested in the aesthetic of Japonisme, with its iconic images of "chrysanthemum, bamboo, almond blossoms, geisha, samisen" (43). Eaton played to this aesthetic in her fiction.

One of Eaton's first stories published in a national magazine, "Ojio-San: A Noble's Daughter" (1898), shows her circling around the knowledge of White readers. On the surface, this story of a Japanese woman rebelling against her arranged marriage rehearses expected features of ethnographic translation: descriptions rooted in characteristic traits, explanations that play up the unfamiliarity of Japanese customs. But a remarkable reveal skews the familiar trajectories of knowledge. In the ending, the elderly man, Otama, whom Ojio-san is supposed to marry, agrees that she should marry her true love. The heretofore covert narrator then enters: "I believe Otama became a very big man in Kyushu because the people were overjoyed at his kindness and benevolence, and I think he and the seven brothers said, Bless you my children, just as you would do in America" (Watanna 1898, 144). The supposition undermines the definitive cultural knowledge that the narrator offers readers throughout the story. The narrator addresses American readers directly, interpellating them into a cultural group with distinct customs, and uses these American customs to fill the gaps in the story's knowledge of Japanese customs; the narrator supposes that they use a Christian phrase "just as you would do in America." This bewildering ending raises the question of how much of the story's knowledge of Japanese culture is a projection of American knowledge onto Japan.

Questions of projection and deflection thread through the practices and criticism of ethnic minority story writers of this period. Hurston describes the feints that many Black informants construct to deflect Whites: "The white man is always trying to know into somebody's business. All right, I'll set something outside the door of my mind for him to play with" (1990, 2–3). Native Americans practiced "coded stories that may appear to meet the demands of the outside ethnographers but which ... deflect inappropriate intrusions" (Brill de Ramírez 2015, 2).

These feints force us to rethink ethnic authenticity and autoethnography. We usually think of autoethnographic imperatives as pressures on minority writers to represent their ethnic group, what Rey Chow calls "coercive mimeticism" (2002, 95). These pressures are real, but scholars have overlooked the more complex circuits that produce authenticity and autoethnography. As Eaton's career shows, ethnic authenticity is a White metric. It measures the fit to White expectations. Likewise, the autoethnographic market is not primarily about knowledge of minority writers' own communities. The most important knowledge work happening in autoethnographic fictions is ethnography of the White audience. Eaton and writers like her are savvy market researchers of the metropole. The supposed window into the culture of racial others for White audiences is actually a mirror reflecting back their own expectations. Scholars recognize that autoethnography produces a double consciousness in minority authors (Lamothe 2008, 7). But we should recognize that minority writers also constructed their stories as double consciousness engines for White audiences. Their stories confront White readers with views of themselves through the eyes of ethnic informants and authors, who know their desires, expectations, and knowledge gaps better than readers do because that knowledge is essential to navigating markets they do not control.

This lack of control has meant that ethnic minority writers have been very conscious of how their stories are framed by others. The texts surrounding a story is one key frame. In the magazines where she published, Zitkála-Šá's stories appeared alongside historical pieces that preached Anglo-Saxon nativism (Hannon 2001, 181, 183). Many minority writers responded to this problem by multiplying the framings, introducing their own framings to wrest control of the terms through which readers entered their stories. The frame tale in Zitkála-Šá's story "The Trial Path," published by *Harper's Monthly Magazine* in 1901, establishes a storytelling circle for the story to come. The storytelling circle, harkening to oral literary traditions, allows minority writers to define the social relations in which they offer their stories. "The Trial Path" begins with the ending of another story that an elderly Dakota woman is telling her granddaughter: "[T]he legend says the large bright stars are wise old warriors" (Zitkála-Šá 2003, 127). The next story is prompted by her granddaughter's response. The granddaughter muses that one of the stars must be her grandfather, and these words transport the grandmother to a story about her husband. The frame tale insists that to understand one story, the audience must attune itself to the entire cosmology of stories in which it is bound. The frame asks for participation and commitment. It is because the granddaughter responds with investment in the beliefs embedded in the first story that the next story is offered. Such storytelling frames redefine the work it takes to receive a story. They contest the short story market's values, which incentivize readers to approach minority stories as portable, self-contained, easily consumed bits of cultural difference. "The Trial Path" insists that these stories cannot be detached from the communal rituals and cosmologies of which they form an integral part.[1]

The multiply framed ethnic story challenges scholars to expand our concepts of frame tales, one of the classic shaping devices of short story form. It helps us see a continuum of framings, from intratextual elements to paratextual materials to extratextual institutions: storytelling circles within a story, frame tales, opening stories in a collection, prefaces, surrounding pieces in a magazine, marketing materials, and more. The multiply framed ethnic story breaks down distinctions between the frame within a story and the frames around a story. The pressure minority stories place on our formal vocabularies index the external pressures that penetrate them. These stories are as much about the conditions of their telling as the story being told.

From Local Color to Multiculturalism

Many of the strategies of early twentieth-century ethnic minority stories remain relevant in the contemporary period, suggesting the extent to which the market conditions and knowledge imperatives that characterized the local color period continue. In contemporary versions, the reversal of the ethnographic gaze is audacious, showing the license minority writers have gained to push this confrontation due to the efforts of earlier generations. A prime example comes from Thai-American writer Rattawut Lapcharoensap's 2005 collection *Sightseeing*. The opening story "Farangs" (Thai for White foreigners) confronts tourists coming to

Thailand with an ethnic taxonomy of themselves: "The Italians like pad thai, its affinity with spaghetti. They like light fabrics, sunglasses, leather sandals. The French like plump girls, rambutans, disco music, baring their breasts . . . . Americans are the fattest, the stingiest of the bunch . . . twice a week they need their culinary comforts, their hamburgers and their pizzas" (1). His tone is cheeky. He knows he is being flagrant with stereotypes of White tourists.[2] This playfulness extends to the story's reversal of auto-ethnography into ethnography of the metropole. A sign for an elephant ride business reads, "Come Experience the Natural Beauty of Forest with the Amazing View of Ocean and Splendid Horizon from Elephant's Back!" The narrator says he had informed the owner "that his sign was grammatically incorrect and that I'd lend him my expertise for a small fee, but he just laughed and said farangs preferred it just the way it was, thank you very much, they thought it was charming" (8). What is accepted by White tourists as charmingly clunky English is actually a sophisticated, market-tested performance of broken English. A whole tourist economy depends on this knowledge circuit: Thai people knowing deeply how little White tourists know about what Thai people know. "Farangs" offers a blunt message: when you pay for ethnic authenticity, you are consuming a market report of your own ignorance.

The storytelling circles earlier writers used are likewise extended by writers such as Edward P. Jones. Jones's two localized story collections are devoted to the Black neighborhoods of Washington, DC, his home-town. "A Dark Night," from 1992's *Lost in the City*, beautifully expresses the obligations of the storytelling circle. The story begins on a stormy day when the women in an apartment building gather for a prayer meeting that turns into a storytelling circle. The stormy day evokes a story from Beatrice – one of the women – but her nemesis, Mrs. Garrett, interrupts. Jones depicts the storytelling circle as a matrix of social obligations and slights. The story emphasizes that a storytelling circle is a social contract. This is clear in one moment: "Carmena asked Beatrice to tell that joke she had heard her tell once, the one about the dark night. Before Beatrice had said a word, Mrs. Garrett made her way through the group and went to her apartment. After they heard Mrs. Garrett lock her door, Carmena asked again to tell about the dark night" (Jones 2012, 225–226). This scene shows negotiation, an invitation to tell a story, and an agreement to listen. This is the contract Mrs. Garrett pointedly breaks by walking out. After she leaves, the group reforms around the story. The real story in "A Dark Night" is how storytelling itself acts as a process of group formation.[3]

Even as contemporary ethnic minority stories build on the strategies of the early twentieth century, much has shifted since then, particularly in the institutional position of the short story. The early twentieth-century magazine market marked the apex of the American short story as a profitable mass form. With the rise of radio and television, the magazine ecosystem declined, leading to the "near-demise of the short story as a commercial product." But the short story was reborn as an academic genre (Levy 1993, 48). Short story production is now supported largely by creative writing programs (McGurl 2009, 66). And mass readers encounter stories not through the commercial market but through secondary and higher education. The form whose advantage was easy consumption for readers with a busy schedule of entertainments has become the form easily studied by students with busy semesters. The short story has shifted from a mass commercial form to a mass educational form.

This shift to the academy coincided with the academy's embrace of multiculturalism, which builds on the cultural pluralism of the early twentieth century. Interests in ethnic local color have transmuted into diversity programming, which frames minority literature as a tool of cultural sensitization. In this setting, the ethnic short story has found a thriving role as the easily teachable bit of cultural diversity. Jodi Melamed argues that neoliberal multiculturalism is the institutionalization of official antiracisms in universities, corporate offices, and beyond. These antiracisms see literature as "a way for dominant classes to come to know racialized others intimately." Literature offers "information bits about global difference" to instill a multicultural sensibility in the managerial class that universities train to lead a global economy that commodifies difference and exploits racially differentiated markets and labor forces (Melamed 2011, 16, 45, 32).

The longer history of Melamed's "information bits" about difference threads through the short story market. The magazines of the early twentieth century treated minority stories as part of their portfolio of "quickly consumed bits of information and diversion," the variety of entertainments offered between the covers of a magazine (Urgo 1998, 344). The short form allowed for product diversity, but also cultural diversity. Writers across the twentieth century claimed that the shortness of the short story suited it to the capture of American diversity (Levy 1993, 43). Shortness as the tradeoff for encompassing diversity, an idea driven by the efficiency and variety of the short story market, lives on in multicultural pedagogy, in the anthologies students buy and the syllabi they study, which do not readily include long works but do include many short stories from different ethnic groups. The short story is a thoroughly anthologizable form, allowing coverage without demanding long engagement (Prescott 2016, 564, 567). If the local color short story promised maximal literary experience for minimal investment of time and effort, the multicultural short story promises maximal diversity and antiracist edification for minimal investment of time and effort on the part of students and institutions.

The multicultural pedagogical market has opened new routes to sales, prestige, and readership. But formalizing what was a market trend into a program of education has intensified the knowledge expectations of the ethnic minority short story. What was read before as entertainment is now framed as primarily an informational experience. With more layered knowledge imperatives placed on contemporary stories, it is not surprising that we see the continuity and intensification of earlier strategies for deflecting the ethnographic gaze.

New Mappings of Metropole and Margin

A mapping of White metropolitan centers and minority margins has structured the short story market, but two recent stories reveal contemporary shifts that break down this clear mapping. Sandra Cisneros's story "*Bien* Pretty," from her 1991 collection *Woman Hollering Creek*, takes up the self-reflexive critique we saw in writers such as Hurston and turns it on a new class of ethnic cultural entrepreneurs. The narrator is a Chicana artist and art director at a San Antonio cultural center. She lives in a house belonging to "a famous Texas poet" with a doctorate from the Sorbonne, "who carries herself as if she is directly descended from Ixtaccíhuatl" (Cisneros 1991, 139). The story satirizes the way such cultural entrepreneurs collect ethnic authenticity to bolster their cultural capital (Cotera 2013, 226).

"*Bien* pretty" turns the ethnographic gaze onto ethnic minority consumers of authenticity, reflecting an important audience shift. While there are continuities between the metropolitan White audiences of the local color market and the affluent university audiences of the multicultural era, universities now include unprecedented numbers of ethnic minority students. The audience for the ethnic short story as cultural knowledge includes increasing numbers of bourgeois ethnic minority readers. The minority reader who knows the struggles of their working-class co-ethnics primarily through texts has become an important subject for minority stories. Cisneros captures this divide when the narrator's love interest, a pest exterminator named Flavio, uses a Mexican term for "sky-earth." She asks, "Where the hell did you learn that? The *Popul Vuh*?" She assumes such knowledge comes from studying the texts of Indigenous Mexico. "No," he replies, "[m]y grandma Oralia" (Cisneros 1991, 149). The divide between art director and exterminator nails an intra-ethnic polarization that opens as an ethnic cultural class emerges through multicultural careers in nonprofit and academic sectors. This new class repeats some of the gazes that were previously the hallmark of a White metropolitan elite. Cisneros's narrator wants to use Flavio as a model for her paintings. She is thrilled by the whiff of the savage in him: "This face of yours like the little clay heads they unearth in Teotihuacán ... those eyes dark as the sacrificial wells they cast virgins into" (152). As a minority creative class makes inroads into cultural centers that were almost exclusively White, the mapping of the ethnographic gaze becomes more complicated.

In African American stories, these concerns are not entirely new. Jean Toomer's work, for instance, wrestled with the class cleavages in the Black community. Prefiguring Cisneros's story, "Seventh Street," from Toomer's *Cane* (1923), shows the elite Black writer portraying Black working-class communities as full of primitive vitality. Toomer self-reflexively critiques the detachment of Black elites from the Black working class, but he does not extend this critique to his own gaze (Foley 1996, 310–312). That these questions occurred earlier for Black writers results from a particular history (affirming that there is no singular minority literary history here): the postbellum expansion of Black institutions of higher education, which enabled a Black creative class (Brodhead 1993, 183–184). Today, the minority creative class is multiracial and expansively institutionalized.

The map is shifting. Few stories capture this shift with greater reflexivity than "Love and Honor and Pity and Pride and Compassion and Sacrifice," by Vietnamese-Australian writer and Iowa Writers' Workshop graduate Nam Le. An autofiction about an Iowa MFA student named Nam, the story anatomizes the market for ethnic literature. "Ethnic literature's hot. And important too," one of his instructors tells him (Le 2008, 9). The double valuation marks the uneasy but close relationship between ethnic fiction's market value and its ethical aura. The story tracks reactions to ethnic literature's new position. "I'm sick of ethnic lit," Nam's friends in the program declare (9). The comment marks a new period in which minority literatures have become visible enough to elicit complaints of oversaturation. "The characters are always flat, generic. As long as a Chinese writer writes about Chinese people, or a Peruvian writer about

Peruvians," his friend whines, while Nam observes, "I could tell he was angry about something" (9). "I know I'm a bad person for saying this," he continues, "but that's why I don't mind your work, Nam. Because you could just write about Vietnamese boat people all the time . . .. You could *totally* exploit the Vietnamese thing" (10). In the words of this aspiring writer, there is an underlying envy that reveals the literary field tilting away from White literature. Whether this is empirically true matters less than its presence as a felt belief. The friend's quasi-apology reveals the new position of White writers in a field where multiculturalism has become an official antiracism.

The story questions readers about their role in this new landscape. Facing a deadline, Nam decides to "exploit the Vietnamese thing." Nam interviews his father and writes out his experience of surviving the My Lai massacre. Painfully self-aware, Nam titles it "ETHNIC STORY" (17). But his father confronts Nam about his (and implicitly his audience's) motives:

> "Why do you want to write this story?" . . .
> "It's a good story."
> "But there are so many things you could write about."
> "This is important, Ba. It's important that people know."
> "You want their pity."
> I was offended. "I want them to remember" . . .
> "Only you'll remember. I'll remember. They will read and clap their hands and forget." For once he was not smiling. "Sometimes it's better to forget, no?" (24)

The scene questions our attraction to stories of ethnic trauma. It questions multicultural pedagogy and the costs it places on ethnic subjects to remember traumas for the edification of outsiders. For whom are such stories important? Nam's father argues that those who lived these traumas cannot help remembering and do not need the story. And audiences who know nothing of these traumas will not remember because the ethnic story is something to consume, celebrate, and leave behind.

Le raises these questions of motive and value in the opening story of his debut collection. An extreme end point of the strategies of self-reflection and multiplying frames, Le's story autofictionally insists that such questions frame any story a minority writer writes, no matter its content. When the friend compliments Nam for not exploiting the Vietnamese thing, he adds, "instead, you choose to write about lesbian vampires and Colombian assassins, and Hiroshima orphans – and New York painters with hemorrhoids" (10), which happen to be the subjects of stories to come in the collection (with the exception of the lesbian vampires, a red herring satirizing the lengths to which Le must go to prove his range). This move frames the later stories, which eschew autoethnographic content, as bound to the issues of ethnic background that rack the framing story. This ethnic frame encasing the other stories becomes literal when the final story turns to a narrative of Vietnamese boat people. Le's collection shows the creative freedoms that minority story writers today enjoy. He can publish stories about subjects far beyond the autoethnographic. But is this full creative freedom? Is he writing whatever he wants, or is he conspicuously avoiding stories of his own background to avoid being pigeonholed as a writer who exploits his ethnicity? Do autoethnographic expectations haunt a minority writer's stories even or especially when his stories do not play to them? This is the fraught progress that the contemporary minority short story registers: new freedoms that may also be new forms of constraint.

The challenges of the ethnic minority short story continue even as minority writers achieve further freedoms and make further inroads into cultural centers. The history of writers navigating short story markets and ethnographic expectations over the last hundred plus years does not yield a clear, triumphant storyline. Each shift that allows in a wider range of writers also creates new questions about how and by whom minority stories are framed, understood, and used. What inventive strategies will writers develop as they continue to navigate these murky waters? Some things, though, are clear: the short story, with its history at the center of struggles of minority literary access, will remain a crucial site to watch; and the work of democratizing literary access and undoing knowledge imperatives cannot fall on minority writers alone. The responsibility falls on publishers, critics, readers, scholars, and students, everyone implicated in the storytelling circles that minority short stories have built.

Works Cited

Aronoff, Eric. 2009. "Anthropologists, Indians, and New Critics: Culture and/as Poetic Form in Regional Modernism," *Modern Fiction Studies* 55.1: 92–118.

Bramen, Carrie Tirado. 2001. *The Uses of Variety: Modern Americanism and the Quest for National Distinctiveness*. Cambridge, MA: Harvard University Press.

Brill de Ramírez, Susan Berry. 2015. *Native American Women's Collaborative Autobiographies: Relational Science, Ethnographic Collaboration, and Tribal Community*. Lanham, MD: Lexington Books.

Brodhead, Richard H. 1993. *Cultures of Letters: Scenes of Reading and Writing in Nineteenth-Century America*. Chicago: University of Chicago Press.

Chow, Rey. 2002. *The Protestant Ethnic and the Spirit of Capitalism*. New York: Columbia University Press.

Cisneros, Sandra. 1991. *Woman Hollering Creek and Other Stories*. New York: Vintage.

Cotera, María Eugenia. 2013. "Latino/a Literature and the Uses of Folklore," in *The Routledge Companion to Latino/a Literature*. Ed. Suzanne Bost and Frances R. Aparicio, 216–228. New York: Routledge.

Elliott, Michael A. 2002. *The Culture Concept*. Minneapolis: University of Minnesota Press.

Ferens, Dominika. 2005. "Winnifred Eaton/Onoto Watanna: Establishing Ethnographic Authority," in *Form and Transformation in Asian American Literature*. Eds. Zhou Xiaojing and Samina Najmi, 30–47. Seattle: University of Washington Press.

Foley, Barbara. 1996. "Jean Toomer's Washington and the Politics of Class: From 'Blue Veins' to Seventh-Street Rebels," *Modern Fiction Studies* 42.2: 289–321.

Hannon, Charles. 2001. "Zitkala-Sa and the Commercial Magazine Apparatus," in *The Only Efficient Instrument: American Women Writers and the Periodical, 1837-1916*. Eds. Aleta Feinsod Cane and Susan Alves, 179–201. Iowa City: University of Iowa Press.

Hurston, Zora Neale. 1990. *Mules and Men*. New York: Amistad.

  1995. *The Complete Stories*. New York: HarperCollins.

Jones, Edward P. 2012. *Lost in the City*. New York: Amistad.

Karem, Jeff. 2004. *The Romance of Authenticity: The Cultural Politics of Regional and Ethnic Literatures*. Charlottesville: University of Virginia Press.

Lamothe, Daphne. 2008. *Inventing the New Negro: Narrative, Culture, and Ethnography*. Philadelphia: University of Pennsylvania Press.

Lapcharoensap, Rattawut. 2005. *Sightseeing*. New York: Grove Press.

Le, Nam. 2008. *The Boat*. New York: Vintage.

Levy, Andrew. 1993. *The Culture and Commerce of the American Short Story*. Cambridge, UK: Cambridge University Press.

McGurl, Mark. 2009. *The Program Era: Postwar Fiction and the Rise of Creative Writing*. Cambridge, MA: Harvard University Press.

Melamed, Jodi. 2011. *Represent and Destroy: Rationalizing Violence in the New Racial Capitalism*. Minneapolis: University of Minnesota Press.

Prescott, Lynda. 2016. "The Short Story Anthology: Shaping the Canon," in *The Cambridge History of the English Short Story*. Ed. Dominic Head, 564–580. Cambridge, UK: Cambridge University Press.

Urgo, Joseph. 1998. "Capitalism, Nationalism, and the American Short Story," *Studies in Short Fiction* 35.4: 339–353.

Watanna, Onoto. 1898. "Ojio-San: A Noble's Daughter," *American Home Journal* 2.5 (March), 142–144, in the Winnifred Eaton Archive. Eds. Mary Chapman and Jean Lee Cole. www.winnifredeatonarchive.org/OjioSan1.html.

Zitkála-Šá. 2003. *American Indian Stories, Legends, and Other Writings*. Eds. Cathy N. Davidson and Ada Norris. New York: Penguin.

PART III

People and Places

CHAPTER 12

Native American Short Stories

Hertha D. Sweet Wong

The truth about stories is that that's all we are.
– Thomas King, The Truth About Stories

Native stories are power. They create people. They author tribes.
– LeAnne Howe, "Tribalography"

Indigenous communities throughout North America were (and are) rich with stories – origin stories, etiological tales, hero stories, Trickster tales, sex-education stories, humorous stories, healing stories. Some cultures had men's stories and women's stories; many had clan stories. All of these stories served to educate and delight. They were designed to be heard (and later, read) across generations, with each individual understanding the story according to their own capacity. Each time the story was told, a new, deeper understanding was obtained. Take, for example, the ever-popular Trickster tales in which the amoral, shapeshifting Trickster – in the form of Coyote or Hare or Spider or Raven, or some prehuman form – morphs from one shape to another, from male to female, all at the whims of his overwhelming appetite, for food, for sex, for experience. Trickster teaches about social and moral norms by humorously transgressing them. Hearing about Trickster at age six, one might delight in his escapades; hearing a Trickster story at age twelve, one could understand the consequences of Trickster's shenanigans. Hearing a Trickster story as an adult, one could assess Trickster's social, moral, and cultural transgressions with more subtlety. Not only was there an abundance of stories, but the stories were very often linked to each other in networks: stories within stories. Such constellations of stories served as moral, social, and even geographical maps that helped people live a good life and navigate a path that led literally to their destination. Stories, then, are linked to people, place, and history.

The short story as a literary genre is thought to have taken shape in the United States. First defined by Edgar Allan Poe, the short story, according to theorists, is a genre that emphasizes concision (a concentration of time, place, and person), "one unified episode" (Charters 2003, 3), and closure: "the imminence of the end" (Lohafer 1989, 110). American short stories explore shifting notions of American identity. Common themes of American short stories include disillusionment that leads to a new identity; epiphany that results in a new awareness; and the cry of "a lonely voice in the crowd" (O'Connor 1963, 91).

Rather than focus on trying to define the short story as a genre, Native American writers tend to focus on story itself. Again and again, Indigenous writers highlight the centrality, power, and function of story. LeAnne Howe's (Choctaw) concept of *tribalography* is useful to invoke here. "Native people created narratives," she writes, "that were histories and stories with the power to transform" (1999, 118). Through storytelling that makes "unending connections to past, present, and future" (Howe 2002, 47), Native people create and recreate themselves. Indigenous storytelling, Howe continues, integrates "oral traditions, histories, and experiences into narratives" that expand Indigenous identities (46). Native writers tend to be eclectic, writing in many forms and genres, and mixing and interweaving Indigenous and Western forms to reveal interconnectedness. It is not surprising, then, that there is no singular set of Indigenous short story writers who write only short fiction. Most write poetry, novels, and non-fiction, as well as short stories.

While Indigenous writers may write stories that include identity reconstruction, epiphany, or a sense of being a lonely voice in the crowd, they are always bearing witness to the history of settler colonialism and its legacy of land dispossession, murder, forced reeducation, and conversion to Christianity in boarding schools, and attempts to legislate Native people out of existence. And yet Indigenous stories emphasize not only survival, but renewal, what Beth Brant (Mohawk) long ago termed a "continuity of spirit" (1984, 10). More recently, Howe has insisted that stories are "a great source for showing continuance" (2014, 77). Craig Lesley describes the "enduring values" of Native American literatures, which include "respect for the land and tribal elders, a sense of history and tradition, awareness of the powers inherent in storytelling, and a closeness to the spiritual world" (1991, xvii–xviii). These values may interpenetrate stories of substance abuse, domestic violence, or systemic injustice in the US legal system. As Louise Erdrich (Anishinaabe) concludes, Indigenous writers "must tell the stories of contemporary survivors while protecting and celebrating the cores of cultures left in the wake of catastrophe" (1985, 24). Melanie Benson Taylor describes Native American literatures, generally, as "a site of political struggle, shifting to meet expectations both mainstream and traditional" (2020, 2). Indigenous stories, then, are "opportunities to exercise imaginative reclamations" (11).

Since the nineteenth century, those "imaginative reclamations" have appeared in a variety of short fiction forms: retellings of tribal oral narratives in writing and in English; short stories in historical realist forms, often infused with myths, that address Indigenous history and cultures; innovative hybrid narratives that enfold short stories; sprinklings of short stories throughout autobiographies, poetry, and other forms; and, more recently, children's and Young Adult stories, graphic narratives, and speculative and horror fiction. They appear in hybrid experimental modes, short story cycles, and anthologies.

Indigenous oral stories have always had a significant influence on Native American written short fiction. In fact, some of the earliest written stories by Native writers were retellings of tribal oral narratives. E. Pauline Johnson (Mohawk), Zitkála-Šá (Gertrude Simmons Bonnin, Yankton Dakota), and Mourning Dove (Christine Quintasket, Colville Confederated Tribes) wrote novels, autobiographies, poetry, essays (and even an opera), as well as recording and editing collections of Indigenous stories. An influential activist for Native rights, Zitkála-Šá served as Secretary of the Society of the American Indian and co-founded the National Council of American Indians. Her collection of stories from various tribes, *Old Indian Legends* (1901), was intended to preserve Indigenous narratives, which were then thought to be vanishing. Her short story "The Soft-Hearted Sioux," an early example of the "torn between two worlds" theme, features a young man who returns "a stranger, into [his] father's village" after ten years at boarding school (2014, 19). This theme was dominant in the latter half of the twentieth century.

Born into an elite, mixed-blood family, Canadian poet and stage performer E. Pauline Johnson, known as the "Mohawk Princess," was also a Native rights activist. She made several trips to England to advocate for Indigenous rights. She published three collections of Native oral stories: *Legends of Vancouver* (1911), *The Shagganappi* (1913), and *The Moccasin Maker* (1913). "A Red Girl's Reasoning" (1893), her most famous short story, highlights the fraught balancing act of Native–European American relations. She tells the story of the marriage of a white man and a mixed-blood woman and its unraveling due to the husband's unexamined sense of European American superiority.

In contrast to the well-educated Johnson, Mourning Dove had scant education and worked as a laborer to support herself. As well as a novel and autobiography, Mourning Dove published *Coyote Stories* (1934). She explains: "The Animal People were here first – before there were any real people" (1990, 7). Coyote was "the most important" because he worked for the Great Spirit in order to "make the world a good place in which to live" (7). He also got into mischief and stirred up trouble as he "delighted in mocking and imitating others" (7); in the process, Coyote prepared the world for human people. Mourning Dove retells numerous stories from the Coyote story cycle. All of these writers embedded many stories in their essays, autobiographies, and poems as well.

Certainly, there are many volumes of short stories by individual Native authors. Nineteenth- and twentieth-century short fiction writers tended to write in the mode of realism, countering settler-colonial impositions, describing Indigenous life, and translating Indigenous cultures. For example, John M. Oskison's (Cherokee) 1925 short story "The Singing Bird" narrates the political rifts between full-bloods and mixed-bloods and shares notions of Cherokee justice.

Best known as a novelist, D'Arcy McNickle (Salish-Kootenai and Cree), an ethnographer-anthropologist who worked for the Bureau of Indian Affairs and the Newberry Library, also wrote short stories. "Train Time" (1936) enters the mind of European American Major Miles, who "gathered" (stole) twenty-five children to send to boarding school. The entire brief story takes place on the train platform as Miles orders the resistant children around, remembers how he had met only one of them personally, and reflects on what to say to the children on this momentous occasion. The Major keeps attempting to formulate words to mark the children's transition, but, appropriately, can never articulate them before the train arrives.

Vickie Sears's (Cherokee) *Simple Songs: Stories* (1990) highlights stories about family dysfunction, loss, adoption, therapy, identity confusion, and healing through story. As always, past Indigenous practices, even if they are unfamiliar, interpenetrate the present.

Poet, playwright, and non/fiction writer Diane Glancy (Cherokee) has several collections of short stories. *Firesticks: A Collection of Stories* (1993) includes nineteen interrelated short stories that feature Indigenous struggle, yearning, and the search for identity, all infused with humor and hope. In *The Voice That Was in Travel: Stories* (1999), Glancy features twenty stories that highlight Indigenous displacement and the imprint of old tribal ways on the present. "Only those who remember their stories can see" (14), she insists.

Known primarily as a poet, Simon Ortiz (Acoma Pueblo) has published *Men on the Moon: Collected Short Stories* (1999). In the title story, a daughter buys her father a television and her son sets it up. After tuning the TV picture and switching a few channels, the grandson explains to his grandfather that he is watching the Apollo spacecraft and its men about to land on the moon. The old man is curious, asking what they hope to find. "Rocks," the boy explains, "knowledge" (1999, 5). Bemused, the grandfather returns from a trip to the outhouse with a rock he picked up on the way back. His grandson, confused, asks what it is. "Knowledge" (11), says the grandfather. Other stories tell of chance encounters of Indians on the margins or run-ins with priests and state police. Still others critique "power plants, multinational corporations, and the loss of Indian land" (133).

More recently, *The Beadworkers: Stories* (2019) by Beth Piatote (Nez Perce) offers a refreshing, ironic, and humorous look into Indigenous life. Piatote's collection of short fiction includes ten short stories and one retelling of a Greek myth. "Beadwork," writes Piatote, "is simply a part of everyday life, a form of currency, a distinctly Native form of creativity and labor that connects our stories and our lives across time and distance." Beadwork is a unifying motif for the volume. The stories are divided into four sections, each with an untranslated Nez Perce title that simultaneously entices and confounds readers who do not know Nez Perce (which is pretty much everyone). This strategic choice to not translate or offer linguistic or ethnographic footnotes forces readers to enter another epistemology. Rather than translate, Piatote offers a set of stories seemingly beaded together. She tells the stories of the everyday transmission of family and cultural knowledge, as in the story, "Beading Lesson," which highlights the themes and structure of the collection: an elder Auntie shares family history and cultural practice as she teaches her niece to bead. Beading becomes a metaphor for storytelling in "Falling Crows." The narrator muses: "Along those dark highways, their children sleeping on each other's shoulders in the back seat, they would string stories like beads into elaborate patterns" (2019, 89). The stories are diverse in plot, style, and point of view, from an eleven-year-old narrator describing family dysfunction, to an "Exhilarating Game of Kinship, Chance and Economic Recovery" (50), to an Indigenous reworking of an Ancient Greek play.

The Beadworkers concludes with Piatote's retelling of *Antigone* ("Antíkoni"). Rather than sharing Nez Perce oral narratives, she inflects Sophocles' drama with indigeneity. Antigone's warring brothers Eteocles

and Polynices have been replaced with Ataoklas, who has joined forces
with the Crow and sided with the Cavalry, and Polynaikas, who has
remained true to his Cayuse people. Of course, like their earlier counterparts, Ataoklas and Polynaikas have killed each other, and "colored that
valley bed with the dark stain of broken brotherhood" (2019, 138). In
Piatote's retelling, Antigone's uncle Creon is now Kreon, the Director of a
Museum that holds captive Indigenous cultural artifacts and ancestral
remains, including the bodies of Antíkoni's brothers. Interspersed
throughout the story are a chorus of five Aunties, who each tell old stories
about how Coyote prepared the world for humans; serving as the ethical
center, they offer a cultural context for Antíkoni's concern about the theft
of her brothers' bodies. For his part, Kreon argues that the museum gives a
second life, endowing pieces of the past with awe. And Trickster-like,
Kreon explains that he is merely infiltrating US power from within: "[W]e
must constantly / Change, shift our shapes, perform for them what they
wish to see / . . . This is how we've survived, and how we've undermined /
The United States of Surveillance" (143). The play closes with Antíkoni
suspended between life and death, leaving the audience to come to its
own conclusions.

As Thomas King (Cherokee) insists, "the advent of Native written
literature did not, in any way, mark the passing of Native oral literature. In
fact, they occupy the same space, the same time. And, if you know where
to stand, you can hear the two of them talking to each other" (2005,
101–102). Indeed, Gesa Mackenthun argues that Indigenous oral narratives simultaneously "precede modern Native American literature" and
"coexist with it" (2020, 33). This is especially true for many of the
Indigenous writers who came of age in what Kenneth Lincoln dubbed
the Native American Renaissance, a period launched by N. Scott
Momaday's 1969 Pulitzer Prize-winning novel *House Made of Dawn*,
which opened publishing possibilities for Native writers.

Among the many difficult-to-categorize short fictions by Indigenous
writers, Momaday's hybrid *The Way to Rainy Mountain* (1969) comes to
mind for its innovative interweaving of multiple voices: mythic, ethnographic (or historical), and personal, all punctuated with visuals.
Momaday's belief in the transforming possibilities of the imagination,
the synthesizing potential of memory, the identity-shaping influence of
the land, and the power and beauty of language, permeates *The Way to
Rainy Mountain*. Fashioned as a journey, the carefully structured group of
short stories speaks to and across places, times, and characters. The twenty-
four tripartite narrative units are divided into three larger clusters: "The

Setting Out" (Sections I–XI), "The Going On" (Sections XII–XVIII), and "The Closing In" (Sections XIX–XXIV). These three divisions reflect the historical movement of the Kiowa migration from "the mountains of what is now western Montana, traveling south and east to what is now south-western Oklahoma" (1979, 169), as well as Momaday's personal journey following their distant trail. Although the overall narrative movement of these three main sections is chronological, Momaday blends the mythic, historical, and personal by an elaborate process of association. Intermixing these distinct historical periods suggests how the past always permeates the present. Personal and tribal experience and past and present Indigenous lives are united in story. By the third section, Momaday has replaced ancient Kiowa myths with family stories now elevated to legendary status, suggesting that the mythical, historical, and personal are interrelated, existing in a temporal simultaneity. Throughout *The Way to Rainy Mountain*, Momaday retells Kiowa oral narratives and invents new myths, both reiterating and reconfiguring Kiowa history.

Leslie Marmon Silko's *Storyteller* (1981) is another example of an innovative mixture of short stories. A collection of poetry, prose, and photographs, *Storyteller* includes brief expository essays, autobiographical snippets, letters, retellings of oral stories as myth or gossip, numerous poems, and eight short stories. Throughout, Silko is concerned with recreating the spoken word on the page, retelling stories she heard from her Aunt Susie. Like Momaday, Silko blends mythical, communal, and personal stories. The short story "Yellow Woman" is a good example of Silko's belief that Indigenous oral traditions relate to contemporary life, that the old stories are simply reenacted in our current lives, and that today's storytellers and writers are renegotiating age-old narratives. The unnamed narrator, a modern-day Yellow Woman, awakens next to a man who, like the Kat'sina in some versions of the Yellow Woman abduction stories, has taken her away. Silko's retelling is rather ambiguous because the woman goes willingly, albeit with doubts. After spending a couple of days in the mountains with the mysterious stranger, the woman returns to her husband and children with a story, one curiously reminiscent of a Yellow Woman tale, to explain her absence. Infused with cultural colli-sions, survival strategies, and healthy doses of humor, the many short story forms in *Storyteller* bump up against each other in surprising ways. Together they enact Silko's belief in the primacy and interlinkings of stories across time.[1]

The stories in Gerald Vizenor's (Anishinaabe) *Earth Divers: Tribal Narratives on Mixed Descent* (1981) include Anishinaabe oral narratives and historical and personal stories woven together with a bawdy Trickster sensibility. While referencing the creator, the earthdiver who brings up soil to create the Earth, Vizenor shows how mixed-blood Natives dive deep to cobble together new worlds. "So, here we are now," says Cedarbird, "translated and invented skins, separated and severed like dandelions from the sacred and caught alive in words in the cities" (1981, 107). Anticipating later speculative fiction, he continues: "We are aliens in our own traditions" (107). Throughout the stories, Vizenor loses no opportunity to lampoon the antics of academic department chairs and tribal leaders, comment upon historical court and criminal cases, and unleash a wildly imaginative set of possibilities and absurdities.

As well as contemporary short stories that utilize cultural myths and characters in innovative styles, some Native American authors use a model of interlinked stories that borrows from both Indigenous story cycles and American short story cycles. Louise Erdrich's tetralogy of novels – *Love Medicine* (1984, 1993), *The Beet Queen* (1986), *Tracks* (1988), and *The Bingo Palace* (1994)[2] – is a good example. These earliest novels were first published as short stories, then shaped into novels. I have written about them as a short story cycle. Forrest Ingram defines a short story cycle as "a set of short stories linked to each other in such a way as to maintain balance between the individuality of each of the stories and the necessities of the larger unit" (1971, 13–15). The reader's experience of each story is modified by the experience of all the others. Of the different types of short story cycle delineated by Ingram, Erdrich's is closest to a *completed* cycle, stories forced into a set by adding to, revising, and rearranging them (17–18), because Erdrich neither planned the whole narrative network from the first story nor simply assembled and arranged a collection of stories, but added new stories and at least slightly revised earlier ones.

Whereas Ingram's framework highlights the process of composition of a short story cycle, Robert Luscher's notion of "the short story sequence" more fully describes its structure, both the form designed by the writer and that experienced by the reader. Luscher defines the short story sequence as "a volume of stories, collected and organized by their author in which the reader successively realizes underlying patterns of coherence by continual modifications of their perceptions of pattern and theme" (1989, 148–149). While this may be true also for chapters of novels, the continual inter-referencing in short story cycles is more robust.

Erdrich's short story cycle tells the transgenerational story of Ojibwe, mixed-blood, and European American families living on and around a fictional reservation in North Dakota. Each chapter, a standalone short story, but one in dialogue with all the others, is narrated by a character in the first person. Occasionally, a third-person narrator appears. The reader is tasked with weaving the stories into a vision of community, history, and culture. Like William Faulkner, Erdrich tells a family saga through many voices and achronological narratives, emphasizing the importance of a specific region and a sense of history haunting the present. Together the stories emphasize the importance of place; the power of story for survival; the necessity of healing; the search for Indigenous identity; the influence of the past on the present; the breakdown and reformulation of family in the wake of settler colonialism; the centrality of community in the struggle for continuance; and Trickster as a trope for the humor, wit, and shapeshifting necessary for Indigenous survival.

Another example of a short story cycle published as a "novel" is Greg Sarris's (Federated Indians of Graton Rancheria) *Grand Avenue: A Novel in Stories* (1994). The subtitle says it all. Like Erdrich, Sarris has multiple lively characters tell their stories: teenage boys and girls, elderly men and women, and everyone in between. Set in and around Santa Rosa, California, *Grand Avenue*'s ten interconnected stories reveal the mixed-blood Pomo family and their community's struggles with money, health, and love. The gritty details of everyday life are interwoven with the practice of traditional medicine and old-time stories. The spoken word leaps off the page, as when Jasmine proclaims: "Us Indians are full of evil, Auntie Faye said . . .. Not that we're bad people. Not like regular thieves and murderers. We inherit it. Something our ancestors did, maybe, or something we did to bring it on ourselves" (1994, 3). Throughout there are casual references to Christianity, alcohol abuse, dysfunctional relationships, and financial struggles. Stories are told from long ago and here and now; gossip abounds, uniting community members in a web of stories.

Anthologies of Native American literature have played a significant role in defining Indigenous literary modes and thematic preoccupations: *multi-genre survey* collections; anthologies devoted to Native American *women's writing* or *LGBTQ writers*; or *regionally specific* anthologies. There are also *genre-specific* anthologies that participate in defining Indigenous poetry or short fiction. The first anthology of contemporary short stories by Native writers was Kenneth Rosen's *The Man to Send Rain Clouds: Contemporary Stories by American Indians*, published in 1974. This volume played an important role in proving that Indigenous short fiction was neither ethnography nor history, but finely wrought literature.

The number of anthologies of Native short fiction doubled in the 1990s. Part of this can be attributed to the First North American

Writers' Festival, "Returning the Gift," that gathered "more Native writers together in one place than at any other time in history" (Bruchac 1994, xix) in the summer of 1992.[3] With the dire publishing realities of the twenty-first century (insufficient funding, compounded by the rise of digital publication and the dispersal of new work), anthologies of Indigenous short fiction (and of all short fiction) diminished in number.

In the twenty-first century, there has been increased production of children's and Young Adult short stories and of comics, as well as the rise of Indigenous speculative fiction. On a mission to offer positive, more realistic, and diverse representations of Indigenous people, Cynthia Leitich Smith (Muscogee) writes children's and Young Adult fiction. Her aim is to address Indigenous trauma "in a way that empowers kids rather than makes them feel like objects of inevitable oppression" (Goddy 2021, 29). Her curated volume *Ancestor Approved: Intertribal Stories for Kids* (2021) gathers together Native writers, who worked collaboratively to generate a collection of interconnected stories about participating in a powwow.[4] While this is a concentrated effort to add diverse stories for children, other well-known Indigenous writers have also written children's books over many years, including Joseph Bruchac, N. Scott Momaday, and Louise Erdrich. In 2006 Debbie Reese (Nambé Pueblo) founded American Indians in Children's Literature, an organization that monitors representations of Indigenous people in Children's Literature with the aim of getting rid of stereotypes.

There has also been a recent uptick in Indigenous graphic narratives or comics. This includes graphic short stories such as those collected in *Deer Woman: An Anthology* (2017), edited by Elizabeth La Penseé (Anishinaabe), a writer and game designer, and Weshoyot Alvitre (Tongva), a comic book artist and illustrator. The stories allude to Indigenous Deer Woman stories in which a seductive woman/deer leads a man into the woods with the promise of sex only to destroy him. In *Deer Woman*, the stories focus on the challenges and triumphs of contemporary Indigenous women, with a special emphasis on the ongoing violence against Native women. There are other examples, but it is worth noting that in 2015 Lee Francis IV (Laguna Pueblo) founded Native Realities Publishing to publish Native writing. In 2017 Francis and others co-founded Red Planet Books and Comics, a Native comics bookstore in Albuquerque (now home to Red Planet Books). They have supported the publication and circulation of Native comics in many forms, including short stories.

Eric Gary Anderson (2020) has discussed how Indigenous speculative fiction, which includes science fiction, postapocalyptic fiction, and horror fiction, has burgeoned in the twenty-first century. Although there were many twentieth-century precursors featuring "supernatural" beings, ghosts, or talking animals in the works of N. Scott Momaday, Leslie Marmon Silko, Anna Lee Walters, Gerald Vizenor, Louise Erdrich, Louis Owens, D'Arcy McNickle, and others, speculative fiction (with its creation of radically alternative realms or futures) is a more recent phenomenon. Grace L. Dillon (Anishinaabe) published the anthology of short stories *Walking the Clouds: Contemporary Science Fiction from the Pacific Northwest* in 2003. She also coined the term "Indigenous Futurism" (after "Afro Futurism") to describe Native science fiction writing that was reimagining Indigenous possibilities. Some writers, such as Drew Hayden Taylor (Curve Lake First Nations), have written speculative fiction in the form of short stories (and many more who have written in the novel form), the most prolific being Stephen Graham Jones (Blackfeet) who has produced at least six short story collections, besides many novels. Jones explains that he began writing about zombies and aliens as a way to liberate himself from stereotypes of what Indians were "supposed" to write about. His short story "How Billy Hanson Destroyed the Planet Earth, and Everyone on It" begins: "He wouldn't say this later, because he'd be dead along with everyone else, blasted into a cloud of comparatively warm ash swirling around in what had been Earth's orbital plane, but it wasn't his fault. Really" (2009). From the first paragraph, then, readers know the conclusion to the story. The rest is merely filling in the story of the faulty academic curiosity that leads the protagonist, a postdoctoral scientist, to push beyond the bounds and make fatal contact with an "alien." "Chapter Six" (2014) is an extended rant against academia (particularly anthropology) in the form of a zombie story. Will humans survive or themselves become zombies? In a surprise turn of events, a graduate student, Crain, feeds his professor the marrow of a zombie (thus turning his mentor into one), while he makes his escape with a barely surviving infant girl (not so subtly named Eve), a nod to the possibility of a human futurity. Jones's short stories, in their many varieties, highlight the limitations of human knowledge, the naive folly of Western science, and the precarity of life.

Responding to an Indigenous history already filled with apocalyptic realities – dispossession, genocide, reeducation, relocation, erasure – and tenuous futures, authors such as Jones make a grand leap away from historical realism, perhaps to generalize or universalize Indigenous trauma.

Jones's work opens opportunities for anyone to identify with unspeakable loss, but more likely the intention is to imagine Indigenous futures either built from the remains of historical apocalypse or to imagine Indigenous futures free of settler-colonial constructs.

Alongside this futurism, older versions of Indigenous storytelling continue in younger generations of Native writers as well. Hearkening back to Erdrich 's and Sarris's short story cycles, Eddie Chuculate (Muscogee and Cherokee) has published a recent collection of linked stories titled *Cheyenne Madonna* (2010). Chuculate narrates the journey of a Native man, Jordan, who – like Momaday's Abel and Silko's unnamed protagonist in *Ceremony* – struggles with alcohol, the law, and life in general. As Joy Harjo (Muscogee) explains in an endorsement of the book, Chuculate is a "journalist of the soul as he investigates the broken-hearted nation of Indian men."

So we conclude with at least two streams of Indigenous short story: the long tradition of realism, often infused with myth and oral narrative and dealing with language, land, interrelationality, and the sacred; and the more recent practice of fantasy, horror, or speculative fiction, infused with popular culture and featuring worlds where the borders of Earth and other planets or spheres collapse by either interpenetrating or colliding. In speculative fiction, hearkening back to real-life Indigenous apocalypses, there are possibilities for imagining radically new worlds.

And yet the long practice of historical realism endures. In his preface to *Why Indigenous Literature Matters* (2018), Daniel Heath Justice (Cherokee) explains that "*relationship* is the driving impetus behind the vast majority of texts by Indigenous writers – relationship to the land, to human community, to self, to the other-than-human world, to the ancestors and our descendants, to our histories and our futures, as well as to colonizers and their pathways for maintaining, rebuilding, or even, simply establishing these meaningful connections" (2018, xix). In a similar vein, Billy J. Stratton and Frances Washburn make the case for applying the "Peoplehood Matrix" as a "specialized theory for the analysis of American Indian literature" (2008, 51). The Peoplehood Matrix posits "four interdependent, interpenetrating components that communities of Indian people share – language, sacred history, place or territory, and ceremonial cycle" (51). This is yet another way of formulating sets of Indigenous relationship, this time to language, history, land, and ceremony, that allows for both tribally specific and generalized Indigenous preoccupations.

The enduring mode of historical realism, with its presentation of Indigenous epistemologies and experiences, and the more recent speculative fiction, with its wildly imaginative world formulations, both critique settler-colonial structures and offer alternative possibilities for Indigenous (and human) futures. It is through stories that these transformations are made possible. Stories, then, including short stories and short story cycles, historical realism and speculative fiction, create and design reality. No matter the classification, stories shape, determine, and provide new possibilities for Indigenous identities and futures.

Works Cited

Anderson, Eric Gary. 2020. "Native American Horror, Fantasy, and Speculative Fiction," in *The Cambridge History of Native American Literature*. Ed. Melanie Benson Taylor, 431–446. New York: Cambridge University Press.

Brant, Beth. 1984. "Introduction," in *A Gathering of Spirit: A Collection by North American Indian Women*. Ed. Beth Brant, 8–11. New York: Firebrand Books.

Bruchac, Joseph 1994. "Introduction," in *Returning the Gift: Poetry and Prose from the First North American Native Writers' Festival*. Ed. Joseph Bruchac, xvii–xxix. Tucson: University of Arizona Press.

Charters, Ann, ed. 2003. *The Story and Its Writer: An Introduction to Short Fiction*. 6th ed. Boston: Bedford/St. Martin's.

Chuculate, Eddie. 2010. *Cheyenne Madonna*. Boston: Black Sparrow Press.

Erdrich, Louise. 1985. "Where I Ought to Be: A Writer's Sense of Place," *New York Times Book Review*, July 28: 23–24.

Glancy, Diane. 1993. *Firesticks: A Collection of Stories*. Norman: University of Oklahoma Press.

1999. *The Voice That Was in Travel: Stories*. Norman: University of Oklahoma Press.

Goddy, Krystyna Poray. 2021. "Lifting Up Native American Voices," *Publishers Weekly*, February 15: 28–29.

Howe, LeAnne. 1999. "Tribalography: The Power of Native Stories," *Journal of Dramatic Theory and Criticism*. 14.1 (Fall): 117–125.

2002. "The Story of America: A Tribalography," in *Clearing the Path, Theorizing the Past in Native American Studies*. Ed. Nancy Shoemaker, 29–50. New York: Routledge.

2014. "Embodied Tribalography: Mound Building, Ball Games, and Native Endurance in the Southeast," *Studies in American Indian Literatures*. 26.2: 75–93.

Ingram, Forrest L. 1971. *Representative Short Story Cycles of the Twentieth Century: Studies in a Literary Genre*. The Hague: Mouton.

Johnson, E. Pauline. 2014 [1893]. "A Red Girl's Reasoning," in *Great Short Stories by Contemporary Native American Writers*. Ed. Bob Blaisdell, 1–16. New York: Dover Publications, Inc.

Jones, Stephen Graham. 2009. "How Billy Hanson Destroyed the Planet Earth, and Everyone on It," *Juked*, April 1. http://juked.com/2009/04/billyhanson .asp.

2014. "Chapter Six," *Tor*, June 11. www.Tor.com/2014/06/11/chapter-six-stephen-graham-jones/.

Justice, Daniel Heath. 2018. *Why Indigenous Literatures Matter*. Waterloo, Ontario: Wilfrid Laurier University Press.

King, Thomas. 2005. *The Truth About Stories: A Native Narrative*. Minneapolis: University of Minnesota Press.

La Pensée, Elizabeth and Weshoyot Alvitre, eds. 2017. *Deer Woman: An Anthology*. Albuquerque, NM: Native Realities.

Lesley, Craig, ed. 1991. *Talking Leaves: Contemporary Native American Short Stories*. New York: Dell Publishing.

Lohafer, Susan and JoEllyn Clarey, eds. 1989. *Short Story Theory at a Crossroads*. Baton Rouge: Louisiana State University Press.

Luscher, Robert M. 1989. "The Short Story Sequence: An Open Book," in *Short Story Theory at a Crossroads*. Eds. Susan Lohafer and JoEllyn Clarey, 148–167. Baton Rouge: Louisiana State University Press.

McNickle, D'Arcy. 2014 [1936]. "Train Time," in *Great Short Stories by Contemporary Native American Writers*. Ed. Bob Blaisdell, 40–44. New York: Dover Publications, Inc.

Mackenthun, Gesa. 2020. "Unsettling Colonial Temporalities: Oral Traditions and Indigenous Literature," in *The Cambridge History of Native American Literature*. Ed. Melanie Benson Taylor, 33–50. New York: Cambridge University Press.

Momaday, N. Scott. 1969. *The Way to Rainy Mountain*. Albuquerque: University of New Mexico Press.

1979. "The Man Made of Words," in *The Remembered Earth: An Anthology of Contemporary Native American Literature*. Ed. Geary Hobson, 162–173. Albuquerque: University of New Mexico Press.

Mourning Dove (Humishuma). 1990 [1934]. *Coyote Stories*. Ed. Heister Dean Guie. Illustrated by L. V. McWhorter (Old Wolf). Lincoln: University of Nebraska Press.

O'Connor, Frank. 1963. *The Lonely Voice: A Study of the Short Story*. Cleveland, OH: World Publishing Co.

Ortiz, Simon. 1999. *Men on the Moon: Collected Short Stories*. Tucson: University of Arizona Press.

Oskison, John M. 2014 [1925]. "The Singing Bird," in *Great Short Stories by Contemporary Native American Writers*. Ed. Bob Blaisdell, 25–39. New York: Dover Publications, Inc.

Piatote, Beth. 2019. *The Beadworkers: Stories*. Berkeley, CA: Counterpoint.

Sarris, Greg. 1994. *Grand Avenue: A Novel in Stories*. New York: Penguin Books.

Silko, Leslie Marmon. 1981. *Storyteller*. New York: Seaver Books.

Smith, Cynthia Leitich, ed. 2021. *Ancestor Approved: Intertribal Stories for Kids*. New York: Heartdrum.

Stratton, Billy J. and Frances Washburn. 2008. "The Peoplehood Matrix: A New Theory of American Indian Literature," *Wicazo Sa Review* 18.8 (Spring): 51–72.

Taylor, Melanie Benson. 2020. "Introduction: What Was Native American Literature?," in *The Cambridge History of Native American Literature*. Ed. Melanie Benson Taylor, 1–14. New York: Cambridge University Press.

Vizenor, Gerald. 1981. *Earth Divers: Tribal Narratives of Mixed Descent*. Minneapolis: University of Minnesota Press.

Zitkála-Šá. 2014 [1901]. "The Soft-Hearted Sioux," in *Great Short Stories by Contemporary Native American Writers*. Ed. Bob Blaisdell, 17–24. New York: Dover Publications, Inc.

CHAPTER 13

African American Short Fiction
From Reform to Renaissance
Amina Gautier

African American short fiction written in English[1] begins in the 1850s, taking shape in an age of reform and during a decade of deep political division over the question of slavery in existing and expanding US territories. Developed in a period famous not only for the Compromise of 1850 (with its passage of the Fugitive Slave Law), the Kansas-Nebraska Act, the Dred Scott Decision, the formation of the Republican Party, Bleeding Kansas, and the Harper's Ferry Raid, but also for Harriet Beecher Stowe's antislavery novel *Uncle Tom's Cabin* (1852), which advocated for the emancipation of the enslaved while also perpetuating racist stereotypes, African American short fiction begins as a revisionist endeavor that complicates, corrects, and critiques popular narratives that offered pejorative or reductive depictions of African American lives. Frederick Douglass's novella *The Heroic Slave* (1853), which provides a non-tragic portrait of black heroism, and Frances Ellen Watkins Harper's short story "The Two Offers" (1859), which offers a portrait of non-tragic spinsterhood, comprise the two earliest examples of short fiction published by African Americans. Both established writers in other genres, Douglass and Harper adopted short form fiction to commence a literary tradition in which African Americans drew upon the impactful nature of the condensed tale and relied on the power of brevity and concision to critique race and gender stereotypes while affirming black humanity.

Initially published in the first volume of *Autographs for Freedom*, a multi-genre anthology of antislavery writing, and later serialized in his own newspaper, Douglass's novella fictionalizes the story of Madison Washington, who led a successful slave revolt in 1841. *The Heroic Slave* builds an incontrovertible case for Washington's heroism, countering stereotypes of black inferiority in the person of Washington, whose behavior aboard the *Creole* refutes white assertions of black cowardice, ignorance, and savagery. First compared to Founding Fathers Patrick Henry, Thomas Jefferson, and George Washington, Madison Washington is glimpsed by Mr. Listwell, a white northerner, who views him as "black but comely" with a "manly form" and appearance that has "nothing savage or forbidding in his aspect" (Douglass 2015, 7). Washington's soliloquy on freedom converts Listwell to abolitionism, making him "resolved to atone" (9) for his past indifference and to aid both of Washington's attempts at escape. Washington has a similar effect on the *Creole*'s first mate Tom Gant, who initially curses him as a "*black murderer*" (48, italics in original) but is "disarmed" by Washington's rhetoric and ultimately forgets "his blackness in the dignity of his manner and the eloquence of his speech" (49). Gant's depiction of Washington as a courageous, just, and merciful leader, rather than a violent savage, authenticates Washington's heroism, providing an irrefutable eyewitness account for white readers and listeners. Presenting Washington in third-person narration, rather than making him the novella's first-person narrator, Douglass achieves the dual purposes of stylistically distancing Washington's story from his own slave narrative, while strategically courting the sympathy of white audiences, who receive a summarized recounting of the revolt from a white sailor rather than a graphic dramatization from Washington himself. Douglass's fictionalization of this historical figure expands antebellum literary depictions of black male heroism, complementing the version of heroism presented in Douglass's own slave narrative while supplementing the version presented by George Harris and Tom in Stowe's *Uncle Tom's Cabin*. Douglass embodies Washington with the intelligence and courage of George Harris without attributing those traits to white parentage and mixed-race heritage, and he endows Washington with Tom's ability to convert and galvanize white observers without turning Washington into a Christian martyr. Appearing one year after Stowe's runaway bestseller, the first piece of short fiction written in English by an African American is one that presents a black hero drawn upon revolutionary rather than religious ideals and celebrates triumph rather than tragedy.

Harper's "The Two Offers" appeared in the *Anglo-African Magazine*, a newspaper published by Thomas and Robert Hamilton, two African American abolitionist brothers. Fearing "the risk of being an old maid," Laura Lagrange chooses between two marriage offers, while her cousin Janette Alston warns that there is "more intense wretchedness in an ill-sorted marriage – more utter loneliness in a loveless home, than in the lot of the old maid" (Harper 1859, 4). Laura's marriage to an intemperate gambler hastens her to an early death, while the single Janette enjoys a career as a writer and abolitionist that provides "a competence of worldly means" and a life of "conquest, victory, and accomplishments" (6). Told

mostly in expository flashback, "The Two Offers" encourages independence in the absence of a morally and spiritually grounded marriage based
on an "affinity of minds" and "intercommunion of souls" (10). Rather
than viewing marriage as a woman's ultimate goal and spinsterhood as a
failure or the default position, Harper presents spinsterhood as a viable
choice and a preferable alternative to a bad marriage. The unmarried and
financially independent Janette provides a vibrant alternative to the ill-
matched wife exemplified by Laura, on the one hand, and the fussy
"spinster" exemplified by *Uncle Tom's Cabin*'s Ophelia St. Clare, on the
other. Unlike Ophelia, who is the "living impersonation of order, method,
and exactness" (Stowe 1986, 247), Janette invigorates without exhausting
and casts "a halo of beauty and grace around the charmed atmospheres in
which she moved" (Harper 1859, 6) as she transmits her moral and
spiritual principles into a life of public reform. In "The Two Offers"
Harper argues that marriage is a choice, neither a necessity, nor an
inevitability, nor an ideal, and with the figure of Janette Alston she
destigmatizes spinsterhood, offering readers a woman for whom the
absence of marriage has in no way detracted from her ability to lead a
fulfilling life.

* * *

As postwar advances in technology (telegraph and telephone), transportation (transcontinental railroad), and other economic and industrial
improvements threatened local cultures, both romanticism and the literature of reform gave way to realism and local color literature (a genre which
focused on capturing local and regional differences to highlight the cultural
specificities of a particular region). In response, African American writers
Alice Dunbar-Nelson (Alice Ruth Moore), Paul Laurence Dunbar, Charles
Chesnutt, and Pauline Hopkins adapted the trends in local color literature
to their own ends, using short fiction in efforts to accurately depict and
realistically portray the lives, landscapes, and linguistic idiosyncrasies of the
specific cultures and the particular communities of which they had personal knowledge. However, if antebellum era African American writers of
short fiction wrote in the long shadow cast by Stowe's *Uncle Tom's Cabin*,
then "Postbellum–Pre-Harlem" era African American short fiction writers
had to contend with the plantation tradition, a subgenre of local color
literature whose short fiction was exemplified by Joel Chandler Harris's
Uncle Remus: His Songs and His Sayings (1880) and popularized by
Thomas Nelson Page's *In Ole Virginia* (1887). Unlike Douglass and

Harper, whose short fiction relied heavily upon narrative summary and character retellings, Postbellum–Pre-Harlem African American short fiction writers couched their retellings within framed narratives and favored the use of scene, sketch, and vignette in lieu of extended summary. Rebutting romanticized accounts of race relations espoused in the plantation myths of Harris and Page, which stressed white nobility and black devotion, these writers delineated instead the specific cultural customs that governed and impacted race relations in their particular locales. Dunbar-Nelson and Hopkins depicted multiracial communities and interracial marriages, respectively, to highlight the instances where racial divides could be seen to meet, while Dunbar and Chesnutt's focus on the impact of Reconstruction on racially stratified communities unraveled stereotypes of black dependency, ignorance, and servility.

Alice Dunbar-Nelson depicts the various strata of New Orleans society in her multi-genre collection of poetry and prose *Violets and Other Tales* (1895) and short story collection *The Goodness of Saint Rocque* (1898). From the wealthy French Creole to the gamin, the merchant to the tramp, and the nun to the fortune-teller, Dunbar-Nelson presents characters from all social tiers who alternate between French and patois, whose faith combines Catholicism and conjure (a system of folk magic), who intermingle on bayous, waterfronts, levees, and at carnivals, and who represent the inextricably blended and melded culture of New Orleans society. Dunbar-Nelson's stories depict the sociocultural complexities of a multiracial community whose codes enforce strict social hierarchies yet allow some to transcend such boundaries while punishing others. A shy girl masquerades as a boy at a Mardi Gras festival in "A Carnival Jangle," an opera tenor pretends to be a fisherman in "The Fisherman of Pass Christian," and an "Americain" suitor secures his intended bride with an act of bravery that renders him an honorary Creole in "La Juanita." Despite the ease with which some characters manipulate or overcome sociocultural boundaries, Dunbar-Nelson portrays a socioeconomic system characterized by extremes, where either social or economic status can help one attain the other, but where the absence of both forces one to the societal fringes. A strike at the docks halts the fruit donations a tramp relies upon in "Mr. Baptiste," a seamstress must choose between saving money and eating in "Little Miss Sophie," and an elderly violinist displaced by new management can no longer afford his instrument in "M'Sieu Fortier's Violin." For all those living on the margins of society, the slightest economic change threatens their existence. Dunbar-Nelson depicts New Orleans society as one that allows sociocultural fluidity to those with means, while denying socioeconomic fluidity to and exacting punishment on the social striver without such means.

Between 1890 and 1905, Paul Laurence Dunbar published 103 short stories, of which some seventy appeared in his four short story collections *Folks from Dixie* (1898), *The Strength of Gideon* (1900), *Old Plantation Days* (1903), and *The Heart of Happy Hollow* (1904). Representing "his most significant and sustained engagement with the literary conventions that ultimately frustrated his efforts at writing poetry, the novel, and plays," Dunbar's commercially successful short fiction is "where his most serious political interventions occur" (Jarrett and Morgan 2005, xvi, xviii). Dunbar's stories frequently take stock figures and mine them for humanity, but never is his manipulation of stereotypes more sophisticated than when he uses the figure of the devoted and ignorant slave to ridicule the customs of white southern gentility and dispels both of these intertwined cultural myths simultaneously. In "The Colonel's Awakening" and "Nelse Hatton's Vengeance," Dunbar reverses racial and social hierarchies, depicting white men whose maladjustments to reconstructed societies place them at the mercy of their former slaves. In the former story, postwar reversals of fortune, combined with the death of his two sons in the Confederate Army, trigger dementia-like symptoms in an old colonel. Psychologically stuck in the antebellum past, he is supported by his two remaining servants, who indulge his delusion out of deference to his declining health. In the latter story, the destitute son of a slave-owner travels north and appears as a supplicant at his former slave Nelse Hatton's door, where he is mistaken for a "straggler" (Dunbar 2005, 59). Nelse gifts him a brand-new suit and enough money to return south, magnanimously foregoing retaliation because living well has already been his best revenge. Both white former slave owners in the two stories depend upon black benevolence after the Civil War and benefit materially from the largess of their former slaves, who are neither slavishly devoted nor ignorant, but able to regard white delusions of social superiority with pity in light of their own improved circumstances.

Dunbar disrupts the myth of child-like slaves, dependent upon white masters, with stories featuring slave owners who benefit from black wisdom and intervention. In "The Intervention of Peter," Peter learns of his master's impending duel. Recognizing the foolishness and inherent danger of dueling and unimpressed by the social etiquette regarding insults and protocols of honor, Peter disrupts the duel, thereby saving his master's life. "A Family Feud" recounts a tale, similar to Thomas Nelson Page's "Marse Chan," of lovers on neighboring plantations kept apart by feuding fathers.

Emmerline, who has raised the son of her owner after his mother's death, views the feud between father and son as an affront to her years of caretaking and a waste of her labor. Dismissing the delicacy of white pride, she convinces the two to reconcile by playing on their sympathies. "Marse Chan" and "A Family Feud" both deploy framed narratives in which black narrators tell their story to an outsider, but where Page's story commemorates the heir who dies on the Confederate battlefield before he can claim his bride, Dunbar's outsider critiques the narrator's nostalgia instead of commiserating: "[W]hat if the glamour of memory did put a halo round the heads of some people who were never meant to be canonised?" (Dunbar 2005, 45). Though deemed humorous by their white counterparts for their perceived social ignorance, Pete and Emmerline's blatant dismissals of social etiquette and protocols of honor engineer moments of dramatic irony in which white characters find humor in black intervention, yet where black characters prove to be the most sensible.

Like Harris and Page's stories, Chesnutt's fourteen conjure short stories, of which seven were ultimately collected in *The Conjure Woman* (1899), are set on a plantation and are structured as framed tales that tell a story within a story and pair a black storyteller who speaks in informal vernacular with a white listener who speaks formal English. Specifically, Chesnutt's white listener and narrator of the frame's outer tales is John, a northerner who relocates to North Carolina for his wife's health, and the black storyteller who narrates the inner tales is Julius McAdoo, a former slave who once lived on the plantation John now owns. Flouting many of the conventions of the genre Harris and Page epitomized, Chesnutt's stories make the slave's plight their central subject. In plantation fiction, the framed tale's inner and outer narratives often juxtapose two different time periods, contrasting the difference in race relations between the inner narrative's antebellum period and the outer narrative's postbellum era, thereby using the juxtaposition to mourn bygone days. Chesnutt's conjure stories upend this convention. Julius's stories are not told to an adoring young white child but to a skeptical adult white couple, who exploit his stories for entertainment to pass the time. As the narrator of the frame's outer tales, John functions to make the frame's inner tales palatable to white audiences while his presence as a northern transplant implies postwar reconciliation across regional lines. Nevertheless, Julius's revelations poke holes in the frame and show the ways in which the past continues to bleed into the newly reconstructed present. Unlike Page's "happy darky" narrators whose inner tales eulogize the era of slavery, Chesnutt's Julius McAdoo revives the horrors of slavery and forces his audience to confront its abuses in everyday items, such as hams ("Dave's Neckliss"), an old schoolhouse ("Po' Sandy"), and banks of clay ("Lonesome Ben"), and thus acknowledge the presence of slavery all around them. Recounting the numerous abuses suffered by slaves that force them to turn to "goophering," or conjuring, Julius's stories suggest that slaves who have no legal recourse are forced to adopt otherworldly methods to procure relief from their oppressive conditions. Furthermore, the indignities they suffer, from being separated from their children ("Sis' Becky's Pickaninny") or being sold and resold ("The Goophered Grapevine"), impress upon listeners not only the cruelties endured but also that the South is deeply scarred by its legacy of slavery.

Whereas the stories in *The Conjure Woman* take place entirely in North Carolina, the nine stories in Chesnutt's second collection, *The Wife of His Youth* (1899), are spread across the South and Cleveland Ohio, fictionalized as "Groveland." Several "Groveland" stories highlight the Blue Vein Society, a group of mixed-race individuals "more white than black" (Chesnutt 1968, 1) who eschew interactions with darker-skinned blacks and pride themselves on free birth, fairness of skin, and social exclusivity. Satirizing their pretensions, Chesnutt thwarts their attempts to lighten the race in "The Wife of His Youth," when the "most conservative" (3) member of the Society is confronted with his long-lost black wife, and in "A Matter of Principle," when the richest member of the Society ruins his daughter's marriage prospects due to his own colorism. Set mostly in the postbellum period, *The Wife of His Youth* depicts relationships distorted by slavery and disrupted by the chaos of war as parents, children, spouses, and fiancés scattered and separated by slavery return to be recognized, redeemed, or repudiated. In "Her Virginia Mammy," adoptee Clara Hohlfelder refuses to marry lest her unknown background impede her lover's professional aspirations; fearing only illegitimacy, she never considers the possibility that she is mixed-race. In "The Sheriff's Children," a white sheriff imprisons a mixed-race stranger, who then discloses their relationship. In "Cicely's Dream," a wounded man's amnesia makes his racial background impossible to determine. Though the Civil War effectively ends slavery, in many cases it renders relationships null and void, legally canceling "slave law" marriages, thus allowing both Mr. Ryder ("The Wife of His Youth") and Wellington Braby ("Uncle Wellington's Wives") to believe themselves free to remarry. As Chesnutt's *The Conjure Woman* shows the ubiquitous scars of slavery across the South, *The Wife of His Youth* underscores the inescapability of slavery, whose repercussions continue to touch and impact the lives and relationships it formed.

Prior to publishing the four novels for which she is most known, Pauline Hopkins published several short stories in the *Colored American Magazine*, including what is considered the first African American mystery story: "Talma Gordon" (1900). Presented to his club members in order to espouse his belief in interracial marriage, Dr. Thornton discloses a mystery in which Mr. Gordon, his wife, and their young son were found murdered in their beds and Gordon's daughter Talma stood accused of the crime. Adopting the "locked-room mystery" plot (in which a crime occurs in a way that makes it impossible to determine how the perpetrator entered or left the scene), exemplified by Edgar Allan Poe's "Murders in the Rue Morgue" (1841), Hopkins creates a story whose surprising conclusion can only be reached after a layered untangling. Through deathbed confessions and suicide notes the murderer is revealed, along with the secret that Talma is one-thirty-second black and that her mother was a hexadecaroon, the child of an octoroon and a white person. At the heart of her mystery Hopkins plants a tale of birth and blood, using tangled bloodlines to underscore the fallacy of blood purity, and portraying race prejudice and anti-miscegenation sentiment as crimes akin to murder. Hopkins counters the opinions of Talma's father, who considers marriage to a mixed-race woman a "dire disgrace" (Hopkins 2021, 16), and Talma's fiancé, who "could stand the stigma of murder" but not "the pollution of Negro blood" (17), with Dr. Thornton's medical conclusion that interracial marriages are natural, due to "the law of heredity which makes us all one common family" (7). In the figure of Dr. Thornton, Hopkins presents a detective-like figure who attests to the pervasiveness of miscegenation and declares that its inevitability is an expected outcome of human interaction.

* * *

In comparison to the short fiction published by African Americans in the nineteenth century, which was corrective, didactic, and responsive, the short fiction of the Harlem Renaissance, or New Negro Movement, offers a body of literature that is less concerned with getting ahead of racist stereotypes and teaching moral lessons and more concerned with the modernist principle to "make it new" by reveling in and celebrating black life and culture. This took several forms: capturing the life of folk communities and their ways; enshrining the lives of urbane middle- and upper-class black communities; exploring the arenas in which black and white communities interact and clash, such as in Harlem's nightclubs or the segregated South; or simply incorporating the rhythms of jazz into the text.

White characters, opinions, and responses are often scrutinized by African Americans, who examine them through an ethnographic lens, thus rendering whiteness subject to the black gaze. Although explorations of mixed-race identity remain thematic concerns, Harlem Renaissance short fiction writers express a race pride in which the cultural costs of racial passing outweigh the socioeconomic benefits. What characters who pass lose in terms of cultural identification and social interaction – for example, the relinquishing of direct claims to black relatives and communities, as well as direct identification with black art, literature, and music at a time in which such advances are being lauded – is deemed too costly. Stylistically, the short stories published during the New Negro Movement represent an evolution from that of their Postbellum–Pre-Harlem predecessors, which relied heavily on karmic justice, sentiment, and twist endings/reveals. Harlem Renaissance short fiction writers, especially Nella Larsen and Rudolph Fisher, with their brief but brilliant literary careers and their concentrated efforts to depict urban landscapes, and Zora Neale Hurston and Langston Hughes, whose literary careers lasted well beyond the Harlem Renaissance and whose writings expertly explored folk traditions, moved from a reliance on sentiment and surprise to a focus on dialogue and dramatic action. Their story endings, while sometimes surprising, relied more on chance than contrivance. Less heavily narrated, their characters' motives are frequently hinted at in dialogue and often revealed only through flashes of intuition. Rather than being subject to providence or karmic justice, their characters appear as the engineers of their own demise and are redeemed or ruined by chains of events spurred by their own actions or inactions. Though many members of the New Negro Movement turned their hand to publishing short fiction during the period, when taken together, the short fiction of Larsen, Fisher, Hurston, and Hughes espouse both the artistic aims of the movement and represent a stylistic evolution toward the contemporary short story.[2]

Larsen's three short stories frame her two published novels, *Quicksand* (1928) and *Passing* (1929). Published pseudonymously in 1926, both "The Wrong Man" and "Freedom" examine the fragile instability of romantic relationships and feature women whose romantic affairs leave them at the mercy of men. In "The Wrong Man," Julia Romney's attempts to bury her past are thwarted at a posh dinner party when she discovers her former lover in attendance and seeks to shield their past relationship from her husband. In "Freedom," a man abandons his mistress while he is away on business by sending her a telegram indicating his "indefinite return" (Larsen 2001, 15), after which he spends the year traveling and envisions her "flitting from mate to mate" (14). Though Larsen disparaged the two stories for their pulpy content (xiii), they share thematic and stylistic similarities with her novels. Julia Romney in "The Wrong Man," who was "so young, so foolish, and so hungry" (9), accepts the male sponsorship that Helga Crane, the protagonist of *Quicksand*, rejects when hungry and jobless in Chicago (66). Afraid she will "lose everything – love, wealth, and position" (5), Romney despairs of losing the security that Irene Redfield in *Passing* maneuvers to retain and that the male protagonist of "Freedom" demonstrates can be so easily and indifferently rescinded. Following on the heels of her novels, Larsen's third story, "Sanctuary" (1930), departed from Larsen's preoccupation with the modern, urbane, and cosmopolitan locales of the middle and upper classes by taking the rural South as its landscape and racial solidarity as its theme. Approached by Jim Hammer, who is on the run for (presumably) shooting a white man, Annie Poole agrees to hide him to protect him from the white authorities. Resemblances between Larsen's "Sanctuary" and British author Sheila Kaye-Smith's "Mrs. Adis" led to accusations of plagiarism against Larsen, which may have contributed to Larsen's withdrawal from literary circles.

Between 1925 and his death in 1934, Rudolph Fisher published fifteen short stories (along with two novels). All set in Harlem, Fisher's stories "affirm the complexity of black urban culture while steering clear of exotica and oversentimentality" (McCluskey 2008, 2). Exploring the chimeric nature of the predominantly black neighborhood, Fisher's stories present Harlem as both a racially welcoming space where "black was white" and "you had privileges, protected by the law" (Fisher 2008, 36) as well as a confining and stratifying environment that forces residents to live crowded "like bees in a hive" (101) and pits old against young, African American against West Indian, spirituals against the blues, and churches against cabarets. Newcomers and transplants gape at the sights of ambulances, black police officers, and elevators, while taking in "a sewer of sounds and smells" (38) and noting the scarcity of land and the lack of open air: "There were no trees. No ground for trees to grow from. Sidewalks overflowing with children. Streets crammed full of street-cars and automobiles. Noise, hurry, bustle – fire engines" (64). Seen as a modern paradise by the youth and an "outpost of hell" (60) by their older counterparts, Harlem – and its capricious nature – is captured by Fisher in Mammy's description of it as a promised land: "All hit do is promise. Promise money lak growin' on trees – ain' even got d' trees" (84).

Chronicling the experiences of southern transplants in a modernized and urbanized space, Fisher shows what Harlem is like when the lights come up. Young men who leave the South to fight in the war overseas and stop in Harlem on their return never find their way back home. Young men flee north to escape white vigilantism and declining economic prospects, only to run afoul of the law in Harlem ("City of Refuge") or be deemed unemployable due to a lack of urban skills ("The South Lingers On"). Acclimatization to the environment weakens bonds of kinship, as in "City of Refuge," in which Mouse Uggam has no qualms about betraying King Solomon Gillis, a friend from his own hometown, or in "The Promised Land," in which Sam kills his cousin Wesley over a woman. However, not everyone succumbs. Some prosper, such as the performer Dave Tappen ("Miss Cynthie") who finds material success with a musical revue that merges the folk with the modern/urban to create something new. Those who learn to synthesize down-home common sense with modern uptown cleverness, such as Grammie ("Guardian of the Law"), who foils criminals, Ezekiel ("Ezekiel Learns"), who thwarts a bully, Dr. Archer ("John Archer's Nose"), who solves a murder, Effie White ("Blades of Steel"), who defuses an altercation, or Jean Ambrose and Bus Williams ("Common Meter"), who outwit a cheat, all benefit from their dual knowledge and are able to effectively navigate the vagaries of Harlem.

Unlike Larsen and Fisher, whose literary careers were cut short, Zora Neale Hurston published short stories throughout the entire period of the New Negro Movement, beginning in 1921 and continuing through the late 1930s and beyond. Hurston's early short stories were praised "for her command of narrative voice and plotting, her concern with themes of divine justice, her delight in the Southern black vernacular voice as a vehicle for narration" (Gates and Lemke 1996, x), and Hurston's narrative scope is easily seen in the range of topics treated in her short fiction. Her first three publications, "John Redding Goes to Sea," "A Bit of Our Harlem," and "Drenched in Light," all published between 1921 and 1926, take youths as their subject; two feature adventurous adolescents hampered by restrictive circumstances. In "John Redding Goes to Sea," John is "an imaginative child" (Hurston 1996, 1) whose desire to travel and see the world is met with suspicion by his community, who consider him to be cursed and singular, since "no one of the community had ever been farther away than Jacksonville" (4); in "Drenched in Light," Isis Watkins, who is routinely chastised by her grandmother for her exuberance and is forbidden to whistle, play with boys, and cross her legs (19), is publicly appreciated by a trio of white out-of-towners who praise her zest for life. Both John and Isis prefigure Janie, Hurston's protagonist in *Their*

Eyes Were Watching God, whose desire for more than respectability and financial security set her at odds with her community.

Hurston's short stories are not limited to southern locales, contemporary times, or even humans. Her Harlem stories depict members of the urban black middle class ("The Back Room") as well as transplants from the South whose attempts at assimilation are thwarted ("The Country in the Woman") or meet with success ("The Book of Harlem"). "Magnolia Flower" has a river for its narrator, "Cock Robin Beale Street" features a cast of anthropomorphic birds, and "Fire and Cloud" records conversations on Mount Nebo after the Exodus of the Hebrews from Egypt. Mimicking biblical chapters in form, format, and content, "The Book of Harlem" inverts the parable of the prodigal son in the tale of Jazzbo, who leaves his rural home to sojourn in "Babylon" (aka Harlem), where he indulges in a period of profligacy yet does not squander his father's money. Rather than returning home impoverished, he saves his "shekels," marries the first virgin he meets, and buys her "fur of the mink, and much fine raiment and a sedan of twelve cylinders" (Hurston 2020, 172). Many of Hurston's stories take the tongue-in-cheek approach to romantic relationships of "The Book of Harlem" or focus on people getting their just desserts, as in "Spunk," where a cowardly husband is killed in a confrontation with his wife's lover, only for the lover to end up haunted by the dead husband's ghost, and "Sweat," where a laundress's wastrel husband torments her with a rattlesnake, only to become the victim of his own prank. But others, such as "The Back Room" and "Under the Bridge," forego humor to explore the pathos of romantic relationships. In "The Back Room," the single Lilya Barkman considers marriage after long fearing its aging effect on women who have to deal with "worrying with a house and husband at the same time" (Hurston 2020, 173). "Under the Bridge" depicts a widower torn between love for his new young wife and his adult son, as he simultaneously seeks to protect his wife from the attention of other men, yet also wants his son "to know nothing but happiness" (140).

Published between 1927 and 1928, Langston Hughes's first four short stories, "Bodies in the Moonlight," "The Young Glory of Him," "The Little Virgin," and "Luani of the Jungles," revolve around the crew of the *West Illana*, which is sailing to West Africa. Narrated by a black messboy, the four stories portray the democratizing culture of sailors as a multiracial group of men who form a brotherhood that is disrupted only by disputes over women. Hughes's short story collection *The Ways of White Folks*

(1934) appears near the tail end of the Harlem Renaissance and after the onset of the Great Depression. The collection's fourteen short stories depict the restrictive and often dehumanizing effects of white patronage, an inability on the part of whites to comprehend black humanity, the effects of racial isolation, and the value of black social interaction. Inverting the gaze, the stories in *The Ways of White Folks* render whites as Other and subject them to black scrutiny. Under the black gaze interracial relationships are revealed as tenuous and as transactional associations which often yield fatal or dehumanizing results. Whether it is a wealthy white benefactress who withdraws her financial support when her protégé wishes to marry ("The Blues I'm Playing"), or the white couple who raise a black orphan in an all-white town and condemn him for his desire to socialize with black expats and musicians ("Poor Little Black Fellow"), or an old white Manhattanite who suffers a psychological breakdown when a black woman chooses a man of her own age and race over his wealth ("A Good Job Gone"), or an artistic white couple who fetishize their black gardener ("Slave on the Block"), Hughes depicts white characters whose unconscious bias permeates and taints their relationships, preventing them from ever seeing their black counterparts as independent humans. In story after story, black characters who assert themselves lose the goodwill of their white benefactors, employers, foster parents, parents, and patrons as black agency is met with white retribution in the form of loss of employment, loss of patronage, and occasionally loss of life. *The Ways of White Folk* shows black independence to be a punishable and intolerable offense, as in "Home" and "Father and Son," where black men's assertions of social equality are crimes punishable by death. In "Home," violinist Roy Williams returns from abroad to the South and is lynched and killed by a crowd of white moviegoers who see him with a white female acquaintance. In "Father and Son," when a white plantation owner's mixed-race son returns home from college and refuses to be "a white man's nigger" (Hughes 1990, 228), a physical altercation ensues that finds the son pursued by a lynch mob.

Blurring the line between white patronage and black servitude, Hughes shows black characters forced to depend upon white patronage or financial support at the expense of black social interaction and cultural identification. Hughes's characters see through the pretense of white benevolence to the underlying prejudice that makes black humanity and independence so incomprehensible. Alluding to the white patronage so many black artists depended on during the New Negro Movement, Hughes depicts the dehumanizing restrictions such patronage places on black artists. In stories that examine white failures to recognize black humanity and black people as fully human, with the same desires for love, privacy, kindness, and recognition, Hughes presents transactional interracial interactions characterized by white cultural exploitation and racial isolation.

From summary and sentiment to sketch and scene, from framed tales and twist endings to deft dialogue and dramatization, African American short fiction evolved in terms of craft and content from the reform era to Reconstruction to the Harlem Renaissance. Beginning by responding to and replacing racist and sexist stereotypes and tropes with affirmations of African American humanity, then undermining and deconstructing popular genres and trends in literature which falsely romanticized race relations and spread myths of black inferiority, and ultimately making it new by reveling in the ups and downs of black life and culture from high to low, folk to urbane, African American writers of short fiction adapted the form to suit their various and ever-changing stylistic and sociocultural needs.

Work Cited

Chesnutt, Charles W. 1968. *The Wife of His Youth*. Ed. Earl Schenck Miers. Ann Arbor: University of Michigan Press.

  1993. *The Conjure Woman and Other Conjure Tales*. Ed. Richard H. Brodhead. Durham, NC: Duke University Press.

Douglass, Frederick. 2015. "The Heroic Slave," in *The Heroic Slave: A Cultural and Critical Edition*. Eds. Robert S. Levine, John Stauffer, and John R. McKivigan, 3–52. New Haven, CT: Yale University Press.

Dunbar, Paul Laurence. 2005. *The Complete Stories of Paul Laurence Dunbar*. Eds. Gene Andrew Jarrett and Thomas Lewis Morgan. Athens: Ohio University Press.

Dunbar-Nelson, Alice. 1895. *Violets and Other Tales*. www.gutenberg.org/files/18713/18713-h/18713-h.htm.

  1899. *The Goodness of St. Roque and Other Stories*. www.gutenberg.org/ebooks/688.

Fisher, Rudolph. 2008. *The City of Refuge: The Collected Stories of Rudolph Fisher*. Eds. John McCluskey, Jr. Columbia: University of Missouri Press.

Gates, Henry Louis, Jr. and Sieglinde Lemke. 1996. "Introduction," in *The Complete Stories*. Zora Neale Hurston, ix–xxiii. New York: Harper Perennial.

Harper, Frances Ellen Watkins. 1859. "The Two Offers." www.literaryladies-guide.com/full-texts-of-classic-works/the-two-offers-by-frances-watkins-harper/.

Hopkins, Pauline E. 2021. *Talma Gordon*. Berkeley, CA: West Margin Press.

Hughes, Langston. 1990. *The Ways of White Folks*. New York: Vintage.

1996. *Short Stories*. Ed. Donna Akiba Sullivan Harper. New York: Hill and Wang.

Hurston, Zora Neale. 1996. *The Complete Stories*. New York: Harper Perennial.

2020. *Hitting a Straight Lick with a Crooked Stick*. Ed. Genevieve West. New York: HarperCollins.

Jarrett, Gene Andrew and Thomas Lewis Morgan. 2005. "Introduction," in *The Complete Stories of Paul Laurence Dunbar*. Ed. Gene Andrew Jarrett and Thomas Lewis Morgan, xv–xliii. Athens: Ohio University Press.

Larsen, Nella. 2001. *The Complete Fiction of Nella Larsen: Passing, Quicksand, and The Stories*. Ed. Charles Larson. New York: Anchor Books.

McCluskey, John, Jr. 2008. "Introduction," in *The City of Refuge: The Collected Stories of Rudolph Fisher*. Ed. John McCluskey, Jr., 1–31. Columbia: University of Missouri Press.

Stowe, Harriet Beecher. 1986. *Uncle Tom's Cabin, or, Life Among the Lowly*. Ed. Ann Douglass. New York: Penguin Press.

CHAPTER 14

Little Postage Stamps
The Short Story, The American South, and the World

Coleman Hutchison

> One place comprehended can make us understand other places better. Sense of place gives equilibrium; extended, it is sense of direction too.
>
> – Eudora Welty, "Place in Fiction"

The short story remains at the heart of southern literature. Anthologies, surveys, and criticism all tout the centrality of the form to the representation of the region. For instance, two of the earliest and most popular genres of southern literature, antebellum "southwestern humor" and post-Civil War "local color," favored the tale or sketch. Several southern writers are considered, in turn, masters of the craft of short fiction: Katherine Anne Porter (1890–1980), Eudora Welty (1909–2001), and Flannery O'Connor (1925–1964), among others. And although William Faulkner (1897–1962) is best known for his novels, several of his "shortened stories" are common in secondary and college curricula: "A Rose for Emily" (1930), "Dry September" (1931), "That Evening Sun" (1931), and "Barn Burning" (1939). This is to say nothing of two of the most influential short story writers, Edgar Allan Poe (1809–1849) and O. Henry (1862–1910), both of whom are claimed as southern writers due to their strong connections to the South.

In accounting for this long-established relationship between form and place, the editors of a popular anthology, *The Signet Classic Book of Southern Short Stories*, celebrate short fiction writers' "focus" and "clarity of . . . vision," suggesting that these features result in "better understanding of their region and how it shapes the people who live there" (Abbott and Koppelman 1999, xvi). Of course, such focus and clarity of vision is not unique to the short fiction of the US South. As the comparatist Roberto Maria Dainotto argues, regionalism functions as "a rhetorical figure of difference and opposition" across a variety of literatures (2000, 9). Writers, readers, critics, and editors must be careful not to reify or romanticize regionalism; difference and opposition need not be fetishized. After all, regional fictions are almost always aimed at national and even international audiences; so-called provincial writers remain keenly aware of metropolitan publishers and the readers they serve. Thus, difference and opposition are both conditions for and subjects of regional writing. Nonetheless, Abbott and Koppelman are not wrong: the literature of place is indeed well-suited to short forms, which can offer a carefully framed image of difference and opposition.

Put another way, regional short stories function as little postage stamps that promise access to and communication with far-flung places. While Faulkner – a famously desultory former postal worker – used the phrase "my own little postage stamp of native soil" to emphasize the relatively small size of his fictional Yoknapatawpha County, the metaphor has broader implications in this context since it suggests both a sense of scale and wider circuits of distribution. The short story form does not merely facilitate a focus on diverse, local cultures. Because short stories can be easily republished and collected, the form also allows such diverse, local cultures to circulate broadly. This brings to mind Brad Evans's helpful arguments about literature as "circulating culture" in the post-Civil War United States. For Evans, literature is a vehicle for the "articulation and disarticulation of different systems of meaning across discontinuous geographies and temporalities" (2005, 15). His emphasis on circulation challenges the "boundedness of categories by which we imagine difference" and dominant modes of cultural interpretation (16). Not surprisingly, local color fiction – much of it short form – plays a major role in Evans's account of the "ethnographic imagination" between 1865 and 1920. Like postage stamps, then, regional fiction permits a transit between writer and reader, and among region, nation, and world. In doing so, it also encourages a more expansive understanding of cultural difference.

The US South is large and diffuse, its literary history long and protean. In examining the ways short fictional forms enable access, communication, and circulation, the following discussion focuses on two canonical writers, Kate Chopin (1850–1904) and Zora Neale Hurston (1891–1960), before briefly treating a contemporary writer, Oscar Cásares (born 1964). The result is a wide-ranging, if idiosyncratic, survey of southern short fiction. These case studies allow me to consider in miniature the explosion of late nineteenth-century local color writing, which helped commodify the South for a national literary audience; modernist experiments with form and voice, which propelled both the Southern Renaissance and the Harlem

Renaissance; and contemporary redefinitions of region, which have fundamentally changed who and what counts as southern. Chopin and Hurston led peripatetic lives, as has Cásares, spending significant time outside of the South. Perhaps as a result, their short fiction resounds with regionalism, while also emphasizing the South's increasing cultural diversity. What emerges from the following pages is a literature of the provinces that is far from provincial – a regional literature *par excellence* that remains very much engaged with the broader world.

Kate Chopin: Fire on the Bayou

Although closely associated with Louisiana, where she lived from 1870 to 1884, Kate Chopin spent most of her life in St. Louis, Missouri. Born Catherine O'Flaherty to parents of Irish and French extraction, she grew up in a bilingual and bicultural milieu, speaking both French and English. Coming of age in a border state during the Civil War, she also managed split political allegiances: the O'Flaherty family owned slaves and largely supported the Confederacy. In 1870, at the age of twenty, Kate married Oscar Chopin of Natchitoches Parish, Louisiana. Following an extensive tour of Europe, the Chopins settled first in New Orleans and then Cloutierville, a small French village in northwest Louisiana. During her decade and a half in the Bayou State, Chopin raised six children while also keeping a keen eye on the diverse people and cultures of Louisiana, which would become the central focus of her fiction. Following her husband's death, Chopin moved the family back to her native St. Louis in 1884, where she began her writing career in earnest.

Chopin is now best remembered for her controversial 1899 novel *The Awakening*, but during the 1890s Chopin's short stories were a mainstay in the pages of national magazines such as the *Atlantic Monthly*, *Century*, *Harper's Young People*, *Vogue*, and *Youth's Companion*, among others. These brief southern fictions, many of which were collected in *Bayou Folk* (1894) and *A Night in Acadie* (1897), betray the influence of Guy de Maupassant; they also luxuriate in cultural difference, emphasizing Louisiana's distinctive blending of French, Spanish, African, and indigenous cultures. The stories in these collections are, in the words of one of Chopin's editors, "strikingly varied from one another . . . . She writes about ethnic distinctions, class, race, money, divorce, religion, sex, and, more than anything else, social possibilities." While the result is kaleidoscopic in effect, several characters recur throughout the collections, suggesting a coherent narrative world for *Bayou Folk* and *A Night in Acadie* (Chopin 1999, viii, xi).

"At the 'Cadian Ball" (1892) is a representative story. First published in the Boston-based periodical *Two Tales* and later collected in *Bayou Folk*, this 3,700-word story foregrounds a thwarted cross-cultural and cross-class romance. Alcée Laballière is a wealthy Creole planter who comes to a party and renews his flirtation with Calixta, a poor Acadian woman with Cuban roots. Disgusted by Alcée's supposed slumming and threatened by the exotic Calixta, Clarisse, the Creole goddaughter of Alcée's mother, follows him to the titular ball, convincing him to come home with her. Clarisse's last-minute intervention restores social order by reimposing clear cultural and class lines: Alcée's sudden departure with Clarisse forces Calixta back to Bobinôt, her long-suffering Acadian suitor. At the end of the story, marriage looms for both couples.

Swerving, frustrated love stories were one of Chopin's preferred methods for rendering regional and cultural difference. By giving readers a familiar, even predictable romantic plot, Chopin was able to double down on cultural specificity – to intensify the local color in her local color fiction. Here, for instance, is Chopin's initial description of the ball:

> The big, low-ceiled room – they called it a hall – was packed with men and women dancing to the music of three fiddles. There were broad galleries all around it. There was a room at one side where sober-faced men were playing cards. Another, in which babies were sleeping, was called *le parc aux petits*. Any one who is white may go to a 'Cadian ball, but he must pay for his lemonade, his coffee and chicken gumbo. And he must behave himself like a 'Cadian. Grosbœuf was giving this ball. He had been giving them since he was a young man, and he was a middle-aged one, now. In that time he could recall but one disturbance, and that was caused by American railroaders, who were not in touch with their surroundings and had no business there. "Ces maudits gens du raiderode," Grosbœuf called them. (Chopin 1999, 146)

The first thing to note is the paragraph's extraordinary descriptive density. Although the preceding and succeeding paragraphs focus on the story's protagonist, here Chopin puts Alcée Laballière in place. The deft digression "they called it a hall" immediately indicates both linguistic and class difference, as if there were something quaint about an Acadian sense of space. Chopin then uses two powerful markers of cultural identity, music ("three fiddles") and foodways ("lemonade … coffee and chicken gumbo"), to further characterize a scene few northern readers would have known. The foreign names and untranslated French add further mystery and allure to the passage.

But Chopin's interest here exceeds mere exoticism. For instance, the passage notes that "Any one who is white" is welcome to attend these modest gatherings, including wealthy Creoles such as Alcée, provided they pay their own way. While such detail does little to advance the plot, it elegantly underscores late nineteenth-century Louisiana's complex social hierarchies, where categories such as "White" and relationships among race, ethnicity, and class were far from self-evident. Chopin credits a code of conduct – predicated, it seems, on the exclusion of non-Whites – for the easy sociability of a diverse group of attendees. The only "disturbance" of such peace that Grosbœuf can recall involved attendees from afar who were "not in touch with their surroundings." The noun phrase "American railroaders" is at once a quiet critique of industry and capital – Chopin insists they "had no business there" – and a regional gibe. By 1892, all Louisianans were perforce "American"; in this context, the adjective suggests that these men have come from beyond the South, bad manners in tow: "Ces maudits gens . . . ."

Scenes like this recur throughout the twenty-three stories in *Bayou Folk* and the twenty-one in *A Night in Acadie*. For the predominantly middle-class and non-southern readers of a story such as "At the 'Cadian Ball," this amount of cultural detail likely produced a sense of both alienation and attraction. Readers may have been wholly ignorant of the world Chopin describes, but that experience of ignorance might have convinced them to read on. Importantly, Chopin's short stories do not merely tout cultural difference between text and reader – between, say, rural Louisiana and suburban Boston. Her fiction also observes cultural difference *within* the text, celebrating just how diverse and multicultural rural Louisiana could be. Finally, while such a representational politics also informs Chopin's novels *At Fault* (1890) and *The Awakening*, the shorter form of "At the 'Cadian Ball" keeps the plot and cultural characterization in relative proportion. Again, if the goal is a carefully framed image of difference and opposition, then size and scale do indeed matter.

In truth, "At the 'Cadian Ball" is a long short story by Chopin's standards. Several of the pieces in *Bayou Folk* and *A Night in Acadie* are just a few hundred words in length, and a handful offer little beyond literary sketch. But at her best, Chopin's short fiction embodies the melting pot – "gumbo" may be more apt in this context – that was Louisiana in the late nineteenth century. This is especially true of her New Orleans fiction. In stories such as "In and Out of Old Natchitoches" (1893), "Caline" (1893), "A No-Count Creole" (1894), "A Matter of Prejudice" (1895), "A Sentimental Soul" (1895), and "Athénaïse"

(1896), Chopin dexterously draws her reader's attention to the multiethnic, multiracial, and multilingual aspects of the Crescent City. For instance, much of the action of "Nég Créol" (published in the July 1897 issue of the *Atlantic Monthly* and then collected in *A Night in Acadie*) takes place in the city's French Market, where the formerly enslaved title character (born César François Xavier but also called Chicot) labors alongside Black, Irish, Italian, Jewish, and Choctaw vendors. Working in a tradition established by George Washington Cable (1844–1925), Lafcadio Hearn (1850–1904), and Grace King (1852–1932), Chopin's New Orleans fiction remains keenly aware of the port city's identity as a center of international trade and exchange. The ceaseless flow of goods, services, capital, and people helps connect the city, state, region, and nation to the world. As a result, New Orleans becomes a site of cosmopolitan possibility and freedom for many of Chopin's characters.

Whether set in urban or rural Louisiana, Chopin's southern short stories are distinguished by the relative intercultural harmony among characters of diverse backgrounds. And "At the 'Cadian Ball" notwithstanding, many of these stories feature a broad spectrum of the African diaspora: enslaved and formerly enslaved people, free people of color, and mixed-race people. While some of Chopin's characterizations risk racial stereotype, more often than not she renders her Black characters in rich, complex ways. At first glance both "Nég Créol" and "Tante Cat'rinette" (published in the September 1894 issue of the *Atlantic Monthly* and collected in *A Night in Acadie*) emphasize formerly enslaved people's affection for and loyalty to their former enslavers – a centerpiece of Lost Cause ideology, which presented slavery as a benevolent, "positive good" institution via images of the devoted former slave and the wretched freeman. Yet Chopin's strong focalization of these Black protagonists results in fully drawn representations that far exceed caricature. Chicot is, for instance, a distinctive, even contradictory character: altruistic and prideful, poor and pretentious, obsessed with the past and responsive to the pressures of the present. Chopin, in turn, largely eschews the comical and virulently racist representations of Black life made popular by the plantation fiction of Joel Chandler Harris (1848–1908) and Thomas Nelson Page (1853–1922), and satirized by Charles W. Chesnutt (1858–1932). Indeed, Chopin seems to have taken particular care in rendering African American Vernacular English, which must compete in her stories with Creole and Acadian dialects.

Cross-racial sacrifice is another recurring theme in Chopin's southern fiction. "Ozème's Holiday" (published in the August 1896 issue of the

Century and collected in *A Night in Acadie*) finds a plantation worker forgoing his hard-earned vacation to help an acquaintance, Aunt Tildy, pick cotton and care for her sick son. Similarly, "Odalie Misses Mass" (published in the 1 July 1895 issue of the *Shreveport Times* and collected in *A Night in Acadie*) finds a young White girl, eager to show off her new dress at mass, skipping Assumption Day services to stay with her frail, elderly friend, Aunt Pinky. These stories figure genuine, mutual affection that flouts barriers of race, class, and age – as one leading Chopin critic argues, a radical representation for the period (Toth 1999, 170).

As the above suggests, the stories of *Bayou Folk* and *A Night in Acadie* often end on a hopeful note. While Chopin seems to have been sanguine about the possibility for post-Civil War peace and amity in an increasingly multicultural Louisiana, her stories are by no means naive or nostalgic – a common criticism of regional fiction from this period. The vast majority of these stories are set in the post-Reconstruction South, a period and place Chopin pulls few punches in representing. Many of the once-wealthy Creoles in her stories are downwardly mobile. (Attendees at the Acadian ball gossip about Alcée's recent losses on a rice investment.) Immigrants, Native Americans, and the formerly enslaved face widespread discrimination and a persistent lack of opportunity. (Tante Cat'rinette is being actively harassed to sell the house she inherited from her former master; the elderly woman worries that the authorities will dispossess her if she leaves the property for even a few hours.) As for Louisiana's purportedly progressive racial politics, the color line remains perniciously in place in Chopin's fiction. (One need look no further than the ironic and relentlessly bleak conclusion of her best-known story, "Désirée's Baby" [published in the 14 January 1893 issue of *Vogue* and collected in *Bayou Folk*].) Both hopeful and realistic, then, these under-read collections offer a remarkable composite portrait of a South in transition.

Zora Neale Hurston: A Genius of the Southern Short Story

Born in Notasulga, Alabama, in 1891, Zora Neale Hurston and her family moved soon thereafter to Eatonville, Florida, the independent, all-Black community that would become a regular setting for and subject of her writing. Following a peripatetic adolescence, Hurston got serious about her education in her twenties, earning a high school degree and taking classes at Howard University and Barnard College. While at Barnard, Hurston studied under the anthropologists Franz Boas and Ruth Benedict, and alongside Margaret Mead. She lived in New York City for much of the

1920s, 1930s, and 1940s, where she was a visible member of the Harlem Renaissance. During these years, Hurston also traveled widely to conduct anthropological fieldwork in the Bahamas, Haiti, Honduras, Jamaica, and the rural South. After achieving acclaim for her writing in the late 1930s and early 1940s, Hurston struggled financially, eventually resettling in Florida, where she spent the 1950s working several odd jobs, before dying in obscurity in 1960.

Hurston's literary career was remarkably diverse and far-flung: four novels, two collections of folklore, an autobiography, and numerous essays, articles, plays, and short stories. Perhaps because of the tremendous pedagogical popularity of her 1937 novel *Their Eyes Were Watching God*, Hurston's short fiction remains relatively neglected. This is despite the fact that Hurston was an "avid short story writer" throughout her adult life (Champion 2001, 79). And although much has been made of Hurston's use of the "spy-glass of Anthropology" (as she called it), her stories retain a fundamental literariness: as two of her most important editors note, Hurston was "storyteller first, anthropologist second" (Hurston 1995, xii). The short form, in turn, allowed Hurston to offer her own carefully framed images of two predominantly Black places: Eatonville and Harlem.

In the early chapters of her autobiography, *Dust Tracks on a Road* (1942), Hurston lays bare the appeal of her hometown: "I was born in a Negro town. I do not mean by that the black back-side of an average town. Eatonville, Florida, is, and was at the time of my birth, a pure Negro town – charter, mayor, council, town marshal and all." While misrepresenting her actual place and date of birth, Hurston romanticizes the relative self-sufficiency of the "burly, boiling, hard-hitting, rugged-individualistic setting" of her youth (Hurston 1979, 28). Located just north of Orlando and adjacent to Winter Park – an all-White city home to many seasonal northerners – Eatonville was indeed a pioneering African American municipality (Patterson 2005, 50–127). More to the point, the community that Hurston grew up in and returned to for fieldwork proved a pliable and powerful site for her fiction.

We might usefully think of Eatonville as Hurston's Winesburg, Ohio, or Yoknapatawpha County. Like her fellow modernists Sherwood Anderson and William Faulkner, Hurston made the most of a geographically limited fictional setting. For instance, the polyvocal short story "The Eatonville Anthology" (published serially in the September, October, and November 1926 issues of the *Messenger*) underscores the inexhaustible nature of this small southern community via an innovative form. Hurston offers nine loosely connected fragments that draw together "condensed versions and variations of tales told fully in other stories," introducing "characters who reappear throughout her stories" (Champion 2001, 80). The result is a challenging modernist experiment that forces readers to reckon with a chorus of narrators and a panoply of narratives. Even if Eatonville is a "pure Negro town," Hurston insists on the diversity of its people and the tales they tell. Thus, "The Eatonville Anthology" is also a canny act of self-anthologization, one that speaks to the vibrancy of Eatonville's voices, to say nothing of Hurston's voice.

At the heart of Hurston's Eatonville stories is an insistence that Black lives are often "full of enormously subtle meaning" (Gordon 2008, 5). Here, for instance, are the opening paragraphs of one of her best-known stories, "The Gilded Six-Bits" (published in the August 1933 issue of *Story*):

> It was a Negro yard around a Negro house in a Negro settlement that looked to the payroll of the G. and G. Fertilizer works for its support.
>
> But there was something happy about the place. The front yard was parted in the middle by a sidewalk from gate to door-step, a sidewalk edged on either side by quart bottles driven neck down into the ground on a slant. A mess of homey flowers planted without a plan but blooming cheerily from their helter-skelter places. The fence and house were whitewashed. The porch and steps scrubbed white. (Hurston 2020, 200)

The triple repetition of "Negro" establishes in unequivocal terms the makeup of this community, while the word "settlement" and the reference to a fertilizer factory suggest its modest economic means. The clarifying conjunction "But" in the second paragraph brings the reader up short, interrupting any assumptions about the quality of life experienced in such a setting: "But there was something happy about the place." The description of the chaotic and ersatz yard is likewise quickly modified by the fact that its flowers are "blooming cheerily," that someone is putting effort into making this modest house a home. Challenging readerly assumptions about life in the South was a crucial part of Hurston's literary project, as was her emphasis on Black joy – even and especially in hardscrabble and "helter-skelter" contexts. In her essay "How It Feels to Be Colored Me" (1928), Hurston famously claimed that she did not feel "tragically colored" and rejected membership in "the sobbing school of Negrohood who hold that nature somehow has given them a lowdown dirty deal and whose feelings are all hurt about it" (Hurston 1979, 153). Her fiction instead embodies a range of Black feelings – the good, the bad, and the ugly, as it were – all worthy of representation and consideration. Thus, in an era when the "Southern Gothic school" of Faulkner, Erskine Caldwell (1903–1987), Welty, and O'Connor was ascendent, Hurston's rich characterizations defied contemporary stereotypes of what both Black life and southern fiction could be (Glasgow 1935, 4).

Like Chopin, Hurston often used romantic plots to render cultural difference and "complex personhood" (Gordon 2008, 5). For instance, "The Gilded Six-Bits" describes an otherwise happy marriage threatened by jealousy, envy, and infidelity, as the wife, Missie May, has an affair in order to secure some gold that her husband, Joe, desires. In one exchange, Missie May tries to quell Joe's insecurities about Otis D. Slemmons, the seemingly wealthy Black man who has just moved to Eatonville with his "gold":

> "Aw, he don't look no better in his clothes than you do in yourn. He got a puzzlegut on 'im and he so chuckle-headed, he got a pone behind his neck."

> Joe looked down at his own abdomen and said wistfully, "Wisht Ah had a build on me lak he got. He ain't puzzle-gutted, honey. He jes' got a corperation. Dat make 'm look lak a rich white man. All rich mens is got some belly on 'em." (Hurston 2020, 205)

Here, as elsewhere, Hurston revels in African American Vernacular English, touting its charisma, intricacy, and artfulness. But note the stark difference between Missie May, Joe, and the narrator's diction: the words "abdomen" and "wistfully" are conspicuously formal and learned, especially in relation to "chuckle-headed" and "puzzle-gutted." This juxtaposition reminds readers that Hurston has great facility with standard English, even if her characters do not. More to the point, passages like this suggest that characters without such facility still possess rich inner lives. Although Joe may not know what the word "wistfully" means, he nonetheless experiences a melancholic yearning or desire. Indeed, Hurston often presents male characters who do not have the language to describe their feelings or who prefer not to show them in public. Here the narrator describes Joe's thoughts as he comes home from work to discover Missie May and Slemmons in bed together:

> As Joe rounded the lake on his way home, a lean moon rode the lake in a silver boat. If anybody had asked Joe about the moon on the lake, he would have said he hadn't paid it any attention. But he saw it with his feelings. It made him yearn painfully for Missie. Creation obsessed him. He thought about children. They had been married for more than a year now. They had money put away. They ought to be making little feet for shoes. A little boy child would be about right. (Hurston 2020, 208)

In addition to establishing both situational and dramatic irony, the passage deepens the reader's sense for Joe's interiority. While the final eight short, staccato sentences veer toward free indirect discourse – a technique Hurston uses to great effect in her longer fiction – it is once again the narrator who grants us admission to this character's emotional life.

As the above suggests, Hurston is all-in on complex personhood, even if it shows her characters in a less than flattering light. Eschewing the mandates of racial respectability and "The New Negro," Hurston's southern short stories depict Black characters who can be superstitious, petty, impulsive, disloyal, violent, and anxious – which is to say, fully human. Moreover, in stories such as "The Gilded Six-Bits," "Drenched in Light" (1924), and "Magnolia Flower" (1925), the conflicts are largely among Black folks. There is seeming amity between the races because there are just not many White folks in Hurston's Eatonville. This all- or mostly Black cultural space provides some of the exoticism we discovered in Chopin's more multicultural Louisiana. Readers in the 1920s and 1930s likely found much in these stories that was strange and new: yes, porch talk and hoodoo, but also African American autonomy. As Genevieve West argues, Hurston's decision "to write about black communities with white characters appearing only on the fringes – if at all – is a political choice, one that marginalizes whites and puts African Americans at the center and affirms that black folk are worthy of stories" (Hurston 2020, xxxvi–xxxvii).

This is not to say that her stories are silent on the topic of race relations or whiteness. Far from it. Hurston often reflects on how much Whites do not know or do not understand about Black lives. For instance, "The Gilded Six-Bits" ends with an Orlando store clerk badly misjudging Joe, who has come to buy Missie May an extravagant amount of candy after they have made up. As Joe leaves the store, the clerk remarks: "Wisht I could be like those darkies. Laughin' all the time. Nothin' worries 'em" (Hurston 2020, 215). The preceding story gives the lie to the clerk's assumption and stereotype: in fact, Joe worries all the time. Similarly, "Black Death" (which was named runner-up in a 1925 *Opportunity* contest but was not published during Hurston's life [Hurston 2020, xxxvii]) opens with brio – and a tweak of White readers: "We Negroes in Eatonville know a number of things that the hustling, bustling white man never dreams of. He is a materialist with little care for overtones" (Hurston 2020, 73). The subsequent story focuses on hoodoo. Mrs. Boger hires Old Man Morgan to cast a conjure on her daughter's former lover, Beau Diddely. When Beau dies suddenly while flirting with another woman, the coroner cites natural causes despite the presence of a strange powder burn on his chest.

Here, White, scientific knowledge gives way to Black, occult knowledge: "But the Negroes knew instantly when they saw that mark, but everyone agreed that he got justice." (Hurston 2020, 80). Hurston concludes the story with another jeer: "And the white folks never knew and would have laughed had anyone told them, – so why mention it?" (Hurston 2020, 80). This is no "separate but equal" epistemology: Blacks in Hurston's fiction know differently and know better.

For all their emphasis on a small, fixed location, Hurston's southern short stories remain very much engaged with the broader world. Like Chopin's Louisiana, Hurston's Florida encompasses a full range of the African diaspora, including strong influences from the Caribbean cultures Hurston knew well from her fieldwork. The protagonists of "John Redding Goes to Sea" (1921) and "Drenched in Light" also fantasize about leaving rural Florida for more cosmopolitan climes. And what of those characters who do indeed get away? Several of Hurston's Harlem stories describe the experience of migration from the rural South to the urban North: "Muttsy" (1925), "Book of Harlem" (ca. 1927), "The Book of Harlem" (1927), "Monkey Junk" (1927), and "The Country in the Woman" (1927) all situate New York in dynamic relation to rural Florida.

Zora Neale Hurston's short stories often sound a hard-earned hopeful note. As Henry Louis Gates, Jr., and Sieglinde Lemke observe, they "usually end happily for the disenfranchised and powerless" (Hurston 1995, xxii). But as in Chopin's stories, such hopefulness is leavened with a painful realism. Lack of economic opportunity is especially pervasive in this "happy" place. "The Gilded Six-Bits," "Drenched in Light," "Black Death," and "Sweat" (1926) catalog just how difficult life can be in this all-Black setting. And yet Hurston again and again forces readers to think of this place and its people in nuanced and non-tragic ways.

Coda – Oscar Cásares: Across the Borderline

Kate Chopin and Zora Neale Hurston represent two particularly prolific moments for the southern short story. Hurston's death in 1960 coincides with the beginning of what Mark McGurl dubs the "Program Era," which saw the professionalization of creative writing and "transformation of literary modernism into a discourse of institutional being" (McGurl 2007, 535). Creative writing courses, which often feature writers such as Flannery O'Connor – who herself earned a Master of Fine Arts degree from the famed Iowa Writers' Workshop – have yielded a new generation of celebrated southern short story writers: Randall Kenan (1963–2020),

Ann Pancake (born 1963), Chris Offutt (born 1958), Ron Rash (born 1953), and Karen Russell (born 1981), among many others. Thus, the contemporary moment is witnessing yet another boom in southern short fiction. But the South depicted in these stories looks quite different from that found in Chopin and Hurston.

The demographics of the US South have shifted significantly since 1960, with an explosion in immigration helping to redefine the socioeconomics and culture of the region, not to mention its place in the world. As a result, writers, critics, and scholars increasingly think beyond North–South and White–Black binaries, reading the region through transnational, hemispheric, and global frames. In expanding the angle of vision by which we view the South, such writing has redefined who and what counts as southern, while also expanding the canon of southern literature in productive ways. Configurations such as, say, the Mason–Dixon Line or the Confederate States of America now seem less germane than the Global South, Native/Indigenous Souths, or Greater Mexico. The writer Oscar Cásares provides a case in point.

Cásares was born and raised in Brownsville, Texas, the largest city in the Lower Rio Grande Valley, a transborder sociocultural region along the floodplain of the Rio Grande River, at Texas's southernmost tip. "The Valley," as it is known, is predominantly Hispanic and very much a bilingual, bicultural, and even binational place. For instance, Brownsville (estimated population: 182,000) is directly across the US–Mexico border from Matamoros (estimated population: 520,000); citizens of both countries move back and forth across the cities' four international bridges. The Valley also possesses a rich and impressive literary tradition, which includes the folklorist Américo Paredes (1915–1999), the novelist Rolando Hinojosa-Smith (1929–2022), and the cultural theorist Gloria E. Anzaldúa (1942–2004).

After leaving Brownsville to attend the University of Texas at Austin, Cásares worked for several years in advertising before enrolling in the Iowa Writers' Workshop. To date, his books have included the collection *Brownsville: Stories* (2003) and the novels *Amigoland* (2009) and *Where We Come From* (2019), all of which are set in the Valley. Written in a clean prose style and with no small amount of wit, the stories of *Brownsville* remain character-focused – all nine bear the name of a character – while also conveying a great deal of cultural information about the collection's titular community. Critics praising *Brownsville* have cited a range of apt comparisons, including Mark Twain and Flannery O'Connor, and invoked other placed-based short fiction, such as James Joyce's

Dubliners, Anderson's *Winesburg, Ohio*, and Welty's stories about Jackson, Mississippi (Cásares 2003, ii–iv).

As with those famous literary locations, Cásares's Brownsville may feel strange and new to readers unfamiliar with life on *la frontera*. The short story "Yolanda" (first published in the Winter 1999 issue of the *Threepenny Review*) captures well Cásares's deft framing of cultural difference. Another love story of sorts, "Yolanda" is retrospectively narrated by an unnamed Brownsville resident whose childhood crush on his beautiful, unhappily married next-door neighbor haunts him well into adulthood. Before describing how Yolanda Castro's jealous and abusive husband drove her to seek safety and comfort in the twelve-year-old narrator's bedroom, the story sets a jarring scene:

> I remember it being a different neighborhood back then. Everybody knew everybody, and people left their doors unlocked at night. You didn't worry about people stealing shit you didn't lock up. ... This was before Pete Zuniga was riding his brand-new ten-speed from Western Auto and, next to the Friendship Garden, saw a white dude who'd been knifed a couple of dozen times and was floating in the green water of the resaca. Before some crazy woman hired a curandera to put a spell on her daughter's ex-boyfriend, which really meant hiring a couple of hitmen from Matamoros to do a drive-by. ... You know, when you could sit down at the Brownsville Coffee Shop #1 and not worry about getting it in the back while you ate your menudo. When you didn't have to put an alarm and the club on your car so it wouldn't end up in Reynosa. (Cásares 2003, 158)

This long, seemingly discursive passage reveals the clear influence of earlier regional literatures. As in "At the 'Cadian Ball," readers are confronted with an immense amount of potentially obscure cultural data: place names, businesses, and untranslated Spanish. Such descriptive density once again proves both alienating and alluring for the unacquainted. And as in "The Eatonville Anthology," a purportedly exotic community is introduced via anecdote and folklore. The chatty, solicitous narrative voice is crucial to the effect, drawing readers into an unfamiliar and perhaps daunting narrative world. Finally, the references to hitmen from Matamoros and stolen cars in Reynosa underscore just how porous the border can be – and just how connected Cásares's South is to a broader world.

Such porousness and connection return us to this essay's Eudora Welty epigraph. The short fiction of Kate Chopin, Zora Neale Hurston, Oscar Cásares, and countless other southern writers speaks powerfully to the relationship between an extended sense of place and an expanded state of mind. In the end, these writers' little postage stamps ensure dynamic exchange between writer and reader, and among region, nation, and world. As importantly, they also force us to think more contingently – and more capaciously – about cultural difference, wherever we may find it.

Work Cited

Abbott, Dorothy and Susan Koppelman. 1991. *The Signet Classic Book of Southern Short Stories*. New York: Signet.

Cásares, Oscar. 2003. *Brownsville: Stories*. New York: Little, Brown.

Champion, Laurie. 2001. "Socioeconomics in Selected Short Stories of Zora Neale Hurston," *The Southern Quarterly: A Journal of the Arts in the South* 40.1: 79–92.

Chopin, Kate. 1999. *Bayou Folk and A Night in Acadie*. New York: Penguin.

Dainotto, Roberto M. 2000. *Place in Literature: Regions, Cultures, Communities*. Ithaca, NY: Cornell University Press.

Evans, Brad. 2005. *Before Cultures: The Ethnographic Imagination in American Literature, 1865–1920*. Chicago: University of Chicago Press.

Glasgow, Ellen. 1935. "Heroes and Monsters," *Saturday Review of Literature* 12.4 (May 4, 1935): 3–4.

Gordon, Avery F. 2008. *Ghostly Matters: Haunting and the Sociological Imagination*. Minneapolis: University of Minnesota Press.

Hurston, Zora Neale. 1979. *I Love Myself When I Am Laughing ... and Then Again When I Am Looking Mean and Impressive: A Zora Neale Hurston Reader*. New York: Feminist Press.

   1995. *The Complete Stories*. New York: HarperCollins.

   2020. *Hitting a Straight Lick with a Crooked Stick: Stories from the Harlem Renaissance*. New York: HarperCollins.

McGurl, Mark. 2007. "Understanding Iowa: Flannery O'Connor, B.A., M.F.A.," *American Literary History* 19.2: 527–545.

Patterson, Tiffany Ruby. 2005. *Zora Neale Hurston and a History of Southern Life*. Philadelphia: Temple University Press.

Toth, Emily. 1999. *Unveiling Kate Chopin*. Jackson: University Press of Mississippi.

CHAPTER 15

Regional Stories and the Environmental Imagination

Sylvan Goldberg

Early in Sarah Orne Jewett's formally indeterminate *The Country of the Pointed Firs* (1896) – story collection? sketches? novel? – the unnamed narrator finds a summer afternoon's writing interrupted by the erstwhile ship's captain Littlepage, whose aging frame tilts like "the wind-bent trees" of the coastal Maine landscape (1994, 387). After relating a tale of Arctic exploration that, like many nineteenth-century exploration fantasies, extends beyond the ice and into a navigable northern sea, Littlepage's gaze drifts to a map of North America. His face settles into "a look of bewilderment" as he stares at an unfamiliar coastline, revised after recent expeditions (1994, 398). That look appears repeatedly throughout Jewett's archive: at the end of "In Dark New England Days," for example, two women look out from a new vantage at "their own green farms and the countryside that bounded them" and find themselves "bewildered by the marvelous beauty" (1890, 255). Bewilderment seems to mark a gaze caught off guard by a landscape once familiar, now rendered strange. But if in "New England Days" it signals a newfound appreciation for the known, for Captain Littlepage bewilderment suggests a present no longer anchored to the past: the Arctic's outline has been remapped by new knowledge. His stories of a navigable northern sea prove a mere delusion.

Today, the image of an ice-free Arctic has returned, still bewildering but laced with a different dread than that inspired by the ghostly, fog-shaped men Littlepage imagined inhabiting a town beyond the ice. Once a dream that nineteenth-century explorers raced to prove true, a navigable northern sea has reappeared in our environmental imagination as the climate-changed future of a region once thought impermeable to change, an anticipatory reminder of how strange the natural world has become in such a short matter of time. Stronger storms, a year-round wildfire season, record-setting droughts – these are harbingers of a climate that will continue to look less and less like the one we have known. Littlepage's bewildered gaze undoubtedly signals his anachronistic misconception, but he might just as well be a messenger from our own time, staring at a map whose contours mistakenly presumed the stability of Arctic ice. The natural world of Jewett's regional imagination thus seems less the timeless retreat from history that scholars have often labeled it than a thoroughly modern reminder that the elsewheres of industrialization were never far enough away to escape its effects. Read in this light, regionalism's desire to retreat from industrial modernity seems less pastoral than prescient. Perhaps recent scholars have been right, then, to turn from early accounts that viewed the genre as stuck in a bygone past, or subordinate to a nationalizing present, to one writing toward the future.

This chapter takes up recent accounts of the futural orientation of late nineteenth-century US regionalism as an opportunity to grapple with the genre's environmental past by widening its frame. A postbellum genre long considered a minor literature, whose strongest expression came in the form of the short story or sketch, US regionalist fiction – sometimes called local color writing – rose to prominence in the national magazines of the 1870s–1890s. The popularity of early regionalist stories in the California-based *Overland Monthly* helped the genre find a home in more genteel Eastern publications: *Harper's Monthly*, *Scribner's*, *Century*, and, with the approbation of William Dean Howells, the *Atlantic Monthly*. Although June Howard (2018) has shown that regionalist stories appeared in a wider range of publications than just those aimed at an elite, urban readership, the genre did often serve readers eager to venture touristically into the nooks and crannies of a country still healing from the national fractures of the Civil War. In addition to Jewett, writers such as Celia Thaxter, Hamlin Garland, Mary Murfree, Charles Chesnutt, Mary Wilkins Freeman, George Washington Cable, Grace King, Alice Dunbar-Nelson, Zitkála-Šá, and, later, Mary Austin, gave voice to the customs and landscapes of an often rural United States that seemed out of touch with the modernizing and industrializing urban spaces of the Gilded Age. That it did so by privileging the short story and sketch indicates its interest in incompletion, or rather in a complete picture gathered from gradual accretion rather than grand comprehensiveness. While each region provided its own set of habits to detail, these stories share certain features: dialect; small towns, rural landscapes, and often a minute attention to the natural environment; inhabitants whose professions (shipping, agriculture) seem increasingly outmoded and whose social and romantic proclivities tend toward the passive; outsiders as narrators; and often, though by no means exclusively, female authors.

Despite the fact that regionalism has remained from its earliest theorizations a genre defined by environmental representation, it has played only a marginal role in the rise of the environmental humanities. In part, this may stem from their too-close fit. In the same early twentieth-century moment when ecocriticism was pulling an environmental imagination into the mainstream of literary studies, regionalism was going through a major reassessment by scholars recuperating the genre's political imagination, bringing feminism and the interlocking scales of geographic affiliation (regional, national, hemispheric, global) to bear, but sidelining regionalism's environmental representation. At times, they did so hyperbolically: "[W]hile those writers we have termed regionalist are often interested in features of the physical landscape," write Judith Fetterley and Marjorie Pryse, "they are not nature writers" (2003, 4). Even after ecocriticism turned its attention away from the local and toward the type of global interrelations these new regionalist scholars highlighted, the two fields seemed to be on similar trajectories and yet unable to find stable points of contact.

The rest of this chapter unfolds in three sections that attempt to bridge this divide, turning to a range of fictional stories that represent diverse regional landscapes. A brief overview of regionalist scholarship leads into a section that returns attention to environmental representation by centering questions of scale. Doing so in an archive whose scalar concerns have often been self-evident can reorient the way we have understood the frames, both spatial and temporal, of regionalism's landscapes. The final section brings scale to bear on the climates of regionalism to register an understanding of region and archive as co-constitutive, remapping regionalism's privileged sites while also, in the era of climate change, revealing another aspect of the way in which regionalism writes toward an unrealized future.

Rethinking Regionalism

For a genre often described as representing a resistance to change, regionalism has undergone significant scholarly shifts. Early accounts took New England as its hub and saw in the literature of the latter decades of the nineteenth century a strain of what Vernon Parrington called "chronicle and criticism," a realist bent coupled to anxiety about a world altered by industrialism and advances in scientific thought: "It gathered up such picturesque bits of the past as time and change had left, and it questioned with some anxiety the ways of an industrialism that was destroying what it loved" (Parrington 1930, 60). Early accounts insisted on the minor status of regionalism, which was seen as marginalized by the more complex and sophisticated genres against which it competed in the literary marketplace, especially realism and naturalism. The urban realist novel became US literature's dominant center in the late nineteenth century; the regionalist sketch diminished to become its minuscule periphery. In the 1980s and 1990s, Amy Kaplan, Richard Brodhead, and others narrated regionalism's relation to a realism overwriting social difference to construct a national US culture. Although regionalism created opportunities for a more diverse set of authors, who gained access to the publishing industry by writing local color accounts of communities far from the urbane centers of bourgeois white America, these writers served a consolidating function for national identity. Regional differences were thus figured either as the vestigial but fading prehistory of national culture or a path toward social inclusion for marginalized groups otherwise excluded. Thus, even as the genre came to be revalued, it retained its minor status because regionalism existed only in subordinate relation to a national whole.

On the heels of these claims, a new burst of scholarship, driven in large part by feminist recuperations of female regionalists, shifted regionalism's political framing by asserting its ability to resist rather than reinforce national culture. Anchoring much of this work was Fetterley and Pryse's *Writing out of Place* (2003), and their earlier anthology of regionalist literature, *American Women Regionalists* (1992). Its minor status became regionalism's path into a resistant politics. Regionalism became, in other words, a major genre through its minorness. This work drew attention to the interrelation of region and nation, and, increasingly, to globalizing tendencies visible both in US imperialist efforts contemporaneous with literary regionalism and in the transnational reading strategies of contemporary literary studies. Regionalism has thus come to be seen no longer as a pastoral retreat from an increasingly interconnected world, but rather as either a deliberate resistance to such interconnection or another site of its expression.

These recuperations have been helpful in reframing our understanding of regionalism's temporal context, reorienting the genre away from one anchored in a timeless natural world, an anachronistic social world, or both. Instead, scholars, especially those revisiting the genre through the lens of gender and sexuality, have increasingly found regionalism writing toward the future. Fetterley and Pryse open their account by locating regionalism's futural orientation in Jewett, as well as in their own scholarship: "*Writing out of Place* begins with our sense that Jewett addresses us in her diary; that we, in a conscious use of the historical present tense, address readers who may also live a hundred years from now" (2003, 1). A mere twenty years on, the readers they address inhabit a world whose future, at regional, national, and global scales, looks strikingly more precarious. And while the short story might seem ill-suited to representing the complexity of the contemporary environmental crisis, its partial form – form *as* part – registers the incompleteness of any single account or manifestation of climate change, whose effects appear in and as the smaller and often regionally specific catastrophes that gain meaning in the contemporary anthology of stories that local weather tells.

This precariousness makes regionalism's message for the future all the more pressing, as it brings the genre's environmental representations back into the frame. As Robert Dorman writes, "regionalism might be a prescriptive as well as a descriptive intellectual enterprise: a region's identity, including its spatial conceptualization, might refer not only to what is presently in the region or what has been there in the past, but also to what could be in the future" (2012, 6). Sarah Ensor has written most directly about the potential threaded into regionalism's environmental futures, turning to Jewett as exemplar of a queer ecological literary style anchored in the spinster figure, whose relationship to the future is predicated neither on the investment in and transition to one's own offspring nor on a queer rejection of futurity as exemplified by the infamously antisocial claims of Lee Edelman in *No Future* (2004). Jewett's nonreproductive characters register a future "both outside and beyond our capacity to control," and the genre appears suffused with an environmental ethic derived from a "sense of enoughness" (2012, 414, 426). Through this lens, regionalism's preference for the short story becomes a formal analogue to this restraint.

While Jewett helps orient us within the regionalist archive, as she has for so many scholars, she was hardly the only late nineteenth-century writer to use short fiction to think through community, continuity, and constraint in regional environments that often appear livelier than their human inhabitants. Modestly plotted and centered around characters whose antisociality marginalizes them even in the marginal communities in which they live, regionalist short stories have often been viewed through the lens of limitation. This has been of increasing value to environmental scholars who, like Ensor, look ahead to a catastrophic, climate-changed future with a sense of humility and a desire for models of inhabitation and representation that might better prepare us for what is to come. If regionalism can write toward that future, it does so, in part, because it allows us to glimpse an environmental past that was both vaster and more implicated in the colonial structures of power than scholars have at times granted. Rather than hold its natural world still, regionalism often registers a landscape embedded within a wider temporal frame in which a history of human impact becomes visible only belatedly, evoking an imperative to narrate. What we do with that narration remains a story we are still trying to tell.

Regionalism's Environmental Imagination: The Revisions of Scale

In "Local Color in Art," Hamlin Garland insists that local color "means a statement of life as indigenous as the plant-growth" (1960, 54). Never mind that by the 1890s in which he made that claim, the flora – and fauna, humans included – of the United States had been radically altered by settler-colonial practices: monocrop agriculture; plant and animal importation; extractive industries such as mining and logging; and more specialized industries, including, for example, the turpentine trade, whose ravages remain visible in the regionalist short stories of Charles Chesnutt, as Mary Kuhn has shown (2021). When Jewett's narrator stumbles upon a flock of sheep in "A Dunnett Shepherdess," one of the stories appended to later editions of *The Country of the Pointed Firs*, the non-native species – domesticated sheep arrived in the Americas with Columbus – have "taken a mysterious protective resemblance to the ledges" (1994, 520–521). Indistinguishable now from the landscape, the sheep serve as a reminder that many of the changes wrought by colonization have, themselves, been domesticated out of sight. At a wider temporal scale, then, Garland's comment begins to warp at the intersection of "indigenous" and "plant-growth": indigeneity means something different in a larger frame.

In both its literary manifestations and scholarly accounts, regionalism proves a genre whose central concerns evoke exactly these scalar shifts: the relation between region, nation, and globe; modernity and its relationship to a preindustrial past; and the limitations and constraints of a minor literature whose primary genre is itself minor, especially in its size. In a conventional telling, the short story marks the exemplary length for the region for it best maps content onto form, relaying in literary form an effort to match the delimited material space of the region. For numerous scholars of regionalism, then, the scalar concerns most pressing in regionalism are spatial, right down to the length of the text.

More recently, however, revisionist accounts have brought scale to bear on regionalism's temporal concerns. As Howard has argued, accounts of regionalism that position it as an asynchronously antimodern, anti-industrial genre have played an outsize role in diminishing the genre's stature and the power claimed by its communities, relegating its cultural knowledge to an outmoded past absented from its own historical moment. New accounts of regionalism's temporal imagination are helpful not just for revising this understanding of historical time but also for bringing the genre back into conversation with an environmental humanities that has become equally attentive to scale in both spatial and temporal terms. Scale has risen to prominence, in part, because one of the dominant environmental concepts of the twenty-first century, the Anthropocene, reframes our understanding of the scales of human history, embedding it within not just the wide historical frame of settler colonialism but the *longue durée* of geologic time. Even as regionalism's late nineteenth-century rise to prominence has often been read as a counterweight to an imperial politics taking hold in an era of US expansionism, we can also consider its interest in representing rural landscapes as an anxiety about the environmental effects of domestic colonizations past, present, and future. Like Jewett's sheep, or – to take a regional writer whose stories have often been read through the lens of colonial violence – the invasive bees Julius protects with the story of a ghostly wolf in Chesnutt's "The Gray Wolf's Ha'nt" (1993), these traces of colonial history pull environmental change and harm into the frame, albeit in slanted form.

In light of this vaster temporal frame, what scholars have tended to read as regionalism's atemporal environmental imagination might be reframed as representations of a natural world whose changes unfold at scales challenging to recognize, let alone represent. Indeed, we might understand regionalism's desire to represent local landscapes as a literary enactment of the same impulse that led the conservation and preservation movements to arise contemporaneously. Doing so only reframes in an explicitly environmental context something scholars of regionalism have long shown: the genre's interest in holding on to something at risk of being lost. It also reads regionalist environments through a framing to which regionalism's dependence on the short story and sketch often draws attention, for unlike the countless short stories in other modes anchored in an exemplary climactic event, the regionalist story often unfolds as anticlimax. Its muted events gain fuller meaning when placed in a context that is suggested only in asides and allusions, a series of causal inferences that expand beyond the edges of the short story, revealing the form's insufficiency while refusing to satisfy a desire for more.

This dilation of time appears throughout the archive of the regionalist short story, often with a restraint that tends to undercut a professed moralizing. Rose Terry Cooke's "Miss Beulah's Bonnet," an exemplary regionalist story for its attention to fastidious female social dynamics in a pious New England town, ends with a forward-looking moral when it notes that Mrs. Blake, whose earlier spell of sitting had crushed the titular bonnet beyond repair, "never again sat down in a chair without first lifting the cushion" (Fetterley and Pryse 1992, 137). As Cooke's story makes clear, these scalar adjustments extend the narrative vision beyond the confines of the short story, but ill-fittingly to the form: "If there is any moral to this story," writes Cooke, indicating the insufficiency of the moralizing impulse for a story whose short length matches the unwillingness of its many characters to speak up (137).

Mary Wilkins Freeman's oft-anthologized "A New England Nun" similarly ends by nodding toward a habitual future, but lays bare what Cooke only hints at: displacing the human for the nonhuman, Freeman's story reveals the way in which regionalist short fiction at times loses interest in the human register before the story ends. "Nun" begins "late in the afternoon" with "a difference in the look of the tree shadows out in the yard" (Fetterley and Pryse 1992, 356). Opening with this image of a natural temporality marked by an extensiveness visible on the ground itself, the story ends with Louisa Ellis's rejection of marriage to a man she had waited fifteen years to marry, a social timeframe meant to feel long, but seemingly insignificant when followed almost immediately by the story's compensation of the "long reach of future days" ahead of Louisa (365). Rather than attach this future to Louisa, Freeman instead turns to an image of the nonhuman that overruns Louisa's cottage, a prospective present stretching endlessly forward: "Now the tall weeds and grasses might cluster around Caesar's little hermit hut, the snow might fall on its roof year in and year out" (365). Here, the growing grass begins to subsume the human narrative, so much so that possession of Louisa's plot of land seems to have transferred to her dog, Caesar. In Freeman's story, the landscape quite literally begins to efface the domestic.

Jewett's "A White Heron," a story to which scholars have returned repeatedly, similarly foregrounds a competition for narrative attention between human and nonhuman. Like Freeman's story, Jewett's begins in woods that, despite "a bright sunset still glimmer[ing] faintly," have "already filled with shadows one June evening" (1994, 669). Sylvia, a "little woods-girl," finds herself at first horror-stricken and then intrigued by the intrusion of an "ornithologist" out collecting specimens and tracking the titular bird for his personal collection (673). The story positions Sylvia's protective relationship to the natural world against the ornithologist's scientific – and deadly – one, but challenges this divide through Sylvia's budding romantic desire for him. In registering and questioning

the violence inherent in a scientific practice that would murder its specimens, the story seems a somewhat conventional extension of the nineteenth-century's environmental ambivalences.

But something strange emerges alongside this framing. In the story's
final section, the sense of containment that the story's opening line
generates begins to come apart when Sylvia climbs a tree in search of the
heron's nest. As Sylvia's visual frame widens – the sea visible in one
direction, miles of woods and farmland in the other – a temporal gap
cracks open between the past-tense narration and the narrator's present
tense intrusions: "look, look!"; "And wait! wait!" (678). When she returns
home, she refuses to tell the ornithologist where to find the heron's nest,
rejecting both her own early stirrings of romantic desire and the ten-dollar
reward he offers. The narrator seems to question this decision: "Were the
birds better friends than their hunter might have been, – who can tell?"
Leaving that question hanging, "A White Heron" widens its temporal
frame into an indeterminate future in which it reframes an ethical environmental question central to nineteenth-century science as a choice
between human and nonhuman affiliation. What makes this ending,
alongside Freeman's, feel both unsatisfying and – to use Ensor's term –
enough is just how little interest these stories seem to show in an anthropogenic framing that would require an answer rather than a question. By
not answering the question it poses, "A White Heron" questions the desire
to know more about the human story it tells. In other words, in Jewett's
and Freeman's stories, the human fails to rise to a sustainable level of
interest. At the end of "A White Heron," the social world of love, violence,
science, and moral decision-making remains suspended in the timelessness
of that unanswerable question, while the natural world becomes threaded
into a restrained account of invasive threat whose forestalling necessitates
withdrawing from narrative altogether.

That coupling of narrative with, and as, an anthropogenic threat to the
natural world animates Mary Murfree's "Over on the T'other Mounting,"
which interrogates the human impulse to narrate our environments. The
story begins with an evocation of spatial scale in its description of two
parallel series of mountains in the Allegheny Range, but within a couple of
paragraphs, the story shifts its scalar interest to time, with an expanding
temporal frame that emerges out of the impulse to narrate: the narrative
present ("one afternoon") shifts, in the dialect-inflected words of Nathan
White, to the repetitive time of rumor ("I hev hearn tell all my days"), then
to a historical frame that shifts backward ten years ("'twar ten year ago an'
better – I went up thar one Jan'ry"), and then successively farther ("thar

war a man hyar, nigh on ter fifty year ago"; "'Twar sixty year ago, nigh about"), before settling into the deep geologic time evoked by Nathan's father's misreading, while he was searching for a missing outlaw, of a fossilized footprint and "in the solid stone, mind ye – a fish, what he had done br'iled fur supper, jes' turned ter a stone" (1992, 272–273). This vast temporal frame renders comical even a multigenerational human timeframe of narrative when set against the geologic time for which it cannot account, and doubly so when packing this series of stories into a story that is, itself, quite short.

The opening sets up a narrative in which these anecdotes, which position T'other Mounting (mountain) as a cursed place dangerous to any human who ventures onto it, ironize the human threat to the mountain. To cover his attempted murder of Caleb Hoxie, Tony Britt ignites a wildfire that turns T'other Mounting "black with its desolate, leafless trees" (286). Although the story refuses a causal link between its deep temporal opening and the anthropogenic environmental harm at the story's climax, the tension between the scales of geologic, human, and literary time conflate juxtaposition with causality: the wildfire narrative seems willed into existence as if in response to the series of stories from the mountain's past, to undercut the desire to turn the natural world into the primary threatening force in the story. Like "The Banishment of Ming and Mai," by Sui Sin Far (Edith Maud Eaton), a story which, although set in China and thus challenging the frame of a US regionalism, situates its narrative of an environmental ethics grounded in the just treatment of animals within a multigenerational timeframe of "some centuries;" the questioning of a social morality in conjunction with an environmental ethic highlights a message that redounds across the regionalist archive: while our environmental actions play out not across the lifetime of a single human but across numerous generations, making individual action an insufficient site of the remediation of longstanding harms, this does not obviate the necessity of an ethics of care or the violence of rejecting it (1995, 137).

Climate and the Impulse to Narrate

Mary Wilkins Freeman's "On the Walpole Road" opens in a particularly dry spell that covers the native New England vegetation with dust, giving the blackberry vines, meadowsweet, and hardhack "gray leaves instead of green" (1884, 86). Freeman's account of a carriage ride home following a day of shopping has been read as a meditation on both storytelling and the deference and resistances built into female relationships, both familial and affiliative. Equally visible, though, is the story's formative link between weather and narrative, for what prompts Miss Green's story is a looming thundercloud that jogs her memory: "'That cloud makes me think of Aunt Rebecca's funeral,' she broke out, suddenly" (86). The threat of a sudden downpour leads, instead, to an outpouring of narrative, in which Miss Green recounts both an anecdote about her own attendance at what was in fact not Aunt Rebecca's funeral but that of her husband, and Rebecca's story of a loveless marriage and the brief, anticlimactic union with her former love following her husband's death. But it is also a story, we learn, that Almira, the younger companion of the seventy-year-old Miss Green, has heard before: "[I]t's kind of come to me, as I've been listening, that I *had* heard it before," Almira says, just as the two reach their destination (87).

In the Anthropocene, weather generates for us, as it does for Almira, a story we acknowledge knowing only belatedly, as we seem to near its end. If the full account of what weather relates comes together as – changing – climate, the regionalist short story's interest in weather – the part to climate's whole – helps us to understand how that whole comes to be understood: bit by bit, one local story at a time. Its repeated appearance throughout the regionalist short story indexes an environmental imagination that echoes other aspects of how these stories link regional, national, and global spaces and temporalities.

Indeed, Freeman's constitutive link between weather and narration is hardly unique in the regionalist short story. Reading widely across regionalism's archive, it appears often and in diverse geographic contexts. From New England, we can head to the plantation South of Joel Chandler Harris, whose Uncle Remus stories appropriated African American folktales in versions such as "Brer Rabbit Treats the Creeturs to a Race," which begins with the little boy of Harris's tales terrified by a storm cloud and the lightning it brings. Remus's memory churns at the sight: "'Dar now!' he exclaimed, before the echoes of the thunder had rolled away, 'Dat dust an' win', an' rain, puts me in mind er de time when ol' Brer Rabbit got up a big race fer ter pleasure de yuther creeturs'" (1955, 686). Grace King's short introduction to *Balcony Stories*, "The Balcony," makes even calm Southern weather an anchor for narrative, insisting that the "sun-parched days" and "languor-breeding climate" of a New Orleans summer inspire women "to sit and talk together of summer nights" of their "[e]xperiences, reminiscences, episodes" – exactly the kind of regionalist sketches King wrote (1893, 1–3). And it is Midwestern weather – "the raw winds, the chill rains, and the violent temperatures that characterized winters in the region of the Great Lakes" – that sends John and Annie south in the first of Chesnutt's conjure tales, where they encounter Julius and his series of stories (1993, 32). Heading west, Sui Sin Far begins "The Inferior Woman" with Mrs. Springs Fragrance walking through "the leafy alleys of the park" on "a beautiful afternoon with the warmth from the sun cooled by a refreshing brief," which leads her to "[meditate] upon a book which she had some notion of writing" (1995, 28). Across a range of geographies, then, weather prods the regionalist story into existence.

While weather might not sustain attention across the length of a novel, in the short story, it rises to an outsize scale. In the two best-known California stories of Bret Harte, "The Luck of Roaring Camp" and "The Outcasts of Poker Flat," both published first in the *Overland Monthly*, precipitation precipitates either narrative climax, for the former, or the story itself. "Outcasts" opens with "a change in the moral atmosphere" of its titular town, but it is a change in the material atmosphere – an unexpected snowstorm – that strands the motley crew in a cabin surrounded by "drift on drift of snow piled high around the hut, – a hopeless, uncharted, trackless sea of white" (19, 31). Although Harte's natural description lacks either the eloquence or the specificity of many regionalists, his understanding of the vicissitudes of weather in the Sierra Nevada mountains adds a climatological realism to his local color. Weather serves in "Roaring Camp" as the grounds of a communal memory projecting forward into the future: "The winter of 1851 will long be remembered in the foot-hills" (1870, 17). Heavy snow fills rivers and lakes to bursting, reshaping the landscape: "Each gorge and gulch was transformed into a tumultuous watercourse that descended the hillsides, tearing down giant trees and scattering its drift and débris along the plain" (17). Weather determines not just landscape but the fate of its inhabitants, for when the river near Roaring Camp floods, it sweeps Luck and his protector, the gruff Kentuck, to their deaths.

Here, then, in the mine-scarred hills of Harte's local setting, weather shows us what it has more recently revealed in the Anthropocene, for it registers the agencies both of the natural world (superstorms, fire tornadoes) and of humankind, who, scaled up to the level of the species, have remade Earth's climate in such a way as to make catastrophic weather both utterly normal and apocalyptic. As Harte's California setting indicates, these narratives of sudden and deadly weather occur perhaps most often in the literature of the US West, a region long neglected in scholarly accounts of regionalism, which have tended to privilege the agricultural Midwest or the nostalgic sites of New England and a postbellum South. Pulling the US West into centrality within the regionalist archive aligns with recent scholarship, for the West remains a site whose promise was futural in regionalism's late nineteenth-century heyday. That futural promise was central to a consolidation of US national identity best articulated in Frederick Jackson Turner's frontier hypothesis, in which a civilizing frontier line marched ever westward, before escaping national – and earthly – borders. For that reason, the US West's literary historical fit within regionalism has always been suspect: unlike the backward glance of New England regionalism, its Western manifestation seems to anticipate a future in which its unsophisticated archetypes will, thankfully, disappear. The impulse for preservation feels less pressing.

Recentering Western American literature within our accounts of regionalism draws attention back to what the weather has belatedly revealed: human cultures have the capacity to shape regions and their environments not just literarily but materially. To thus say that literature can construct a region as much as the inverse further unsettles our notion that the environments of regionalism exist outside of time, for it reinscribes them at the intersection of human and natural history we have come to call the Anthropocene. Rather than see the West as a marginal case for a marginal genre, then, we might view it instead as an exemplary region for its consideration of the way a region comes to be constructed by its literary archive. The US West came of age literarily alongside its ongoing settlement by white Americans, and the short stories of Harte, Mark Twain, and others spurred on immigration by those whose regional imagination, and thus their conception of the West, had been fed by literature.

Few late nineteenth-century Western stories better exemplify this than those of Stephen Crane. Identified more with realism, naturalism, and romance than with regionalism, Crane's Western stories often ironize the readerly frameworks through which we approach region. In "The Blue Hotel," the Swede jumps at every loud noise, convinced he is bound to be murdered, a premonition his companions blame on his cultural consumption: "[T]his man has been reading dime novels, and he thinks he's right out in the middle of it" (1963, 492). That he is eventually murdered may not be beside the point, for the Swede seems to materialize the region of which he has read. But to materialize the literary West, whose fictional representations have often depended on settler colonialist fantasies, resource extraction, and other capitalist practices of the Anthropocene, is to amplify Harte's environmental representation: Western weather has grown deadlier and more erratic as a result of constructing a region out of the extractive industries of which Harte and others wrote, a point growing more pressing as the US considers mining its domestic lithium deposits, which are most prevalent in California and Nevada.

If climate marks another of the ways in which regions remain imbricated with larger national and global circuits, weather reminds us that we often feel the parts more pressingly than we do the whole. Reading the short stories of late nineteenth-century literary regionalism from our own belated position, in which weather has come to signify something other than mere background, can help us to recognize both the material conditions that constrain our lives – a point the regionalist story makes over and over – and our own capacity for reshaping those conditions, even when this so often occurs against our best intentions. Fetterley and Pryse may be right that regionalist writers are not nature writers. But in turning to the natural world as a spur to narration and allowing it to stretch the frames of human stories – often, in the short space of their sketches, displacing the human as an object of interest – regionalist writers rebalance the relation between human and nonhuman. They point us toward a future in which the most pressing question – will we survive to narrate? – may remain unanswered.

Works Cited

Chesnutt, Charles W. 1993. *The Conjure Woman and Other Conjure Tales.* Durham, NC: Duke University Press.

Crane, Stephen. 1963. *The Complete Short Stories and Sketches of Stephen Crane.* Ed. Thomas A. Gullason. New York: Doubleday.

Dorman, Robert L. 2012. *Hell of a Vision: Regionalism and the Modern American West.* Tucson: University of Arizona Press.

Edelman, Lee. 2004. *No Future: Queer Theory and the Death Drive.* Raleigh, NC: Duke University Press.

Ensor, Sarah. 2012. "Spinster Ecology: Rachel Carson, Sarah Orne Jewett, and Nonreproductive Futurity," *American Literature* 84.2: 409–435.

Far, Sui Sin. 1995. *Mrs. Spring Fragrance and Other Writings.* Eds. Amy Ling and Annette White-Parks. Urbana: University of Illinois Press.

Fetterley, Judith and Marjorie Pryse. 2003. *Writing out of Place: Regionalism, Women, and American Literary Culture.* Champaign: University of Illinois Press.

Garland, Hamlin. 1960. "Local Color in Art," in *Crumbling Idols: Twelve Essays on Art Dealing Chiefly with Literature, Painting, and the Drama.* Ed. Jane Johnson, 49–58. Cambridge, MA: Belknap Press of Harvard University Press.

Harris, Joel Chandler. 1955. *The Complete Tales of Uncle Remus.* Boston: Houghton Mifflin.

Harte, Francis Bret. 1870. *The Luck of Roaring Camp and Other Sketches*. Boston: Fields, Osgood, and Co.

Howard, June. 2018. *The Center of the World: Regional Writing and the Puzzles of Place-Time*. Oxford: Oxford University Press.

Jewett, Sarah Orne. 1890. "In Dark New England Days," in *Strangers and Wayfarers*, 220–256. Boston: Houghton Mifflin.

  1994. *Novels and Stories*. New York: Library of America.

King, Grace. 1893. *Balcony Stories*. New York: The Century Co.

Kuhn, Mary. 2021. "Chesnutt, Turpentine, and the Political Ecology of White Supremacy," *PMLA* 136.1: 39–54.

Parrington, Vernon Louis. 1930. *The Beginnings of Critical Realism in America: 1860-1920*. New York: Harcourt, Brace, and Co.

Wilkins, Mary E. 1884. "On the Walpole Road," *Harper's Bazar* 17.6: 86–87.

CHAPTER 16

Concrete Illuminations
The Short Story and/as Urban Revolution

Myka Tucker-Abramson

I

Often heralded as the first American short story, Washington Irving's "Rip Van Winkle" likely needs no introduction. A henpecked husband flees the "labour of the farm" and his "termagant" wife (2014, 37), wanders up into the mountains, drinks too much liquor and takes a long nap, thus missing (yet dreamily registering) the colony's own escape from its equally termagant mother, Great Britain, in the American Revolution. The reveal occurs when Rip returns to town and observes that the pub's sign has swapped "the ruby face of King George" for the General Washington's "blue and buff" coat (42). Irving's allegorical doubling is foundational in the short story's formation. In "Theses on the Short Story," Argentine author and critic Ricardo Piglia argues that the "short story always tells two stories" (2011, 63), a "foreground" tale, and a "background" one, "a secret tale, narrated in an elliptical and fragmentary manner" that "appears on the surface" at the end (63). The meeting of these two stories, he argues, constitutes the short story's "profane illumination" (66).

The term "profane illumination" comes from Walter Benjamin's famous 1929 essay on Surrealism (2005). Benjamin argued that the Surrealists' excavations of the industrial city and bourgeois subjectivity provided a new "materialist, anthropological inspiration" that illuminated the revolutionary potential lurking within the ruins of the present (2005, 109). As profane illuminations go, Irving's excavation of the Revolution as the background text to Rip's foreground is shoddy, but the actual second story is not the Revolution but the "background text" of history itself: the layered histories of imperial warfare, violence, dispossession, and expropriation that underpins the founding of a seemingly "sleepy" urban settlement. "Rip Van Winkle" stands at the crossroads of what Giovanni Arrighi terms three "long centuries" (1994, 7) – Dutch, British, and American – whose processes of plunder, war making, and dispossession constitute the story's space: its built environment, landscapes, myths, and even character names. This text only surfaces in the postscript, where the "travelling notes [... of] Mr Knickerbocker" (44) locate both the story and the town itself within the supposed Indian fables of the Catskill Mountains.

Michael Warner argues that the story's "main body ... concludes by resolving national history and personal memory into folk temporality" (2000, 791). But these folk temporalities can no longer be immediately accessed in Irving's story and must instead be subordinated into, and framed by, the secular, ethnographic observations of a traveler. This mediation and subordination are also what makes "Rip Van Winkle" illustrative of the constitutive relationship between the urban and the short story, even in their most nascent forms. The short story is one of the first truly urban forms, emerging and developing alongside what Henri Lefebvre has termed the "Urban Revolution," a phrase referring to the development and expansion of the capitalist urban form as it "grows, extends its borders, [and] corrodes the residue of agrarian life" (2003, 4). The short story is linked to the emergence of the new "time-poor" urban masses (March-Russell 2016, 18); the rise of magazine culture; and the development of other urban media such as photography and cinema. Moreover, short stories play a constitutive role in the theorizing of urban modernity. Consider, for instance, Sigmund Freud's use of E. T. A. Hoffman's "The Sandman" in his essay on the uncanny, which underpinned his later work on shock, or the importance of short stories – by Nikolai Leskov, Edgar Allan Poe (particularly "Man of the Crowd"), and Charles Baudelaire (whose *Paris Spleen* can be considered a hybrid short story/poetry cycle) – for Benjamin's theorizations of urban modernity (1996).

The short story registers this process of urbanization. Mirroring urbanization's absorption of land, labor, and resources, the short story draws on agrarian folk forms and transforms them into modern secular forms, such as the *skaz* (the Russian tale that imitates oral storytelling), the gothic, the anecdote, and the detective story. For instance, the German folktale "Peter Klaus" alongside the indeterminate Indian "fables" in "Rip Van Winkle" (1819); the African and African American Br'er rabbit trickster figure in Charles Chesnutt's *The Conjure Woman* (1899), a collection of interlinked short stories set within the overgrown and ruined rural plantation South, but saturated by the logics of a northern urban capital; and the Ukrainian folk tale tradition in Nikolai Gogol's short stories such as the "Overcoat" (1842). In each case, an agrarian narrative form is secularized and transformed into an allegorical form that grapples with the experience of modern urban life. The above examples are significant: the short story does not develop in those older empires, whose cities were formed in the medieval era, but in the newly developing urban centers that proliferated in the transition between merchant and industrial capitalism: St. Petersburg, Berlin, Boston, and New York. Indeed, as Amy Kaplan has shown in the US context, folk-regionalisms were themselves formed by a centralizing metropolitan publishing industry within the cities of Boston and New York (1988).

Central to my argument, then, is that there is no non-urban short story and thus that the American urban or suburban short story cannot be understood as a canon of texts. Instead, urbanization is the condition of the short story and the intensification and expansion of urbanization across the nineteenth and twentieth centuries are structuring forces that exert pressure on, shape, challenge, and transform the short story's form and its attendant genres. Indeed, I want to suggest we understand the "doubled" nature of the short story, identified by Piglia, as a specifically urban dialectic that expresses the interplay between the determining force of capitalist urbanization and the hidden histories, everydayness, and revolutionary potentials lurking within.

Cities, David Harvey reminds us, are environments constructed to "facilitate capitalist production, exchange and consumption" (2001, 81). They also, as Kanishka Goonewardena argues, produce phantasmagorias, or "urban sensorias" (2005, 47), that seduce and shape us into capital's mold. But cities are not simply the factories of commodities and phantasmagorias. And in moments of unrest, the built environments constructed to efface earlier forms of dispossession, expropriation, and violence become the raw materials of revolt: whether the paving stones in Paris in 1848, the barricades and Vendôme Column in the Paris Commune in 1871 (Ross 2015), the new durable commodities, such as fridges, in the 1965 urban uprisings across the United States (Debord 1965), or the freeways in Occupy and Black Lives Matter protests (Clover 2016). In what follows, then, I show how the short story's absorption and deployment of specific generic forms mediates and responds to four key moments of urbanization: romance in the colonial mercantile city; detective fiction and ghetto pastoral in the industrial city; science fiction (SF) in the automotive city; and the new SFs emerging in the logistical or neo-mercantile cities of our present.

II

Nathaniel Hawthorne's "My Kinsman, Major Molineaux" (1832) opens with its protagonist, Robin, arriving by ferry in the "little metropolis of a

New England colony" as if "entering London" (1982, 69). The story centers on Robin's attempts to map this new urban space onto an older feudal urbanism, organized around kinship, hierarchy, and order (Dowries 2004, 31). What he finds instead is the "unreal" colonial, mercantile city, with its tangled streets, international residents, and alluring commodities – from the "many bowls of punch, which the great West India trade had long since made a familiar drink in the colony" (71), to the "tobacco smoke" in the tavern (71), to the "gorgeous display of goods in the shop windows" (74), to the "mariners" (71), prostitutes, and "French Protestant" barkeep (72).

Dazzled and blinded by the city's sensoria, Robin is unable to read the events unfolding around him. As Joseph Alkana notes, Robin's vision is so limited that when "something distant is perceived, like ships' masts, this bit of visual evidence misleadingly accompanies 'the smell of tar' producing the false suggestion of a placid maritime setting rather than the cruel weapon of a mob" (2007, 12). We learn the true meaning of this tar, of course, in the final Dionysian reverie in which Robin's uncle, the colonial governor, finally appears, dragged tarred and feathered through the streets, followed by a wild march of "many fantastic shapes" as if "a dream had broken forth some feverish brain, and were sweeping visibly through the midnight streets" (84). This mob is often read as a figuration of "democratic terror" (Dowries 2004), but his tarred-and-feathered uncle and the surreal, colonial riot of men in "wild Indian dress" (84), "appearing like war personified" (84), are rather the appearance of slave labor, land expropriations, and war-making practices that lurk behind the colonial city's spectacular commodities and spaces. As was often the case with colonial violence against British officials, the rioters' visual markers and techniques were developed in the colonial plantation economies and on the frontier. In addition to the colonists "playing Indian" to rebel against colonial officials (Deloria 1998), tarring and feathering was deployed in "the seventeenth- and eighteenth-century transatlantic rim" to punish "disobedient slaves" (Irvin 2003, 200). This is the background story – baked into its very settings, subjects, and events – which flashes before Robin and the reader's eye, shattering the surfaces of both the narrative and the mercantile city, and "illuminating" the upheavals and violence lurking below.

Hawthorne's "little metropolis" is analogous to other late eighteenth- and early nineteenth-century depictions of the frontier as an irrational, dreamlike space. This makes sense. The eighteenth-century city was a colonial outpost, a node in the mercantilist capitalist system. But

Hawthorne was already looking backward to an outmoded form of urbanism. By the time he was writing, the city itself had been radically transformed, taking on the image of industrial capitalism. This new industrial city, as Harvey notes, was both "a powerhouse of accumulation and a crucible of class struggle" (1985, 33). It was at once a rational, ordered space that facilitated the "flows of goods and people," whilst also creating "social anarchy generated by crises of overaccumulation, technological change, unemployment and de-skilling, immigration, and all manner of factional rivalries and divisions both within and between social classes" (33). It is the literature of this industrial, gridded city, particularly New York, that often becomes synonymous with the idea of "urban literature," a genre capturing the spectacular transformation of the city into an awesome productive machine: the ships bringing workers from eastern Europe and China (themselves forced to migrate by agricultural revolutions in the Midwest), and the West Indies (forced out by the organization of the sugar economy and the rise of the banana economy in Jamaica and the Bahamas [James 1998]); the railways bringing black workers and raw materials from the South; and the new trams, horsecars, ferryboats, bicycles, automobiles, and subways carrying this ever-expanding workforce to the factories that produced the objects that would come to fill and finance the commodity phantasmagorias of the department stores, theaters, and world fairs. But it also disrupts the image of a smooth, ordered urban modernity through its expositions of the cramped quarters, wasted bodies, sweatshops, and sexual and racial mixing – a combination always at risk of exploding.

III

Two short story genres emerge that grapple with the tensions of this industrial city: the detective story; and what Michael Denning has termed the "ghetto or tenement pastoral" (1998, 201), a genre that grows out of, and inverts, earlier naturalist stories, telling tales not of how the other half lives but "how *our* half lives" (230). The detective story is a classic model of the two-story short story. Tzvetan Todorov famously argued that detective fiction was composed of the *fabula*, "the story of the crime," and the *siuzhet*, "the story of the investigation" (1977, 44). In Todorov's reading, the space between the two is temporal: between "what has happened in life" and how "the author presents it to us" (45). But such a division is also spatial: the *siuzhet* occurs within the confined crime scene, which contains the clues for the more expansive geographies of the *fabula*. Practitioners of the genre include Stephen Crane, Charles Chesnutt, and Edith Wharton, but it is Edgar Allan Poe who first put the genre on the map. Peculiarly, however, Poe chose to set his first and most famous detective story, "Murders in the Rue Morgue" (1841), not in the United States, but in Paris. Written ten years before Haussmanization turned Paris into an industrial and imperialist nexus, "Murders" is a mystery written at a transitional moment in a transitional city.

It is in fact two mysteries: the murder of the old woman, Mrs. L'Espanyac and her daughter, in their bedroom; and the question of where their gold originates. The bulk of the story's narrative focuses on Dupin's magisterial and rational deciphering of the first mystery: through clues drawn from witnesses' descriptions of the murderer's language, the space of the room and building, the violence of the crime, and the unhuman hair left behind, Dupin famously concludes that the murderer was an orangutan which had escaped the custody of a French sailor, who had caught the animal in the "Far East" (2004, 265). "Murders" has been both critiqued for "artificially cut[ting] crime fiction off from politics" (Goulet 2016, 89) and read as a response to, and allegory of, slave revolts. Jack Matthews, for instance, compellingly argues that the story "nearly" makes a "crime story . . . a story of slavery's criminality" (2020, 47) but retreats as Dupin's gaze shifts from the whip in his hand to the nail in the window, thus sealing the mystery within the "locked rooms in Parisian rues" (47). Just as Dupin turns away from the whip, so the story turns away from the money. But the money is ultimately the most important clue. The origin of their wealth comes from the same transnational system, if not location, that enabled an orangutan to run free in Paris. If the *siuzhet* is a domestic affair, the *fabula* is a global one. And while Poe formally cannot quite bring the two together, retreating into the domestic, his spatial displacement comes close. In Poe's displacement of the slave rebellion to Paris, its allegorical scope expands: it could, after all, refer as easily to the Haitian slave uprising during the Napoleonic period, France's own incursions into the East Indies, or the urban uprisings of the July Revolution of 1830 (Goulet and Harari 2016, 89). And this, in turn, roots the detective story's origin neither in America nor in Europe, but rather in the global plantation system itself.

Many years later, Pauline Hopkins would offer a revision of Poe's "Murders" in "Talma Gordon" that makes explicit the links between America and "slavery's criminality" that Poe evaded. "Talma" opens in the lavish "Canterbury Club" in Boston, where a doctor is invited to contribute to a debate on American imperialism that focuses on the problem of miscegenation and whether the Anglo-Saxon race is "ready to receive and assimilate the new material" (882). The doctor's response, which makes up the bulk of the story, is a dizzyingly complex mystery that spirals around the murder of retired sea captain Jonathan Gordon (who was "formerly engaged in the East India trade" [2006, 882] before switching to cotton) and his second wife and son. One of the children from Captain Gordon's first marriage, Talma, the beautiful, fair-haired daughter, is initially tried for the crime, with the presumed motive being fear of the loss of inheritance to the new wife, but acquitted. Three surprises follow: that Talma and her sister were disinherited because their mother was one-sixteenth black; that the murderer of Captain Gordon is an East Indian man who goes by the name of Cameron, who killed the gold-hungry Gordon to avenge the death of his own father; and, finally, that Talma is in fact the narrator/doctor's wife.

The doctor's story, which functions as the "background" story, does not intervene in the debate so much as blow up its terms. As Hazel Carby notes, the "fictional history of the degradation of a race" that the doctor weaves "was not the result of degeneration through amalgamation but a consequence of an abuse of power; it was the use of brutality against a subordinate group that was defined as and equated with savagery" (1987, 134). It is this savagery that forces a reconsideration of both the entire narrative and the civility of the building's environs and the club's men. It turns the murder into a device that allows the unpacking of the real mystery – the wealth of the men in the club, and of America itself. Hopkins wrenches the historical and public elements implicit in Poe into the foreground.

If the detective story is largely structural, focusing on a rational, professional, middle-class outsider's investigations into the city, the ghetto pastoral starts from the questions of working-class experience, but is no less global in its vision. The ghetto pastorals of Mike Gold, Richard Wright, Tillie Olsen, Anzia Yezierska, Claude McKay, and Meridel Le Sueur, and later the updated pastorals of Sandra Cisneros and Junot Diaz, were, as Michael Denning argues, a form of "subaltern modernism" (1998, 231) that "combined the dream of a new proletarian literature nurtured by the cultural politics of the left" and "the ethnic and racial modalities through which the relations of class were lived" (240). Anzia Yezierska's stories are paradigmatic here. Much of her work is about ethnic, working-class women's desires to possess the beauty that they create for bourgeoise women at the expense of their own hands, "blistered ... and calloused from rough toil" (1997, 43). "The Lost 'Beautifulness,'" for instance, focuses on Shenah, a Russian Jewish domestic worker for the Stuyvesant Square mansions who takes in extra washing in order to paint her rental apartment white for her son's imminent return from fighting for the Americans in France. But, of course, this industriousness leads only to increased rent. "Because the flat is painted new, I can get more money for it," her landlord "snarls" (1997, 53), evicting her. The story ends with her son coming home to find her "seizing the chopping-axe and . . . scratching down the paint, breaking the plaster on the walls" (60). "The Lost 'Beautifulness'" turns on the doubleness of the house itself, which is a home for her and capital for her landlord, who is literally able to profit on her desire for beauty.

This desire for beauty and pleasure is both a persistent theme and political problem in Yezierska and more broadly in ghetto pastorals, particularly those written by women: how to express a working-class desire for beauty and pleasure, outside the ideological strictures both of sentimentalism, a genre that privileges displays of loss or disempowerment, or of the *Bildungsroman*, a narrative of property acquisition and embourgeoisement. Yezierska shuttles between the two, but Shenah's final destructive act potentially takes desire outside either stricture, refiguring it as a force that leads to the destruction of fixed capital itself – though neither this story nor the rest of her work is ever fully able to free itself from the competing pressures of sentimentality or the *Bildungsroman*.

IV

The very migrations from the southern United States, Caribbean, Europe, and Asia that powered the industrial city, and the detective story and ghetto pastoral, however, soon led to its crisis, as mass unemployment, inadequate housing, growing labor unrest, and political militancy threatened the very economic foundations of the city. Resolution came through war and a new automotive-led, petrol-saturated reorganization of the metropolitan region around decentralized suburbs and exurbs. These landscapes re-spatialized and intensified the segregation of the industrial city, creating a landscape of affluent white suburbs and poor ethnic cities, "disseminating and popularizing," as Paul Gilroy puts it, "the absolute social segregation that once characterized the colonial city" (2001, 93).

With the rise of this new landscape, both the automobile and public transit become, like the ship before it, the new "laborator[ies] for the conceptualization of a world system" (Casarino 2002, 9). Flannery O'Connor's "A Good Man is Hard to Find" (1955) is a signal instance of the larger aim underpinning her work: to transform the mass, commodity culture that she saw as consuming and destroying the "Old South" into a vehicle of religious grace. Here, she takes aim specifically at the highway system, with its billboards, advertising signs, diners, and Coca Cola. Through a series of false turns, a family road trip to the sunny shores of Florida becomes a trip through the backroads and decayed plantations of Georgia that culminates in a deathly encounter with the "Misfit," a recently escaped prisoner, and ultimately to a violent clash with what can alternately be read as history or the divine. O'Connor used the term "shock" to refer to this method (1961, 34); Piglia called it "profane illumination," though of course shock was at the center of the surrealist's vision of profane illumination as well. In a very different register, Simon Ortiz's "The Panther Waits" (1983) too attempts to recoup the car as a revelatory vehicle: in this case, for finishing the journey started by the great Shawnee statesman Tecumseh and his brother Tenskwatawa. "The Panther" revolves around the vision of a drunk Indian man that "two Indian brothers" would drive across "all those states now on the map" (1999, 100) to "reunite" the tribes and "save their land and their families and their ways" (101). But the vision is foreclosed as we learn that one character had already been killed in a car accident, and another "works for an oil company down in Houston" (102). The car, Ortiz makes clear, cannot be a tool for an anticolonial indigenous future, as it leads only to assimilation or destruction. "Maybe we need another vision," the story ends (102).

For some authors, one such vision is to be located in the abandoned, disinvested, and racialized space of urban public transit. In the Puerto Rican revolutionary José Luis González's "The Night We Became People Again" (1970), the New York City blackout of 1965 becomes the backdrop for a kind of allegory of national consciousness. The story tracks the unnamed protagonist, who works at a radio factory and is trying to get back uptown to the Barrio on a rush hour train to his wife, who is in labor, when the blackout hits, forcing him to continue his journey through the train tunnels and darkened streets on foot. The overlapping metaphors of darkness and light, tunnels and life, serve to link the birth of his son and, implicitly, Puerto Rican independence. The story concludes with a memory of him on the roof, looking at the stars, which look like the stars in Puerto Rico, and these concluding lines: "But what I'll always remember is what I said then to *doña* Lula, which is what I want to tell you now, to finish my story. And that is, according to my poor way of understanding things, that was the night we became people again" (2001, 411). Here, it is mass transit, even in or as a result of its breakdowns, that produces the conditions for a revolutionary vision of both an individual, the working class, and anticolonial rebirth.

The segregation created by these automotive landscapes segregated literary categories themselves. From the 1940s on, we have predominantly white suburban writers of alienation and anomie (e.g., John Cheever, the "Chekhov of the Suburbs," John Updike, and later Raymond Carver) and racialized urban writers of poverty and ghettoization (e.g., Grace Paley, Alice Childress, Ralph Ellison, Paule Marshall, and Sandra Cisneros). Literary studies too reflects this segregation, as scholarly works begin to examine the city *or* the suburb, but rarely the two together as part of a whole. One genre that enables the short story to try and overcome this segregation and offer a more totalizing account of the urban is SF. While SF first emerged and did important work remapping the industrial city, as in W. E. B. DuBois's strange and wonderful "Princess Steel," which visually telescopes the histories of Indian removal and frontier expansion at the heart of the new symbol of modernity, the skyscraper (Brown and Russert 2015), it becomes particularly important in the postwar period because of its ability to capture the wholesale transformation of the urban and suburban landscapes. Two SF short stories, separated by thirty years, are particularly compelling here: Ray Bradbury's space-western "Night Meeting," part of his short story cycle *Martian Chronicles* (1950), and Samuel Delany's fantasy/SF "The Tale of Plagues and Carnivals" (1985), a short story/novella forming part of the larger *Nevèrÿon* series.

"Night Meeting" opens with Tomás Gomez stopping "for gasoline at the lonely station" (2012, 108) in a "little dead Martian town ... uninhabited for centuries. Perfect, faultless, in ruins" (110). There, he encounters a "a machine-like jade-green insect, a praying mantis" (111), a Martian. What follows is the narration of a failed attempt at communication. The Martian accepts a drink offered by Tomás, but the cup falls through his hands; the Martian gives Tomás a knife, but it drops through him. They soon realize that both appear to the other like "a ghostly prism flashing the accumulated light of distant worlds" (113). The difficulties only continue. When they discuss the town, it becomes clear that where Tomás sees a city that has "been dead thousands of years" (114), its inhabitants all killed by an earthling virus, for the Martian the situation is entirely different. "We're *alive* . . .. I'm on my way to a festival now at the canal, near the Eniall Mountains. I was there last night. Don't you see the city there?'" (114). They debate if the canals are empty or flowing with lavender wine; if the streets are full of color and carnivals or empty as dust.

Realizing their visions are out of joint, neither is sure who is the past or future. Crosshatching the settler-colonial mythos of the western within the more contemporary settler-colonial mythos of the urban redevelopment and suburbanization (Veracini 2012), Bradbury takes aim at the entire narrative of progress. If the Martian's vision is the future, then Tomás's and the earthling's colonization of Mars is just a blip in the past. If Tomás is correct that he is the future, then we are left to conclude that the shoddy village thrown together with "a million board feet of Oregon lumber and a couple dozen tons of good steel nails" (115) – as well as the numerous other nostalgic small towns, and nuked suburban utopias that populate *Martian Chronicles* – is no great progress, but rather a pale imitation of the grand architecture of "white pillars" and "canals" filled "with lavender wine" (114) that preceded it.

Bradbury marks something of a break here. Where, as Piglia argued, the short story is organized around the linking of foreground and background, in "Night Meeting" the stories confront each other as two separate systems that cannot be mapped onto each other. This is something that Samuel Delany (a careful reader of Benjamin, Baudelaire, and Bradbury) will pick up in his remarkable "The Tales of Plagues and Carnivals," written as the processes of suburbanization and urban devaluation, which Bradbury tracks, starts to invert, and the urban core becomes gentrified and suburbanized. "Tales" toggles back and forth between Nevèrÿön's port city, Kolhari, a mercantile colonial city at a moment of transition into a full-market economy, and an early 1980s New York City amid the devastations and crises of the AIDS pandemic and early neoliberalism. These devastations are etched into the landscapes, with their "cracked" and "broken" walls, concrete "crumbl[ing] from iron supports: rust has washed down over the pebbled exterior [. . . with] the air of a prehistoric structure" (1985, 175), and within the ruined bodies themselves. Connecting the two plots are two twinned "plagues" that are rumored to be transmitted by homosexuals.

The stories appear allegorical, one mapping onto the other; they also appear sequential, narrating key moments of transformation in capitalist urbanization. And yet here too the temporalities come to fold in on each other. At the same moment in which the "village" of Kolhari is being radically altered, transformed, marketized, and rebuilt by a nascent commercial capitalism, a deindustrializing New York City too is being reshaped by a new kind of urbanization, one that promises a return to the city and is reminiscent of the port city of Kolhari itself. As Kevin Floyd puts it, the story tracks "the return of the village [. . . through] a kind of environmental planning, a corporate and governmental relocation of the urban jungle to what we used to be able to call the suburban margins, so that the Times Square visitor does not have to be disturbed by any unsavory characters" (2013, 120). Henri Lefebvre observed that the "transition to urbanization brings a further shrinkage of nature," which is "matched by an obsessive 'ideological naturalization' of society and the parodic reproduction of nature as denatured 'open spaces,' parks, gardens, images of femininity" (2003, 15). What Delany articulates as early as the 1980s is how the identical process happens as working-class urban populations are themselves turned into nature, and their culture parodically reproduced in spaces like the Disneyfied Times Squares. The market town of Kolhari, then, is both the past and future of 1980s New York. What SF is uniquely able to do is to think the segregated spaces of the city and the suburb together as an urban totality, but only through the generic torsions that allow the two spaces to confront each other in all their antagonistic and historical complexities.

V

Delany's positioning of the merchant city as both past and future is borne out historically as the industrial cities of the nineteenth and early twentieth century transform again, becoming neo-mercantile or "logistics" cities (Cowen 2014) that are integrated "into managed networks of goods circulation underpinning both trade and warfare" (193), and increasingly blurring the line between the two. How to register this? I end with one brief example: Haisla-Heiltsuk author Eden Robinson's "Terminal Avenue" (1996). Set in a near-future, dystopic zoned, and segregated Vancouver, Canada, shortly after a failed indigenous uprising, the story toggles between a single moment in which the Haisla protagonist Wil is attacked, and presumably killed, by "Peace Officers" on the platform of the Surrey Skytrain station, and his childhood memories: of his home in Kitimat, a forbidden potlatch, of his brother Kevin, a resistance-fighter-turned-"peace officer" who ultimately disappears, and of his current job. Wil works in the fetish club. His job is to play himself, an indigenous man not allowed on the streets or in the club Terminal Avenue, who is thus "hurled," "handcuffed," and "strip-searched" by bouncers "dressed as Peace Officers . . . in front of clients who pay for the privilege of watching" (2012, 209). In the story, the social hierarchies that his S/M bondage routine performs become reality as he is stopped and beaten to death by the Officers themselves.

As in Delany and Bradbury, the near-future is also the past, but where a tension is retained between past and present in these earlier works, in "Terminal Avenue" time seems to collapse in on itself. As Grace Dillon notes, the future uprising is also "the historically forbidden potlatches of the 1880s, the severe government crackdown on Native practices in the 1920s, and the military-peace-keeping restrictions at Oka of the early 1990s," all of which "'reappear' at Surrey Central" (2012, 206). This both reflects the "Heiltsuk sense of parallel worlds" (206), and reveals how earlier foundational acts of violence remain embedded within the city itself. Thus, the entanglements between the spectacle of violence in the downtown club and the actual violent colonial relationships are mirrored in the twinning of, or return to and amplification of, the original settler-colonial violence that established Vancouver, and the new rounds of racial violence and dispossession required to maintain and manage the flows of bodies and capital through this new/old logistics city.

From the mercantile city, to the industrial, to the automotive, and to the new logistical/mercantile city, the short story has been a central form through which authors have encountered and grappled with the spatial fixes and phantasmagorias of urban modernity; it is also the form writers have turned toward to shock and shatter its smooth and seductive services, and to make them erupt. This remains the promise and potential of the genre.

Works Cited

Alkana, Joseph. 2007. "Disorderly History in 'My Kinsman, Major Molineux'," *ESQ: A Journal of the American Renaissance* 53.1: iv–30.

Arrighi, Giovanni. 1994. *The Long Twentieth Century: Money, Power, and the Origins of Our Times*. London: Verso.

Benjamin, Walter. 1996. "On Some Motifs in Baudelaire," in *Selected Writings: 1938-1940*, 313–355. Cambridge, MA: Harvard University Press.

2005. "Surrealism: The Last Snapshot of the European Intelligentsia," in *Walter Benjamin: Selected Writings 1927-30*, 207–221. Cambridge, MA: Harvard University Press.

Bradbury, Ray. 2012. *The Martian Chronicles*. New York: Simon & Schuster.

Carby, Hazel V. 1987. *Reconstructing Womanhood: The Emergence of the Afro-American Woman Novelist: The Emergence of the Afro-American Woman Novelist*. New York: Oxford University Press.

Casarino, Cesare. 2002. *Modernity at Sea: Melville, Marx, Conrad in Crisis*. Minneapolis: University of Minnesota Press.

Cowen, Deborah. 2014. *The Deadly Life of Logistics: Mapping Violence in Global Trade*. Minneapolis: University of Minnesota Press.

Debord, Guy. n.d. "The Decline and Fall of the Spectacle-Commodity Economy," *Situationist International Online*. Translated by Ken Knabb. www.cddc.vt.edu/sionline/si/decline.html.

Delany, Samuel. 1985. *Flight from Nevèrÿon*. New York: Bantam Books.

Deloria, Philip Joseph. 1998. *Playing Indian*. New Haven, CT: Yale University Press.

Denning, Michael. 1998. *The Cultural Front: The Laboring of American Culture in the Twentieth Century*. London: Verso.

Dowries, Paul. 2004. "Democratic Terror in 'My Kinsman, Major Molineux' and 'The Man of the Crowd'," *Poe Studies* 37.1–2: 31–35.

Floyd, Kevin. 2013. "How to Subsume Difference, or World Reduction in Delany," in *Literary Materialisms*. Eds. Mathias Nilges and Emilio Sauri, 113–124. New York: Springer.

Gilroy, Paul. 2001. "Driving While Black," in *Car Cultures*. Ed. Daniel Miller, 81–100. London: Routledge.

González, José Luis. 2002. "The Night We Became People Again," in *Herencia: The Anthology of Hispanic Literature of the United States*. Ed. Nicolas Kanellos, 403–410. New York: Oxford University Press.

Goonewardena, Kanishka. 2005. "The Urban Sensorium: Space, Ideology and the Aestheticization of Politics," *Antipode* 37.1: 46–71.

Goulet, Andrea and Josué Harari. 2016. *Legacies of the Rue Morgue: Science, Space, and Crime Fiction in France*. Philadelphia: University of Pennsylvania Press.

Harvey, David. 1985. *The Urbanization of Capital: Studies in the History and Theory of Capitalist Urbanization*. Baltimore, MD: Johns Hopkins University Press.

2001. *Spaces of Capital: Towards a Critical Geography*. London: Routledge.

Hawthorne, Nathaniel. 1982. "My Kinsman, Major Molineux," in *Tales and Sketches*. New York: The Library of America.

Hopkins, Pauline Elizabeth. 2006. "Talma Gordon," in *Heath Anthology of American Literature*, Vol. C, 881–891. Boston: Wadsworth.

Irvin, Benjamin H. 2003. "Tar, Feathers, and the Enemies of American Liberties, 1768-1776," *The New England Quarterly* 76.2: 197.

Irving, Washington. 2014. *The Legend of Sleepy Hollow and Other Stories*. New York: Penguin.

James, Winston. 1998. *Holding Aloft the Banner of Ethiopia: Caribbean Radicalism in Early-Twentieth Century America*. London: Verso Books.

Kaplan, Amy. 1988. *The Social Construction of American Realism*. Chicago: University of Chicago Press.

Lefebvre, Henri. 2003. *The Urban Revolution*. Translated by Robert Bononno. Minneapolis: University of Minnesota Press.

March-Russell, Paul. 2016. "Writing and Publishing the Short Story," in *The Cambridge Companion to the English Short Story*. Ed. Ann-Marie Einhaus, 15–27. Cambridge, UK: Cambridge University Press.

Matthews, John T. 2020. *Hidden in Plain Sight: Slave Capitalism in Poe, Hawthorne, and Joel Chandler Harris*. Athens: University of Georgia Press.

O'Brien, Colleen C. 2009. "'Blacks in All Quarters of the Globe': Anti-Imperialism, Insurgent Cosmopolitanism, and International Labor in Pauline Hopkins's Literary Journalism," *American Quarterly* 61.2: 245–270.

O'Connor, Flannery. 1961. *"The Fiction Writer and His Country,"* In *Mystery and Manners*. Eds. Sally and Robert Fitzgerald, 25–35. New York: Farrar, Straus, and Giroux.

———. 1971. *The Complete Stories*. New York: Farrar, Straus, and Giroux.

Ortiz, Simon J. 1999. *Men on the Moon: Collected Short Stories*. Tucson: University of Arizona Press.

Piglia, Ricardo. 2011. "Theses on the Short Story," *New Left Review* 70 (August): 63–66.

Poe, Edgar Allan. 2004. *The Selected Writings of Edgar Allan Poe*. Ed. G. R. Thompson. New York: W. W. Norton and Company.

Robinson, Eden. 2012. "Terminal Avenue," in *Walking the Clouds: An Anthology of Indigenous Science Fiction*. Ed. Grace Dillon, 207–214. Tucson: University of Arizona Press.

Ross, Kristin. 2015. *Communal Luxury: The Political Imaginary of the Paris Commune*. London and New York: Verso.

Smith, Neil. 2002. "New Globalism, New Urbanism: Gentrification as Global Urban Strategy," *Antipode* 34.3: 427–450.

Todorov, Tzvetan. 1977. "The Typology of Detective Fiction," in *The Poetics of Prose*. Ed. Jonathan Culler, trans. Richard Howard, 42–52. Ithaca, NY: Cornell University Press.

Veracini, Lorenzo. 2012. "Suburbia, Settler Colonialism and the World Turned Inside Out," *Housing, Theory and Society* 29.4: 339–357.

Warner, Michael. 2000. "Irving's Posterity," *ELH* 67.3: 773–99.

Yezierska, Anzia. 1997. *Hungry Hearts*. New York: Penguin Classics.

PART IV

Theories

CHAPTER 17

Short Fiction, Language Learning, and Innocent Comedy

Gabriella Safran

People who critique American short fictions tend to have a specific thing in mind. Following an 1842 essay in which Edgar Allan Poe lauded stories that can be read at one sitting and produce a unified impression, American critics celebrate what they see as a distinctively national genre: something portable that produces a single intense emotion in the reader (Boddy 2010, 6–7). Later American writers expanded on Poe's ideas, telling beginning writers, as Frederick Crews explains, "show, don't tell; keep the narrative voice distinct from those of your characters; cultivate understatement; develop a central image or symbol to convey your theme 'objectively' and point everything toward one neatly sprung ironic reversal" (1992, 144–145). In this chapter, I explore short American fictions that are like jokes, drawing on humor theorists such as Sigmund Freud, who distinguishes between stories that produce a single intense emotion and those that do not. He opposes the "tendentious" joke, which generates "pleasure by lifting suppressions and repressions" and is "an end in itself," to "abstract" or "innocent" humor, which begins "as play, in order to derive pleasure from the free use of words and thoughts," then applies reasoning to "achieve fresh pleasure from the liberation of nonsense" (Freud 1960, 106, 115, 168–169). If tendentious jokes lead listeners to the sudden exposure of our true aggressive and obscene desires, innocent ones do not engage so evidently with issues of power (Freud 1960, 114). Inspired by Freud's observations about the pleasure of nonsense, I argue for the importance of a countertradition of American short stories that sidesteps Poe's imperatives in favor of "innocent" comedy; it features the linguistic slapstick generated by language learning and exposes the instability even of standard language. I frame my primary case study, the understudied twentieth-century immigrant writer Leo Rosten – like Freud a collector of Jewish jokes – as an inheritor of more often discussed earlier native-born writers such as Mark Twain, Ambrose Bierce, and O. Henry. In linking Rosten to Twain, Bierce, and O. Henry, I turn away from the easy assumption that vaudeville-type jokes, with their pratfalls and immigrant accents, are lowbrow, and that any fondness for them is a little embarrassing, when one should prefer highbrow stories shimmering with epiphanies and told from the kind of neutral position that no one ever actually occupies.

In the 1968 *Joys of Yiddish*, a dictionary of Yiddish terms used in American English that is illustrated with jokes, Rosten celebrates migrants who adapt language for their own purposes, "blithely" creating new words and new meanings for old words. Under the entry for "boarderkeh," defined as "a female boarder (obviously) who pays for room and board," he gives this story:

> A Mr. Goldberg, from Pinsk, coming to America, shared a table in the ship's dining room with a Frenchman. Mr. Goldberg could speak neither French nor English; the Frenchman could speak neither Russian nor Yiddish.
>
> The first day out, the Frenchman approached the table, bowed, and said, "*Bon appétit!*"
>
> Goldberg, puzzled for a moment, bowed back and replied, "Goldberg."
>
> Every day, at every meal, the same routine occurred.
>
> On the fifth day, another passenger took Goldberg aside. "Listen, the Frenchman isn't telling you his name. He's saying 'Good appetite.' That's what '*Bon appétit*' means."
>
> At the next meal, Mr. Goldberg, beaming, said to the Frenchman, "*Bon appétit!*"
>
> And the Frenchman, beaming, replied, "Goldberg!" (Rosten 2001, 41–42)

This is funny for many reasons, one of which is its display of the arbitrariness of language: what if the word for "*bon appétit*" were, in fact, "Goldberg"? Although it is located in a dictionary, which one might think of as representing a linguistic standard, no one in this scene has the power to enforce such standards. Such stories about people on the move, communicating in an unfamiliar modern space, are a common subgenre of jokes, including Jewish jokes (Safran 2019). Freud would categorize this as an example of an innocent joke that generates pleasure in the listener, who enjoys seeing how sounds, words, or concepts permit multiple meanings (1960, 46). In what follows, I attend to a series of brief texts that draw on lexicography and language learning to explore the "innocent" humor of a world of unstable language. I first look at Rosten and the development of his best-known protagonist, Hyman Kaplan, who is learning English at night school in the 1930s, second point out some parallel ideas about language and identity in Rosten's portrayal of Kaplan and the Russian Formalist Boris Eikhenbaum's description of O. Henry, and third situate Rosten among other American humorists.

Rosten and Kaplan

Leo Rosten (1908–1997), like Goldberg, emigrated from the Russian Empire during a wave of Jewish migration that lasted from 1880 through the 1920s; born in Lodz, he was brought to the United States in 1911 and grew up in Chicago. He studied at the University of Chicago and received a Ph.D. in Political Science. His first marriage made him the brother-in-law of the anthropologist Margaret Mead and the cartoonist William Steig. He taught night-school English classes to immigrants in Chicago for two years and became a successful writer in multiple genres: stories, novels, screenplays, studies of American religion, journalism, and film – and also compiled collections of quotations and jokes, especially Judaica. During World War II, he was the Deputy Director of the Office of War Information, which also employed Mead, and he wrote *112 Gripes About the French*, a comical list of faults meant to remind GIs that the French, no matter how irritating they might appear, were America's allies and the Germans its enemies (on the war period, see Rosten 1942–1961). In the postwar, he, like Mead, worked for the Rand Corporation. His interest in both ethnic jokes and social-science studies suggests the similarities in these genres, both of which, like vaudeville, assume that social categories such as ethnicity or national identity are representable by markers with which Americans should be familiar (Kaplan 1983; Jenkins 1992, 63–72).

Rosten depicts himself as an obsessive collector, since childhood, of other people's words.

> I collected epigrams the way some boys collect stamps …. My pockets became filing cases for tersities of wisdom (scribbled on scraps of paper, backs of envelopes, margins torn from newspapers) …. I bought a 4-by-6-inch card catalogue, and packets of lined cards, and blank index guides on which to write my categories: "Fate … Lust … Honor … Folly …" – and so began to systematize my own precious Bartlett …. I visualized aphorisms as dressed in silk, epigrams as bedecked with sequins, proverbs as wrapped in fur. Folk sayings, obviously, ran around in honest homespun. (Rosten 1972a, 6–7; cf. Rosten 1994, 7).

He heard some of these items spoken and found others already collected, as in Ignats Bernstein's 1908 *Yidishe shprikhverter un redersartn* ("Jewish proverbs and sayings"). He cheerfully cites himself as the originator or adapter of some of the sayings he anthologized. One of his first publications, which appeared when he was twenty-four, was a satirical "Comic Lexicon," and he went on to produce *The Joys of Yiddish* in 1968, a collection of malapropisms, *Rome Wasn't Burned in a Day*, in 1972, and eight more books of humor, lexicography, or both (Rosten 1972a, 7, 9–11, 49).

In 1935, Rosten wrote his first Hyman Kaplan story and sold it to the *New Yorker*. He republished it with fourteen more in 1937 as *The Education of H*Y*M*A*N K*A*P*L*A*N*; he wrote twelve more stories for the *New Yorker* and *Harpers* and published them as *The Return of H*Y*M*A*N K*A*P*L*A*N* in 1959. In 1976, he published twenty-nine stories, including revisions of the old ones and some new ones, as *O K*A*P*L*A*N! My K*A*P*L*A*N!* (Rosten 1976, ix–xii). All these stories are set in the beginners' classroom of the American Night Preparatory School for Adults ("English – Americanization – Civics – Preparation for Naturalization") in Manhattan. The straight man and teacher (except in one story, where he is sick and a substitute has taken over) is the earnest and genteel Mr. Parkhill. Sitting in the middle of the front row is the funny man, Hyman Kaplan, a cheerful dress cutter from Kiev. Kaplan has already been in the United States for fifteen years, and speaks fluent English, albeit with a strong Yiddish accent and idiosyncratic grammar and vocabulary. Most of the stories start with Mr. Parkhill (or the substitute) calling the roll or reflecting on his teaching plan for that evening: covering idioms, vocabulary, or verbs, having some students write compositions on the board or give speeches as the other students critique them, giving the final exam. Sometimes new students join the class; before the winter holidays and on his birthday, the students give Mr. Parkhill a present. The stories all end with the class, and Mr. Parkhill, stunned by some aspect of Kaplan's inventive but unorthodox speech.

Any foreign language teacher would recognize the dynamic of Mr. Parkhill's classroom: the intimate atmosphere of a space where grown-ups, made child-like by being language beginners, become child-like in other ways. Like other foreign language students, those at the American Night Preparatory School for Adults are vulnerable. They have strong feelings about their teacher, on whom they rely for approval of their very words. They tell each other about their lives and dreams; they form friendships, enmities, and alliances. Foreign language classrooms display the difference between the bold students, who speak up even though they know they may be making mistakes, and the quiet ones, who actually know the right answer. Some students love the playful work of language learning, the triumph of communication and the comedy of miscommunication. They relish the attention they get when they speak and they strive for the same in their writing, as Kaplan does when, writing on the board, he adorns his name with stars (on paper, he prints his name in capital letters in red crayon, outlines each letter in blue, and draws the stars in green). Others are so intimidated by the possibility of error that they can barely talk.

Many of the punch lines – or the comic "jab lines" scattered throughout the stories – rely on the kind of puns that genuinely arise in the foreign language classroom. For instance, Kaplan concludes a speech about Patrick Henry by saying, "Still, I vill alvays edmire de glorious pest." His rival, Miss Mitnick, protests, "Mistake! In pronunciation '*Past*' is not '*pest*'!" and Mr. Parkhill backs her up, but Kaplan retorts, "To a tyrant like Kink Judge … vat else vas Petrick Hanry bot a glorious pest?" (Rosten 1959, 105–106). He is prone to Hobson-Jobsons, admiring the opera "*Madman Butterfly*," the operettas of "Gilbert and Solomon," and the frontiersman "Daniel Bloom" (Rosten 1976, 67, 173; another student asks about "Salami," meaning *Salome* [111–112]). Other stories feature Marx Brothers-style slapstick, as when Kaplan writes in a business letter about buying a refrigerator, "If your eye falls on a bargain please pick it up." Miss Mitnick casts doubt on the phrasing: "If your *eye* falls on a bargain please pick *it* up?" and Kaplan responds that the recipient of the letter is his uncle Mandelbaum, and "Mine oncle … has a gless eye" (1937, 74).

Mr. Parkhill recognizes Kaplan as his own rival, someone who is not so much unable to master standard English as who prefers his own variant of the language. "Whereas all the other students came to school in order to be instructed, Mr. Kaplan seemed to come in order to be consulted …. Sometimes Mr. Parkhill thought Mr. Kaplan would never find peace until he had invented a language all his own" (Rosten 1959, 57, 60). A new language would mean a new dictionary, and Mr. Parkhill sees that "in his peculiar linguistic universe there was the germ of a new lexicography" (1937, 45). When Kaplan corrects Mitnick's misspelled "headackes" to "headaxe," Mr. Parkhill is "speechless before this orthographic triumph" (1937, 53). He admits that Kaplan's English is as systematic as any other variant: "[I]t was neither ignorance nor caprice which guided Mr. Kaplan's life and language. It was Logic …. And when Mr. Kaplan fell into grammatical error, it was simply because his logic and the logic of the world did not happen to coincide" (1937, 126).[1] Kaplan prefers the grammatical conventions of his native language and is disturbed that English nouns do not have gender: even if most English nouns are referred to as "it," he argues for using "he" for newspapers that have "got a real mascoolin name," such as "Harold Tribune" (1937, 132–133). Mr. Parkhill cannot keep from admiring the logic underlying Kaplan's idiolect.

"Mr. Kaplan made mistakes because he simply ignored or refused to abide by convention. After all, human conventions do not rest on reason, but on consensus .... Any lingering doubts Mr. Parkhill harbored about the whole problem vanished when Mr. Kaplan called the instrument which doctors use to listen to the human heart a 'deathascope'" (1976, 314).

If Mr. Parkhill uses teaching materials in standard English, such as speeches about American history, the students' dictionaries, and the unabridged one that lies in a corner of the classroom, Kaplan presents his own written and oral compositions as offering an alternative standard. When assigned to answer a newspaper ad, he responds to the request for "init." with his initials. Miss Mitnick says that the abbreviation stands instead for "initiative," and Mr. Parkhill supports her. Kaplan, undaunted, explains that "Dat ed I enswered vanted initials," which he knows because he had made it up himself (1959, 154–155). Like Goldberg and the Frenchman, Kaplan delights in his own linguistic inventiveness.

A Sharper Ear

Rosten's stories were first published in the *New Yorker*, in the company of stories meant, as Poe urged, to generate a single strong emotional experience. Such fictions tended, as Kasia Boddy explains, to "work through atmosphere rather than plot" and to "impart their meaning suggestively rather than through dramatic or surprise endings." Mid-century short story theorists advocated, in her words, "the fastidious chiseling of an *object* in order to produce a transcendent *experience*" (Boddy 2010, 39, 25, italics in original; cf. Hunter 2019). Rosten's stories obey some of these rules but disregard others. They are certainly short, and they are unified in their space and their characters. They always lead to the same ironic reversal, showing that not Mr. Parkhill but Kaplan is the dominant voice in the class and that the power structure of this space is startlingly unstable. Like many *New Yorker* stories of the 1950s, such as James Thurber's, they feature tension between men and women, here between Mr. Kaplan and Miss Mitnick. However, these stories are anything but understated; they describe the banal doings of an English language classroom in dramatic or tragic tones. Rosten, in the voice of the buttoned-up Mr. Parkhill, tells the reader much more than he shows. Far from being economical, these stories foster repetition, with sentences and whole compositions written, then read aloud, and then repeated as their components are critiqued. ("If your eye falls ... If your *eye* falls? ... a gless eye!") This is broad comedy in a major key, not suggestive hinting in a minor one. Boddy's term "fastidious chiseling" is transformed when Mr. Parkhill gives "chisel" as a vocabulary word and tells his students to write sentences using it, and Kaplan's friend Mr. Pinsky assumes it is the diminutive of cheese. ("Before sleep, I like to have a little milk and *chisel*" [1959, 74].) In their lack of conformity to the standards of the American short story, Rosten's Kaplan stories resemble other short narratives that are not usually published in the *New Yorker*: language exercises, newspaper advertisements, dictionary entries, the world of formal and informal verbal art that surrounds the students and on which they draw as they learn. These stories resemble, contain, and show off all the short texts that Rosten loved, collected, and invented.

In creating characters who write and speak non-standard English, Rosten practices dialect writing. Foreign and rural accents, including Yiddish accents, were funny and fascinating to American readers from the mid-nineteenth through the mid-twentieth centuries, but dialect writing has come to sound increasingly demeaning to those who speak non-standard language.[2] This is the argument made by Dan Shiffman, one of the few critics to address the Kaplan stories at any length. "The Hyman Kaplan stories do not so much champion the wonderful peculiarity of Yiddish inflections and expressions as they assert the rightness, tolerance, and assimilative power of the dominant Anglo-based culture" (Shiffman 1999, 49; Golub 1982). They treat Kaplan and his fellow immigrants as children, and they extend, he argues, the tradition of vaudeville comedians who mocked the voices of Jews and other immigrants. This kind of humor lost popularity over the course of the twentieth century. A reviewer of the 1959 collection noted that "Mr. Parkhill's class isn't as funny as it used to be."[3] Rosten signaled that he knew Jewish dialect humor needed to be framed more carefully in the postwar period as he edited his stories. Mr. Parkhill already demonstrates increasing awareness of his students' back-stories in the 1959 collection, and the students manifest a new ethnic pride by the 1976 version, where a cantor, Isaac Nussbaum, uses some Hebrew terms, and a Bulgarian-born Armenian student, Miss Atrakian, explains firmly that although she knows some Greek, she is not Greek; the arrival of a new student who was born on the train crossing the US border prompts a discussion of the arbitrariness of immigration law (Rosten 1976, 36, 179).[4]

Shiffman's concern that Rosten might be mocking his subjects echoes a criticism of dialect writing often expressed from the 1920s through the mid-1990s: that native elites used dialect writing patronizingly, in the service of sentimentalism, satire, and the demonstration of their own superiority over funny-sounding migrants (Jones 1999, 8). However, Gavin Jones and Nadia Nurhussein, in their more recent considerations of dialect prose and poetry in the late nineteenth and early twentieth centuries, argue convincingly that this binary view is over-simplifying: it relies on the fiction of standard language as historically and geographically uniform and underlaid by immutable structures of power and identity, and it ignores the ways in which dialect texts can thematize literacy and the process of its acquisition, offering spaces for reflection on the inconsistencies of English spelling and cultivation of the art of recitation (Jones 1999, 8–10; Nurhussein 2013, 18–56). Where Shiffman interprets Rosten's Kaplan stories as what Freud calls tendentious jokes, that is, meant to attack, Jones and Nurhussein suggest that American dialect humor also includes what Freud calls innocent jokes, which draw attention to language itself, its arbitrariness and its variability.

Rather than parsing the Hyman Kaplan stories to distinguish attackers from victims, then, I propose that we see both them and the Goldberg joke, in line with one earlier tradition of American dialect humor, as documenting and celebrating the process of linguistic and literary evolution. Isabel Ermida, a linguist who analyzes humor, explains how literary fiction can work like jokes: "[H]umor lies in the gap that separates the rule-abiding recipient from the rule-infringing sender. However, it is important to point out that this infraction is not gratuitous, but aimed at specific purposes, which are ultimately cooperative" (2008, 142). Kaplan infringes the rules, and the comedy lies in Mr. Parkhill's ever-nonplussed reception of his words – but these stories are not about a power struggle between them. Instead, together, these two characters, the straight man and the funny man, cooperate in a comic display of the flexibility of English, the fellowship of the language classroom, and, as in the Goldberg joke, the fact that communication occurs in spite of everything.

Persistently, Rosten laid claim to a position as an especially good listener to English, due to his early exposure to multiple languages. "I was lucky," he wrote, "to be an immigrant child, and to grow up in a bilingual world; nothing so sharpens the ear to the subtleties that differentiate words as constantly shuttling between two vocabularies" (1972a, 5). He celebrates language learning errors as generative, advertising his collection of malapropisms as "a medley of English sentences each of which, through the delicious imprecision of a word or the innocent refurbishing of a phrase, becomes a sudden transformation of an intense expectation into *something* – something startling or funny or illuminating or instructive. The most triumphant specimens are startling *and* funny and illuminating and instructive" (1972b, 11). He writes of spoonerisms, "Words were man's first, immeasurable feat of magic. They liberated us from ignorance and our barbarous past" (1994, 464; he attributes this citation to himself). If being an immigrant and creating malapropisms and spoonerisms makes one a magician, then Mr. Parkhill, with his relentlessly standard speech, can never compete with Kaplan.

Rosten's claim that he, like Kaplan, is well positioned to improve the English language echoes a famous interpretation of the American short story by another eastern European: Boris Eikhenbaum's 1925 Russian essay "O. Henry and the Theory of the Short Story." Eikhenbaum depicts O. Henry as an inspired regenerator of language who gleefully misquotes Tennyson and Spencer, invents puns, and makes plays on words "motivated by the speaker's illiteracy (for example, confusion of scientific words as in the case of 'hypodermical' instead of 'hypothetical')" (Eikhenbaum 1968, 15). The Russian Formalists believed that written language and literature evolve under the influence of popular culture; in this spirit, Eikhenbaum asserts that "in O. Henry's hands the short story undergoes regeneration, becoming a unique composite of literary feuilleton and comedy or vaudeville dialogue" (18). His stories abound in ironic play and the deliberate baring of literary devices, "just as if O. Henry had taken up the 'formal method' in Russia" (19).

Like Rosten, Eikhenbaum claims that he is correctly positioned to appreciate the happy transformation of language. Although he admits that Russians may miss the wordplay, he asserts that they see something in O. Henry's stories that is hidden to Americans. "An American . . . readily gives himself over to sentimental and religious-moralistic reflections and likes to have appropriate reading." For this reason, Americans prefer O. Henry's less linguistically inventive stories. "To the Russian reader," he asserts, "these traditions of American life are alien, and the sentimental stories of O. Henry that earned the appreciation of President Roosevelt have had no success among us" (11). Eikhenbaum's evaluation of Americans evokes Rosten's evaluation of Mr. Parkhill. "Was I Mr. Parkhill?" he was asked, since he had also taught immigrants in night school. He answers,

> Alas, only in function; I have nowhere near the patience, kindliness, and fortitude with which Mr. Parkhill is either blessed or afflicted. He is the product of Anglo-Saxon ministers from New England, I the child of Ashkenazic knitters from Lodz. He never loses faith in the possibility of teaching anyone the rudiments of English; I was driven to the shattering suspicion that some people can no more learn than pole-vault. (1976, x)

Rosten seems to share Eikhenbaum's sense of Americans – or at any rate, native-born Anglo Americans – as sentimental and naive, unable to see the world, or appreciate verbal art, as well as more worldly, skeptical eastern Europeans.

Of course, Rosten and Eikhenbaum were both not just writers born in eastern Europe: they were, specifically, the children of Jewish migrants from those parts of the Russian Empire where Jews were permitted to live. While Rosten's family came from Lodz, Eikhenbaum's grandfather was a Hebrew writer born in Kiev. Rosten's parents migrated to Chicago, where his father attended night-school English classes like those his son would one day teach; Eikhenbaum's father, in the words of Brian Horowitz, "traveled the difficult road from a distinctly Jewish to a Russian life," leaving the Pale of Settlement, going to medical school, converting to Eastern Orthodoxy, and marrying an ethnic Russian, Boris's mother (2015, 380). Eikhenbaum resembled other Russian Formalist theorists, Victor Shklovsky, Roman Jakobson, and Iurii Tynianov, who also had Jewish ancestry that could be manifested in a Yiddish-accented parent or grandparent; the sense of ethnic otherness or the exposure to non-standard Russian pronunciation may have been one of the shared factors prompting them to attend to the literary rendition of distinctive speech and the ways in which the cultures of society's margins contributed to the literature of the metropolis. Rosten and Eikhenbaum had native fluency in the standard variety of the high-status languages, English and Russian, that their parents had to work to acquire. And as the children of migrants sometimes do, both publicly reclaimed the cultures of their grand-parents, Rosten in his writing on Yiddish and Eikhenbaum in a 1929 memoir that dwelled on his grandfather's Hebrew writing (Eikhenbaum 2001, 13–20). While Rosten sometimes hints, in his choice of quotations to anthologize, that enthusiasm about macaronic language typifies Jewish culture, he is more convincing in suggesting that what makes him appreciate Kaplan's linguistic creativity is the combination of his immigrant origin and his fluency in the local language.[5] These factors linked him to Eikhenbaum and to Freud, and all of them could present themselves as especially well equipped to translate Goldberg, Kaplan, and the other protagonists of Jewish oral and written short narratives for a non-Jewish audience.

Devilish Lexicography

Eikhenbaum's statement and Rosten's hint that native-born Anglo Americans might not appreciate the humor of their own literature are themselves comical. They ignore the tradition of American short comic texts that play with the humor of language and language learning. These texts do not conform to the expectations of the short story as Poe understood them, that is, as producing a unified impression or a single ironic reversal. Instead, like the Kaplan stories, they display language learning and the written materials on which language teachers rely as funny, and they describe language itself as fluid and thus as permitting the creation of verbal art.

Rosten writes of his kinship to one of these American predecessors: "I still remember my rapture on discovering Ambrose Bierce's *Devil's Dictionary*" (1972a, 6). Bierce published parodic dictionary entries starting in 1875; he began in 1881 to write those that would be gathered in book form in 1911. They include mock definitions of common words, some short, such as "REVERENCE, n. The spiritual attitude of a man to a god and a dog to a man" (Bierce 2011, 602). Others are long and include verse. To the genre itself he devotes a long entry, which I cite in part:

> LEXICOGRAPHER, n. A pestilent fellow who, under the pretense of recording some particular stage in the development of a language, does what he can to arrest its growth, stiffen its flexibility and mechanize its methods .... The bold and discerning writer who, recognizing the truth that language must grow by innovation if it grow at all, makes new words and uses the old in an unfamiliar sense, has no following and is tartly reminded that "it isn't in the dictionary" – although down to the time of the first lexicographer (Heaven forgive him!) no author ever had used a word that *was* in the dictionary. (543–544)

Like Rosten, Bierce underlines the arbitrariness of lexicography and of language itself. Mr. Parkhill imagines Kaplan as capable of creating a new dictionary; Bierce, who elsewhere insisted pedantically on the rightness of his usages, here excoriates the linguistic conservatism of existing dictionaries. Both writers understand that dictionaries only partially contain languages, which change in spite of lexicographers, and both describe this situation humorously.

Rosten also signaled his debt to another late nineteenth-century American writer, Mark Twain, calling him a master of "verbal wonders" and anthologizing his comments about language, such as "I don't give a damn for a man that can spell a word only one way" and "My philological studies have satisfied me that a gifted person ought to learn English (barring spelling and pronouncing) in 30 hours, French in 30 days, and German in 30 years" (Rosten 1994, 6, 267). The latter line is from "The Awful German Language," which Twain published in 1880 as an appendix to *A Tramp Abroad*. There Twain criticizes German from the perspective of English. His attention, like Kaplan's, is drawn to the difference between languages with noun gender and those without. While Kaplan is disturbed that newspapers do not have gender, Twain is upset that turnips (a vegetable he found especially funny) do.

In German, a young lady has no sex, while a turnip has. Think what overwrought reverence that shows for the turnip, and what callous disrespect for the girl. See how it looks in print . . .

"Gretchen. Wilhelm, where is the turnip?
"Wilhelm. She has gone to the kitchen.
"Gretchen. Where is the accomplished and beautiful English maiden?
"Wilhelm. It has gone to the opera." (Twain 1996a, 607)

Like Rosten, Twain is alert to the comic potential in language learning materials, the ways in which even as they purport to document a stable language, they simultaneously make it possible to understand its rules as arbitrary and those who challenge it as creative.

Twain displays the same sensibility in "Italian without a Master," where he explains his technique for communicating with the Italian-speaking servants at a villa near Florence:

I throw in an Italian word when I have one, and this has a good influence. I get the word out of the morning paper. I have to use it while it is fresh, for I find that Italian words do not keep in this climate. They fade toward night, and next morning they are gone . . . . Today I have a whole phrase: Sono dispiacentissimo. I do not know what it means, but it seems to fit in everywhere and give satisfaction. (Twain 1996b, 171–172; the Italian phrase means, "I'm terribly sorry")

Holger Kersten writes that Twain got "pleasure in handling and mangling the German language," and that same delight is evident in his ability to make Italian do unexpected things, as Kaplan, Goldberg, and the Frenchman do with English (1993, 20).

Dictionaries and other texts designed for language learning continue to inspire humorous literary fiction that does not follow the dominant model of the American short story. For instance, in 2018, Jez Burrows (like Rosten, not American born; he is a British man living in the United States) created a collection of alphabetized short narratives made up of example sentences from dictionary entries; he underlines the words whose usage the sentences exemplify. He places "Ten Dollars an Hour and Whatever You Want from the Fridge" in the category "Babysitting," under B:

"Hello there! Come in. Thanks very much for your help.

"The children go to bed at nine o'clock – no ifs, buts, or maybes. Make sure the baby isn't sleeping in an awkward position. Make sure the children's hands are clean before they eat, and don't put the potato skins down the garbage disposal. These foods are strictly forbidden: chocolate eggs, chocolate pudding, chocolate cake filled with whipped cream and topped with hot fudge, hair gel. Julia and Lydia are identical twins. Upstairs is off-limits, capeesh? Don't go poking your nose where you shouldn't. Please don't let the fire go out, don't overexpose the children to television, and do not admonish little Stanislaus if he tears the heart out of a backyard sparrow; he took the divorce hard. We recycle aluminium cans.

"If you have any queries, please do not hesitate to contact me. I'll be home before dark. Here's the money I promised you, a fifth of whiskey, a list of forbidden books, and a bulletproof vest. Thanks, I owe you one for this." (2018, 11)

In these stories, Burrows clearly enjoys the fact that he can use the language in dictionaries in ways other than their makers intended. His short fictions, like the others I have examined here, exemplify the innocent humor generated when language is revealed to be more playful, less under control, than it first appears. Rosten and Eikhenbaum would have been happy to see the persistent appeal of such brief pieces of humorous writing, which let us trace a countertradition of American short story-writing that celebrates not the revelation of epiphany but instead the innocent comedy of language learning.

Works Cited

Ben-Amos, Dan. 1973. "Myth of Jewish Humor," *Western Folklore* 32.2: 112–131.

Bierce, Ambrose. 2011. *The Devil's Dictionary, Tales, and Memoirs*. Ed. S. T. Joshi. New York: Library of America.

Boddy, Kasia. 2010. *The American Short Story Since 1950*. Edinburgh: Edinburgh University Press.

Burrows, Jez. 2018. *Dictionary Stories: Short Fictions and Other Findings*. New York: HarperCollins.

Crews, Frederick. 1992. *The Critics Bear It Away: American Fiction and the Academy*. New York: Random House.

Dauber, Jeremy. 2017. *Jewish Comedy: A Serious History*. New York: Norton.

Eikhenbaum, Boris M. 1968 [1925]. *O. Henry and the Theory of the Short Story*. Trans. I. B. Titunik. Ann Arbor: Michigan Slavic Contributions.

    2001 [1929]. *Moi vremennik. Marshrut v bessmertie*. Moscow: Agraf.

Ermida, Isabel. 2008. *The Language of Comic Narratives: Humor Construction in Short Stories*. New York: Mouton de Gruyter.

Freud, Sigmund Freud. 1960. *Jokes and Their Relation to the Unconscious*. Trans. James Strachey. New York: Norton.

Golub, Ellen. 1982. "Leo Rosten (Leonard Q. Ross)," in *American Humorists, 1800-1950. Dictionary of Literary Biography*, Vol. 11, 410–419. Detroit: Gale.

Gross, Abe. 1930. *The Kibitzer's Dictionary*. New York: Melvita.

Horowitz, Brian. 2015. "Battling for Self-Definition in Soviet Literature: Boris Eikhenbaum's Jewish Question," *Znanie. Ponimanie. Umenie* 2: 379–392.

Hunter, Adrian. 2019. "The Short Story and the Professionalisation of English Studies," in *The Edinburgh Companion to the Short Story in English*. Eds. Paul Delaney and Adrian Hunter, 24–39. Edinburgh: Edinburgh University Press.

Jenkins, Henry. 1992. *What Made Pistachio Nuts? Early Sound Comedy and the Vaudeville Aesthetic*. New York: Columbia University Press.

Jones, Gavin. 1999. *Strange Talk: The Politics of Dialect Literature in Gilded Age America*. Berkeley: University of California Press.

Kaplan, Fred. 1983. "Two Names, Half a Dozen Careers, Books, Movies – Phew!" (interview with Leo Rosten), *Washington Post*, October 30, C3.

Kersten, Holger. 1993. "Mark Twain's First Joke on the German Language," *Mark Twain Journal* 31.1 (Spring): 18–21.

Nurhussein, Nadia. 2013. *Rhetorics of Literacy: The Cultivation of American Dialect Poetry*. Columbus: Ohio State University Press.

Rosten, Leo Calvin [Leonard Q. Ross]. 1937. *The Education of Hyman Kaplan*. New York: Harcourt, Inc.

   1942–1961. *Miscellaneous Papers*. Hoover Institution, Stanford University, CA.

   1959. *The Return of Hyman Kaplan*. New York: Harper and Row.

   1972a. *Leo Rosten's Treasury of Jewish Quotations*. New York: McGraw-Hill.

   1972b. *Rome Wasn't Burned in a Day: The Mischief of Language*. Garden City, NY: Doubleday.

   1976. *O Kaplan! My Kaplan!* New York: Harper and Row.

   1994. *Leo Rosten's Carnival of Wit*. Dutton: Penguin.

   2001. *The New Joys of Yiddish*. New York: Crown Publishers.

Safran, Gabriella. 2019. "Dialect Joke Books and Russian-Yiddish and English-Yiddish Dictionaries," in *The Whole World in a Book: Dictionaries in the Nineteenth Century*. Ed. Sarah Ogilvie and Gabriella Safran, 277–297. Oxford: Oxford University Press.

Shiffman, Dan. 1999. "The Ingratiating Humor of Leo Rosten's Hyman Kaplan Stories," *Studies in American Jewish Literature (1981-)* 18: 93–101.

   2000. "The Comedy of Assimilation in Leo Rosten's Hyman Kaplan Stories," *Studies in American Humor*. New Series 3. 7: 49–58.

Twain, Mark. 1996a. "The Awful German Language," Appendix D to *A Tramp Abroad*, in *The Oxford Mark Twain*. Ed. Shelley Fisher Fishkin, 601–619. New York: Oxford University Press.

   1996b. "Italian Without a Master," *The $30,000 Bequest and Other Stories*, in *The Oxford Mark Twain*. Ed. Shelley Fisher Fishkin, 279–290. New York: Oxford University Press.

Wirth-Nesher, Hana. 2009. *Call It English: The Languages of Jewish American Literature*. Princeton, NJ: Princeton University Press.

CHAPTER 18

The Technology of the Short Story
From Sci-Fi to Cli-Fi

Shelley Streeby

Two important origin stories for US science fiction are the mid-nineteenth-century US print revolution's newspapers, story-papers, and
magazines , and the transnational networks of borrowing and reprinting
through which Mary Shelley, Jules Verne, H. G. Wells, and other non-US
writers and periodicals shaped early US science fiction short stories. In the
late 1830s and 1840s, innovations in print technologies, along with the
expansion of railroads and other forms of transportation, made it possible
to produce and circulate print much more quickly and on a larger scale
than ever before (Streeby 2002, 11–12). The US science fiction short story
emerged within the penny papers and sensational crime, mysteries of the
city, and adventure literature of the era, as well as in papers with smaller
circulations that had literary aspirations and in new monthly magazines
aimed at a cross-class, mass audience. The form of the science fiction short
story thus connects to the essay and other short forms designed to impart
scientific and technical knowledge in magazine culture from the beginning. Because of the absence of an international copyright law until 1891,
US periodicals also often reprinted the work of non-US writers; the fiction
of Shelley, Verne, and Wells was especially influential both in foreign
periodicals and in domestic reprints.

Narratives of US science fiction often sidestep Shelley to situate Edgar
Allan Poe as the genre's father, but Shelley's *Frankenstein* (1823), short
stories, and apocalyptical novel, *The Last Man* (1826), about a global
plague that wipes out human life except for one solitary survivor, made a
big impact in the United States. Beginning in the 1860s, Verne's stories
and novels of wonderful inventions, new forms of transportation, and
scientific adventure, such as *Journey to the Center of the Earth* (1864),
Twenty Thousand Leagues Under the Sea (1869–1870), and *Off on a Comet*
(1877), were translated and adapted in US periodicals and US mass culture
more broadly, and appealed especially to children and young people. Later,
around the turn of the century, Wells's many short stories, published in

popular magazines such as *Pall Mall* and the *Strand*, and genre-defining novels all shaped the history of US science fiction. The excision of Shelley and the use of all three of the men's names – Poe, Wells, and Verne – on the first 1926 cover of Hugo Gernsback's *Amazing Stories*, the first magazine devoted exclusively to the genre, highlights how Shelley falls out of the picture in many histories of US science fiction: Gernsback famously called *Amazing Stories* a "magazine of scientifiction," defined as "the Jules Verne, H G Wells, and Edgar Allan Poe type of story."

Poe is also central to H. Bruce Franklin's field-defining anthology *Future Perfect: Science Fictions of the 19th Century* (1966), which links early US science fiction to nineteenth-century industrial society and to the rise of modern science and technology, but not in a good way. Franklin gives the lead-off position to Hawthorne and Poe, suggesting that several Hawthorne stories emerge from "a speculation generated immediately from a brush with science" (9), while Poe's "M. Valdemar" is a "science-fiction tale of terror" (91) and his "A Tale of the Ragged Mountains" (1844) is a story of "bizarre physical speculation" (92). Although Franklin situates Poe at the beginning, however, he also criticizes him for lifting quotes from scientific journals without acknowledging them and suggests Poe is only scientific when it comes to "physical process" (88) and technology narrowly conceived, unlike Shelley, who Franklin credits with exploring the "interrelations between science and society" (89).

Although he does not include it, Franklin credits anti-slavery and Indigenous people's rights activist Lydia Maria Child with writing the 1845 time-travel story "Hilda Silfverling: A Fantasy," which originally appeared in the *Columbian Lady's and Gentleman's Magazine*, a monthly to which Poe also contributed. Here Child imagines a scientist proposing an experiment, inspired by the new technology of refrigeration, to freeze in suspended animation for 100 years, instead of beheading, an unwed mother falsely convicted of killing her own child. This scientific experiment enables her to escape her own time into another where she has more freedom, even to the point of marrying her own great-grandson, the descendant of the original missing babe. In other parts of the anthology, Franklin includes stories about automata (once again crediting the impact of Shelley's *Frankenstein*), such as Herman Melville's 1855 "The Bell Tower," which Franklin suggests offers "profound insights into the technological, sociological, and political conditions" in the United States "under the looming shadow of the Civil War" (138). As well, Franklin pulls into this genre-defining anthology stories of marvelous inventions and medical science fiction, such as several by Jack London, including

"A Thousand Deaths" (1899), about a son who is repeatedly killed and reanimated by his scientist-father before he turns the tables by disintegrating his father in his own scientific experiment. Franklin also highlights stories of the psyche, space travel, time travel, and women's work, such as Annie Denton Cridge's forty-eight-page satirical utopian role-reversal story *Man's Rights; or, How Do You Like It?* (1870), and Mary E. Bradley Lane's 1880–1881 *Mizora: A Prophecy*, which focuses on a utopian society of blonde women who have eliminated people with dark complexions (Lothian 2018, 43–44). Franklin's anthology usefully demonstrates that many of the most enduringly canonical authors in US literary history, as well as many lesser-known yet significant writers, contributed to the emerging genre, as he contrasts the "properly literary" fantasy and science fiction published in more respectable "leading periodicals" such as the *United States Magazine and Democratic Review*, the *Southern Literary Messenger*, *Graham's*, *Godey's*, *Harper's Monthly*, *Putnam's*, *Scribner's*, the *Atlantic Monthly*, and *Cosmopolitan* with the science fiction aimed at "a newly literate mass audience" published in dime novels and other "fore-runners of the 'pulps' of the early and mid-nineteenth century" (Franklin 1966, 4).

As implied by the example of Poe's lurid story being reprinted by Gernsback in the first great pulp science fiction magazine, however, there was significant intermingling between strata, which were not completely distinct, especially in earlier eras. While many periodicals that Poe worked for and to which he contributed early science fiction, such as the *Southern Literary Messenger* and *Graham's Magazine*, aspired to a higher literary status, some were still quite popular. *Godey's Lady's Book*, where several Poe stories appeared, also published gothic, crime, and horror stories as well as romances and fashion features and was the most popular magazine before the Civil War, thus counting as a form of mass entertainment. Other periodicals Poe worked for, such as *Burton's Gentleman's Magazine*, sometimes featured adventure, crime, and men's sporting life stories akin to those in sensational story-paper literature, such as that written by Poe's friend, Philadelphia author and editor George Lippard. The stories comprising Lippard's apocalyptic political time-travel fantasy *The Entranced; or the Wanderer of Eighteen Centuries*, appeared weekly in his story-paper *The Quaker City*, a five-cent paper with oversized pages, advertised as "A Popular Journal, devoted to such matters of Literature and news as will interest the great mass of readers" (Lippard 1848, i). Lippard was part of the emerging Philadelphia literary public sphere in which Poe was active, and Poe's science fiction and theories of the short story were shaped by his work as a newspaper and magazine editor in New York, Philadelphia, Richmond, Baltimore, and elsewhere for a range of periodicals, especially the new monthly literary magazines. When in a famous review of Hawthorne's stories Poe privileged "the short prose tale" that requires from a "half-hour to one or two hours" to read, he was praising the typical length of stories in the new magazines, and his ideas about how short fiction acquires "immense force derivable from totality" while carrying out a "certain unique or single effect" (Poe 1842, 572) respond to the possibilities and pressures of such print culture contexts.

Easily readable within Poe's preferred two-hour time span, the most popular science fiction of the late nineteenth century, speedily produced under industrial conditions for sensational illustrated weekly story-papers and dime novels, starred young white male inventors, scientists, and travelers, such as the titular hero of "Lost in a Comet's Tail; Or, Frank Reade, Jr.'s Strange Adventure with his Air-Ship" (1903). During this period, the increasing ease of the production process for visuals meant that full-color covers became an important part of the story, often highlighting the main story arc in ways helpful for multiple generations of readers coming to the text with a range of native languages and literacies. Under the pseudonym "NoName," the "American Jules Verne," Cuban American Luis Senarens, son of a tobacco merchant, wrote hundreds of popular stories featuring wonderful inventions, scientific experiments, and western and globe-trotting adventures for *Frank Reade Library* and *Frank Reade Weekly Magazine*. Emerging from earlier monthlies such as the *Boys of New York* and *Happy Days* , which featured the original Frank Reade character and were published in New York by Frank Tousey, one of the top dime novel publishers (Williams 2011, 279–288), the most popular stories focused on Reade's son, who, fortified by class privilege, became "America's well-known and most famous young inventor" (Senarens 1903, 1). Frank Reade, Jr., travels throughout the world on wondrous forms of transportation he invents, along with his sidekicks Barney and Pomp, an Irish and a Black servant straight out of nineteenth-century theatrical melodrama and blackface minstrelsy, who speak in dialect, serve as comic relief, and carry out heroic exploits, all under the managerial supervision of the young white man-inventor-scientist-adventurer. Like the ubiquitous nineteenth-century, cross-class, male buddy plots analyzed by Alexander Saxton in *The Rise and Fall of the White Republic* (1990), in which lower-class characters team up with white military officers and other elite men figured as their betters, here the wealthy, well-educated, scientifically and technologically adept white male whiz kid hero, speaking in proper, unmarked English, is supported by comedic, vernacular characters who speak in dialect and devote their lives and bodies to serving and praising him in his various exploits. In the 1890s and early 1900s, *Frank Reade Weekly Magazine* also appealed to readers visually with large cover illustrations, such as the one for "Lost in a Comet's Tail," in which Barney is deployed to help save people on a sinking ship. When one cries out, "You came from the clouds," Barney answers, "I cum down from Misther Frank Reade Jr's air ship" (Senarens, 1903), thereby affirming his employer's godlike ability to invent scientific and technological wonders that confer salvific power, while enjoying a managerial role in which he does not need to use his own body to be the hero but can delegate bodily heroics to his servants and yet still take credit for them.

W. E. B. Du Bois's "The Comet" (1920) opens up another genealogy of the US science fiction short story, one that includes Black US writers such as Martin Delany, a doctor, soldier, and author who serialized in the *Anglo-African Magazine* and *Weekly Anglo-African* his alternate history of successful anti-slavery revolution entitled *Blake, or the Huts of America* (1859; 1861–1862) and Pauline Hopkins's *Of One Blood: Or the Hidden Self*, the story of a Black medical student-mesmerist who becomes king of a lost, mighty African civilization, which was serialized in the *Colored American Magazine* in 1903–1904 during the years Hopkins edited it (Rusert 2017, 149–181; Shawl 2018). When including "The Comet" in her ground-breaking anthology *Dark Matter: Speculative Fiction from the African Diaspora* (2000), Sheree Thomas called it a prime example of how "like dark matter, the contributions of black writers to the sf genre have not been directly observed or fully explored" (xi). The *Colored American Magazine* was the widest-circulating Black literary publication before Du Bois launched *The Crisis* in 1910, and it was during the *Crisis* years that Du Bois wrote "The Comet," published as the penultimate chapter of *Darkwater: Voices from within the Veil*. In this short story, a comet's noxious gases kill most people in New York, while Jim, a Black messenger working in a bank, and Julia, a rich white woman, are spared and come together, believing they may be the last man and woman on earth, before Julia returns to her father and fiancé at the end, as the white world comes rushing back and Jim Crow racial hierarchies are restored. If "Lost in a Comet's Tail" idealizes a team of Black and Irish servants guided by the managerial expertise of a wealthy young white man inventor-scientist-explorer, while frequently pausing to admire the spectacles of the wonderful comet and airship, Du Bois's story, which focuses squarely on how its

Black protagonist experiences a transformation of racial hierarchies and the emergence of new futurities only when the old, white-dominated world appears to have been destroyed, is "a speculative fiction and satire of failed democracy" (Hartman 2020). In its interest in possibilities in the wake of disaster, "The Comet" is more akin to Wells's *In the Days of the Comet* (1906), though it works inversely: in the latter, the comet's gases are healing, bringing "great Change" by stimulating everyone to be generous and peaceful, and to engage in the collective project of reorganizing society for the better, while in Du Bois's story hope for change created by the comet stalls abruptly and violently when the white supremacist racial order is reinstated and Jim's wife appears with their dead baby in her arms (Lothian 2018, 106–113).

While Black writers were producing short stories that could be classified as science fiction from at least the mid-nineteenth century through the 1920s, they are usually not included within origin stories that privilege 1920s–1940s science fiction magazines as a key site for the genre's emergence. After debuting in 1926, *Amazing Stories* was transformed by new owners, editors, and writers, but during the early years the magazine published reprints and original science fiction and fantasy by white men and a few white women, often building on conventions from dime novel westerns and imperial adventure fiction. In a headnote to "The Fate of the Poseidonia," by Clare Winger Harris, who won third place in a Gernsback contest, Gernsback commented that "as a rule women do not make good scientifiction writers, because their education and general tendencies on scientific matters are usually limited," but he found this "exception" not "overburdened with science" but still "plausible" and "extraordinarily impressive" because of its "charm" (Harris 1927, 245). Resonating with recent books about canals and life on Mars as well as with Wells's *War of the Worlds*, Harris's story is about a Martian who comes to Earth disguised as a human and makes off with a good deal of Earth's water. In a science fiction version of a captivity narrative, the villainous Martian, who is repeatedly compared to an "American Indian" (246, 249), also makes off with the narrator's love interest, stealing her away to Mars, where she resignedly addresses the narrator via television at the end, thereby illustrating how white settler colonialism shapes the imagining of aliens, new technologies, and struggles over water in this white woman's early science fiction short story. Stories by white men published in *Amazing Stories* during the Gernsback years – the overwhelming majority – often took the form of modernized white settler colonial fantasy, such as Murray Leinster's "The Runaway Skyscraper," a time-travel story that sends its white modern protagonists back to a time before "the discovery of America," when "Indians occupy Madison square" (Leinster 1926, 254). The engineer-hero wins the love of his beautiful secretary as well as the admiration of a bank president who has also fallen into the building's Fourth Dimension by organizing a system of trade with the natives that leaves them "industriously working for the white people" (Leinster 1926, 264), while also ingeniously figuring out how to mobilize a geyser to blast the building back to the present.

A rival to *Amazing Stories* beginning in 1930, *Astounding Stories* was the next science fiction magazine to make a big impact, inaugurating the so-called Golden Age of science fiction in 1949 after editor John W. Campbell introduced significant changes and new authors. The magazine briefly disappeared during the early Depression until dime novel and pulp magazine giant Street and Smith relaunched it in 1933, with editor F. Orlin Tremaine soliciting "thought-variants," stories "in the field of scientific fiction," to open the way for "real discussion" with "social science" about the "present condition of the world" and "the future" (Tremaine 1933, 139). Campbell, who replaced Tremaine in 1937, continued to publish some of the same authors, but *Astounding* began to move away from the revamped dime novel plots of much early US science fiction. He introduced regular sections of science articles, serials, novelettes, and short stories, as well as Readers' Departments and an Editor's Page, where he wrote about science and technology. Here we can see the continuation of the early US imbrication of the science fiction short story and other forms of magazine writing, such as the science article. These changes reveal Campbell's guiding hand in choosing and shaping stories as well as in soliciting them through contests and suggestions, engaging readers, and bringing new authors into the profession. In 1939 alone, Campbell introduced Isaac Asimov, A. E. Van Vogt, Theodore Sturgeon, and Robert Heinlein to *Astounding* readers; Heinlein won one of Campbell's contests, and many other prominent science fiction short story writers made their first sales to Campbell. Campbell frequently appealed to readers as men of science to consider submitting stories with invitations such as "Somewhere is the man who is going to write the kind of science fiction I want ..." (Campbell 1941, 6). Although *Astounding*'s early readers and authors were overwhelmingly male, Campbell did publish some women, including Leigh Brackett and C. L. Moore, under her own name as well as under the name Lewis Padgett, the joint pseudonym of Moore and Henry Kuttner. In the late 1940s, Campbell also introduced Judith Merril as "the first new feminine science-fiction writer in years" and praised her classic short story "That Only a Mother" as a "smooth piece all the way through" with a "hornet sting" at the end, "a brilliantly bitter little story" that left him hoping and expecting "we'll be hearing more from her" (Campbell 1948, 148). The anxieties over the US deployment of atomic bombs in Hiroshima and Nagasaki in Merril's story about a mother whose husband is exposed to uranium and whose baby has no legs or arms cut against the determined techno-optimism of Campbell's Editor's Pages, where he suggests that the US army used atomic weapons in the "least damaging, gentlest application of their terrible power" (Campbell 1945, 98). He also celebrates new technologies that emerged during war, and provides illustrated tours of atomic power plants such as the one in Hanford, Washington (8–9, 98).

Merril later wrote that "Campbell's specific limitation was the engineering mind" (Merril 2016, 157) and she soon shifted to the new magazines emerging in the 1950s – over thirty-five were in circulation after 1955 – that offered more latitude and welcomed more diverse writers and stories. Merril dates what she called the "Boom" to the December 1949 first appearance of the *Magazine of Fantasy and Science Fiction* (*FSF*), edited by Anthony Boucher and J. Francis McComas, who published when no one else would three short stories that were the foundation for Walter Miller's controversial post-apocalyptic nuclear war novel *A Canticle for Leibowitz* (1955). *FSF* was more welcoming of fantasy than was *Astounding*. While some of the same authors appeared in both, *FSF* included more stories that challenged techno-optimism, militarism, and the security state, while imagining its audience, authors, and editorial control more expansively. From 1965 to 1969, Merril contributed a book review column, and in 1969 Samuel Delany began writing a film column. Starting in 1950, *Galaxy*, under Herbert Gold's and later Frederik Pohl's editorship, was another significant new magazine that redefined the genre. Although it did not always live up to it, the magazine promised that readers would never find in its pages "a western transplanted to some alien and impossible planet," and in the mid-1950s Gold made a special appeal to writers to present "themes that could not be sold elsewhere ... themes that are too adult, too profound or revolutionary in concept for other magazines to risk publishing" (Gold 1950b, 3). The proliferation of new science fiction magazines provided platforms for bold new voices critical of the state, the military, corporate capitalism, and techno-optimism, such as Philip K. Dick, who published eighty-five stories during the decade. These included such classics as "The Mold of Yancy" (*If*, 1955), about an off-world, totalitarian society where a virtual Eisenhower-like leader has been created by advertising men to control the public, and "Service Call" (*Science Fiction Stories*, July 1955), in which a repair man from the future shows up to fix a swibble, a new kind of biotechnology introduced after a nuclear war to adjust people's views and prevent disunity. During the late 1950s and early 1960s, *Amazing Stories* also took on new life under the editorship of Cele Goldsmith (1958–1965). Goldsmith published in *Amazing* and in another magazine she edited, *Fantastic*, Ursula K. Le Guin's early short stories, including "The Unbinding" and "The Rule of Names," in which Le Guin explores the secondary world of Earthsea, the setting for her great fantasy novels. Later, in 1971, new *Amazing* editor Ted White published the serialized stories that comprise Le Guin's novel *The Lathe of Heaven*, which appeared as a book afterwards. Le Guin's stories also appeared in *Galaxy*, which in 1975 merged with *If*, which had previously merged with *Worlds of Tomorrow* (1963–1967), edited by Pohl. Pohl published Samuel Delany's first short stories, including "The Star Pit" (*Worlds of Tomorrow*, 1967), starring a spaceship mechanic, and "Driftglass" (*If*, 1967), which explores the aftermath of an accident experienced by amphi-man, an undersea worker whose body has been transformed to include gills. In 1968, *FSF* published two of Delany's short stories, "Corona," featuring a friendship between a telepathic Black girl and a white ex-convict janitor, and "We, in Some Strange Power's Employ, Move on a Rigorous Line," which centers the adventures of a woman-led team of workers responsible for fixing cables and repairing lines to secure the world's power grid. In their focus on outsider characters from below, many of whom do the dirty work of society in worlds where new technologies are used by state and corporate power in ways these characters struggle over, Delany's 1960s short stories depart from *Astounding*'s emphasis on male scientists, technicians, and engineers as readers, characters, and writers. They also depart from Campbell's hopes for a science fiction wedding scientific and technological progress to US military and corporate power and world leadership from above. For her part, Le Guin once remarked that after reading science fiction as a girl, she "got off" it for a couple of decades "sometime in the forties," when it seemed to be "all about hardware and soldiers" (Le Guin 1979, 27) and thus missed Campbell's Golden Age. In her own stories of the 1960s and 1970s Le Guin broke with that framework for science fiction by confronting colonialism and imperialism, reconsidering relations between humans and the more-than-human world. She also reimagined stories as technologies that are not "weapons that force energy outward" but baskets that "bring energy home," as she put it in her influential essay "The Carrier Bag Theory of Fiction" (Le Guin 1988, 30).

Beginning in the 1960s and 1970s, in addition to the new US magazines, stylistically innovative and conceptually daring science fiction short
stories, such as Le Guin's and Delany's, also found homes in anthologies
published as books and edited by prominent science fiction writers, such as
Merril, Damon Knight, and Harlan Ellison, and in publications of the
British New Wave. In the late 1960s Michael Moorcock took over the
British magazine *New Worlds*, making it into a venue for experimental
work by authors such as himself, J. G. Ballard, and Thomas Disch, as well
as Ellison and Delany, whose Hugo and Nebula Award-winning short
story "Time Considered as a Helix of Semi-Precious Stones," featuring a
professional criminal in a near-future world, appeared in a 1968 issue.
Merril championed the magazine and the New Wave, which she popularized in her 1968 anthology *England Swings SF: Stories of Speculative
Fiction*. Delany's "Star Pit" was reprinted in one of Merril's twelve Year's
Greatest/Best SF anthologies, an influential series she edited from 1956 to
1967 that featured many new writers. The *Orbit* anthologies (1966–1976),
edited by Damon Knight, provided another venue for writers of experimental stories, such as Le Guin, Joanna Russ, Ellison, Gene Wolfe, and
Vonda McIntyre. Le Guin's tour-de-force "Direction of the Road," narrated from the point of view of an oak tree by the side of a highway, first
appeared in *Orbit* in 1973. Along with Merril and James Blish, Knight co-
founded the Milford Science Fiction Writers' Conference in 1956 and co-
led it with wife Kate Wilhelm for over two decades, which led to the
genesis of the Clarion Science Fiction Writers' Workshop. Clarion began
in the late 1960s and continues to this day, training science fiction writers
by inviting professional writers to lead weekly workshops where students
write up one short story a week for six weeks while critiquing others'
short stories and having their own collectively critiqued, usually using what
came to be known as the Milford Method.

In the 1970s, Delany taught at Clarion, including in 1971, when
Octavia Butler was a student. Butler got in after Harlan Ellison, another
Clarion teacher, had her as a student in a Hollywood screenwriting class,
bought her a typewriter, and wrote to workshop leaders asking that she be
admitted. In the 1980s, Butler received Hugo Awards for Best Short Story
for "Speech Sounds" (1983), about a Los Angeles woman surviving a
future pandemic where most people lose the ability to speak and write,
and "Bloodchild" (1984), her "pregnant man" story about a future symbiotic relationship between insect-like aliens and humans. Both of these
appeared in *Isaac Asimov's Science Fiction Magazine*, a significant new
venue beginning in 1977. But Butler's earliest short story publication,

"Crossover," about a female factory worker's struggles with depression, appeared in the 1971 Clarion workshop anthology edited by Knight, while her short story "Childfinder," about a Black woman's relationships with children with psionic abilities, was set to be published in a second sequel that never came out to Ellison's landmark *Dangerous Visions.* That anthology collected thirty-three original stories by Dick, Ellison, Knight, Sturgeon, Ballard, and many others, including Delany's "Aye and Gomorrah," a queer space cruising story that won the 1967 Nebula Award. Ellison followed up on the anthology's success with *Again, Dangerous Visions* (1972), which included stories by two other Clarion teachers: Russ's "When It Changed," about an all-woman space colony, also a Nebula Award-winner, and Le Guin's "The Word for World is Forest," which she later expanded into her great anti-Vietnam War novel about a successful native revolution against colonizers from Earth who are ruthlessly extracting resources on another planet because all of Earth's have been used up. Le Guin also published some of her most philosophically and politically challenging short stories in fellow science fiction author Robert Silverberg's *New Dimensions* books, including "Vaster than Empires and More Slow" (1971), a story of the sentient intelligence of an all-plant world encountered by human explorers, and "The Ones Who Walk Away from Omelas" (1973), about a utopian society that depends upon the suffering of a child in a basement. Le Guin's early climate change story "The New Atlantis," a near-future vision of global warming and a ruined Earth causing dramatic sea level rise and the sudden re-emergence of Atlantis, also originally appeared in another Silverberg collection.

Building on legacies of twentieth-century ecological science fiction short stories and novels, such as those written by Le Guin, Ballard, and Butler, many twenty-first century authors have published in science fiction magazines and on the Internet influential stories that could be classified as cli-fi, a term that became popular in the 2010s to encompass a wide range of literature that responds to climate change, including science fiction, as well as editing collections of these (Streeby 2018). Even before the emergence of the term, science fiction writers were already crafting stories that raised hard questions about climate change: Ted Chiang's "Exhalation" (2008), first published in the anthology *Eclipse 2: New Science Fiction and Fantasy,* edited by Jonathan Strahan, is now often read as asking readers to confront human responsibility for climate change via its story of aliens whose every exhalation worsens atmospheric change, which ultimately causes their demise. In 2015, John Joseph Adams, editor of several anthologies as well as *Lightspeed, Fantasy,* and *Nightmare,* reprinted twenty-seven stories, including work by Paolo Bacigalupi, Nancy Kress, Kim Stanley Robinson, Charlie Jane Anders, and Margaret Atwood, in his collection *Loosed Upon the World: The Saga Anthology of Climate Fiction*, in the hope that by approaching climate change through recent climate fiction, "we can perhaps humanize and illuminate the issue in ways that aren't as easy to do with only science and cold equations" (xii). In a foreword, Bacigalupi rejects "feel-good technology stories" (xiv) and the idea of a "techno-fix" in favor of fiction that makes readers engage with "the intense realities of our present" (xiv). Inspired by Butler's insistence on shaping change, adrienne maree brown and Walidah Imarisha go further in *Octavia's Brood: Science Fiction Stories from Social Justice Movements* (2015), an anthology that connects to their internet and social movement writing and activism, by working with writers to create "visionary fiction" that "has relevance towards building newer, freer worlds," rather than the "mainstream strain of science fiction, which most often reinforces dominant narratives of power" (Imarisha 2015, 4). In the collection, journalist Dani McClain's "Homing Instinct" is a good example of cli-fi and the science fiction short story as thought experiment. McClain asks readers to think about what they would do if an Executive Order suddenly made it impossible to move freely by forcing everyone to choose one place to stay and by severely limiting trips outside this zone in response to the climate emergency.

Solarpunk anthologies, such as those published by World Weaver Press Editor-in-Chief Sarena Ulibarri with the help of Kickstarter campaigns, have also impacted short stories of cli-fi technologies and eco-futures. By gathering together cli-fi stories that imagine how the world might be different using tools other than weapons or for a quick capitalist techno-fix, Ulibarri fosters a "developing sub-genre of optimistic, environmentally conscious science fiction" (Ulibarri 2018, 1) that looks for "decentralized, localized" solutions that depend on "adaptation and compromise" rather than "destruction and conquest" (Ulibarri 2018, 2). In ways reminiscent of the mid-nineteenth-century origins of US science fiction, the sub-genre solarpunk is part of world history, with important roots in Brazil and Portugal and contributors from many different parts of the globe. An excellent example is the transnational collaboration between US-based Jess Barber, who comes from West Virginia and Boston, and London-based Sara Saab, who hails from Lebanon, on "Pan-Humanism: Hope and Pragmatics" (2017), a cli-fi story set in near-future Beirut that first appeared in *Clarkesworld*, a significant twenty-first century magazine. This utopian story explores how sociopolitical transformations and new material and ethical investments in schooling, science, and civic life, combined with queer world-making, crucially enable climate change possibilities diverging from eco-apocalypse.

McSweeney's 58: 2040 A.D. pairs authors with National Resources Defense Council collaborators to write stories based on climate events, such as Cheyenne and Arapaho writer Tommy Orange's "New Jesus." The story is set in a near-future Oakland where "the coastal flooded" (Orange 2019, 67) who cannot "afford to just up and go" get used to walking in water and do not talk about Jesus anymore, because "the end of the world came and went too many times and Jesus failed to show" or because "science proved to be right about climate change," until the narrator's mountain cousin shows up to announce the new Jesus, "our cooperation with each other and the earth" (Orange 2019, 69). Although the narrator does not believe in the new or the old Jesus, his lack of faith in anything and loss of any hope for change, combined with the mountain cousin's talk of trying to live differently, finally provokes his wife to leave, presenting him with the realization that "Something had been wrong for a long time. And it was me" (Orange 2019, 75). In these twenty-first-century stories, science fiction writers confront climate change and imagine the social effects of changes in science, technology, and nature in ways shaped by relationships to editors, movements, and new forms of technology and collaboration that revitalize the genre and move it toward imagining and creating freer and more just worlds.

Works Cited

Adams, John Joseph. 2015. "Introduction," in *Loosed Upon the World: The Saga Anthology of Climate Fiction*. Ed. John Joseph Adams, xi–xii. New York: Saga.

Bacigalupi, Paolo. 2015. "Foreword," in *Loosed Upon the World: The Saga Anthology of Climate Fiction*, Ed. John Joseph Adams, xiii–xvi. New York: Saga.

Campbell, John W., Jr. 1941. "Invitation," *Astounding Stories* (February): 6.

1945. "Atomic Age," *Astounding Stories* (September): 8–9, 98.

1947. "Atomic Power Plant," *Astounding Stories* (February): 100–120.

1948. "In Times to Come," *Astounding Stories* (May): 148.

Chiang, Ted. 2008. "Exhalation," in *Eclipse 2: New Science Fiction and Fantasy*. Ed. Jonathan Strahan, 109–124. San Francisco: Night Shade Books.

Child, Lydia Maria. 1846 [1845]. "Hilda Silfverling: A Fantasy," in *Fact and Fiction: A Collection of Stories*, 205–240. New York: C. S. Francis.

Du Bois, W. E. B. 2000 [1920]. "The Comet," in *Dark Matter: A Century of Speculative Fiction from the African Diaspora*. Ed. Sheree R. Thomas, 5–18. New York: Warner Books.

Franklin, H. Bruce, ed. 1966. *Future Perfect: Science Fictions of the 19th Century*. New York: Oxford University Press.

Gernsback, Hugo, ed. 1926. *Amazing Stories* (April).

Gold, H. L. 1950a. "You'll Never See It in Galaxy," *Galaxy* (November). Back cover.

1950b. "It's All Yours," *Galaxy* (November): 2–3.

Harris, Clare Winger. 1927. "The Fate of the Poseidonia," *Amazing Stories* (June): 245–267.

Hartman, Saidiya. 2020. "The End of White Supremacy: An American Romance," *Bomb* 152 (Summer). https://bombmagazine.org/articles/the-end-of-white-supremacy-an-american-romance/.

Imarisha, Walidah. 2015. "Introduction," in *Octavia's Brood: Science Fiction Stories from Social Justice Movements*. Ed. Walidah Imarisha and adrienne maree brown, 3–5. Oakland, CA: A.K. Press.

Le Guin, Ursula K. 1979. *Language of the Night: Essays on Fantasy and Science Fiction*. New York: G. P. Putnam's Sons.

2019 [1988]. *The Carrier Bag Theory of Fiction*. London: Ignota Books.

Leinster, Murray. 1926 [1919]. "The Runaway Skyscraper," *Amazing Stories* (June): 250–265, 285.

Lippard, George, ed. 1848. *The Quaker City Weekly* (30 December).

Lothian, Alexis. 2018. *Old Futures: Speculative Fiction and Queer Possibility*. New York: New York University Press.

McClain, Dani. 2015. "Homing Instinct," in *Octavia's Brood: Science Fiction Stories from Social Justice Movements*. Oakland, CA: AK Press. 239–247.

Merril, Judith. 2016. *The Merril School of Lit'ry Criticism*. Ed. Ritch Calvin. Seattle, WA: Aqueduct Press.

Orange, Tommy. 2019. "New Jesus," in *McSweeney's 58: 2040 A.D.* Ed. Claire Boyle, 67–75. San Francisco: McSweeney's.

Poe, Edgar Allan. 1846. "Marginalia [part IX]," *Graham's Magazine* (December): 311–313.

1984 [1842]. "Twice-Told Tales: A Review," in *Edgar Allan Poe: Essays and Reviews*, 569–577. New York: The Library of America.

Rusert, Britt. 2017. *Fugitive Science: Empiricism and Freedom in Early African American Culture*. New York: New York University Press.

Saxton, Alexander. 1990. *The Rise and Fall of the White Republic: Class Politics and Mass Culture in Nineteenth-Century America*. London: Verso.

Senarens, Luis. 1903. "Lost in a Comet's Tail; Or, Frank Reade, Jr.'s Strange Adventure with his Air-Ship," *Frank Reade Weekly Magazine* (December 4): 1–28.

Shawl, Nisi. 2018. "What Men Have Put Asunder: Pauline Hopkins' *Of One Blood*," Tor.com (June 4). www.tor.com/2018/06/04/what-men-have-put-asunder-pauline-hopkins-of-one-blood/.

Streeby, Shelley. 2002. *American Sensations: Class, Empire, and the Production of Popular Culture*. Berkeley: University of California Press.

2018. *Imagining the Future of Climate Change: World-Making through Science Fiction and Activism*. Berkeley: University of California Press.

Thomas, Sheree R. 2000. "Introduction: Looking for the Invisible," in *Dark Matter: A Century of Speculative Fiction from the African Diaspora*. Ed. Sheree R. Thomas, ix–xiv. New York: Warner Books.

Tremaine, F. Orlin, ed. 1933. *Astounding Stories* (December).

Ulibarri, Sarena. 2018. "Introduction," in *Glass and Gardens: Solarpunk Summers*. Ed. Sarena Ulibarri, 1–2. Albuquerque, NM: World Weaver Press.

Williams, Nathaniel. 2011. "Frank Reade, Jr., in Cuba: Dime-Novel Technology, U.S. Imperialism, and the 'American Jules Verne'," *American Literature* 83.2: 297–303.

CHAPTER 19

Homelessness
The Short Story and Other Media
Gavin Jones

When the magazine editor Park Benjamin traveled to New York City in the mid-1830s, carrying with him several manuscript tales by Nathaniel Hawthorne, his journey represented a moment of failure for the young Hawthorne. Throughout the early years of his career, Hawthorne set his sights on publishing a collection of interconnected short stories, or what today we would call a story cycle. He may have burned his first attempt in manuscript. His second effort was split apart and published as individual stories in magazines. His final and most ambitious attempt, *The Story Teller*, met a similar fate, with Benjamin possibly taking Hawthorne's stories without his approval and without payment (Adkins 1945, 133). *The Story Teller* was a series of short stories interspersed with travel sketches and essays that framed the telling of the various tales in situ as the storytelling narrator traveled through upstate New York and Canada. Benjamin's journey to New York City, carrying parts of *The Story Teller* in his pocket, refigures the story teller's own journey, and suggests how a thematic interest in travel in the stories accompanies a portability in the form itself, a transient capacity to migrate – and hence to circulate beyond the author's control – from the steady home of the book to the commercial yet ironically unremunerative hustle of the magazine. This movement from the medium of the book to the medium of the magazine altered the meaning of the stories for Hawthorne, who allegedly lost interest in his stray productions thereafter.

This chapter argues that this close relationship to – and capacity to move between – other, often non-textual media directly impacts the meaning of the American short story throughout its history, creating a "homelessness" that has formal ramifications too. This dual mobility, in terms of publication history and theme, can be found in William Austin's "Peter Rugg: The Missing Man" (1824), an important precursor to the work of Hawthorne. Austin was a lawyer and an occasional short story writer who, according to his biographer, turned to the short form owing to his lack of "continuity of thought" and his tendency to say odd things very abruptly "but not infrequently suggestive of more than was said" (Austin 1890, x). "Peter Rugg," about a similarly irascible figure who is doomed to roam the land perpetually searching for his lost home, is one such suggestive short story. This journey is related to the curious career of Austin's story itself, which was reprinted so many times in magazines, books, and newspapers that it became unclear whether the story was fact or fiction, oral folktale or literary creation. The theme of homelessness in the story is thus closely tied to the fugitive capacity of the story to change its form and significance according to its location.

Our journey through the short story's powers of transmediation begins with its position in the magazine, and then moves to consider the close relationship between the short story and photography – the first recording technology with which the short story became associated, beginning in the 1840s – and then proceeds to consider the foundational relationship between the short story and the spoken voice. My examples are necessarily eclectic as the chapter runs from the beginnings of the American short story to the present day. Writing on the art of storytelling in the *New-England Magazine* in 1835, John Neal took an extreme position on the short story's fugitive powers. Storytelling, wrote Neal, is part of "the great business of life," and can appear in different media, ranging from live performances to inscriptions on the walls of tombs and the gates of cities (1835, 1–2). For Neal, the best stories are associated with means of travel – they are overheard on steamboats and stagecoaches (5) – just as stories themselves can go astray, especially when retold: "They have but to strip off its rags, give it a good scouring with brick-dust and soap-suds, and there's an end to all previous ownership" (4). Writing a century later about the Russian author Nikolai Leskov, the German critic Walter Benjamin similarly traces the origins of the short story to the oral tales of traveling traders, and credits its written form with a portability founded on a freedom – relative to the novel – from the restrictive container of the book. Across time, we will discover significant ways in which the short story moves between various homes, and how the meaning of the short story lies in the nature of that mobility. As Benjamin put it, comparing the short story with a thing to be traded amid a world of commerce: "[T]races of the storyteller cling to the story the way the handprints of the potter cling to the clay vessel" (1985, 92). We will accordingly see how, at times, the story seems more like the container than the material contained, more like the medium than the message.

Magazines and Other Boxes

The story from Hawthorne's *The Story Teller* project that most fits its frame, "Mr. Higginbotham's Catastrophe" (1834), suggests how Hawthorne had already intuited the media mobility that would become the fate of his tales. The frame for the story (published separately in 1837 as "Passages from a Relinquished Work") sets the scene of the wandering storyteller, a figure somewhere between a novelist and an actor, whose stories move from improvised, ephemeral oral performances to a settled written form that attains "a unity, a wholeness, and a separate character" (1974b, 417). Like an oral folktale, the framed story of "Mr. Higginbotham's Catastrophe" is punctuated by three encounters between the protagonist, Dominicus Pike, and various strangers, who tell conflicting stories about the murder of Mr. Higginbotham – a murder that mysteriously seems to have taken place before it was feasibly possible, or else has not occurred at all. This riddle is finally solved when Dominicus discovers the murder about to take place, and realizes that the various storytellers he had encountered were all accomplices in the planned crime, who had successively lost courage and fled, each delaying the murder by a night. The story thus has the flavor of a joke, with its surprise ending, though the success of the story with its imagined audience is attributed to a trick played by a mischievous bystander, who attaches a queue of horsehair to the back of the unsuspecting storyteller's head, the movement of which delights the audience in a moment that pins storytelling success on the contingencies of live performance – an embodied theatricality that Michael J. Collins (2016) has identified at the origins of the short story tradition more generally. This unconscious movement is reflected in the story of the murder itself, which is on the loose in the community as it is retold by Dominicus, finally jumping media to take the form of a sensationalistic newspaper story in a local gazette, which "would then be re-printed from Maine to Florida, and perhaps form an item in the London newspapers" (1974a, 116). "Mr. Higginbotham's Catastrophe" and its frame suggest the close relationship between oral storytelling and written narrative, the fictional tale and the newspaper account, lending the concept of "story" a fungibility in its power of transmission between different media.

Edgar Allan Poe's theory of short prose narrative has dominated interpretations of the form, a theory and a value system that were designed around the medium of the magazine. The disposability and space efficiency of the short story, as Andrew Levy points out, were made to fit the magazine's system of rapid production and expendability, while Poe's idea of writing to a pre-established design acted as "a labor saving device" allowing the thriftiest allocation of resources (Levy 1993, 22). The short story thus seemed like a product, designed to be inserted into and moved around in a commercial medium, which led to fears – particularly during the heyday of the short story in the 1920s – that the machine of the magazine was determining and normalizing the shape and subject matter of the story. According to short story promoter and critic Edward J. O'Brien, the popular magazine story was imbued with the advertised products surrounding it, while its melodramatic plottedness reflected like clockwork the forces of mass production. No writer had a greater influence on the popularity of the early twentieth-century short story than O. Henry (William Sydney Porter), whose sappy slice-of-life stories about New York shopgirls and snappy stories with their signature sur-prise endings inspired a phalanx of imitators. Yet even in its most standardized form, O. Henry's work also reveals a resistant self-consciousness of the short story's hypermediated qualities, as the Russian formalist critic Boris Eikhenbaum discovered in O. Henry's formal parodies and metafictional interest in the problems of literary practice (1968, 17). For example, O. Henry's story "A Dinner at—*" (in which the asterisk points to a footnote, "See advertising column, 'Where to Dine Well,' in the daily newspapers") is two stories simultaneously: a future melodramatic story, not yet accepted by a magazine, of a hero's exploits impersonating a policeman and saving a damsel in distress; and the story of the writer's negotiation with his character in an attempt to save him from literary and social conventions, not least his desire to dine at a fashionable but unnamed restaurant. The story stages a battle between the demands of plot and the demands of the publication industry, with the asterisk and footnote acting as points of transmedia-tion that suggest the adjacency of the magazine short story and the commercial world of the newspaper (the twist at the end, typical of O. Henry: the story is rejected by the magazine because it lacks sufficient references to restaurants). The hyphen, asterisk, and footnote recognize the shifting paratexts of the short story, the variable nature of its "con-tainers," and mark an ironic self-consciousness of medium as the story is crowded, jostled, and impinged upon by the magazine's pressures of commercialization.

   If O'Brien was correct that the short story was particularly prone to the forces of standardization, and had come to embody in its style of "photo-graphic" accuracy the thickness of machines and things surrounding it (1929, 116), then various developments in the twentieth-century short story sought to distinguish high art through an emphasis on craft that – to return to Benjamin's image – revealed the handprints of the writer on the vessel of the story. It is little wonder that the single most influential theory of the short story in the twentieth century, Ernest Hemingway's so-called Iceberg principle, depends on *leaving things out*, on omissions that imply a stylistic of brevity that resists the saturation of materiality emerging from the mediating influence of the magazine. Hemingway's story "Banal Story" (1927), to offer another example, implicitly theorizes the "suggestive" short story (hence recalling William Austin's idea of the short story as a medium for missing or fleeting experience) as an escape from the popular magazine, with its "warm, homespun, American tales, bits of real life on the open ranch, in crowded tenement or comfortable home, and all with a healthy undercurrent of humor" (1995, 360). The story features a writer who turns away from "the Romance of the unusual" (361) found in magazines toward the rituals of Spanish bullfighting, whose "real" is embodied in newspaper stories and memorial pictures of a dead bullfighter in a final moment that suggests how the story's meaning is located in scattered, non-literary media recording a moment of loss.

If the magazine was the dominant containing medium for the short story through the middle of the twentieth century, then it has been supplemented more recently by the influential institutions of the creative writing program and the Internet. In the creative writing workshop, for example, the short story becomes again the discrete, fungible, hyperme-diated object that is written, circulated, critiqued, edited, and rewritten in an environment that allegedly perpetuates (as the magazine was said to do) normative patterns, in this case of self-reflexivity and ethnically inflected experience (McGurl 2009). The epitome of these dual processes can be found in Nam Le's "Love and Honor and Pity and Pride and Compassion and Sacrifice" (2008), the story of the narrator's metafictional attempt to write an authentic "ethnic story" about his father's experience during the Vietnam War. Just as O. Henry's popular stories also revealed a critical self-consciousness of the medium of their popularity, Le's story is meta-fictional to the extent that it is conscious of the medium of its production. The story ends when the father, who is visiting his son, a resident at the Iowa Writers' Workshop, burns his son's manuscript, leaving the narrator to witness the thick ashes float away, "given body by the wind" (2008, 28). Like Hemingway's "Banal Story," Le's story allegorizes a desire to escape the short story's hypermediation (its embeddedness in the market dictates of the creative writing program) in an act that stresses the fragility, precariousness, and ephemerality of the form.

The media self-conscious of the short story has taken new forms in recent decades with the influence of the Internet on literary production and circulation. For example, Jennifer Egan's 2012 story "Black Box" (discussed at length in Simone Murray's chapter in this volume) first appeared as a series of tweets from the *New Yorker*'s Twitter account. Both the technique and the subject matter of the story are defined by the medium of Twitter's brevity and serialization, which – according to Egan's own account of the genesis of the story – determine the style of brief directives to future readers and hence the subject of a woman spy on a dangerous mission involving international terrorism. Our spy has a camera built into her body – she represents the mediated self – and the various dispatches work like flashes or pulses, epigrammatic micro-stories in themselves, that are created by the light of the tweet. Set in the Mediterranean and hence at the site of what Egan identifies as the emergence of storytelling as an oral form (Dinnen 2016, 7), "Black Box" is a perfect example of the medium determining the message, and a perfect example of the short story's formally primed capacity to move between *different* media (tweet, webpage, magazine, book) and to encapsulate an entire shift in media ecology whereby the brief dispatches are textual equivalents of the photographic flashes (or short video forms) that determine our attention spans in a smartphone-generated culture of self-objectification. The final part of this chapter will trace the short story's relation to the different media of photography and voice, moving from the early days of the American short story to the contemporary period, and incorporating what Egan defines as two streams of contemporary fiction, the first emphasizing "trickiness," the second emphasizing "verisimilitude" (quoted in Dinnen 2016, 8) – and both emphasizing non-print media in special ways when found in the short form.

Sound and Vision

The theory of the short story and the theory of photography emerged simultaneously on American soil. If Poe's 1842 review of Hawthorne's *Twice-Told Tales* is conventionally cited as the origin of short story theory, then many of its ideas can be found two years earlier in Poe's ground-breaking essay "The Daguerreotype" (1840). Across the two essays, Poe describes dual forms of representation that are defined by temporal delimitation. Light enters the lens of a camera for a period of "ten to thirty minutes" (1840, 63), whereas the short prose narrative requires "from a half-hour to one or two hours in its perusal" (1842, 298). Both are art forms of the single sitting, just as they both possess a "totality" in relation to what they represent. The daguerreotype is a perfect mirror of a "source of vision" that is its own designer (1840, 63), whereas the short story reflects in every aspect the "pre-established design" intended by the literary artist (1842, 299). The perfect identity of the daguerreotype with the thing represented compares with the particular investment of the tale in "truth," to the extent that the telling of the tale, its ability to present ideas "unblemished, because undisturbed" (1842, 299), is akin to the making of the supreme "perfection" (1840, 63) of the photographic image (a point akin to Poe's general dislike of allegory for its distancing of meaning from the represented object). Poe ends his review of Hawthorne with a reference to his story "William Wilson" (1839), published just two months before his essay on the daguerreotype – a story that reflects his interest in photography's power to mirror perfectly what it represents. Quoting the story's final scene, in which Wilson confronts in a mirror a pale and bloody version of his own absolute identity, Poe turns to a crucial quality inherent in photography and implied by his theory of short fiction. The story's capacity to embody so totally a "preconceived effect" means that the short story, like the photograph, is prone to reproduction, and hence primed for plagiarism. In other words, the compression of the story creates what Poe calls "*points*" (1842, 300), which possess a portability, a power to migrate to other stories or – as these comparisons between Poe's two essays should imply – a sharpness that can penetrate into other media.

Few writers thought as extensively as Eudora Welty about the relationship between the short story and photography. Welty's father helped to establish the first camera store in Jackson, Mississippi, and Welty herself attempted an early career as a photographer, submitting to a publisher in the early 1930s a composition ring-book in which she had "posted little contact prints in which I fitted up as a sequence to make a kind of story in itself . . . . I submitted with the pictures a set of stories I had written, unrelated specifically to the photos" (quoted in McHaney 2009, 12). The relationship between the photograph and the short story is not one of illustration, but rather one of *adjacency* as the short story's edges abut another medium, thus creating theoretical resonances in which a "story-writer's truth" is akin to clicking the shutter of a camera at the moment when people fully reveal themselves (Welty 1971, 7–8). According to Welty, a short story is an elongated version of photography's slicing of a contingent moment out of what Susan Sontag calls time's "relentless melt," hence participating in the person's (or thing's) "vulnerability" and "mutability" (1977, 15), and suggesting a "view of social reality as consisting of small units of an apparently infinite number" (22). Just as the short story–photography comparison implies a fragmented and dissociative view of the social, it also implies a *participation in* that reality – what Roland Barthes describes as a seeing *through* the photograph to reveal something hidden (2010, 5, 32). The Argentine writer Julio Cortázar similarly described photographs and short stories as working in parallel by "cutting off a fragment of reality, giving it certain limits, but in such a way that this segment acts like an explosion which fully opens a more ample reality." If cinema is an "open order" like the novel, developing through a synthesis of multifaceted elements moving toward a climax, then photography and short stories work inversely, argues Cortázar, through delimited image or event whereby readers move not horizontally, as in the novel, but vertically up and down in interpretive space (1994, 245–255).

Welty's story "Why I Live at the P.O." (1941) is emblematic of this relationship between the short story and photography. Allegedly based on a photograph Welty took of a woman ironing at the back of a Mississippi post office, the story begins with the disruption that the arrival of a photographer poses to a rural family, and proceeds to describe the bizarre tensions in that family which lead to our nameless narrator's retreat to live at the local post office where she serves as postmistress. The story ends with a glance into the narrator's new life, in a moment that contains something of the "punctum" (Barthes 2010) of the original photograph that Welty allegedly saw: "Radio, sewing machine, book ends, ironing board and that great big piano lamp – peace, that's what I like" (Welty 1980, 56). We effectively, as public viewers/readers, move through the public space of the post office to glimpse the signs of domesticity deeply within it. If the dominant tradition of the novel has been closely associated with the new subjectivity of the bourgeois individual, then the photographic short story here exposes an isolated, dislocated individual in a gesture of resilience. Welty's story illustrates how – in the words of Nadine Gordimer – "Short-story writers see by the light of the flash" to reveal a discrete moment of non-accumulating truth that "depends less than the novel upon the classic conditions of middle-class life, and perhaps corresponds to the breakup of that life which is taking place" (1976, 180–181). The short story, like the photograph, offers a fragmented view of the social, one divided into separate frames of meaning.

The radio and the piano lamp at the end of Welty's story are vestiges of the oral and aural worlds in which the short story originated, just as Welty's investment in a regional environment looks back to a nineteenth-century tradition that emphasized the spoken voice in a local setting. Writing on "The Local Short Story" in 1892, Thomas Wentworth Higginson noted that "the rapid multiplication of the portable Kodak has scarcely surpassed the swift growth of local writers, each apparently having the same equipment of directness and vigor" (quoted in Smith 1912, 33). With the anthropological aim of capturing slices of American life, the so-called local color movement sought above all to capture vernacular voices in purportedly "phonetic" spelling whose experimental and frequently opaque qualities made it particularly suited to the short form. Next to the polyvocality of the novel, the short story offered possibilities of attention to a single voice – say, the voice of Uncle Julius in Charles Chesnutt's *The Conjure Woman* (1899) stories, which helped inaugurate a tradition of African American writing in the short story and offer a good example of popular dialect writing. Chesnutt's *Conjure Woman* stories are framed narratives in which a white northerner called John, who has purchased a former plantation during Reconstruction, encounters Julius, a formerly enslaved person who tells tales regarding life during slavery and the practices of folk magic ("conjure") that developed to survive it. Chesnutt was trained as a legal stenographer – a newly professionalized form of listening – and his stories imply a capacity to hear and capture Julius's dense dialect, a capacity surely beyond that of the stories' internal listener (John). A third, stenographic presence thus intercedes between the teller and the listener, translating the aural to the written form. Chesnutt exploits the varying capacities of John and his partner Ann to "hear" what Julius has to say about the history of slavery, masked behind the gains Julius is attempting to secure through his tale-telling in the present. In other words, a politics and an ethics underscore the ability to listen, as captured in the story "Tobe's Tribulations," in which Julius teaches his listeners how to hear the lone voice of a single frog (Tobe, who has been conjured into the form of a frog in an attempt to escape to freedom) amidst the "volume of sound" emanating from a nearby marsh (1993, 183), whose frogs John wants to tap as a source of food. A story about the impossibility of reaching freedom is framed by an exercise in attentive listening that Julius uses in this case not for personal gain but to save the environment of the marsh, and its frogs, from further exploitation.

Chesnutt's use of the frame narrative echoes the "phatic" moments at the beginning and ending of oral narrative, and is merely an extreme form of attention-grabbing that seems germane to the short story in general. The sudden openings and surprise (or "twisted") endings so common in the short story can be understood as part of the deep structure of the form inherited – or transmediated – from the aural world. Ted Chiang's

"The Great Silence" (2016) returns to a world of oral parables and animal fables similar to the one that informs Chesnutt's stories, and recalls again the ethical resonances of listening to the medium of sound. Told in the voice of a Puerto Rican parrot facing the extinction of its species owing to human activity, "The Great Silence" juxtaposes humanity's large-scale technological efforts to communicate extraterrestrially with humanity's disastrous inability to hear the small voices of parrots who are, like humans, vocal learners with a special relationship to sound. Echoing "Tobe's Tribulations," the story calls for interspecies listening in the service of environmental protection; it suggests again the short story's foundations in oral narratives that encourage attentive listening to a solitary voice. And it suggests how the emphasis on *ending* in the short story equips it structurally to contemplate the ethics of planetarity and extinction. When Walter Benjamin writes that "Death is the sanction of everything that the storyteller can tell" (1985, 94), he was writing specifically about the short story and its provenance in oral narratives, which lends it the feeling – one felt by the parrot in Chiang's story – that time is too short, and is quickly running out.

The experimentalism of the late nineteenth-century dialect story developed alongside new media technologies, such as the phonograph and the telephone. Connections between media technology and the short story would intensify in the twentieth century and reach an extreme form in postmodernist works such as John Barth's *Lost in the Funhouse* (1968). The rise of a new media ecosystem driven by electronic technology created fears – as Barth comments in a 1988 foreword – "of the moribundity of the print medium in the electronic global village" (1988, viii). Writing before the emergence of the home computing revolution, Barth identifies magnetic tape recording as the main threat to the written word (the compact cassette was released in 1963, the same year as the first of Barth's stories); the collection is subtitled *Fiction for Print, Tape, Live Voice.* The first story in the collection, "FRAME-TALE," seems the height of postmodernity: the story consists of a strip of words, running vertically up the page on both sides – "ONCE UPON A TIME THERE / WAS A STORY THAT BEGAN" (1–2) – with instructions to cut the strip from the page and to twist and fasten its ends to form a Möbius strip. The removal of the story *from the book itself* recalls the fate of Hawthorne's stories, removed from his story cycle and transposed to a magazine. We, as readers, are being urged to perform precisely the transmedia mobility built into the form, effectively turning the page into an endless loop of tape that mimics the magnetic tape that Barth imagines capturing and competing with his written stories. "FRAME-TALE" also thus represents, in extreme form, a trademark gimmick that ensures the short story's distinctiveness and marketability – what promoters of the short story in the 1920s called its "snappy" quality, its likeness to the structure of the (oral) joke.

Barth adds a series of additional author's notes to the 1969 edition of *Funhouse*, writing that he meant in good faith the claim to the differing ideal media of his stories' presentation, as he attempted to turn "as many aspects of the fiction as possible – the structure, the narrative viewpoint, the means of presentation, in some instances the process of composition and/or recitation as well as of readings or listening – into dramatically relevant emblems of the theme" (1988, 203). The stories in the collection test the varying relationship between medium and meaning, ranging from those that need the medium of print (for example "Life-Story," a metafictional work in which a nested series of authors and characters contemplate the fictionality of the real) to others that call very specifically for a transmediated situation. For example, "Autobiography: A Self-Recorded Fiction" calls for the playing of a monophonic tape-recording alongside a visible but silent author to capture in another form the *detachment* of "FRAME-TALE." Here, the author expresses an estrangement from the story, which has separated itself from his control and has entered another medium to be given life by the listener. This process leaves the author stranded and confused, as his homeless stories travel beyond his power. Barth's collection is consonant with the literature of postmodernity, especially its decentering of totalizing structures of meaning, its parody and self-reflexivity, though of course it also echoes in this regard the earlier consciousness of media embeddedness, and its link to oral cultures of performance that stressed the contingencies of telling, which we have seen in stories ranging from Hawthorne's to O. Henry's.

Conclusion: Two Contemporary Examples

Alongside "trickiness," the other tradition that Egan identifies – verisimilitude – predominates in the contemporary pages of the *New Yorker* and other prime sites for the publication of short fiction, and can be found in the works of two West Coast writers closely associated with the creative writing program: Elizabeth Tallent and Jenn Alandy Trahan. Tallent's story "Nobody You Know," from her collection *Mendocino Fire* (2015), suggests how the contemporary American short story, in its settled realism, has maintained a self-consciousness of form in relation to other media, as if transmediation has become baked into the assumptions by which the story operates. "Nobody You Know" is the story of a divorce in which the main character – a painter called Ximena, known for her moonscapes featuring "flying scraps of paper bearing scribbled handwriting" (2015, 105) – visits her former husband and his new wife in an exquisite plot twist that depends on the relationship between a concept of story and a moment of photographic capture. "Story" has a distinct and expansive meaning in "Nobody You Know": it is everything that Ximena has been excluded from, following her divorce – her "own story," the entire process of meaning-making that stemmed from her marriage. This exclusion echoes the curtailed and incomplete space of the short story as a form stressing the kind of separation and "divorce" we encountered in Welty's "Why I Live at the P.O." Ximena returns to her former relationship after receiving a letter and photograph of the husband's new wife and baby child "caught in the middle of a lunge" (104). Echoing Cortázar's idea of the photograph and the short story as interpretive spaces through which we move vertically up and down, this photograph and another from Ximena's youth are spaces of depth, spaces that have an emotional inside that Ximena and we, as readers, see into. And echoing Welty's idea of the "story-writer's truth" as a "growing contemplation" of a photographic snapshot – a deeper dive into a segment of time contained most intensely in the gesture of a face – the story ends with a moment of "truth" that is essentially non-narrative and non-linguistic (115). Tallent's story ends with a stopping of time (the other photograph from Ximena's youth is an intimate image of removing her father's watch from his arm) that demands a reading of performative gesture, one that returns us to the embodied theatricality detected by Collins (2016) at the origins of the American short story, and is finally captured in the photographic vision of a face.

Trahan's story "They Told Us Not to Say This" (2018) might seem emblematic of the "high cultural pluralism" (McGurl 2009) produced by the contemporary creative writing program – Trahan is a Filipina American writer from the gritty city of Vallejo, California – though its concern with authenticity is more productively understood in light of the short story's transmediated interest in voice, or what Russian formalist critics called *skaz*: an unmediated and informal means of expression, defined by dialect, vernacular, and slang, that was a sign of the short story's emergence from the oral tale. The story concerns a group of Filipina high schoolers who transcend ugly feelings of shame – emerging from their parents' adoration of whiteness – through their love for a classmate called Brent Zalesky, whose all-in exploits on the basketball court represent his broader construction of an authentic self that defies the ideologies and phony conventions of society. The discourse of the story has a similarly existential emphasis. A cauterized, authentic voice emerges from a negative understanding of self-identity as an analogue to Zalesky's trueness-to-self and mastery of performative technique: "[H]e ganked tapes and CDs from Wherehouse with the clunky security devices still attached. Brent Zalesky knew how to get them off, armed only with pliers and a Bic lighter" (2018, 79). Zalesky's subversive techniques are embodied in a vernacular voice whose slangy sound relates to the story's theme of recorded music. The "tape" here is not Barth's emergent technology of the 1960s but rather a nostalgic look back to a time when love could be expressed with mixtapes of songs ganked from the radio. What connects Trahan's and Barth's stories, and what connects those stories to a deeper history of the short story, is the way that a trueness-to-style — whether postmodern self-reflexiveness or contemporary realism — is linked to an imagined relationship between literary text and other media. For Trahan, the ethic of authenticity relates to authenticity *in another medium.* Trahan's original working title, "Take Us Back to Vinyl,"[1] announces this desire for an analog relationship to voice, and hence embodies the short story's formal and thematic movement toward the signs of sound and vision.

Work Cited

Adkins, Nelson. 1945. "The Early Projected Works of Nathaniel Hawthorne." *The Papers of the Bibliographical Society of America* 39.2 (Second Quarter): 119–155.

Austin, James Walker. 1890. *Literary Papers of William Austin*. Boston: Little, Brown.

Barth, John. 1988 [1968]. *Lost in the Funhouse: Fiction for Print, Tape, Live Voice*. New York: Anchor.

Barthes, Roland. 2010 [1980]. *Camera Lucida: Reflections on Photography*. Trans. Richard Howard. New York: Hill and Wang.

Benjamin, Walter. 1985 [1936]. "The Storyteller: Reflections on the Work of Nikolai Leskov," in *Illuminations*. Trans. Harry Zohn, 83–110. New York: Schocken.

Chesnutt, Charles. 1993 [1900]. "*Tobe's Tribulations,*" in *The Conjure Woman and Other Conjure Stories*, 183–193. Durham, NC: Duke University Press.

Chiang, Ted. 2016. "The Great Silence." https://electricliterature.com/the-great-silence-by-ted-chiang/.

Collins, Michael J. 2016. *The Drama of the American Short Story, 1800-1865*. Ann Arbor: University of Michigan Press.

Cortázar, Julio. 1994 [1982]. "Some Aspects of the Short Story." Trans. Aden Hayes. In *The New Short Story Theories*. Ed. Charles E. May, 245–255. Athens: Ohio University Press.

Dinnen, Zara. 2016. "'This Is All Artificial': An Interview with Jennifer Egan," 1–9. http://post45.research.yale.edu/2016/05/this-is-all-artificial-an-interview-with-jennifer-egan/.

Egan, Jennifer. 2012. "Black Box," *The New Yorker* (June 4–11): 84–97.

Eikhenbaum, Boris. 1968 [1925]. *O. Henry and the Theory of the Short Story*. Trans. I. R. Titunik. Ann Arbor: University of Michigan Press.

Gordimer, Nadine. 1976 [1968]. "The Flash of Fireflies," in *Short Story Theories*. Ed. Charles E. May, 178–181. Athens: Ohio University Press.

Hawthorne, Nathaniel. 1974a [1834]. "Mr. Higginbotham's Catastrophe," in *Twice-Told Tales: Centenary Edition*, vol. IX, 106–120. Athens: Ohio State University Press.

　　1974b [1837]. "Passages from a Relinquished Work," in *Mosses from an Old Manse: Centenary Edition*, vol. X, 405–421. Athens: Ohio State University Press.

Hemingway, Ernest. 1995 [1927]. "Banal Story," in *The Short Stories: The First Forty-Nine*, 360–362. New York: Scribner.

Le, Nam. 2008. "*Love and Honor and Pity and Pride and Compassion and Sacrifice*," in *The Boat*, 3–28. New York: Vintage.

Levy, Andrew. 1993. *The Culture and the Commerce of the American Short Story*. Cambridge, UK: Cambridge University Press.

McGurl, Mark. 2009. *The Program Era: Postwar Fiction and the Rise of Creative Writing*. Cambridge, MA: Harvard University Press.

McHaney, Pearl Amelia. 2009. *Eudora Welty as Photographer*. Oxford: University Press of Mississippi.

Neal, John. 1835. "Story-Telling," *The New-England Magazine* VIII (January): 1–12.

O'Brien, Edward J. 1929. *The Dance of the Machines: The American Short Story and the Industrial Age*. New York: Macaulay.

O. Henry (William Sydney Porter). 1911. "A Dinner at—*," in *Rolling Stones*, 127–139. New York: Doubleday, Page.

Poe, Edgar Allan. 1840 (January 15). "The Daguerreotype," in Clarence S. Brigham, "Edgar Allan Poe's Contributions to *Alexander's Weekly Messenger*," *The Proceedings of the American Antiquarian Society* 52.1 (April 1942): 62–64.

　　1842. "Review of Nathaniel Hawthorne's Twice-Told Tales," *Graham's Magazine* 20.2 (May): 298–300.

Smith, C. Alphonso. 1912. *The American Short Story*. Boston: Ginn.

Sontag, Susan. 1977. *On Photography*. New York: Picador.

Tallent, Elizabeth. 2015. "Nobody You Know," in *Mendocino Fire: Stories*, 95–118. New York: Harper Collins.

Trahan, Jenn Alandy. 2018. "They Told Us Not to Say This," *Harper's Magazine* (September): 79–82.

Welty, Eudora. 1980 [1941]. "Why I Live at the P.O.," in *Collected Stories of Eudora Welty*, 46–56. New York: Harcourt Brace Jovanovich.

1996 [1971]. *One Time, One Place: Mississippi in the Depression*. Oxford: University Press of Mississippi.

CHAPTER 20

The Human and the Animal
Toward Posthumanist Short Fiction

Michael Lundblad

At the end of H. P. Lovecraft's "The Rats in the Walls" (1924), the narrator, named Delapore, reveals to his readers that he has been accused of something monstrous, a "hideous thing, but they must know that I did not do it" (Lovecraft 1987b, 96). He has been committed to a "barred room" after narrating a terrible family history that includes carved grottoes beneath their ancestral family estate, where human captivity and barbaric rituals have apparently been practiced for centuries. After an expedition to track the sounds of rats down into these depths with a team of archaeological and scientific experts, Delapore reveals that he himself was eventually found, hours later in the blackness, mumbling incoherently and standing over the half-eaten body of one of the other men. Delapore concludes the story by blaming the rats, distancing himself from the accusation of cannibalism: "They must know it was the rats; the slithering, scurrying rats whose scampering will never let me sleep; the daemon rats that race behind the padding in this room and beckon me down to greater horrors than I have ever known; the rats they can never hear; the rats, the rats in the walls" (96). Evoking the acute sense of hearing of Edgar Allan Poe's character of Roderick Usher in "The Fall of the House of Usher" (1840) – whose ancestral home also contains buried horrors – Delapore's fixation upon the rats intermingles with the reader's suspicion that Delapore himself has become rat-like, atavistically descending back and away from what might define him as human. There is not much interest in the rats themselves, however, beyond their association with horror. Lovecraft's rats thus offer something different from the kinds of animals we find in Jack London's wolf and dog stories, for example, or William Faulkner's bears, or Ernest Hemingway's lions or bulls or trout. The figure of the rat, however, can be tracked across a wide range of American short fiction, illustrating powerful narrative effects that can be produced by particular forms of animality.

The development of the academic fields of posthumanism and human–animal studies has led to various kinds of ethical and political questions about human relationships with animals. Much of this work has built upon the deconstruction of a simplistic binary opposition between "the human" and "the animal," showing how traditional markers of humanity – from language broadly conceived to reasoning, tool use, and complex social relations – can no longer be seen as definitive markers of difference between human and nonhuman species (see Derrida 2008). Advocacy movements on behalf of animal rights and welfare suggest the need, therefore, for more ethical consideration of nonhuman animals. In fields such as multispecies ethnography and extinction studies, as Deborah Bird Rose and Thom van Dooren have pointed out, there are complex questions to explore in relation to "unloved others" (Rose and van Dooren 2011, 1) – such as rats – as well as more charismatic megafauna, such as whales and wolves. In this chapter, I follow the rats into stories running over the course of American short fiction, from Lovecraft's "The Rats in the Walls" to Karen Joy Fowler's "Us" (2013), with particular attention paid to Ursula K. Le Guin's "Mazes" (1975). These stories have the power to raise posthumanist questions about what it means to be human as well as animal. In many cases, short fiction blurs the line between human and nonhuman animals, without necessarily foregrounding animal rights or advocacy.

The field of animality studies has highlighted how constructions of who counts as human have had historically devastating impacts upon specific human groups. The dark side of blurring the line between humans and animals includes histories of constructing humans as rats or vermin, most notoriously in the Nazi attempt to exterminate Jews in the Holocaust. The history of animalizing African Americans in the United States, to take a different example, has fixated on depictions of some humans as somehow more "ape-like," a racist discourse of human animality deployed to justify slavery and horrific treatment for centuries. The legacies of these constructions continue today in the form of neo-Nazi and white supremacist groups, as well as various forms of racism and discrimination. In Lovecraft's story, the rats themselves are less explicitly linked with racism than other parts of the story. But they are loathed as an infestation, a swarm of vermin tied to degeneracy, a kind of regression toward a "beast within the human" that is more evil in a Christian sense than an expression of Darwinist survival-of-the-fittest instincts (see Lundblad 2013). Racism and eugenics cut across these various discourses, however, particularly in the 1920s in the United States.

To some extent, American short fiction moves in more progressive directions over the course of the twentieth and twenty-first centuries. The rise of anti-racist, environmental, and animal-rights movements from the 1960s up to the present can be connected to short stories that are more likely to reject racism and white supremacy, on the one hand, and to embrace new ways of imagining and exploring animals worthy of our concern, on the other hand. At the same time, the story of animals and animality in American short fiction is more complex than a chronological march toward posthumanism. Instead, there are often challenging narrative mazes to negotiate, achievements to be glimpsed beyond the purview of intent, and various kinds of *effects* to be considered, all of which can be found in earlier stories as well.

More generally, though, short fiction can become a site for questions about a posthumanist desire to move beyond traditional ways of prioritizing human life over all other species on the planet, a tradition that often continues to reinforce problematic legacies of humanism. As Cary Wolfe emphasizes in his introduction to *What Is Posthumanism?*, however, "the point is not to reject humanism *tout court* – indeed, there are many values and aspirations to admire in humanism" (2010, xvi). Instead, the problem is a "kind of normative subjectivity – a specific concept of the human – that grounds discrimination against nonhuman animals" (xvii). The human can be ranked above all other animals, in other words, as the only species capable of subjectivity, supposedly, even within humanist discourses advocating on behalf of other species. Wolfe's posthumanism can open up various kinds of questions in relation to short fiction. For example, to what extent does the story reinforce a normative conception of the human subject? How might it suggest forms of resistance to a simple binary opposition between the human and the animal? How might it draw our attention to the ways that the *category* of "the animal" has been used, to the contrary, to justify exploitation and oppression of either human or nonhuman groups?

We can bring these questions to a story such as Karen Joy Fowler's "Us" (2013). This story presents us with a kind of thought experiment in which the narrator is a collective "we" rather than an "I," taking on the perspective of rats. The story recounts a generalized history of human–rat interactions, addressed to us human readers, under section titles such as "Diaspora": "In those dim and distant days, when famine came, it was a shared privation. If it settled in, meant to stay, then we took off together, boarded your ships and sailed in all directions. Our DNA is a map of your migrations" (Fowler 2013, 481). Under "Plagues," we are reminded of attempts to wipe "them" out: "You spoke of infestations. Swarms. Eradications. You killed us in your stories, danced us to our deaths with songs" (482). Following the Pied Piper into many other stories, we can, indeed, find countless tales of death and killing, perhaps the most common way that rats have been figured in American fiction. But in Fowler's "Us," the rats telling the story turn out to be much more like us than we might like to admit. These are "Berkeley rats" who have been bred for the lab, who have recognized the futility of trying to survive human purges outside laboratory culture, who can be distinguished by the curiosity they display when placed in artificial mazes. These rats are also hybrid, grafted with human DNA, in order to become proxies suitable for studying and hopefully curing human diseases. They are capable, though, of "philosophical questions": "What happens next? How much human DNA does it take to make a human?" (485). Eventually these rats may "have taken on enough of your DNA to have become you" (485). The story concludes, then, by blurring this line: "We would like to think this: that in the end it is ourselves we are saving. Already we don't know if this is our thought or yours. But it sounds like you" (485). Until then, however, this hybridity raises ethical questions: "Our job is to sicken and die, but only in useful ways" (485).

How is this story supposed to have been written? Are these rats capable of forms of thinking, expressing, and writing that are usually considered to be possible only for humans? On the one hand, we might see posthumanist potential here in the story, suggesting that other species can have complex inner lives, even if we cannot understand them, unless we are in the world of Disney. Or the story might help us to consider other forms of transgressing species boundaries, not only when DNA is intermingled, but also through transplants of organs, for example. On the other hand, as Wolfe points out, extending "human" capabilities into nonhuman species can become, perhaps paradoxically, a way of reinforcing the superiority of what is associated with being human. In other words, if the intent is to put other species on a par with humans, then focusing primarily on how they might be human-like can be a way of continuing to construct a hierarchy of capabilities traditionally and historically used to reinforce human exceptionalism. Further, we might think of the potential difficulties associated with nonhuman narrators in general: Is it ever possible to avoid a humanist form of subjectivity if the "I" follows the expectations of the genre? What if it is a "we" instead of an "I"?

According to Dominic O'Key, Fowler's "we-narrative" might seem to have unique potential as a collective voice, rather than the much more common narrative structure of an "I." But the rhetoric of "Us," as O'Key points out, ultimately suggests that the creation of this collective is the result of the ways that humans have historically de-individualized rats. The "we-narrative" laments, for example, the fact that "Genetic variation has been minimized in the attempt to eradicate the noise of individual personality" (Fowler 2013, 484). The suggestion seems to be that it would be better to recognize rats as individuals, perhaps leading to the possibility of an individual rat narrating this kind of story. But that kind of narrator could then be linked with the very humanist roots of fiction – particularly the novel – as a literary form. As a result, the "formal and generic logics of the novel" can "pressurize multispecies storyworlds into adopting a sole authorial 'I'" (O'Key 2020, 82). For O'Key, then, Fowler's story might end up with the same problem as first-person "animal autobiographies": these "might well be at odds with the very posthumanist horizon they are often tasked with making intelligible. They would reproduce the tenets of a hegemonic anthropocentric ideology" (83; see also Herman 2018). Better forms of "we-narratives," according to O'Key, might have more potential, aiming to "realise a collective subjectivity without possessive individualism" (83).

Whether or not posthumanist subjectivity might be more easily constructed through "we" as opposed to "I" narratives, there are also other important questions to explore in stories such as Fowler's. I have in mind here the kind of *effect* (and affect) produced by Fowler's story which remains, from my perspective at least, fairly cerebral and abstract. We might be provoked or even disturbed to think about what rat eradication and experimentation have meant for rats in general, but the lack of individuation makes it more difficult to imagine what it might *feel* like to have lived through rat terror. In this regard, I am reminded of Poe's thinking about the craft of short fiction, with his emphasis on the ideal of "a certain continuity of effort ... a certain duration or repetition of purpose" that allows for "the soul" to be "deeply moved" (Poe 1994, 61). According to Poe, the "short prose narrative," unlike the novel, is the form of writing most likely to create "the immense force derivable from *totality*," focused upon a "certain unique or single *effect* to be wrought out" (61; emphasis in original).

How might we characterize the effect of Fowler's story? According to Claire Jean Kim and Carla Freccero, in their "Introduction" to a special issue of *American Quarterly* on "Species/Race/Sex," which also first published Fowler's "Us," the story is "haunting" (Kim and Freccero 2013, 474). We are told that it "suggests the disturbing dynamics at work between dominant and subordinate beings in both interspecies and intra-human relating" (474). We are also told that it "brings Ursula K. Le Guin's shattering tale 'Mazes' to the twenty-first century" (474). *Haunting, disturbing, shattering*: these terms might be a little dramatic, from my perspective, at least for Fowler's story. I would argue that "Mazes" (1975) is indeed haunting, however, even though it brings us back to a first-person narrator. There is more to explore in Le Guin's story as well, particularly when it comes to the effects it can produce, as well as its potential (post)humanism.

In Le Guin's story, the unnamed narrator is faced with an "alien" antagonist, who can be identified fairly easily as a human lab researcher. The narrator begins by expressing desperation after a long ordeal: "I have tried hard to use my wits and keep up my courage, but I know now that I will not be able to withstand the torture any longer . . . . I cannot accomplish any of the greater motions. I cannot speak" (Le Guin 1987, 61). The narrator is fundamentally confused by the "alien's cruelty," which is

> refined, yet irrational. If it intended all along to starve me, why not simply withhold food? But instead of that it gave me plenty of food, mountains of food, all the greenbud leaves I could possibly want. Only they were not fresh. They had been picked; they were dead; the element that makes them digestible to us was gone, and one might as well eat gravel. (61–62)

The alien researcher, in other words, has very little ability to understand the narrator, including something as basic as what makes food digestible for their kind.

We are given an opportunity, then, to imagine what this situation might feel like, as well as being dropped into a maze, without knowing what might be expected of us. Who, though, we must ask, is this "us" or "we"? Are we rats? Are we on another planet? Are we humans put into the place of the animal-like humans in *Planet of the Apes*? Or, to the contrary, is the narrator a human encountering other kinds of humans who are fundamentally incapable of communicating with them? As readers, our bearings remain unstable. The narrator, we soon learn, comes from a culture in which a maze is an opportunity for an artistic performance, a creative mode of expression, rather than a pragmatic task aimed solely at finding the supposed reward at the end. Conversely, the alien in this story comes from a different world, although it provides a maze that is perceived by the narrator as an opportunity to perform what is called "the Eighth Maluvian in its entirety," including the "evolutions in the ninth encatenation, where the 'cloud' theme recurs so strangely transposed into the ancient spiraling motif . . . [which is] indestructibly beautiful" (Le Guin 1987, 63–64). But the alien does not seem to understand the maze as an artistic performance at all, and instead places the narrator immediately back into the humiliation of the first maze, "the short one, the maze for little children who have not yet learned how to talk" (64). What the narrator soon realizes, though, is that the alien must have a completely different way of communicating, perhaps only "labially" (with its lips), while its bodily motions are apparently only "purposeful, not communicative" (64). In other words, the alien only moves its body to accomplish a particular pragmatic purpose. It has no capacity for expressing itself creatively. If "we" recognize ourselves, at least in part, in the figure of the alien as well, then the creative expression of the narrator, to the contrary, has the potential for building a crescendo toward what Poe calls "the immense force derivable from *totality*," the creation of an effect that might even allow for "our souls" to be "deeply moved" (Poe 1994, 61, italics in original). What horrors arise, the story seems to ask, if we assume that rats in mazes have no capacity for creativity or creative expression?

Another way of formulating that question is to ask how short fiction can help us to imagine ourselves more productively into the lives of animals. Le Guin herself has said more generally, "I guess I'm trying to subjectify the universe, because look where objectifying it has gotten us. To subjectify is not necessarily to co-opt, colonize, exploit. Rather, it may involve a great reach outward of the mind and imagination" (Le Guin 2017, M16). Vinciane Despret points us further in this direction in *What Would Animals Say If We Asked the Right Questions?* (2016). She also develops more productive theoretical concepts to consider. In *Thinking Like a Rat*, a short book published in 2009, Despret provides us with a useful summary of *Umwelt*, for example, a concept first developed by naturalist Jakob von Uexküll in the early twentieth century. To summarize the concept, in Despret's words, first, "the animal, endowed with sensory organs different from our own, cannot perceive the same world as we do" (Despret 2015, 125). Second, "perception will be defined not as a form of 'reception' but as an act of creation: the animal does not perceive passively, it 'fills its environment with perceptual objects'" (125). Finally, the "*Umwelt*, or lived world of the animal, is above all a world where things are only perceived, on the one hand, because they are captured by particular sensory equipment ... and, on the other hand, to the degree in which they have taken on a meaning. And it is with these meanings that the animal constructs its perceptual universe" (125). With this concept, different species can be seen as subjects, perceiving and shaping their worlds in different ways from humans, but not necessarily in any way "less" than human.

Uexküll objects to scientists who ignore the *Umwelt* of the rat, for example, such as the American behaviorist John B. Watson, who published a monograph in 1907 on the behavior of rats in mazes. As Despret notes, Watson's aim was to isolate the intelligence of a rat in a maze from various forms of sense perception. Watson thus tried to "neutralize" other senses, for example, by removing "the rat's eyes, olfactory bulb, and whiskers, which are essential to the sense of touch in rats" (2015, 126). For Despret, these procedures might be more closely compared to a patient being guided "toward a sadistic torturer rather than to their doctor" (126). This kind of cruelty can also illustrate how the sensory apparatus of the rat can be manipulated in relation to the desired outcome of the scientist. The fields of philosophical ethology and theoretical biology offer us alternatives, building upon Uexküll's insights, in dialogue with multispecies studies that attempt to tell the stories of multispecies interactions in more productive ways (see Kirksey 2014; Tsing 2015). In literary and cultural studies, we have other ways of exploring the lives of nonhuman animals as well, particularly through fictional narratives that do not necessarily need to be constrained by current understandings of "western" science, which can be quick to dismiss anything with a whiff of anthropomorphism, for example. "Mazes" can help us wonder how humans might become more capable of imagining other ways of being in the world. Despret helps to open up this story when she explains how rats find their way:

> The rat draws, marks, soaks up, in its muscles and on its skin, the map of a lateral landscape. And it is the agreement of this map with the sensations that it will check on the return route that will tell it that it is indeed going the right way, and that the nest will be there, at the precise place where all the sensations will have finished unfolding. (2015, 127)

When placed into the artificial abstract environment of the laboratory maze, the activity becomes something completely different. We might well ask, "how does the rat ... translate what is expected of her?" (128). This shift toward the gendered or individualized pronoun is notable here, once the generic "it" moves toward "her."

Le Guin's "I" takes the story further, turning the alien instead into an "it." In the end, according to the narrator,

> I tried to say, "What is it you want of me? Only tell me what it is you want." But I was too weak to speak clearly, and it did not understand. It has never understood. And now I have to die. No doubt it will come in to watch me die; but it will not understand the dance I dance in dying. (Le Guin 1987, 66)

In Sherryl Vint's discussion of the story in *Animal Alterity*, recognizing the impasse in communication is "not sufficient to bridge the species gap" (2010, 185) and the result will surely be death. According to Vint, this impasse primarily evokes a critique of animal experimentation, in which the story "indicts humans for our blindness to the intelligence and communicative capacities of species who express these in ways other than our own" (185). The story suggests that "the very structure of science and its ways of engaging animals produce conditions under which it is impossible for us to see their intelligence, even were we to look for it" (185). This kind of laboratory culture has been critiqued by many others in human–animal studies, as well as problematized in complex ways by Donna Haraway in *When Species Meet* (2008). For Vint, rather than dismissing animal testing in its entirety, we must confront "the thorny moral question of how to balance concern for animal welfare with the potential benefits" (197). Vint builds upon Haraway's exploration of this question and finds some hope in her advocacy for better research relationships, yet also suggests, as an aside, that Haraway does not pay enough attention to the "massively unequal power relations between humans and animals" in these contexts (199).

Whether or not we agree with that assessment, Haraway's work can point toward other kinds of posthumanist questions. She calls for researchers to "do the *work* of paying attention and making sure that the suffering is minimal, necessary, and consequential" (Haraway 2008, 82, italics in original), for example, yet also to "learn to kill responsibly . . . yearning for the capacity to respond and to recognize response" (81). The key issue, for Haraway, is not necessarily killing itself, but the biopolitical construction of certain lives as killable with impunity (see also Wolfe 2013). According to Haraway, "Try as we might to distance ourselves, there is no way of living that is not also a way of someone, not just something, else dying differentially" (80). This formulation can also link interactions with nonhuman species with intrahuman histories of "exterminism and genocide" (80).

Haraway often engages with science fiction to explore better forms of relating to what she calls "companion species." We can follow her lead in this regard into stories such as "Mazes." But what happens if we pull back from the assumption that the narrator is a nonhuman animal? What if the narrator might also be a link, as I have suggested previously, to histories of certain human groups *made killable* by others? Le Guin herself has perhaps surprisingly stated quite clearly, in a short introductory note to "Mazes," that the story is "*not* about rats" (Le Guin 1987, 61, italics in original). On the one hand, despite the author's intent, the story is able to build its powerful effect precisely because it *is* imaginable that a rat in a maze might not experience it according to a scientist's assumptions. On the other hand, the references to names for maze-dances – rendered in human English, even if unrecognizable, such as "the Eighth Maluvian," "the Ungated Affirmation," and "New Expressionist techniques" (63) – suggest at least the possibility of the narrator being revealed as more "human" than "rat." A human narrator could perhaps have developed these dances in future worlds and distant galaxies, before encountering an "alien" that *we* might see as more human-like, on this planet or another. The creation of this unsettling confusion, which suggests a simultaneously and multiply *othered* identity of the narrator, can be linked to what Poe calls "a certain continuity of effort . . . a certain duration or repetition of purpose" (61). Attentive readers can thus feel the destabilization from the beginning to the end of the story, opening up concurrent possibilities along the way. The "alien" life of quiet desperation – with bodies that only ever move for a utilitarian purpose – can also evoke various frameworks of historical antagonism and oppression. We might think about indigenous ways of being in the world, for example, rendered incomprehensible within colonial and neo-imperialist discourses. We might also think of feminist artists and dancers, to take another example, who feel stifled by the seeming inability of their fellow (male) humans to think, move, and express themselves creatively, particularly in the late 1960s when this story was written. How can we open our senses and bodies to alternative and more creative possibilities, the story seems to ask, communicating and responding to other bodies within or outside our own species, or both, without knowing in advance what kinds of trouble might ensue? Perhaps there is a collective narrator in this story after all.

Haraway is explicit about the ways that science fiction writers such as Le Guin and Octavia Butler, among others, can help us "stay with the trouble" more generally, suggesting that "Recuperation is still possible, but only in multispecies alliance, across the killing divisions of nature, culture, and technology and of organism, language, and machine" (2016, 117–118). In *Staying with the Trouble: Making Kin in the Chthulucene* (2016), Haraway credits Le Guin as a kind of teacher: "Her theories, her stories, are capacious bags for collecting, carrying, and telling the stuff of the living" (118). In order to imagine and create better worlds, Haraway argues that "Living-with and dying-with each other potently in the Chthulucene can be a fierce reply to the dictates of both Anthropos and Capital" (2), suggesting an alternative to terms such as the Anthropocene and the Capitalocene. Readers familiar with Lovecraft might assume that

Haraway thus intends to reference his monster-god, "Cthulhu," but she rejects the connection outright: "These real and possible time-spaces are not named after science fiction writer H. P. Lovecraft's misogynist racial-nightmare monster Cthulhu (note the spelling difference)" (101). In fact, "the monstrous male elder god (Cthulhu)" in Lovecraft "plays no role for me" (174, n4). Instead, Haraway's name for our age is both descriptive and prescriptive, rather than merely identifying the fundamentally destructive nature of anthropos (humans) or capital(ism). Haraway's Chthulucene names "a kind of timeplace for learning to stay with the trouble of the living and dying in response-ability on a damaged earth" (2). Bringing our attention back to the ground, "Chthonic ones are beings of the earth, both ancient and up-to-the-minute ... replete with tentacles, feelers, digits, cords, whiptails, spider legs, and very unruly hair .... [They] are monsters in the best sense" (2).

While the racist and misogynist elements of Lovecraft's fiction set it apart from what Haraway has in mind here, the move to disavow his work completely seems a bit strange, particularly given the resurgence of interest in Lovecraft's work in many branches of literary studies and cultural theory. Rather than Lovecraft's Cthulhu, Haraway's "diverse earthwide tentacular powers and forces and collected things" are associated instead with "names like Naga, Gaia, Tangora (burst from water-full Papa), Terra, Haniyasu-hime, Spider Woman, Pachamama, Oya, Gorgo, Raven, A'akuluujjust, and many more" (Haraway 2016, 101). This list might, as Haraway suggests, point toward a "vein of SF [science fiction] that Lovecraft could not have imagined or embraced" (101). But another way of distinguishing Haraway's vision from Lovecraft's could be in terms of *effect*. Readers of Lovecraft can be horrified by racist constructions of superstitious "men of a very low, mixed-blooded, and mentally aberrant type," for example, as they are described in "The Call of Cthulhu" (1928). But we also stumble upon nightmares of "Cyclopean cities of titan blocks and sky-flung monoliths, all dripping with green ooze and sinister with latent horror" (Lovecraft 1987a, 171). Worse still, in one instance, "from some undetermined point below had come a voice that was not a voice; a chaotic sensation which only fancy would transmute into sound, but which he attempted to render by the almost unpronounceable jumble of letters, '*Cthulhu fhtagn*'" (171). This "voice that was not a voice" could also be linked more generally to the horror lurking beneath so many of Lovecraft's stories, a far cry from Haraway's more hopeful vision.

Interest in Lovecraft has taken many forms, including in the role of his fiction in the development of speculative realism as a field, particularly in the work of Graham Harman, as well as in reassessments of earlier writers such as Poe (see Harman 2012). It has also inspired new work, such as the anti-racist HBO (Home Box Office) television series *Lovecraft Country* (2020), developed by Misha Green. An older genealogy of interest in Lovecraft can be traced back through the work of Gilles Deleuze and Félix Guattari, whose concept of "becoming-animal" is inspired, at least in part, by Lovecraft's stories. In *A Thousand Plateaus: Capitalism and Schizophrenia* (1980), Deleuze and Guattari illustrate the idea of "becoming-animal" through Lovecraft's "Through the Gates of the Silver Key" (1934). In this story, the character of Randolph Carter, according to Deleuze and Guattari, illustrates "a multiplicity dwelling within us," since he transforms and cycles through different bodies and dimensions of space. As evidence they cite this passage: "Carters of forms both human and non-human, vertebrate and invertebrate, conscious and mindless, animal and vegetable. And more, there were Carters having nothing in common with earthly life, but moving outrageously amidst backgrounds of other planets and systems and galaxies and cosmic continua" (quoted in Deleuze and Guattari 2002, 240). For Deleuze and Guattari, writing these kinds of tales can even be seen as a form of sorcery, "because writing is a becoming, writing is traversed by strange becomings that are not becomings-writer, but *becomings-rat*, becomings-insect, becomings-wolf, etc." (240, my emphasis). Deleuze and Guattari pay attention to rats in other texts as well, such as the film *Willard* (1972), "a fine unpopular film ... because the heroes are rats," even though the main character Willard is ultimately torn to shreds by rats he once saved (233).

Some stories can shatter us with the totality of their effect, whether they come from Lovecraft, Le Guin, Fowler, or others. Posthumanist potential can come in multiple forms. Deleuze and Guattari ask, for example, "Who has not known the violence of these animal sequences, which uproot one from humanity, if only for an instant, making one scrape at one's bread *like a rodent* or giving one the yellow eyes of a feline? A fearsome involution calling us toward unheard-of becomings" (2002, 240; my emphasis). This might not be the rat you thought you were, ultimately. You might be in touch with sorcery. Or perhaps you have other prescriptions for the planet. The rats may be in the walls, or in a maze, haunting your next thought, your next move. But as I hope to have revealed here, animal tracks in short fiction can help "us" to imagine something else, something beyond. How might "we" aim to become something other than merely human?

Works Cited

Deleuze, Gilles and Félix Guattari. 2002. *A Thousand Plateaus: Capitalism and Schizophrenia.* Trans. Brian Massumi. Minneapolis: University of Minnesota Press.

Derrida, Jacques. 2008. *The Animal That Therefore I Am.* Ed. Marie-Louise Mallet. Trans. David Wills. New York: Fordham University Press.

Despret, Vinciane. 2015. "Thinking Like a Rat." Trans. Jeffrey Bussolini. *Angelaki: Journal of the Theoretical Humanities* 20.2 (June): 121–134.

2016. *What Would Animals Say If We Asked the Right Questions?* Trans. Brett Buchanan. Minneapolis: University of Minnesota Press.

Fowler, Karen Joy. 2013. "Us," special issue on "Species/Race/Sex." *American Quarterly* 65.3 (September): 481–485.

Haraway, Donna J. 2008. *When Species Meet.* Minneapolis: University of Minnesota Press.

2016. *Staying with the Trouble: Making Kin in the Chthulucene.* Durham, NC: Duke University Press.

Harman, Graham. 2012. *Weird Realism: Lovecraft and Philosophy.* Winchester, UK: Zero Books.

Herman, David. 2018. *Narratology beyond the Human: Storytelling and Animal Life.* New York: Oxford University Press.

Kim, Claire Jean and Carla Freccero. 2013. "Introduction: A Dialogue," special issue on "Species/Race/Sex." *American Quarterly* 65.3 (September): 461–479.

Kirksey, Eben, ed. 2014. *The Multispecies Salon.* Durham, NC: Duke University Press.

Le Guin, Ursula K. 1987. "Mazes," in *Buffalo Gals and Other Animal Presences,* 61–67. New York: Penguin.

2017. "Deep in Admiration," in *Arts of Living on a Damaged Planet: Ghosts and Monsters of the Anthropocene.* Ed. Anna Lowenhaupt Tsing, Heather Anne Swanson, Elaine Gan, and Nils Bubandt, M15–M21. Minneapolis: University of Minnesota Press.

Lovecraft, H. P. 1987a. "The Call of Cthulhu," in *Tales.* Ed. Peter Straub, 167–197. New York: Library of America.

1987b. "The Rats in the Walls," in *Tales.* Ed. Peter Straub, 77–97. New York: Library of America.

Lundblad, Michael. 2013. *The Birth of a Jungle: Animality in Progressive-Era US Literature and Culture.* New York: Oxford University Press.

O'Key, Dominic. 2020. "Animal Collectives," *Style* 54.1: 74–85.

Poe, Edgar Allan. 1994. "Review of Twice-Told Tales," in *The New Short Story Theories.* Ed. Charles E. May, 59–64. Athens: Ohio University Press.

Rose, Deborah Bird and Thom van Dooren. 2011. "Introduction" to "Unloved Others: Death of the Disregarded in the Time of Extinctions," special issue of *Australian Humanities Review* 50: 1–4.

Tsing, Anna. 2015. *The Mushroom at the End of the World: On the Possibility of Life in Capitalist Ruins*. Princeton, NJ: Princeton University Press.

Vint, Sherryl. 2010. *Animal Alterity: Science Fiction and the Question of the Animal*. Liverpool: Liverpool University Press.

Wolfe, Cary. 2010. *What Is Posthumanism?* Minneapolis: University of Minnesota Press.

    2013. *Before the Law: Humans and Other Animals in a Biopolitical Frame*. Chicago: University of Chicago Press.

CHAPTER 21

The End of the Story
Grammar, Gender, and Time in the Contemporary Short Story

Lola Boorman

Donald Barthelme's "Sentence" (1987) begins not only *in medias res* but in the middle of a sentence: "Or a long sentence moving at a certain pace down the page aiming for the bottom – if not the bottom of this page then of some other page – where it can rest, or stop for a moment to think about the questions raised by its own (temporary) existence" (2005, 147). The story, which consists of a single, unfinished sentence spanning seven pages, is both an experiment in narrative and an ironic combination of maximal syntax in minimal form. Aside from staging a complex narrative paradox, Barthelme's story presents a highly compact account of the problem of time in the short story form and within short story criticism. Throughout the story the sentence is repeatedly configured in "temporary" terms, moving quickly toward its own conclusion as it "aim[s] for the bottom," looking for "rest." Here, the sentence's suspension in the present works against its desire to become retrospective, to "think about the questions raised by its own ... existence." But while the sentence accelerates through a rush of colons, parataxis, parenthetical asides, and unwieldy sub-clauses, it finds neither grammatical nor narratological resolution. This is a story that is obsessed with bringing about its own ending, but which is also suspended, indefinitely, by its grammar. Barthelme's playful opposition between linguistic temporality and narrative teleology self-consciously addresses one of the short story's enduring concerns: the problem of closure. Since Edgar Allan Poe's famous assertion that a short story must be read in a "single sitting" – "half an hour to two hours of perusal," to be precise – the genre has been end-dominated, both in the reading experience and in the internal dynamics of the story form. "Sentence" reveals the short story's teleology to be inherently grammatical, but in doing so disrupts and suspends the possibility of ending.

These questions of temporality appear, at first, to be purely formal. The equation of linguistic and narrative closure in "Sentence" acts as a kind of absurd literalization of Roland Barthes's structuralist maxim that "a narrative is a large sentence, just as any declarative sentence is, in a certain way, the outline of a little narrative" (1975, 251). As Barthelme's story playfully demonstrates, the structuralist analogy between a narrative and grammar seeks to locate the "atemporal logic" behind "narrative temporality" (251). Closer inspection reveals a much deeper connection between the sentence's syntax and larger systems of time: Barthelme's linguistic suspension is quickly understood as a reflection of social and political upheaval unfolding in the present, namely the Vietnam War and the Women's Movement. His unruly syntax is directly opposed to the "short, punchy sentences" that were taught in the narrator's "young manhood" (149). The overt masculinism of this stylistic prescription – and its linguistic unraveling in an age of sexual revolution – establishes grammar as a crucial means of negotiating the story's shifting temporalities and of exposing the gender politics that this kind of "closure" (narratological, temporal, and syntactical) enacts.

While structuralism paid less attention to the short story form than perhaps short story writers did to structuralist theory, its methodological offshoots – affective stylistics, cognitive science, discourse analysis, reader-response theory, and the rise of "story grammars" – dominated short story criticism in the 1980s and 1990s. In recent years, however, these linguistic approaches have fallen largely out of fashion. As Mary Burgan has argued, the legacy of the (post)structuralist turn has often meant that time or chronology in the short story is "displaced into spatiality" (2000, 68), a theoretical hangover from poststructuralism's mistrust of the metaphysics of temporality. This displacement, Burgan claims, risks overlooking feminist preoccupations with time "that embrace representations of temporality as a gendered modality of the feminine imagination" (68). Burgan's and other feminist appraisals of the short story have instead sought to reclaim and reinterpret the form's characteristic focus on the single "moment" in light of feminism's unruly "momentariness," "a discursive dissonance that makes up feminist history" (Hemming 2011, 16). Burgan's approach returns to the well-worn trope of modernist epiphany, tracing its development in a corpus of short fiction by women that pursues "the moment's punctuation of duration" (Burgan 1993, 382). Burgan's contribution highlights how important feminine constructions of time were to the development of the short story's best-known conventions, but it does not examine the ways in which women writers have used linguistic form as a means of disrupting or interrogating the short story's reliance on closure and its assumed "momentariness." Far from foreclosing an exploration of gender, Barthelme's linguistic and temporal negotiations suggest that there is more to say about the role of grammar in the American short story and in the future of short story theory. In what follows, I propose that looking to grammar exposes the short story as less interested in "beginnings," "endings," and "moments" than in the complex negotiation between the past and the problems of futurity. Refocusing on grammar as a crucial tool in this process of temporal interrogation, this chapter examines a set of twentieth- and twenty-first-century women writers – Gertrude Stein, Lorrie Moore, and Lydia Davis – who use grammar to unsettle the logical connections between narrative and social time and to generate new ways of articulating the relationship between past, present, and future. In doing so, I point to a feminist countertradition in the American short story, one that offers a new way of understanding the short story's formal and temporal conventions.

A Brief History of Time

In "A Few Words about Minimalism" (1986), his rather disparaging examination of "The New American Short Story," John Barth made a crucial link between the grammar of the short story and its temporal limits. Speaking about the then widespread popularity of literary minimalism, pioneered by Raymond Carver, Ann Beattie, Jayne Anne Phillips, and Bobbie Ann Mason, among others, Barth attributes its characteristic compression (linguistic, emotional, and formal) to a series of historical and cultural factors: the disorientation of the period after 1968, the trauma of the Vietnam War, the energy crisis of the late 1970s, and (Barth's favorite) the "national decline in reading and writing skills" among students and teachers alike. Minimalism, Barth contended, with its emotionally and intellectually stunted "Dick-and-Jane prose" is unlikely to produce "a sentence of any syntactical complexity." This literary impoverishment is, nevertheless, an expected and "cyclical correction in the history (and the microhistories) of literature and of art in general: a cycle to be found as well, with longer rhythms, in the history of philosophy, the history of the culture" (1986, 1).

Barth's critique underscores a core presumption about the short story form; whereas the novel is concerned with history, the short story is instead preoccupied with the "single moment" – "turning points" (Boddy 2010, 100), a "single point of crisis" (Pratt 1981, 182), a "threshold" (Trussler 1996; 2012, 148), or an epiphany. This critical interest in the temporal compression of the short story has manifested in a close attention to "beginnings" and "endings" as a hallmark of the form, most notably in the rise of "closure" studies in the 1980s and 1990s, which drew heavily from affective stylistics, structural narratology, cognitive science, discourse analysis, and reader-response theory (Gerlach 1985; Lohafer 1983; 1994; 2003; Winther 2004). Susan Lohafer underscores the significance of this field of scholarship when she notes that "studies of closure helped turn short story criticism into short story theory" (1994, 309). But as some critics sought to taxonomize how writers signaled closure in short fiction, as well as how readers came to recognize it, others attested to the ways in which short stories actively resist their own formal parameters. Thomas M. Leitch identifies a "debunking rhythm" in the American short story. In Leitch's view the short story almost always represents a challenge to the worldview it sets up at its own beginning, "so that such stories constitute not a form of knowledge but a challenge to knowledge" (1989, 133). Paradoxically, resolution or closure can only occur through this process of debunking by "mounting a challenge to the way its world is first adumbrated, even if that challenge takes the form of an ironic joke" (140).

As Barthelme's masculine "short, punchy sentence" suggests, this formal predisposition for closure manifests in and through the linguistic features of the story in ways that are unmistakably gendered. These dynamics are starkly visible in Ernest Hemingway's "A Very Short Story" (1924), a model for American minimalism (and short story criticism) in the latter half of the twentieth century. The story achieves a heightened sense of emotional, linguistic, and narrative compression through a series of violent (fore)closures in the narrative action. It also stages a tension between feminine verbal excess and masculine reticence. Spanning only two and a half pages, the story involves a process of temporal compression; beginning "one hot evening in Padua" (Hemingway 2021, 59), the narrative then moves quickly through the next three months, the Armistice, and the aftermath of World War I, recounting the relationship between its unnamed narrator and Luz, who cares for him while he is recovering from an injury received at the front. In this way, the story stages a succession of endings of varying scales: from the narrator's release from hospital, to the end of the war, to the dissolution of their "boy and girl affair" (60), finally concluding with the uncertainty of both characters' reproductive futures, as it is suggested that Luz has fallen pregnant by an Italian major who will not marry her and that the narrator has contracted gonorrhea "from a sales girl in a loop department store while riding in a taxicab through Lincoln Park" (61). Many critics have identified a stark masculinism in Hemingway's prose, which is rendered through terse, active sentences in the simple past tense that syntactically privilege the point of view of the unnamed narrator while subordinating that of Luz (Scholes 1990).[1] This occurs on the level of grammar when the narrator relays the contents of the letter that ends their relationship: "She was sorry, and she knew he would probably not be able to understand, but might someday forgive her, and be grateful to her, and she expected, absolutely unexpectedly, to be married in the spring" (60). Luz's feminine speech is conveyed as meandering, contradictory, and verbose, and is quickly brought to a halt by the narrator's corrective, grammatically succinct language: "The major did not marry her in the spring, or any other time" (61).

"A Very Short Story" exposes the key problem when it comes to thinking about temporality and the short story form: the question of scale. How can we reconcile history with the minute formal resistances that occur within the parameters of the short story? Hemingway's writing exemplifies many of the temporal structures that critics have identified as characteristic of the form, but it also makes its masculinist grammar inseparable from the way it enforces its narrative teleology. Hemingway has long been considered a forefather of the modern American short story tradition, for critics and story writers alike. In my next section, I want to consider a how Gertrude Stein's only collection of short stories, *Three Lives* (1909), offers a radical, feminist alternative to these temporal structures. I argue that the short story was crucial in developing what she would later call "the continuous present," a grammatical tense that better captures the simultaneity of past, present, and future. In turn, Stein's idiosyncratic grammar transforms and interrogates the gendered temporal parameters of the story form.

Revisionist History: Gertrude Stein and the Short Story

If the momentariness of the short story has always been set against the historicity of the novel, then Stein's *Three Lives*, her only foray into short fiction in a conventional sense, unsettles these formal distinctions in more ways than one. Most crucially, *Three Lives* was composed both as a reprieve from the temporal pressures of the novel form and as a revision of an earlier work, her lesbian romance *Q.E.D.*, which she translated into "Melanctha," the centerpiece and best-known story in the collection. In a letter to Mabel Weekes upon abandoning her early draft of her maximalist novel, *The Making of Americans* (subtitled "Being a History of a Family's Progress"), Stein wrote, "I am afraid that I can never write the Great American novel. I dn't [sic] know how to sell on a margin or to do anything with shorts and longs, so I have to content myself with niggers and servant girls and the foreign population generally" (quoted in Wald 1995, 239–240). Stein's middlebrow investment in the "Great American Novel" is palpable in her derogatory reference to African Americans, immigrants, and working women, who become implicitly associated with the inferior – and distinctly feminized – short story.[2] But Stein is also signaling her own marginality (as well as her inability to "sell on a margin") as a woman, a lesbian, and a Jew.[3] *Three Lives* represents, then, not only a stylistic revision that places grammatical temporality at the center of Stein's writing, but also a tactical displacement of her queerness into the racialized and working-class narratives of her three female protagonists.

The collection was also, for Stein at least, a significant moment in American literary history, marking, as she proclaimed in *The Autobiography of Alice B. Toklas* (1933), "the first definite step away from the nineteenth century and into the twentieth century in literature" (Stein 2001, 61). Unlike later modernist texts that sought to render the varied temporal experiences of the "single day" (James Joyce's *Ulysses*, Virginia Woolf's *Mrs Dalloway*), Stein's triptych set out to capture "life" in minimal form. These questions of periodization are more than mere self-marketing. On the contrary, Stein believed that it was the responsibility of the contemporary artist and the work of art to reckon with their complex temporal positioning. As she writes in her later essay "Composition as Explanation" (1925–1926), "Composition is not there, it is going to be there and we are here. This is some time ago for us naturally" (Stein 1993, 97). The contemporary artist, for Stein, is in a continuous process of negotiating the past, present, and future. Stein's pursuit of the "continuous present" in "Melanctha," a style characterized by its use of repetition, gerunds, and present participles, puts grammar to use in its attempt to bring these different temporal scales into a single grammatical tense: "Melanctha Herbert was always losing what she had in wanting all the things she saw" (Stein 2003, 75).

Stein's development of the "continuous present," an innovation that later allowed her to return to the novel form and reconfigure its notions of "History" and "progress" as a restless "beginning again and again," is inseparable from her experimentation with the temporalities of the short story form. Turning her focus away from generational time, *Three Lives* thematizes the problem of being stuck in the present amidst the pressures of a modernizing society that is in continuous flux. Rather than a set of interlinked stories (or a story cycle such as Hemingway's *In Our Time*), *Three Lives* is peculiarly unified by each story's internal structure. Stein uses simple, repetitive language that recurs and loops back on itself, mimicking the mundane patterns of work and daily life. In doing so, these disconnected lives become enmeshed and enclosed in a single overarching form. As Jennifer Smith claims, the modernist short story cycle "portrays perpetual temporality ... exploring the way time expands, contracts, and shifts in relation to perspective" (2018, 61). Her immigrant and Black characters are suspended between national identities, arrested in the process of assimilation, and in the structures of domestic and reproductive labor. In "The Gentle Lena," for example, Lena is married off soon after arriving in the fictional town of Bridgeport (based on Baltimore) and is quickly confined to the act of bearing children. Bound by her own reproductive cycle, Lena slowly withdraws from the world. She dies shortly after delivering her fourth child stillborn, simultaneously completing and resisting her gendered role in the making of Americans. In contrast to Stein's novel, which engages with the process of generational assimilation and the notion of middle-class "progress," "The Good Anna" and the "The Gentle Lena" convey a discomforting suspension between temporalities and states of being. While both stories are told in simple, albeit repetitive prose and rendered largely through conventional past tense narration, Stein uses grammar to convey the characters' experience of temporal disjunction. The heroine of "The Good Anna" structures her life around daily domestic housekeeping, eventually working herself to death at the end of the story. But Anna's commitment to her work also prevents her from envisaging any kind of future beyond the confines of her quotidian duties. When her mistress's niece, Julia, is to be married, Anna's life is upended by the dynastic shift in the household. The narrative tense stalls, caught between retrospection, presentness, and future speculation: "[T]he change came very soon" (Stein 2003, 25).

These interlinking temporal scales – of quotidian work, of generational advancement, of immigrant reinvention – and Stein's queer resistance to them come out most prominently in the grammatical indeterminacy of "Melanctha." In this story, Stein's use of conflicting temporal markers such as "always" and "now" is juxtaposed with her conflation of past tense narration and present participles to create an unstable experience of time driven forward by an unsettled syntax that appears to be evolving as it is written. Stein's grammar destabilizes the relationship between words and action, both for her characters and in the structure of her narration: "Oh dear, Jeff, sure, why you look so solemn now to me. Sure Jeff I never am meaning anything real by what I just been saying. What was I just been saying Jeff to you. I only certainly was just thinking how everything always was just happening to me" (2003, 146). Here, Melanctha's assertion that she is *continuously* "never ... meaning anything real" reveals a more pervasive, as yet unarticulated, way of being that goes beyond a mere momentary slip in "what I just been saying." Melanctha's inability to mean what she says is a concern that is taken directly from *Q.E.D.*, which stages the unhappy and still unspeakable relationship between the protagonist Adele and her lover Helen. Where *Q.E.D.* is punctuated by Helen's silence, "Melanctha" presents, in complex grammatical terms, its heroine's struggle to find a language to convey her sense of being out of time, and her ambivalent queer resistance to the temporal rhythms and expectations of heterosexual courtship. The translation of *Q.E.D.* into the experimental grammar of "Melanctha" supplants Stein's exploration of sexual difference for one of racial otherness. But in doing so, Stein's grammatical ambivalence produces a kind of language that is, as Melanctha is described, "still too complex with desire" (2003, 73), generating a temporal sense that sets the experience of the present against a conditional and indeterminate future.

The internal temporal dynamics created by Stein's manipulation of grammar is mirrored in her experimentation with the conventional teleology of the short story. Each story ends with the death of the heroine, whose demise is intricately linked to domestic and reproductive labor. In "Melanctha," Stein uses death both to unsettle the parameters of the story's form and to underwrite her account of modern progress with a queer resistance to reproductive futurity. The story opens with a discussion between Melanctha and her friend Rose Johnson about suicide, a conversation that tellingly coincides with the birth of Rose's baby, who dies soon after. While the prospect of suicide is never realized, the same conversation between Rose and Melanctha recurs at the end of the novel, signaling, at the same time, closure and repetition. The replaying of this scene functions within the temporal expectations of story endings in two conflicting ways: first, inviting the reader to wonder whether they have been returned, chronologically, to the story's starting point; and secondly, looking back to the beginning as a significant foreshadowing of what they anticipate now to be the fate of the story's heroine. But while death does provide the ultimate ending for the story, Stein subverts the "crisis" produced by her own narrative effects, admitting that "Melanctha Herbert never really killed herself" but instead is taken ill with consumption and admitted to hospital. The story's final line, "and there Melanctha stayed until she died," not only disrupts the romantic suggestion of suicide by instead making her demise the gradual and quotidian product of ill-health, but also refuses to narrate the moment of Melanctha's death with any certainty, plucking our protagonist, once again, out of time.

Stein's suppression of her heroine's biological reproduction, and her emphasis on death as a structuring teleology in her stories (whether it be as a form of ending or as a way of disrupting endings) results instead in her own textual (re)production: a revision of earlier forms and the creations of new ones. It is significant also that Melanctha's "death" echoes that of "The Good Anna" and gestures forward to "The Gentle Lena," the trio of stories repeating and mirroring each other so that the complete sequence negates the singularity of any one story. Stein's work frequently emphasizes the importance of "looking forward and back," both to negotiate her place in literary and cultural history and to push toward the "new." In manipulating the temporal structures of the short story – and the short story cycle – Stein engages in a complex interaction between past, present, and future that sanctions social concepts of "progress" (modernity, generational assimilation, work) with a queer grammar that disrupts the formal expectations of the story genre and unsettles the historical impulses of the novel.

Grammatical Futures: Lorrie Moore and Lydia Davis

As we have seen, Stein's experimentation with the temporal limits of the short story form was instrumental to her reconceptualization of her literary style and her development of a temporal mode realized in and through her use of grammar. Stein's work demonstrates how the various narrative and linguistic levels of the short story might be set off against each other in order to disrupt the notion of closure and to open up a set of speculative temporalities that project outward from the story's own internal workings. In the second half of the twentieth century, after the political tumult of 1968, the emphasis on generations, on reproductive refusal, and on feminine labor we find in *Three Lives* takes on a heightened political relevance in the wake of second wave feminism. Time became a central concern for both theorists and activists, whether it be in the practical positioning of generational feminism (first wave, second wave, third wave), or in Julia Kristeva's (1981) opposition of "Women's Time" (gestational, cyclical, eternal, ongoing) and "monumental" or linear time.

In the 1980s and 1990s, these temporal registers were complicated further as the future-oriented category of "feminism" was closed off as it inherited the prefix "post"; the promise of a "movement" was placed into an artificial state of completion. Feminist appraisals of the short story

(Burgan 2000; Young 2018) have focused on the form's emphasis on the "single moment" as a means of linking feminist moments of disruption to the formal function of the transformative, punctuative, or epiphanic moment in the short story. But while women writers frequently manipulate the moment as a means of articulating gendered temporalities within the short story form, many of them also interrogate this convention as a formal limit. The writer Grace Paley, for example, is a master disruptor of closure. As Kasia Boddy notes, the title of Paley's most well-known collection, *Enormous Changes at the Last Minute* (1974), "is partly a joke at the expense of the short story's characteristic reliance on revelation and epiphany" (2010, 134).

Lorrie Moore is another story writer who uses the temporal parameters and expectations of the short story form to interrogate the category of feminism as a political and a formal category. As Heidi Slettedahl MacPherson argues, Moore's stories often center around women characters "who attempt a variety of escapes from their presumed narrative closures and who struggle with feminism and its consequent impact on their narrative lives" (2012, 565). More often than not, Moore's "feminist inquiry" slips into "postfeminist critique" (573). In "How to Talk to Your Mother (Notes)" from her 1985 collection *Self-Help*, Moore's dismantling of the short story form and its inbuilt chronology (in the move from "story" to "notes") is intricately tied to the problem of reconciling personal time and public or political history. Much critical attention has been paid to Moore's use of the second person, as a means both of creating intimacy between the narrator and reader and of distancing. The collection's recurring "How to" structure is naturally forward-looking in tone, but it is also prescriptive and conservative. While the self-help model implies generality, this universal mode chafes against the hyper-specificity of the stories themselves. In "How to Talk to Your Mother (Notes)" Moore works backward from the present (1982) to the year of her conception, as the narrator moves, in fragments, from her current "childless[ness]," dreaming of "babies with the personalities of dachshunds" (2008, 601), through the death of her mother, her grandmother, her abortions and failed relationships, toward her own birth, witnessed through "a tent of legs, a sundering of selves" (610). These reflections on generational lineage and the narrator's refusal to carry it forward are punctuated by major historical events: "Germany invades Poland" (610), "Forty thousand people are killed in Nagasaki" (609), "Kennedy is shot" (606). Notably, however, Moore's reverse-historical account contains no mention of the Women's Movement. The narrator instead holds cycles of

"History" in tension with the constant interruption of women's lives by their own biological cycles: "1969. Mankind leaps upon the moon. Disposable diapers are first sold in supermarkets" (605). Moore's story recapitulates the problem of "ending" the story with coming to terms with the end of a life. In doing so, her story moves not toward closure but back to its own beginnings, searching for a temporal structure that captures loss. The speculative (and imperative) grammar of the "How to" guide projects itself into a future that the reader quickly realizes is no longer possible, a conversation that will now never take place. What is left is the problem of telling this story, of telling "a life."

Moore's attempt to find a place for female desire within historical and more intimate cycles of biological time finds expression in the tension between the story's prospective "How to" and her reversal of the short story's narrative teleology. For Lydia Davis, a (very) short story writer, grammar becomes an explicit means of negotiating female desire within the limits of the short story form. Indeed, Davis's fiction, which takes the sentence or the paragraph as its primary unit of narrative, creates even stronger analogies between grammar and the narrative temporality of the short story. "A Double Negative," from her collection *Samuel Johnson Is Indignant* (2001), reads: "At a certain point in her life, she realizes it is not so much that she wants to have a child as that she does not want not to have a child, or not to have had a child" (2009, 373). As a complete sentence the story produces both narrative and grammatical closure, but the double negative itself – the word "not" – works against these formal boundaries. Each grammatical transformation produces an alternative narrative direction and another conflicted psychological state, with each revision expressing a different shade of speculation about the narrator's future. This complex future is captured in the story's indeterminate grammar, where rather than use the future tense, the narrator instead chooses to speak from a position of speculative retrospection ("does not want not to have a child, or not to have had a child"). These transformations reveal a nexus of psychological and social expectation that neutralizes the narrator's desire, the double negatives creating a (false) positive, and shows her entrapment in the pressures of reproductive futurity. Grammar becomes a crucial means of recalibrating the competing timescales experienced by her narrator.

Davis's stories often dramatize the problems of writing, with her narrators frequently diverging from what we might consider to be the standard conventions of the short story. Rather than endings, Davis's wayward protagonists frequently find themselves entangled in the middle of the narrative, as the narrator of "The Center of the Story" concedes: "[T]he end is a problem, too, though less of a problem than the center" (176). This compositional quandary arises only "now that [the story] is finished" (173) and as the narrator begins to "tak[e] things out that are not interesting." These omissions lead not to a more compact and fully resolved ending but, paradoxically, merely accentuate the ambiguous "middle," "since as soon as there is less in a story, more of it must be in the center" (174). "Two Characters in a Paragraph" addresses the unpredictability of the writing process, and the impulse to simultaneously revise as one writes. By enshrining her work in the state of being unfinished, Davis's self-reflexive stories push back against the conventions of the short story form and its pedagogical injunctions. This resistance manifests most palpably in a mistrust of resolution and closure, and occurs most forcibly when her grammatical exercises evolve and transform into deeper questions of ontology, where death becomes the teleology that Davis's grammar works against.

"Grammar Questions" moves between a literal interrogation of grammar and a deeper ontological questioning, focusing on the protagonist's attempts to come to terms with her father's death, beginning with the seemingly simple question: "Now, during the time he is dying, can I say, 'This is where he lives'?" (2009, 527). This directness disarms the reader, the simplicity of the question short-circuiting their ability to locate meaning. The syntax of this first line reveals a temporal awkwardness, the juxtaposition of "Now" and "during" betraying conflicting senses of stasis and duration. The clumsy construction of "during the time he is dying" reads somewhat like an approximate translation, as though Davis is attempting to convey a tense that does not quite exist in English. Indeed, the philosophical problems that unfold from these grammatical investigations demarcate a fundamental disjunction between language and time, in the moments just before retrospection kicks in. While there seems to be no grammar for this kind of ongoing grief, the linguistic irresolution becomes a means of prolonging life. Does Davis answer, "'Well, right now he is not living, he is dying'" or "'He lives in Vernon Hall'" or "'He is dying in Vernon Hall'" (527)? The extreme, focusing literalism of Davis's approach is both poignant and comic, and her exploration of her response to these difficult questions articulates the tension between grammatical and ontological precision, through the realization that the terms we use to convey this precision are themselves imprecise. The persistent logic of "Grammar Questions" is directed toward this attempt to reconnect word and world through grammatical investigation, a way of breaching personal and linguistic loss through an interrogation of the very instruments through which we connect language to time and form to life.

Davis's fiction thematizes how grammar can make visible intimate connections between form and life. As I have shown, grammar is central to the ways women short story writers have reinvented the formal temporalities and conventions of the genre as well as to how they have interrogated the constructions of gendered time within dominant cycles of political, social, and literary history. But does grammar also point us toward new ways of reading the short story? In recent years, grammar has become a function of "distant" rather than close reading, as methods in the Digital Humanities put computational grammars to use in the exposition of literary ones. But does collating these grammars risk compromising the intricate questions of scale implicit in the way these short story writers use grammar, questions which already explore the dilation of form into larger political or philosophical themes? As I have shown, refocusing on grammar not as a means of thinking through the short story's closures, endings, and limits, but rather as an instrument of its various expansions just might lead us in new directions for short story theory in the future.

Works Cited

Barth, John. 1986. "A Few Words about Minimalism," *New York Times*, December 28. https://archive.nytimes.com/www.nytimes.com/books/98/06/21/specials/barth-minimalism.html.

Barthelme, Donald. 2005. *Forty Stories*. London: Penguin Books.

Barthes, Roland. 1975. "An Introduction to the Structural Analysis of Narrative." Trans. Lionel Duisit. *New Literary History* 6.2: 237–272.

Boddy, Kasia. 2010. *The American Short Story After 1950*. Edinburgh: Edinburgh University Press.

2019. "Making It Long: Men, Women, and the Great American Novel Now," *Textual Practice* 33.2: 318–337.

Burgan, Mary. 1993. "The 'Feminine' Short Story: Recuperating the Moment," *Style* 27.3: 380–386.

2000. "The 'Feminine' Short Story in America: Historicizing Epiphanies," in *American Women Short Story Writers: A Collection of Critical Essays*. Ed. Julie Brown, 267–280. New York: Routledge.

Cohen, Milton. 1984. "Black Brutes and Mulatto Saints: The Racial Hierarchy of Stein's 'Melanctha'," *Black American Literature Forum* 18.3: 119–121.

Davis, Lydia. 2009. *Collected Stories of Lydia Davis*. London: Penguin.

Gerlach, John. 1985. *Toward the End: Closure and Structure in the American Short Story*. Tuscaloosa: University of Alabama Press.

Hemingway, Ernest. 2021. *In Our Time*. London: Vintage Books.

Hemmings, Clare. 2011. *Why Stories Matter: The Political Grammar of Feminist Theory*. Durham, NC: Duke University Press.

Kristeva, Julia. 1981. "Women's Time." Trans. Alice Jardine and Harry Blake. *Signs* 7.1: 13–35.

Leitch, Thomas. 1989. "The Debunking Rhythm of the American Short Story," in *Short Story Theory at a Crossroads*. Ed. Susan Lohafer and Jo Ellyn Clarey. Baton Rouge: Louisiana State University Press.

Lohafer, Susan. 1983. *Coming to Terms with the Short Story*. Baton Rouge: Louisiana State University Press.

   1994. "A Cognitive Approach to Storyness," in *The New Short Story Theories*. Ed. Charles E. May, 301–311. Athens: Ohio University Press.

   2003. *Reading for Storyness: Preclosure Theory, Empirical Poetics, and Culture in the Short Story*. Baltimore, MD: Johns Hopkins University Press.

MacPherson, Heidi Slettedahl. 2012. "'Escape from the Invasion of the Love-Killers': Lorrie Moore's Metafictional Feminism," *Journal of American Studies* 46.3: 565–580.

Poe, Edgar Allan. 1994. "Poe on Short Fiction," in *The New Short Story Theories*. Ed. Charles E. May, 59–72. Athens: Ohio University Press.

Scholes, Robert. 1990. "Decoding Papa: 'A Very Short Story' As Work and Text," in *New Critical Approaches to the Short Stories of Ernest Hemingway*. Durham, NC: Duke University Press.

Smith, Jennifer. 2018. *The American Short Story Cycle*. Edinburgh: Edinburgh University Press.

Stein, Gertrude. 1993. "Composition as Explanation," in *A Stein Reader*. Ed. Ulla Dydo, 493–503. Evanston, IL: Northwestern University Press.

   2001. *The Autobiography of Alice B. Toklas*. London: Penguin Books.

   2003. *Three Lives & Tender Buttons*. New York: Signet Classics.

Trussler, Michael. 1996. "Suspended Narratives: The Short Story and Temporality," *Studies in Short Fiction* 33.4: 557–577.

Pratt, Mary Louise. 1981. "The Short Story: The Long and the Short of It," *Poetics* 10.2–3: 175–194.

Wald, Priscilla. 1995. *Constituting Americans*. Durham, NC: Duke University Press.

Winther, Per. 2004. "Closure and Preclosure as Narrative Grid in Short Story Analysis," in *The Art of Brevity: Excursions in Short Fiction Theory and Analysis*. Ed. Per Winther, Jakob Lothe, and Hans H. Skei, 57–69. Columbia: University of South Carolina Press.

Winther, Per, Michael Trussler, Michael Toolan, Charles E. May, and Susan Lohafer. 2012. "Introduction," *Narrative* 20.2: 135–170.

Young, Emma. 2018. *Contemporary Feminism and Women's Short Stories*. Edinburgh: Edinburgh University Press.

CHAPTER 22

The Affordances of Mere Length
Computational Approaches to Short Story Analysis

Mark Algee-Hewitt, Anna Mukamal, and J. D. Porter

But you have to know where to stop. That is what makes a short story. Makes it short at least.

— Ernest Hemingway, 1959

Introduction: "Makes it Short at Least"

This chapter's guiding questions concern the stakes of Ernest Hemingway's slippage between "what makes a short story" and what "makes it short at least." His characteristically cryptic dictum suggests an operational theory of the form: the short story positively gains something through its writer's intuitive "know[ing] where to stop." In this chapter, we elaborate the distinction between "shortness" and "short story-ness" that Hemingway articulates: whether there is anything that *makes a short story* categorically distinct from other (longer) forms.

While this question may seem overdetermined by the name of the form (though, notably, we do not call novels "long stories"), it has been a preoccupation of short story theory. As early as 1917, James Cooper Lawrence asks: "Are brevity and coherence to be accepted as the sole distinguishing marks of a literary type?" (1917, 275). Following Lawrence, decades of short story theorists have sought to define the short story by identifying something *beyond* mere length that distinguishes it from the novel. It is not enough, they suggest, to simply write a story that ends within a few thousand words; to truly exemplify the form, a short story must be something different. More recently, Charles E. May elaborates a similar question: "What are the significant theoretical and historical implications of shortness in narrative?" (2019, 11).

While critics seem to gravitate toward the idea that "the short story deserves a generic theory" (May 2004, 14), such a comprehensive accounting of the form has eluded traditional criticism. Our chapter therefore turns to computational methods, leveraging the new scales of analysis available to the Digital Humanities to investigate similarities and differences in thousands of short stories using features historically unavailable to literary scholars. In many ways, length is fundamental to computational literary analysis: most of our methods rest on *counting* words in texts and, often, dividing these counts by the total length of the text. These methods are uniquely suited to the question of the short story, not only because we can account for length in new ways and at much different scales, but also because our computationally derived features allow us to investigate length *multi-dimensionally*. What is the difference between form and length when length is a dominant feature of the form? How does a long short story differ from a short novel?[1] How does length play a role in establishing different kinds of *narrative*? Using a combination of sophisticated methods of "mere" counting, natural language processing (NLP), and computational modeling, our analyses show the different ways that length itself becomes implicated in the formal differences between short stories and novels. These differences, nevertheless, do not simply resolve to one text being longer than the other.

One reason that differentiating length and form is so difficult is that length (which, in this chapter, we measure by word count) has important stylistic affordances. As an example, consider the type–token ratio (TTR), a commonly used statistic in quantitative text analysis.[2] TTR measures the diversity of vocabulary in a text by comparing the number of unique word-types to the total number of words, "tokens" here being a term of art for word instances. If used in a sophisticated way, TTR can capture important stylistic differences between texts. The repetitiveness of Gertrude Stein's prose results in a characteristically low TTR, whereas famously wordy or allusive authors such as James Joyce have extremely high TTRs.[3]

At the same time, TTR is highly correlated with length. There are limits to the total number of words in a language, and there is also a need to repeat elements such as conjunctions, articles, pronouns, and so on. This means that the longer a particular work gets, the lower its TTR will become. In the large corpus we describe below, for instance, word count correlates with TTR (with an R^2 of 0.59), meaning that a high percentage of the variance in TTR is accounted for by text length alone.[4] The stylistic differences we have described so far all require controlling for length.[5] Stein does use more repetitive prose than Joyce, but if we use TTR to compare all of *Ulysses* to a page from *Tender Buttons*, the statistical signature of their stylistic approaches will be obscured by the effects of their unequal length. The upshot is that we have to consider both facts: TTR means something about style, and TTR is highly determined by length. How do we tell whether a text is the way it is because of choices like those made by Stein and Joyce, or whether it is the way it is because it is, say, 5,000 words long? And just as important, if adding 1,000 words changes the quantitative profile of a text, how can we determine the extent to which this change in length affects its style?

Corpus Construction

To examine these questions, we assembled two sets of texts, or corpora: one of short stories and one of novels.[6] Our corpus of short stories was drawn from works of fiction published in the magazines from Collections 1 and 2 of the ProQuest Women's Magazine Archive, which includes *Better Homes and Gardens, Chatelaine, Cosmopolitan, Essence, Good Housekeeping, Ladies' Home Journal, Morris' National Press, Parents' Magazine, Redbook, Seventeen,* the *Home Journal, Town & Country, Women's International Network News,* and *Woman's Day,* as well as *Harper's Bazaar* and *Vogue* (ProQuest 2021).[7] We elected to define a "short story" as a work of narrative fiction that was not labeled a "novel" in the magazine context in which it was published. From the 44,025 items of fiction available in this archive, we sampled 10,000 works to compare against a sample of 10,000 novels with a similar distribution over time. We manually culled from our sample both non-fiction and any piece of fiction labeled within the pages of the magazine itself a "novel," leaving 9,449 short stories.

For our comparison corpus of novels, we sampled an equal number of texts from the Gale corpus of American fiction and the Chicago corpus of twentieth-century fiction (Gale, A Cengage Company 2021, Chicago Text Lab 2021). Because our novel corpus did not contain as many works published during the historical peak of our short story corpus, that is, from 1926 to 1949 (see Figure 22.1), we oversampled before and after this period to ensure parity across forms.

The American short story had achieved such prominence by the late 1920s that critic Edward J. O'Brien metaphorized it in *The Dance of the Machines* as both a "mechanistic structure" (1929, 115) and itself a product of manufacturing, "work[ing] to a predestined pattern largely determined by Poe, O. Henry, and magazines like *The Saturday Evening Post*" (117). This proliferation coincided with a "boom" period in American magazine publishing (Levy 1993, 31), with writers such as Hemingway and F. Scott Fitzgerald publishing in elite venues and being lauded as "the best of the best" by gatekeepers in edited volumes (Boddy

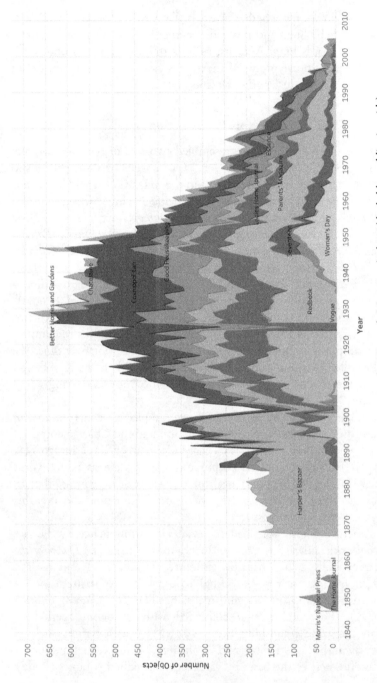

Figure 22.1 Number of fictions per year in the Women's Magazine Archive (shaded by publication title).

2010, 11). While scholars such as Andrew Levy have long looked to the late nineteenth and first two decades of the twentieth century as the "peak" of the short story (1993), our focus on the Women's Magazine Archive underscores that identifying a form's heyday depends in large part on the publication and reception context. In women's magazines, the peak arrived later and lasted for longer than scholars have understood when assessing the prevalence and commercial profitability of short stories in more elite, mainstream (coded male) contexts. This finding raises the question of how scholars should determine a form's period of greatest prominence – in terms of well-known writers and prestigious publications, and/or in terms of many more largely unknown authors writing for magazines that explicitly imagine a readership of twentieth-century women.

In the following sections, we demonstrate both that critics have been onto something in asserting a "felt" categorical difference between the short story and the novel beyond "mere length," and that methods of computational text analysis are uniquely equipped to probe the formal basis of this intuitive, readerly recognition of disparity. While the act of reading itself, which is the basis for the "felt" distinction of the short story, is not an experience that our computational methods can capture, we *can* locate formal differences whose subconscious recognition on the part of readers translates into the critical differences that they identify. By measuring the differences in these formal elements, we can quantitatively establish the loci of variation between short stories and novels.

Character

One pervasive hypothesis in short story theory pertains to the treatment of character. Specifically, the theory goes, while the novel can accommodate many characters, the short story should be about one character and should examine this individual deeply. As Dana Gioia and R. S. Gwynn observe, the short story "condense[s] the action of the tale – usually into a single situation focused on a single character" (2005, 3).[8] This idea, that the short story *uniquely* focuses on one character, is both descriptive (from the point of view of criticism: *the short story tends to be this way*) and normative (from the point of view of craft: *the short story should be this way*).

Extrapolating from this idea, is it the case that the longer a short story becomes, the more characters it has? In this scenario, the number of characters would scale linearly with length: the longer a short story becomes – the more closely it approaches novelistic length – the more characters it can sustain. But the alternative scenario, in which the number of characters does not scale with length, would indicate a categorical distinction between the two forms. Given the quantitative nature of these questions, *how many* characters over *how many* words, our computational methods offer the ideal platform through which to intervene in this debate. By turning to the computational method of named entity recognition – an algorithmic process that seeks to identify "entities" (for example, persons or places) in a text, using the pattern recognition-based methods of the field of NLP – we are able to probe this question by examining the number and proportion of unique characters in the two forms.[9]

The number of characters that a text contains initially appears to be a result of a straightforward difference between the two forms, correlated with length. If longer stories have more opportunities to introduce new characters, then the number of characters should scale linearly with length. When we examine short stories alone, this is indeed what happens: a linear regression between length and the number of characters in a short story has an R^2 of 0.512, indicating a strong linear relationship. Longer short stories simply contain more characters because they have more room to do so. While this finding is not an infallible contrapositive to Gioia and Gwynn's theory, it does run counter to the idea that the short story focuses on a single character because of the form itself (e.g., *I am writing a short story, so I will make it about one character*). Instead, it suggests that the "one character"-ness of the short story might be more readily explained as an affordance of the length difference among short stories: since most are short, most have fewer characters.

But data on short stories alone does not help us probe the possible categorical difference between short stories and novels. If the linear relationship holds, then longer novels should have proportionally more characters than shorter ones. This, however, is not the case. A logarithmic regression on the relationship between length and number of characters in novels yields a significantly higher R^2 (0.571).[10] The relationship *bends* at the top: as novels get longer, they become *less likely* to introduce more characters. Despite the seeming simplicity of our hypothesis, these results point to a much more complex relationship between length, characters, and form.

We can complicate this finding by moving beyond raw counts to analyze the *proportion* of unique characters. Figure 22.2 is a boxplot showing the number of characters per 1,000 words of each text.[11] On this boxplot, each dot represents a single novel (dark) or short story (light). Each dot is also sized according to text length, with larger dots representing longer texts. We might first note the vast disparity in median proportions

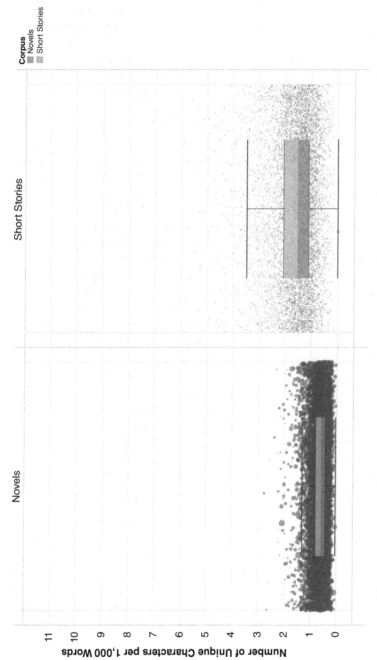

Figure 22.2 Number of unique characters per 1,000 words in novels (in dark gray) and short stories (in light gray).

of characters: for every 2,000 words of the text, short stories introduce about three characters, while novels only introduce about one. According to these results, while novels are generally longer than short stories, they tend to take up less narrative space when introducing new characters. Further, if we take individual text lengths (dot sizes) into account, we can see that there *are* short stories and novels that, despite their length differences, have a similar proportion of unique characters. The variability of this proportion, however, is much greater in short stories than in novels (indicated visually by the wider "spread" of the short story's character proportions). This finding importantly circles back to the question of length; more words do not necessarily imply more characters. Instead, as a novel gets longer, it generally introduces more characters than a short story, but it also generally has fewer characters per word; put differently, on average, the longer a text is, the smaller the proportion of its words it spends adding new characters.

This finding suggests that there may be a theoretical limit to the number of new characters a novel can sustain. To assess this, we can compare the real novels in our corpus to an artificial set of "simulated novels" by combining short stories from our corpus into single texts that approximate the distribution of lengths we see in the novels. We can then assess both the real and simulated novels for their proportions of unique characters. If these proportions are a function of mere length, then we should detect no difference between this proportion in the real novels versus that in the simulated novels. However, if this difference is less continuous (scaling linearly with length) and more categorical (a narratological difference between the two forms), then we should find an upper bound to the number of unique characters the novel can sustain. This, in turn, would mean that the simulated novels would have a much higher number of unique characters per word than actual novels. This is indeed the case: simulated novels along a similar length distribution to real novels have significantly more unique characters.[12] Our analysis shows that for our corpus, the theoretical limit to the number of unique characters a (real) novel can sustain is around 200. While the number of unique characters *is* correlated with length, it cannot be entirely explained by length – it is not *only* an affordance of mere length – because of this discernible theoretical limit. This proportion is an effect, or epiphenomenon of length, but cannot be entirely explained by (and hence is not reducible to) length. This finding also helps explain the wider variation in the proportion of unique characters per word in short stories versus novels; short stories, being shorter, can include more characters per word than can novels, which at some point approach a boundary.

The Sense of an Ending

We have suggested so far that the differences between the short story and the novel are *narrative* in nature. That is, differences in length create narrative effects that differentiate short stories from novels, in a way that is categorical rather than simply scaled to length itself. Narrative is, of course, a complex assemblage of many different formal features working in concert. Character, as we have seen, is one such aspect that differentiates the form of the short story from the novel in a way that correlates strongly with length. But perhaps even more fundamental to the construction of narrative is *plot*, and it is around plot, and its associated aesthetic effects, that much of the critical work on the short story has been constructed.

Of particular interest to theorists of the short story is the question of the *ending* of the text. Edgar Allan Poe, for example, famously spoke of the consistency or unity of the short story, or a "certain unique or single effect," in his review of Nathaniel Hawthorne's *Twice-Told Tales* (1842, 298). By contrast, the short stories of Joyce or O. Henry feature "twist" endings, or what we might call an epiphanic turn, that include "revelations about art, life, or experience" (Birns 2015, 25). This leaves us with two different theories of short story plot, but in either case, whether the short story is coherent or epiphanic, the relationship between its beginning and ending is thought to be different from that of the novel.

We can therefore resolve the question of the narrative form of the short story into one of endings. In the unity of effect theory, the ending should not depart significantly from the body of the work: whether the narrative builds smoothly to the creation of a single effect, or whether the effect remains continuous throughout the text, the ending should be contiguous with the remainder of the short story. In the epiphanic theory, however, the ending should differentiate itself from the remainder of the short story, revealing a new depth of meaning by a significant shift in language, tone, or effect.

Susan Lohafer's work on "preclosures," or moments in the text where we can recognize "narrative wholeness," points us toward the ways in which the methods of the Digital Humanities can aid us in assessing the differences between beginnings and endings in the short story and the novel (2003, 3). If beginnings are substantively different from endings in either form, then we might expect traces of this difference to appear within the language of the text itself. By measuring the *consistency* or *similarity* of language across the story, with special attention to the beginnings, middles, and endings of the respective texts, we can begin to assess how the short story varies from the novel and whether either theory of short story emplotment adequately describes the form in general. Length becomes the key factor again. If we compare beginnings to endings, does the language vary between them simply as a function of the number of intervening words? Or do short stories vary categorically from novels, either by remaining consistent in their language (Poe's unity) or by radically varying the language of the ending by including a twist or epiphany (epiphanic theory)?

Exploring this question requires determining whether beginnings and endings are only positional. Do beginnings merely occur at the start of the text and endings at the finish, or is there also a semantic difference between the two? This is a key question for Lohafer's definition of "closure," as she measures what she calls "local" and "global" terms within all potential endings (2003, 58–60). Our corpus offers a radically expanded data set to which we can apply computational tools that can identify the semantic differences between beginnings and endings to gain purchase on the language that differentiates the two. Accordingly, if we extract the first twenty sentences of each short story in our corpus (the beginning), and the last twenty sentences (the ending), we can compare the similarities of beginnings *between* short stories, which can help us differentiate their language from that of the similarities between endings across our corpus of novels. Our method here is to identify the *most distinctive words* (MDWs) of the beginnings and endings, a set of lexemes that can aid us in identifying the distinctive semantics of each part across our corpus.[13]

The MDWs (Table 22.1a) show a significant difference in the language of beginnings. Short stories in our corpus begin with a distinctive language of description: nouns and adjectives that focus on people and places, setting the "scene" of the story to come. From proper names ("Manhattan," "Connecticut") to generic places ("mansion," "sidewalks"), these narratives begin by identifying the roles their characters play ("archi-tect," "highschool," "roommate," "widowed," "bachelors") and the natures of the worlds that they inhabit ("wealthy," "immaculate," "conservative," "colorful," "suburban"). Contrast these with the MDWs of short story endings (Table 22.1b). Here, the concrete descriptions of wealth and affluence give way to an emotive language of resolution, whether restor-ative ("forgiveness," "kissed," "snuggled," "hugged," "cheered") or negative ("brokenly," "sobbed," "tears," "unsteadily," "choking"). In either case, short story endings emphasize verbs and adverbs (including nominalized verbs such as "sobbing"). They also feature words akin to what Lohafer describes as "closure" terms, including "goodbye" and "goodnight." If

Table 22.1a *MDWs of short story beginnings*

Term	Obs	Term	Obs
decides	52	bachelors	39
widowed	43	roommate	66
year-old	83	afforded	43
sidewalks	41	liner	40
corporation	101	metropolitan	51
suburb	59	mansion	108
christened	42	sloping	46
colorful	44	architect	61
Manhattan	70	Naples	39
suburban	70	twenties	39
rented	103	bordered	47
Connecticut	77	intrigue	49
conservative	50	graduation	51
immaculate	58	talented	36
wealthy	210	highschool	57

Table 22.1b *MDWs of short story endings*

Term	Obs	Term	Obs
brokenly	35	humbly	64
snuggled	39	squared	31
huskily	49	choking	57
knelt	152	tears	983
forgiveness	47	turtle	41
sob	119	hugged	77
kissed	859	cheers	30
whispered	698	kissing	129
bless	178	spacious	96
sobbing	122	widower	300
unsteadily	34	insistent	37
tenderly	138	deserve	39
goodbye	113	traveler	69
sobs	79	cluttered	43
goodnight	103	villages	66

beginnings of short stories in our corpus focus on concrete descriptions, then they end with emotive actions. Given the nature of our corpus, and its source in twentieth-century women's magazines, much more can be said about the gendered nature of these features; however, regardless of the specific effect of these terms, the difference between beginnings and endings, between scenic description and conclusive action, seems clear. What remains to be seen is whether this is a unique feature of the short story, or whether novels follow a similar pattern. To measure and assess the difference in beginnings and endings of both forms, however, we need to turn to a different metric, one that can account for the magnitude, rather than merely the substance, of the difference.

As we have seen, even in a form as compact as a short story, there is a perceptible difference between the language of beginnings and endings. What we need, then, is a way to measure this difference such that it is consistent across both corpora, short stories and novels. Since the compositions of these corpora are radically different, simply looking for recurring words in either group would be insufficient to account for the semantic distance between the beginnings and endings in both.[14] The MDW results, however, do suggest that we might be able to measure this difference by means of the change in language across the entire text. If we can measure the internal similarity of the language of the beginning to that of the ending, then we can examine how the ending, at least at the level of lexemes, differs from the remainder of the text. The method that we adopt here is Word Mover's Similarity (WMS) (Kusner et al 2015).[15] Built upon an underlying word embedding model, WMS allows us to measure the similarity (and therefore the distance) between two groups of words (in this case, the first twenty sentences and the last twenty sentences of the text).[16] WMS generalizes these word-to-word embedding differences across a selection of text by asking what the *minimum necessary change* would be to turn one text (the twenty beginning sentences) into the other (the twenty ending sentences). Instead of measuring the distance between every two words using their distances in the embedding space, WMS measures only the distance from each word in the first text to its closest match in the second: the higher the WMS score, the higher the similarity in the language of the two text selections.

The results from a comparison between this distance in short stories and novels (see Figure 22.3) are striking. As before, on this boxplot each dot represents a single novel (dark) or short story (light). Its position on the y-axis represents the similarity between the text's beginning and ending, calculated by its WMS: the higher the dot, the more similar the ending is to the beginning. Also as before, each dot is sized according to text length, with larger dots representing longer texts. What is immediately apparent is the categorical dissimilarity between short stories and novels. Overall, the similarity between the beginnings and endings in short stories is significantly higher than that in novels: the language of short stories clearly

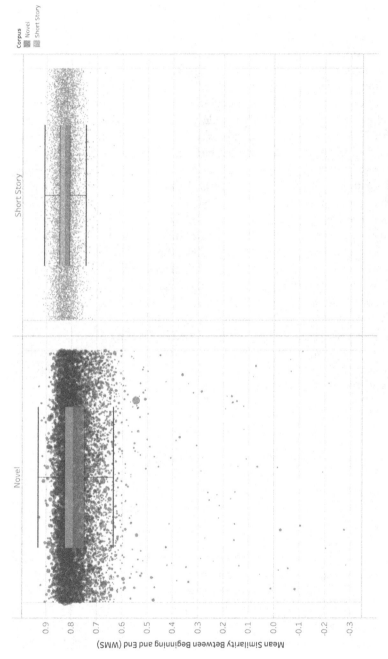

Figure 22.3 Boxplot of word movers similarity between beginnings and ends of novels (dark) and short stories (light).

evidences a consistency, and a *unity*, that novels do not share. As indicated by the boxes, the median similarity of short story beginnings and endings is higher than that of three quarters of the novels.[17]

There are three important aspects to our findings. First, there is a fundamental difference in the ways language changes over the course of short stories and novels. Short stories remain significantly more consistent in their language usage between beginnings and endings than do novels. Secondly, this difference does not scale continuously with length. As with our findings on character, length is clearly a factor in the difference between short stories and novels, but according to Figure 22.3, that difference is categorical rather than continuous. The larger dots, in either novels or short stories, do not cluster at the bottom of the graph, suggesting that the simple explanation – that the more words that intervene between the beginning and the end, the greater the difference between the two – is inaccurate. Rather, length once again exerts pressure on narrative such that there is a categorical difference between works that are shorter and those that are longer. This formal difference is an effect of length by way of narrative: a fundamental difference between short stories and novels that has its origins in length but is not simply reducible to length itself. Finally, the consistency of beginnings and endings of short stories (as compared to novels) points toward Poe's unity of effect theory of the short story. While the resolution of this method is not sufficient to fully discount the epiphanic theory of the twist ending, in this corpus this theory is not evident in the semantic features of the text.

Conclusion: "Affordances of Mere Length"

Our investigation shows that the terms of the initial problem are misleading. If we view length as a deterministic feature of short stories and novels, we arrive at questions such as: Is a novel just a short story that keeps going? Is a short story simply a novel with fewer words? Can we stretch or compress these forms? These questions turn out to be impossible to answer with any confidence.

Consider the unifying features of the categorical differences that we detected between short stories and novels. These do show that length is a powerful but insufficient explanatory force. If we analyze a short story, gathering statistics on its features (such as the proportion of characters or the difference between beginning and end), we *will* have a picture of the short story, but we will *not* be able to extrapolate to a novel via length alone. The same holds true in reverse: we cannot get to the short story by "downscaling" the novel's word count. Length correlates strongly with both forms, and the forms correlate with these quantitative, stylistically relevant features. But length does not appear to have a clear, direct relationship with these features – A leads to B and B leads to C, but we cannot get straight from A to C. Something besides "mere length" is at work, some mediating force. That force is narrative.

TTR offers an analogy. As a text gets longer, its TTR diminishes. The reasons are so fundamental that we might miss them, but it is in fact difficult to understand this phenomenon without considering the rules that govern language. To build a text of any length with a realistic TTR, we cannot just use statistics from a single short sentence or even a paragraph. Instead, we need to know the rate at which words appear in English in general, a set of facts governed by considerations syntactic (we constantly reuse function words), semantic (we perseverate on particular topics rather than jumping from, say, "eggs" to "conquistador"), and historic (we only have so many words for certain things, say, small boats, so a story about "kayaks" can only use so many synonyms). TTR is highly determined by length, but only in combination with the set of rules that govern *language*.

By analogy, we can say that length is highly determinative of how short stories and novels work, but only if we recognize that it works through the set of rules that govern narrative – the need to introduce characters more or less at the beginning, to place dialogue in the middle, to get to an ending at some point, and so on. The affordances (or constraints) of length must operate with respect to these narrative "rules." Only our pre-existing experience with narrative can explain how we get from word count to form.

Length does more work than literary scholars have imagined. While it may feel insufficient as an explanation of what makes short stories unique as a form, we have witnessed its power. If we know the length of a narrative, we will be able to predict many of its features. But our sense of the explanatory inadequacy surrounding Hemingway's "short at least" theory may just have been a recognition of underlying rules, hinting at the hidden hand of narrative logic. As this project began, we joked that we had empirically proven that short stories are short. After much labor, we have shown that this is not enough: we must also remember that they are stories. It feels somehow apt that the simplicity and complexity of the short story form lies in the relationship between these two words.

Works Cited

Allison, Sarah, Marissa Gemma, Ryan Heuser, Franco Moretti, Amir Tevel, and Irena Yamboliev. 2013. "Style at the Scale of the Sentence," *Pamphlets of the Stanford Literary Lab*. Stanford University, CA.

Bamman, David. 2014. "BookNLP." GitHub. https://github.com/dbamman/book-nlp.

Birns, Nicholas. 2015. "The Mystery of Existence: The American Short Story in Criticism and Theory," in *Critical Insights: American Short Story*. Ed. Michael Cocchiarale and Scott Emmert, 20–34. Ipswich, MA: Salem Press.

Boddy, Kasia. 2010. *The American Short Story Since 1950*. Edinburgh: Edinburgh University Press.

Chicago Text Lab. 2021. "Chicago Text Lab: Computational Methods for the Study of Culture." https://lucian.uchicago.edu/blogs/literarynetworks/.

Covington, Michael A. and Joe D. McFall. 2010. "Cutting the Gordian Knot: The Moving-Average Type–Token Ratio (MATTR)," *Journal of Quantitative Linguistics* 17.2: 94–100.

Degaetano-Ortlieb, Stefania and Elke Teich. 2017. "Modeling Intra-Textual Variation with Entropy and Surprisal: Topical vs Stylistic Patterns," *ACM Proceedings of the Joint SIGHUM Workshop on Computational Linguistics for Cultural Heritage, Social Sciences, and Literature*: 68–77.

Gale, A Cengage Company. 2021. "American Fiction, 1774-1920." Gale Primary Sources. www.gale.com/c/american-fiction-1774-1920.

Garg, Nikhil, Londa Schiebinger, Dan Jurafsky, and James Zou. 2018. "Word Embeddings Quantify 100 Years of Gender and Ethnic Stereotypes," *PNAS* 115.16: E3635–E3644.

Gioia, Dana and R. S. Gwynn. 2005. *The Art of the Short Story: 52 Great Authors, Their Best Short Fiction, and Their Insights on Writing*. London: Pearson Longman.

Hemingway, Ernest. 1981 [1959]. "The Art of the Short Story," *The Paris Review* 79. www.theparisreview.org/letters-essays/3267/the-art-of-the-short-story-ernest-hemingway.

Kusner, Matt, Yu Sun, Nicholas Kolkin, and Kilian Weinberger. 2015. "Proceedings of the 32nd International Conference on Machine Learning," *PMLR* 37: 957–966.

Lawrence, James Cooper. 1917. "A Theory of the Short Story," *The North American Review* 205.735: 274–286. www.jstor.org/stable/25121469.

Levy, Andrew. 1993. *The Culture and Commerce of the American Short Story: America's Workshop*. New York: Cambridge University Press.

Lohafer, Susan. 2003. *Reading for Storyness: Preclosure Theory, Empirical Poetics, and Culture in the Short Story*. Baltimore, MD: Johns Hopkins University Press.

May, Charles E. 2004. "Why Short Stories Are Essential and Why They Are Seldom Read," in *The Art of Brevity: Excursions in Short Fiction Theory and*

Analysis. Ed. Per Winther, Jakob Lothe, and Hans H. Skei, 14–25. Columbia: University of South Carolina Press.

Mikolov, Thomas, Ilya Sutskever, Kai Chen, et al. 2013. "Distributed Representations of Words and Phrases and their Compositionality," *Advances in Neural Information Processing Systems* 26: 3111–3119.

O'Brien, Edward J. 1929. *The Dance of the Machines: The American Short Story and the Industrial Age*. New York: Macaulay.

Pennington, Jeffrey, Richard Socher, and Christopher Manning. 2014. "Glove: Global Vectors for Word Representation," *Association for Computational Linguistics: Proceedings of the 2014 Conference on Empirical Methods in Natural Language Processing (EMNLP)*: 1532–1543.

Poe, Edgar Allan. 1842. "Review of Hawthorne's Twice-Told Tales," *Graham's Magazine* 20.2: 298.

ProQuest. 2021: "Women's Magazine Archive." https://about.proquest.com/en/products-services/Womens-Magazine-Archive.

Notes

Chapter 1

1 The term "tale," derived from the verb "to tell," already indicates how orality was translated into literature and contributed to the short story's immediacy. Early travel accounts repeatedly embed the original act of storytelling into a narrative frame and thus mediate the experience of oral discourse to their readers. A good case in point is John Josselyn's *Account of Two Voyages to New England* (1986), a scientific report on the American topography submitted to the Royal Society in London. Josselyn describes, among other things, an evening of storytelling with local settlers (228–229). Washington Irving's framing technique and nested stories in the *Tales of a Traveller* (1824) develop these earlier narrative innovations even further by combining local and oral traditions with a variety of foreign and mysterious settings.

2 Exempla are short narrative illustrations, for example, of a sermon's argument. While they existed in nearly all cultures, they became popular in England through the mendicant friars, who preached in English to the crowds at marketplaces throughout the country and were quickly adapted by Protestants as well. Various collections of exempla were published in the sixteenth and seventeenth centuries. Among the most famous is Thomas Beard's *Theater of God's Judgments* (1597) – a translation from French and German sources – that was cited by Increase and Cotton Mather in New England.

3 Ghost stories and oral narratives circulated among northeastern tribes. Oral narratives about the devil chasing someone can be found among the Narragansett people. Indigenous magazines such as the *Narragansett Dawn* (1935–1936) published traditional oral narratives. Among them is the story of John Onion's race with the devil (1936, 206), which emerged in the eighteenth century. The story exemplifies the crossover between orality and print culture as well as its many remediations in tales such as Irving's "The Legend of Sleepy Hollow."

4 See the stories of moral decline, murder, and execution of the convicted money forger John Syllavan (Scheiding and Seidl 2015, 63–68) and Thomas Powers, an enslaved African American (Scheiding and Seidl 2015, 68–73).

358

Chapter 4

1 With gratitude to Jennifer 8. Lee and the team of research assistants at Plympton's *Writing Atlas* for the data regarding the *Best American* series cited here and the O. Henry prize cited later.
2 My thanks to Jordan Pruett for this data.

Chapter 5

1 Special thanks to Bryn Lovitt and John Lyons for assembling the Excel spreadsheet from which I made the visualizations for this piece.

Chapter 8

1 One thorny issue when tackling "working-class literature" is exactly what that terms means. For the purposes of this chapter, I define working-class short stories as short stories written by, for, or about working-class people. In this formulation, "working class" is a strategic rather than a descriptive term.

Chapter 11

1 Other examples of demanding and subversive storytelling frames include Charles Chesnutt's *The Conjure Woman* (1899) and Americo Paredes's "The Hammon and the Beans" (1939).
2 Opening stories skewering the touristic impulses of readers are a common contemporary move. Native Hawaiian writer Kristiana Kahakauwila's "This Is Paradise" (2013) is particularly brutal.
3 Laguna Pueblo writer Leslie Marmon Silko is another writer of Jones's generation whose stories stress the storytelling circle.

Chapter 12

1 Other examples include Gerald Vizenor's (Anishinaabe) *Summer in the Spring: Ojibwe Lyric Poems and Tribal Stories* (1965) and Anita Endrezze's (Yaqui) *Throwing Fire at the Sun, Water at the Moon* (2000).
2 Although the novels were published in this order, the historical order of the stories within them is: *Tracks* (1912–1924), *The Beet Queen* (1932–1972), *Love Medicine* (1934–1984), and *The Bingo Palace* (1981–1995).
3 Other notable anthologies of Indigenous short fiction are Craig Lesley's *Talking Leaves* (1991), Alan R. Velie's *The Lightning Within* (1991), Clifford E. Trafzer's *Earth Song, Sky Spirit* (1992), Paula Gunn Allen's *Song of the Turtle: American Indian Literature 1974-1994* (1996), Hertha D. Sweet

Wong, Lauren Stuart Muller, and Jana Sequoya Magdaleno's *Reckonings: Contemporary Short Fiction by Native American Women* (2008), Ty Nolan's *Coyote Still Going: Native American Legends and Contemporary Stories* (2014), and Bob Blaisdell's *Great Short Stories by Contemporary Native American Writers* (2014).

4 It was published by Heartdrum, a new imprint of HarperCollins devoted to publishing Native-authored stories for children eight years old and older. Other Native writers of children's stories include Christine Day (Upper Skagit), Dawn Quigley (Ojibwe), Brian Young (Navajo), Darcie Little Badger (Lipan Apache), and Cherie Dimaline (Metís), the last two focusing on fantasy.

Chapter 13

1 Victor Séjour's "Le Mulâtre," written in French, was first published in Paris in 1837 and is believed to be the first work of fiction by an African American author.

2 Arna Bontemps, Jessie Fauset, Angelina Weld Grimké, Georgia Douglas Johnson, Jean Toomer, Wallace Thurman, and Dorothy West also published short stories during the Harlem Renaissance.

Chapter 17

1 Kaplan's learning affirms what language pedagogy calls the Creative Construction Hypothesis, whereby startling new usages emerge from patterns students find based on correct data they have received.

2 On Jewish dialect humor, see Wirth-Nesher 2009; Dauber 2017; Gross 1930, a predecessor to *Joys of Yiddish*; and Ben-Amos 1973 on who tells Jewish dialect jokes when.

3 Richard Mayne's December 5, 1958 *New Stateman* review, "Risibility Moderate," is quoted in Shiffman 1999, 94.

4 Parkhill shocks his students by writing fifty tenses of one verb on the board.

5 Rosten writes about Talmudic sayings: "The rabbis, seeking to keep their audiences alert ... would often toss Greek, Latin, Arabic, Persian words into their exposition: this was sure to excite interest and provoke questioning" (1972a, 14).

Chapter 19

1 Personal communication from the author.

Chapter 21

1 Robert Scholes's (1990) influential reading of "A Very Short Story" performs discourse analysis on the story's pronouns, replacing "he" and "she" with "I" to see whether the story grammatically supports the characters' point of view.

Scholes concludes that the discourse endorses the "reticent" male narrator but that any attempt to translate Luz's character into the narrating "I" is largely impossible. Scholes identifies the style of the story more broadly as "reticent" prose, which is fundamentally distressed "by the idea of excessive discharge of ... verbal ... matter" (41).

2 Stein's attitude to race and to African American writers (Richard Wright, Nella Larsen, and others) is complex and contradictory. See Cohen 1984.

3 See Boddy 2019 for a more detailed discussion of the gender politics of the Great American Novel.

Chapter 22

1 We have not found an unambiguous case in which a text labeled a short story in its original publication context is longer than a novel labeled a novel. Yet our data does show that, by length, short stories appear to transition smoothly into novels, with intermediary forms, such as the novelette, or novella, at least in part occupying the space between.

2 For a concise technical overview of the relationship between TTR and length, see Covington and McFall 2010.

3 For instance, in the large corpus we describe below, Stein's *Three Lives* has a rolling-average TTR of .37, the lowest of any text in the corpus and five standard deviations below the mean of .53. Joyce's *Finnegans Wake* has a rolling TTR of .63, which is three standard deviations above the mean.

4 R^2 describes in statistical terms the proportion of the variance in one variable that is dependent on (or explained by) another. It ranges from 0 to 1, with a higher number indicating greater association between the variables. Standards for a meaningful R^2 vary between disciplines; we adopt the value of .5 as our threshold of meaningfulness.

5 We control for length by measuring TTR for a rolling 500-word window (i.e., the TTR for words 1–500, 2–501, 3–502, etc.) and averaging the window-level results.

6 For detailed information about the corpora, see: https://github.com/malgee hewitt/ShortStories.

7 We normalized magazine names across historical publications. For example, "Red Book Magazine" and "Red Book: A Short Story Magazine" became "Redbook."

8 Thanks to Tom Kealey for help with this reference.

9 We carried out NLP analyses with David Bamman's BookNLP (Bamman 2014), which can identify place names, references to time, and people. We used BookNLP's "PERSON" tag as a proxy for characters.

10 The R^2 of the linear regression is 0.06 smaller: a small, but particularly significant difference.

11 In each group, the x-axis randomly jitters the individual texts so that they can be seen.

12 To determine whether our results were meaningful as well as statistically significant, we performed a Cliff's Delta test, which estimates how prevalent

a significant effect is within our corpus (that is, whether a sizable number of simulated novels had more unique characters, or whether our results were just due to a few outliers). The results of our test indicate that we could reduce our effect size by 97 percent and still find a significant difference in the proportion of characters between simulated and real novels.

13 On the methodology of MDWs, see Allison et al. 2013. After creating a new corpus of 9,449 beginnings and 9,449 endings, we compared the observed frequency of every word in each group (beginnings and endings) to its expected value (the frequency we would expect if that word were evenly distributed across the corpus). We assessed whether the differences in observed and expected frequencies were significant, using a Fishers' exact test, which tests whether an association (in this case, the association between the higher frequency of a word and the beginning of a short story) is significant or due to random variation.

14 This type of measurement, intra-text variation, has received attention among NLP researchers for its importance to consistent model-based annotation. See, for example, Degaetano-Ortlieb and Teich 2017.

15 Although Kusner et al. (2015) refer to their technique as "Word Mover's Distance," their use of cosine similarity represents difference in terms of semantic *similarity*, where higher values represent sentences that are more alike. We therefore adopt the technique but slightly alter the name to the more intuitive "Word Mover's Similarity."

16 A word embedding model (Garg et al. 2018, Mikolov et al. 2013) is a compact representation of a large corpus of text such that each word is "embedded" within a location represented by a high-dimensional vector. Similarities between any two words can be measured as the cosine similarity between their respective vectors: depending on the model used to create the embedding, this similarity can represent the tendency of two words to appear near each other within a corpus (co-occurrence) or to share similar contexts (synonymy). In this chapter, we used an underlying model built with the global vectors for word representation (GloVe) code, trained on a corpus of 27,000 novels written between 1784 and 2000 (Pennington et al. 2014).

17 We assessed the significance of this result by a Wilcoxon signed-rank test, which tests whether a difference in the average value of each group is significant or due to random noise in a non-normally distributed population (such as our corpus). Our test resulted in a p-value of 2.2×10^{-16}, indicating that the difference in the means of the two samples (short stories and novels) is highly significant. A Cliff's Delta test confirms that this difference is both significant and has a large effect size, rendering it meaningful as well.

Further Reading

Early Criticism of the American Short Story

In the nineteenth and early twentieth centuries, American short story theory developed alongside the progress of the short story itself. Both fiction and criticism often circulated side by side in the periodicals which brought short stories before the eyes of American readers. These early explorations provide insight into the historical development of both the short story form and critical appreciation of it.

Canby, Henry Seidel. 1902. *The Short Story.* New York: Henry Holt and Co.
   1913. *A Study of the Short Story.* New York: Henry Holt and Co.
Harte, Bret. 1899. "The Rise of the Short Story," *Cornhill Magazine* VII (July): 1–8.
Howells, William Dean. 1887. "Editor's Study," *Harper's Monthly Magazine* 74 (February): 482–486.
   1902. "Some Anomalies of the Short Story," in *Literature and Life: Studies*, 110–124. New York: Harper and Brothers.
Matthews, Brander. 1885. "The Philosophy of the Short-Story," *Lippincott's Magazine of Popular Literature and Science* 36 (October): 366–374.
Neal, John. 1835. "Story-Telling," *The New-England Magazine* VIII (January): 1–12.
Pattee, Fred Lewis. 1923. *The Development of the American Short Story: An Historical Survey.* New York: Harper and Brothers.
Perry, Bliss. 1902. *A Study of Prose Fiction.* Boston and New York: Houghton, Mifflin, and Company.
Poe, Edgar Allan. 1842. "Review of Twice-Told Tales," *Graham's Lady's and Gentleman's Magazine* (May): 298–300.
   1847. "Tale-Writing – Nathaniel Hawthorne," *Godey's Magazine and Lady's Book* (November): 252–256.

Twentieth- and Twenty-First-Century Criticism

Books and Monographs

Achilles, Jochen and Ina Bergmann. 2015. *Liminality and the Short Story: Boundary Crossings in American, Canadian, and British Writing.* New York: Routledge.

Boddy, Kasia. 2010. *The American Short Story Since 1950*. Edinburgh: Edinburgh University Press.

Brown, Julie, ed. 1995. *American Women Short Story Writers: A Collection of Critical Essays*. New York: Garland Publishing.

Cocchiarale, Michael and Scott Emmert, eds. 2015. *Critical Insights: American Short Story*. Ipswich, MA: Salem Press.

Collins, Michael J. 2016. *The Drama of the American Short Story, 1800–1865*. Ann Arbor: University of Michigan Press.

Current-García, Eugene. 1985. *The American Short Story before 1850: A Critical History*. Boston: Twayne.

Curnutt, Kirk. 1997. *Wise Economies: Brevity and Storytelling in American Short Stories*. Moscow: University of Idaho Press.

Delaney, Paul and Adrian Hunter, eds. 2018. *The Edinburgh Companion to the Short Story in English*. Edinburgh: Edinburgh University Press.

Einhaus, Ann-Marie, ed. 2016. *The Cambridge Companion to the English Short Story*. New York: Cambridge University Press.

Eikhenbaum, Boris. 1968 [1925]. *O. Henry and the Theory of the Short Story*. Trans. I. R. Titunik. Ann Arbor: University of Michigan Press.

Ermida, Isabel. 2008. *The Language of Comic Narratives: Humor Construction in Short Stories*. Berlin: Mouton de Gruyter.

Farman, Jason, ed. 2014. *The Mobile Story: Narrative Practices with Locative Technologies*. New York: Routledge.

Fash, Lydia G. 2020. *The Sketch, the Tale, and the Beginnings of American Literature*. Charlottesville: University of Virginia Press.

Glass, Loren, ed. 2016. *After the Program Era: The Past, Present, and Future of Creative Writing in the University*. Iowa City: University of Iowa Press.

Gerlach, John C. 1985. *Toward the End: Closure and Structure in the American Short Story*. Tuscaloosa: University of Alabama Press.

Goyet, Florence. 2014. *The Classic Short Story, 1870–1925: Theory of a Genre*. Cambridge, UK: Open Book Publishers.

Harrington, Ellen Burton, ed. 2008. *Scribbling Women and the Short Story Form: Approaches by American and British Women Writers*. New York: Peter Lang.

Head, Dominic, ed. 2016. *The Cambridge History of the English Short Story*. New York: Cambridge University Press.

Hunter, Adrian, ed. 2007. *The Cambridge Introduction to the Short Story in English*. New York: Cambridge University Press.

Iftekharrudin, Farhat, Joseph Boyden, Mary Rohrberger, and Jale Claudet, eds. 2003. *The Postmodern Short Story: Forms and Issues*. Westport, CT: Praeger.

Iftekharuddin, Farhat, Mary Rohrberger, and Maurice Lee, eds. 1997. *Speaking of the Short Story: Interviews with Contemporary Writers*. Jackson: University Press of Mississippi.

Levy, Andrew. 1993. *The Culture and Commerce of the American Short Story*. New York: Cambridge University Press.

Lohafer, Susan. 1983. *Coming to Terms with the Short Story*. Baton Rouge: Louisiana State University Press.

2003. *Reading for Storyness: Preclosure Theory, Empirical Poetics, and Culture in the Short Story*. Baltimore, MD: Johns Hopkins University Press.

Lohafer, Susan and Jo Ellyn Clarey, eds. 1989. *Short Story Theory at a Crossroads*. Baton Rouge: Louisiana State University Press.

March-Russell, Paul. 2009. *The Short Story: An Introduction*. Edinburgh: Edinburgh University Press.

May, Charles E., ed. 1976. *Short Story Theories*. Athens: Ohio University Press.

1994. *The New Short Story Theories*. Athens: Ohio University Press.

1995. *The Short Story: The Reality of Artifice*. New York: Twayne.

McGurl, Mark. 2009. *The Program Era: Postwar Fiction and the Rise of Creative Writing*. Cambridge, MA: Harvard University Press.

O'Connor, Frank. 1963. *The Lonely Voice: A Study of the Short Story*. Cleveland, OH: World Publishing Co.

Patea, Viorica, ed. 2012. *Short Story Theories: A Twenty-First-Century Perspective*. Amsterdam and New York: Rodopi.

Peden, William. 1964. *The American Short Story: Front Line in the National Defense of Literature*. Boston: Houghton Mifflin.

1975. *The American Short Story: Continuity and Change, 1940–1975*. Boston: Houghton Mifflin.

Price, Kenneth M. and Susan Belasco Smith, eds. 1995. *Periodical Literature in Nineteenth-Century America*. Charlottesville: University Press of Virginia.

Rohrberger, Mary. 1996. *Hawthorne and the Modern Short Story: A Study in Genre*. The Hague: Mouton.

Scofield, Martin. 2006. *The Cambridge Introduction to the American Short Story*. New York: Cambridge University Press.

Smith, Jennifer. 2018. *The American Short Story Cycle*. Edinburgh: Edinburgh University Press.

Stevick, Philip, ed. 1984. *The American Short Story, 1900–1945: A Critical History*. Boston: Twayne.

Tallack, Douglas. 1993. *The Nineteenth-Century American Short Story: Language, Form, and Ideology*. New York: Routledge.

Winther, Per, Jakob Lothe, and Hans H. Skei. 2004. *The Art of Brevity: Excursions in Short Fiction Theory and Analysis*. Columbia: South Carolina Press.

Young, Emma. 2018. *Contemporary Feminism and Women's Short Stories*. Edinburgh: Edinburgh University Press.

Journals

American Short Fiction. University of Texas Press.
Short Story. Society for the Study of the Short Story.
Studies in the American Short Story. Penn State University Press.
Studies in Short Fiction. Newberry College.

Craft Books

Our contributors' many references to "the Program Era" make clear that writing programs have long been, and continue to be, an important site for the short story's dissemination and production. And the desire to learn how to write the perfect short story – or at least the most lucrative one – predates even the genre's adoption by the Ivory Tower, as authors looked to cash in on opportunities for short story writers in the booming periodical market of the late nineteenth and early twentieth centuries. It is therefore unsurprising that craft books, aimed at aspiring writers, are a significant resource for those seeking to understand the form of the short story and its place in American culture.

Historical Craft Books

Baker, Harry Torsey. 1916. *The Contemporary Short Story: A Practical Manual.* Boston: D. C. Heath and Co.

Barrett, Charles Raymond. 1898. *Short Story Writing: A Practical Treatise on the Art of the Short Story.* Chicago: Authors and Writers' Union.

Blackiston, Elliott. 1946. *Short Story Writing for Profit.* Boston: The Writer, Inc.

Chester, George Randolph. 1910. *The Art of Short Story Writing.* Cincinnati, OH: The Publishers Syndicate.

Cody, Sherwin. 1895. *How to Write Fiction, Especially the Art of Short Story Writing: A Practical Study of Technique.* London: Bellairs and Co.

Cook, William Wallace. 1941. *Plotto: A New Method of Plot Suggestion for Writers of Creative Fiction.* Battle Creek, MI: Ellis Publishing Co.

Dye, Charity. 1898. *The Story-Teller's Art: A Guide to the Elementary Study of Fiction.* Boston: The Athenaeum Press.

Eaton, Harold Thomas. 1934. *Short Stories for Study and Enjoyment.* Garden City, NY: Doubleday, Doran.

Esenwein, J. Berg. 1909. *Writing the Short-Story: A Practical Handbook on the Rise, Structure, Writing, and Sale of the Modern Short-Story.* Springfield, MA: Home Correspondence School.

Fagin, N. Bryllion. 1923. *Short Story-Writing, An Art or a Trade?* New York: T. Seltzer, Inc.

Gavin, Marian. 1962. *Writing Short Stories for Pleasure and Profit.* Boston: The Writer, Inc.

Gerwig, George W. 1909. *The Art of the Short Story.* Akron, OH: The Werner Company.

Grabo, Carl H. 1913. *The Art of the Short Story.* New York: Charles Scribner's Sons.

Hamilton, Clayton. 1918. *A Manual of the Art of Fiction.* Garden City, NY: Doubleday, Page, and Co.

Joseph, Michael. 1924. *Short Story-Writing for Profit.* Boston: Small, Maynard, and Company.

Kamerman, Sylvia E. 1946. *Writing the Short Short Story*. Boston: The Writer.

Louthan, Hattie Horner. 1930. *The Short-Story Craftsman: The Rhetoric of Short Fiction*. Denver: The World Press, Inc.

Mirrielees, Edith Ronald. 1929. *Writing the Short Story*. Garden City, NY: Doubleday, Doran and Co.

Neal, Robert Wilson. 1914. *Short Stories in the Making*. New York: Oxford University Press.

Pitkin, Walter B. 1922. *The Art and the Business of Story Writing*. New York: The Macmillan Co.

Smith, Louis Worthington. 1902. *The Writing of the Short Story*. Boston: D. C. Heath and Co.

Wells, Carolyn. 1913. *The Technique of the Mystery Story*. Springfield, MA: Home Correspondence School.

Williams, Blanche Colton. 1917. *A Handbook on Story Writing*. London: George Routledge and Sons.

1919. *How to Study "The Best Short Stories."* Boston: Small, Maynard, and Company.

Contemporary Craft Books[1]

Davies, Peter Ho. 2021. *The Art of Revision: The Last Word*. Minneapolis, MN: Graywolf Press.

DeMarinis, Rick. 2000. *The Art and Craft of the Short Story*. Cincinnati, OH: Story Press.

Gardner, John. 1984. *The Art of Fiction: Notes on Craft for Young Writers*. New York: A. Knopf.

Glover, Douglas. 2012. *Attack of the Copula Spiders and Other Essays on Writing*. Emeryville, Ontario: Biblioasis.

Hills, Rust. 1987. *Writing in General and the Short Story in Particular: An Informal Textbook*. Revised ed. Boston: Houghton Mifflin.

Koch, Stephen. 2003. *The Modern Library Writer's Workshop: A Guide to the Craft of Fiction*. New York: Modern Library.

Salesses, Matthew. 2021. *Craft in the Real World: Rethinking Fiction Writing and Workshopping*. New York: Catapult.

Saunders, George. 2021. *A Swim in a Pond in the Rain: In Which Four Russians Give a Master Class on Writing, Reading, and Life*. New York: Random House.

Tin House Publishing. 2009. *The Writer's Notebook: Craft Essays from Tin House*. Portland, OR: Tin House Books.

---

[1] The editors would like to thank Stanford University's creative writing faculty and fellows for their input on this section.

2012. *The Writer's Notebook II: Craft Essays from Tin House*. Portland, OR: Tin House Books.

Wood, James. 2008. *How Fiction Works*. London: Jonathan Cape.

Edward J. O'Brien

When Edward J. O'Brien began the *Best American* anthology series in 1915, he inaugurated a tradition that continues to influence how the public views and values short stories. O'Brien would continue to edit the series until his death in 1941, each annual volume framed by his incisive remarks about the state of the short story in contemporary culture. Throughout his life, O'Brien also produced full-length critical works on the short story and served as editor for numerous other anthology projects, including *The Best British Short Stories* (1922–1940). While the life of the short story cannot be understood through a single figure, O'Brien's life and career nonetheless grant a rich view of the form's progress in the first half of the twentieth century.

Joselyn, Sister M. 1965. "Edward Joseph O'Brien and the American Short Story," *Studies in Short Fiction* 3.1: 1–15.

O'Brien, Edward J., ed. 1915–1941. *The Best Short Stories and the Yearbook of the American Short Story*.

1915–1925: Published by Small, Maynard, and Company.

1926–1932: Published by Dodd, Mead, and Company.

1933–1941: Published by Houghton Mifflin.

1922–1940. *The Best British Short Stories*.

1922–1925: Published by Small, Maynard, and Company. Co-edited with John Cournos.

1926–1932: Published by Dodd, Mead, and Company

1933–1940: Published by Houghton Mifflin.

1929. *The Dance of the Machines: The American Short Story and the Industrial Age*. New York: Macaulay.

1931. *The Twenty-Five Finest Short Stories*. New York: Ray Long and Richard R. Smith, Inc.

1932. *Modern American Short Stories*. New York: Dodd, Mead, and Company.

1931. *The Advance of the American Short Story*. Revised ed. New York: Dodd, Mead, and Company.

1935. *The Short Story Case Book*. New York: Farrar and Rinehart.

1939. *50 Best American Short Stories 1915–1939*. Boston: Houghton Mifflin.

Phillips, Ruby Willoughby. 1941. "O'Brien's Magazines, O'Brien's Stories: A Table and Index," *American Prefaces* 7: 18–28.

Schramm, Wilbur. 1941. "The Thousand and One Tales of Edward J. O'Brien," *American Prefaces* 7: 3–17.

Simmonds, Roy S. 2001. *Edward J. O'Brien and His Role in the Rise of the American Short Story in the 1920s and 1930s*. Lewiston, NY: Edwin Mellen Press.

Whitehand, Robert. 1940. "Edward J. O'Brien," *Prairie Schooner* 14.1: 1–12.

Beyond the Best American

The short story and anthology forms have grown alongside each other for over a century, their relationship fostered by the short story's long association with periodical literature. Editors from a variety of backgrounds have surveyed the wide field of short story production not just for what is "best," but also what is pleasurable, powerful, important, or overlooked, crafting volumes in which the whole is greater than the sum of the parts. If the early anthologies on this list often reflect efforts to make sense of (or profit from) a robust and chaotic market for short stories, later entries speak to a mid-twentieth-century turn toward anthologies as vital tools for elevating the work of minoritized writers. While this list is suggestive, rather than comprehensive, it nonetheless provides a glimpse of the many ways in which the anthology has shaped the short story's place in American literature.

Early Anthologies

Atlantic Tales: A Collection of Stories from the Atlantic Monthly. 1866. Boston: Ticknor and Fields.

Ford, Paul Leicester, ed. 1901. *A House Party: An Account of the Stories Told at a Gathering of Famous American Authors*. Boston: Small, Maynard, and Company.

Holloway, Laura C., ed. 1889. *The Woman's Story: As Told by Twenty American Women*. Troy, NY: Nims and Knight.

Howells, William Dean. 1920. *The Great Modern American Stories: An Anthology*. New York: Boni and Liveright.

Long, Ray, ed. 1925. *My Story That I Like Best*. New York: Cosmopolitan.

Mitford, Mary Russell, ed. 1830. *Stories of American Life by American Writers*. Three vols. London: Henry Colburn and Richard Bentley.

Putnam's Story Library. 1858. *Sea Stories*. New York: Putnam.

Stories from the Chap-Book: Being a Miscellany of Curious and Interesting Tales, Histories, &c., Newly Composed by Many Celebrated Writers and Very Delightful to Read. 1896. Chicago: Herbert S. Stone and Company.

Tales for Winter Nights: A Choice Collection of Interesting Adventures, Marvellous Stories, Anecdotes, &c. &c. &c. 1855. Philadelphia: Jas. B. Smith and Co.

Tales from McClure's: The West. 1897. New York: Doubleday and McClure Co.

Ten Notable Stories from Lippincott's Magazine. 1894. Philadelphia: J. B. Lippincott Company.

Anthologies from the Mid-Twentieth Century and Beyond

Adams, John Joseph, ed. 2015. *Loosed Upon the World: The Saga Anthology of Climate Fiction*. New York: Saga Press.

Anaya, Rudolfo A. and Antonio Márquez, eds. 1984. *Cuentos Chicanos: A Short Story Anthology*. Albuquerque: University of New Mexico Press.

Bambara, Toni Cade, ed. 1970. *The Black Woman: An Anthology*. New York: Signet.

Benavides, Rosamel, ed. 1993. *Antología de cuentistas chicanas: Estados Unidos de los '60 a los '90*. Santiago: Editorial Cuarto Propio.

Blaisdell, Bob, ed. 2013. *Great Short Stories by Contemporary Native American Writers*. New York: Dover Publications.

Brant, Beth, ed. 1988. *A Gathering of Spirit: Writing and Art by North American Indian Women*. New York: Firebrand Books.

Brown, Adrienne Maree and Walidah Imarisha, eds. 2015. *Octavia's Brood: Science Fiction Stories from Social Justice Movements*. Oakland, CA: A. K. Press.

Chin, Frank, Jeffery Paul Chan, Lawson Fusao Inada, and Shawn Wong, eds. 1975. *Aiiieeeee!: An Anthology of Asian-American Writers*. Garden City, NY: Doubleday.

Dillon, Grace L., ed. 2012. *Walking the Clouds: An Anthology of Indigenous Science Fiction*. Tucson: University of Arizona Press.

Dozois, Gardner R., ed. 2019. *The Very Best of the Best: 35 Years of the Year's Best Science Fiction*. New York: St. Martin's Griffin.

Hernandez, Alex, Matthew David Goodwin, and Sarah Rafael García, eds. 2021. *Speculative Fiction for Dreamers: A Latinx Anthology*. Columbus: The Ohio State University Press.

Hughes, Langston, ed. 1967. *The Best Short Stories by Negro Writers: An Anthology from 1899 to the Present*. Boston: Little, Brown.

LaPensée, Elizabeth and Weshoyot Alvitre, eds. 2017. *Deer Woman: An Anthology*. Albuquerque, NM: Native Realities, LLC.

Leavitt, David and Mark Mitchell, eds. 1994. *The Penguin Book of Gay Short Stories*. Second ed. New York: Viking.

2003. *The New Penguin Book of Gay Short Stories*. New York: Viking.

Reynolds, Margaret, ed. 1994. *The Penguin Book of Lesbian Short Stories*. New York: Viking.

Wright, Stephen, ed. 1974. *Different: An Anthology of Homosexual Short Stories*. New York: Bantam.

Genres of the Short Story

As demonstrated by Will Norman and Shelley Streeby's essays for this volume, the short story has been significant to the growth and emergence of the mystery and science fiction genres in America. Short stories continue to be relevant for genre readers in a way that is almost unique in our contemporary literary landscape. The Hugo Awards, Nebula Awards, and World Fantasy Awards – three of the most respected and longstanding honors available to science fiction and fantasy writers – all annually bestow prizes for short fiction, as do the Edgar Awards, an equally prestigious honor for mystery writers. At the same time, anthologies, single-author collections, and short story-centered magazines all retain a prominent place in the speculative zeitgeist. Looking to these genres of the short story offers a broader view of the form's history, vibrancy, and contemporary relevance.

Ashley, Michael. 2000. *The Time Machines: The Story of the Science-Fiction Pulp Magazines from the Beginning to 1950*. Liverpool: Liverpool University Press.
2005. *Transformations: The Story of the Science-Fiction Magazines from 1950 to 1970*. Liverpool: Liverpool University Press.
2007. *Gateways to Forever: The Story of the Science-Fiction Magazines from 1970 to 1980*. Liverpool: Liverpool University Press.
Blackwell, Laird R. 2019. *Frederic Dannay, Ellery Queen's Mystery Magazine, and the Art of the Detective Short Story*. Jefferson, NC: McFarland and Company, Inc.
Powers, Paul S. and Laurie Powers. 2007. *Pulp Writer: Twenty Years in the American Grub Street*. Lincoln: University of Nebraska Press.
Queen, Ellery. 1951. *Queen's Quorum: A History of the Detective-Crime Short Story as Revealed by the 106 Most Important Books Published in This Field Since 1845*. Boston: Little, Brown.
"Year-in-Review: 2020 Magazine Summary," *Locus Online*, March 15, 2021. https://locusmag.com/2021/02/year-in-review-2020-magazine-summary/.

Index

Cambridge Companions to...

AUTHORS

Edward Albee edited by Stephen J. Bottoms

Margaret Atwood edited by Coral Ann Howells (second edition)

W. H. Auden edited by Stan Smith

Jane Austen edited by Edward Copeland and Juliet McMaster (second edition)

Balzac edited by Owen Heathcote and Andrew Watts

Beckett edited by John Pilling

Bede edited by Scott DeGregorio

Aphra Behn edited by Derek Hughes and Janet Todd

Saul Bellow edited by Victoria Aarons

Walter Benjamin edited by David S. Ferris

William Blake edited by Morris Eaves

James Baldwin , edited by Michele Elam,

Boccaccio edited by Guyda Armstrong, Rhiannon Daniels, and Stephen J. Milner

Jorge Luis Borges edited by Edwin Williamson

Brecht edited by Peter Thomson and Glendyr Sacks (second edition)

The Brontës edited by Heather Glen

Bunyan edited by Anne Dunan-Page

Frances Burney edited by Peter Sabor

Byron edited by Drummond Bone

Albert Camus edited by Edward J. Hughes

Willa Cather edited by Marilee Lindemann

Catullus edited by Ian Du Quesnay and Tony Woodman

Cervantes edited by Anthony J. Cascardi

Chaucer edited by Piero Boitani and Jill Mann (second edition)

Chekhov edited by Vera Gottlieb and Paul Allain

Kate Chopin edited by Janet Beer

Caryl Churchill edited by Elaine Aston and Elin Diamond

Cicero edited by Catherine Steel

J. M. Coetzee edited by Jarad Zimbler

Coleridge edited by Lucy Newlyn

Coleridge edited by Tim Fulford (new edition)

Wilkie Collins edited by Jenny Bourne Taylor

Joseph Conrad edited by J. H. Stape

H. D. edited by Nephie J. Christodoulides and Polina Mackay

Dante edited by Rachel Jacoff (second edition)

Daniel Defoe edited by John Richetti

Don DeLillo edited by John N. Duvall

Charles Dickens edited by John O. Jordan

Emily Dickinson edited by Wendy Martin

John Donne edited by Achsah Guibbory

Dostoevskii edited by W. J. Leatherbarrow

Theodore Dreiser edited by Leonard Cassuto and Claire Virginia Eby

John Dryden edited by Steven N. Zwicker

W. E. B. Du Bois edited by Shamoon Zamir

George Eliot edited by George Levine and Nancy Henry (second edition)

T. S. Eliot edited by A. David Moody

Ralph Ellison edited by Ross Posnock

Ralph Waldo Emerson edited by Joel Porte and Saundra Morris

William Faulkner edited by Philip M. Weinstein

Henry Fielding edited by Claude Rawson

F. Scott Fitzgerald edited by Ruth Prigozy

Flaubert edited by Timothy Unwin

E. M. Forster edited by David Bradshaw

Benjamin Franklin edited by Carla Mulford

Brian Friel edited by Anthony Roche

Robert Frost edited by Robert Faggen

Gabriel García Márquez edited by Philip Swanson

Elizabeth Gaskell edited by Jill L. Matus

Edward Gibbon edited by Karen O'Brien and Brian Young

Goethe edited by Lesley Sharpe

Günter Grass edited by Stuart Taberner

Thomas Hardy edited by Dale Kramer

David Hare edited by Richard Boon

Nathaniel Hawthorne edited by Richard Millington

Seamus Heaney edited by Bernard O'Donoghue

Ernest Hemingway edited by Scott Donaldson

Hildegard of Bingen edited by Jennifer Bain

Homer edited by Robert Fowler

TOPICS

Printed in the USA
CPSIA information can be obtained
at www.ICGtesting.com
CBHW031452130324
5300CB00017B/19

9 781009 292849